Book Club Plus!

A Literacy Framework for the Primary Grades

Taffy E. Raphael

Susan Florio-Ruane

MariAnne George

Nina Levorn Hasty

Kathy Highfield

SMALL PLANET COMMUNICATIONS, INC.

Lawrence, Massachusetts

Acknowledgments

Editorial: Melinda T. Hobausz, Kim L. Beaudet, Fiona O'Connor, Carol A. Griffin

Design and Production: Natalie MacKnight

We gratefully acknowledge the following teachers and literacy professionals who reviewed portions of this guide and provided valuable feedback.

Jeri Cramer, Bernice Mathews School, Reno, Nevada; Lori Helman, University of Nevada, Reno, Nevada; Cathy A. Hummel, Kelly Elementary School, Lewisburg, Pennsylvania; Wendy Hummel, Kelly Elementary School, Lewisburg, Pennsylvania; Dawn Kuntz, West Wendover Elementary School, Wendover, Nevada; Angie Jo Laubach, Kelly Elementary School, Lewisburg, Pennsylvania; Kim Lorson, Elimsport Elementary School, Elimsport, Pennsylvania; Paula Reber, Kelly Elementary School, Lewisburg, Pennsylvania; Mechiel D. Rozas, Pine Shadow Elementary School, Houston, Texas; Stephanie Wellons, Reno, Nevada

We gratefully acknowledge the contributions to this book (in the form of classroom vignettes and samples) of the following teachers from the Chicago, Illinois, area.

Cammy Anderson, Christine Cimino, Karen Eisele, Barbara Naess, Jeni Ness, Janine Rodrigues, Julia Stern

Visit www.PlanetBookClub.com.

Small Planet Communications, Inc.
15 Union Street
Lawrence, MA 01840
www.smplanet.com

ISBN: 1-931376-35-2   2 3 4 5   08 07 06

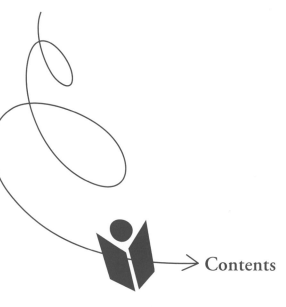

Contents

About the Authors

Taffy E. Raphael, Ph.D.

Taffy E. Raphael is a member of the Literacy, Language, and Culture faculty in Curriculum and Instruction at the University of Illinois at Chicago. Dr. Raphael has also held faculty positions at the University of Utah, Michigan State University, and Oakland University. Dr. Raphael's work in teacher education was recognized by her receipt of the Outstanding Teacher Educator in Reading Award from the International Reading Association, May 1997. Dr. Raphael's research has focused on Question Answer Relationships and strategy instruction in writing, and Book Club. She has studied professional development and received Oakland University's Research Excellence Award in September, 2000. Dr. Raphael has published in the leading research journals. She has also co-authored and edited several books, including *Book Club: A Literature-Based Curriculum* (Small Planet Communications 1997, 2002) and, with Kathy Au, *Literature-Based Instruction: Reshaping the Curriculum* (Christopher-Gordon Publishers, Inc., 1998) and *Super QAR for Testwise Students* (Wright Group, 2002). In 2002, she was selected for the International Reading Association Reading Hall of Fame.

Susan Florio-Ruane, Ed.D.

Susan Florio-Ruane is Professor of Teacher Education at Michigan State University. Her research includes studies of "Schooling and the Acquisition of Written Literacy," "Reading Culture in Autobiography," and "Re-engaging Low-Achieving Readers by Innovative Professional Development." Her paper "The Social Organization of Classes and Schools" won the Division K Research in Teacher Education Award of the American Educational Research Association. Dr. Florio-Ruane publishes in journals including *American Educational Research*

Journal, Research in the Teaching of English, Language Arts, and *English Education.* Her book, *Teacher Education and the Cultural Imagination,* won the National Reading Conference Ed Fry Book Award. In 2003, she received the Michigan State University Distinguished Faculty Award.

MariAnne George, M.A.

MariAnne George received her B.S. in early childhood education and elementary education from Michigan State University. She has a masters degree in reading and is currently working on her doctorate in Reading and Language Arts from Oakland University. She has taught primary grades for 27 years and is a Learning Consultant with the Rochester Community Schools. Ms. George became involved with the Book Club *Plus* project in 1998 as a member of the Teachers Learning Collaborative. She has been a frequent presenter at the National Council of Teachers of English, National Reading Conference, and International Reading Association. She has also published the results of her Book Club *Plus* research in professional journals and books. Her continuing research focus is in language, literacy, and culture.

Nina Levorn Hasty, M.A.

Nina Levorn Hasty is currently a Ph.D. candidate at Michigan State University in Teaching, Curriculum, and Educational Policy. She received her B.S. in elementary education and her M.A. in instructional technology from Wayne State University. Nina has seven years of teaching experience within urban school districts. She has worked with CIERA since 1999, researching literacy strategies for struggling readers within her classroom. She has spoken at the National Council of Teachers of English, the National Reading Conference, and the International Reading Conference to share her experiences and outcomes of her research. Nina has also co-authored articles on her research findings and continues to expose her students to rich and meaningful literature to increase their literacy skills.

Kathy Highfield, Ph.D.

Kathy Highfield received her B.A. in elementary education and French and her M.A. in Literacy Instruction (1994) from Michigan State University; and she received her Ph.D. in Reading Education (2003) from Oakland University. Kathy's more than fourteen years of teaching experience include teaching students from second to sixth grade and being involved in curriculum coordination. She is currently teaching fourth grade at Rose Pioneer Elementary School in Holly, Michigan. Her research interests include in-service teacher learning (professional development), Book Club, and test preparation. Kathy has been a frequent presenter at the Michigan Reading Association and the International Reading Association annual conferences. She enjoys consulting with schools that are seeking to improve their literacy instruction and student achievement.

Preface

This book is the result of a collaborative effort by members of the Teachers Learning Collaborative (TLC), a network of teachers sponsored in part by the Center for the Improvement of Early Reading Achievement. Building on almost a decade of research and practice with Book Club, we were interested in adapting the existing Book Club framework to address two important concerns. The first concern was to identify a way to connect students' Book Club activities using texts written for their age group to their guided reading activities using texts written at their instructional level. The second concern was to connect literacy instruction to the substantive study of other school subjects. Organizing students' learning around key thematic questions, the Book Club *Plus* framework is designed to help teachers coordinate their literacy activities, link them to their state literacy and related content area standards, and bring a sense of coherence to students' school reading, writing, and talk.

Members of the Teachers Learning Collaborative were particularly concerned about students who have become disengaged from school literacy events. We saw in our students a variety of reasons for turning away from school literacy activities. Some of our students—often those least able to decode print or write letters—were offered the least meaningful and interesting texts to read and the fewest opportunities to express themselves in writing and speech. Thus, by learning more about the fundamentals of literacy they were paradoxically learning less about the purposes and nature of literacy. Given the lack of meaningful literacy in these students' lives, it is not surprising that they turn away. In working to engage all students in literacy learning, we created a yearlong organizing theme—Our Storied Lives. We worked within this theme to develop the Book Club *Plus* framework, as illustrated by the many examples throughout this book. We wanted the framework to support a community of learners conducting inquiry into their own lives, understanding their families, and situating themselves and their families within the study of their cultural heritage, values, and traditions. The theme provided an important "hook" for linking students' activities between literacy and other student subjects across the year. Working within a broad theme, such as Our Storied Lives, can make it easier for both teachers and students to make meaningful connections across the many texts they encounter.

Young children love to talk, ask questions, and engage in language play. Most young children enter school excited about books and the prospect of learning to read and write. Literacy educators long to harness this enthusiasm as they introduce students to the wonders of language and to the concepts that will lead to their becoming successful, independent readers and writers. It is essential to capitalize on the enthusiasm of young readers if we are to meet the goals laid out in recent initiatives at the federal level, such as the No Child Left Behind Act of 2002. Unfortunately, neither standards documents nor textbooks offer the individual teacher all she or he needs to know and do in order to create a learning environment in which all youngsters learn to read at grade level and also understand and use literacy as authentic communication. It is the teacher's responsibility to provide much of the planning, instruction, and assessment, as well as the "on the spot" decisions made in interactions with youngsters. We need to provide both the necessary instructional support and meaningful experiences with literacy to accelerate literacy growth. We must start early and implement procedures of diagnosis, assessment, instruction, and curriculum development throughout the early grades (especially Kindergarten through 3) to ensure that none of our students are "left behind." With this book, we hope to support teachers' efforts in making curriculum meaningful for all their students.

We gratefully acknowledge our colleagues in the Teachers Learning Collaborative: Dara Bacher, Jennifer Berne, Karen Eisele, Kristin Grattan, Nina Hasty, Amy Heitman, Jacquelyn Jones-Frederick, Marcella Kehus, Molly Reed, Earlene Richardson, Jennifer Szlachta, Andy Topper, Jo Trumble, and LaToya Wilson. Working together has been challenging, exciting, and always fun. The support from the Educational Research and Development Centers Program (PR/Award Number R305R70004) to the Center for the Improvement of Early Reading Achievement (CIERA), as administered by the Office of Educational Research and Improvement, U.S. Department of Education was critical to our research on implementing Book Club *Plus* in a variety of grade levels and school districts. Particular recognition is due to the tireless work of the Small Planet team, including Joe Buschini, Melinda Hobausz, Kim Beaudet, and Natalie MacKnight.

What Is
Book Club *Plus*?

Meeting the Dual Obligations of Literacy Instruction

In literacy instruction today, there are a variety of new dilemmas and new ways of thinking. Janine Rodrigues, featured in Classroom View to the left, is typical of many excellent primary teachers—recognizing state and district standards and benchmarks, knowing young children and their literacy abilities, and hoping that all her students leave first grade ready to continue with a lifelong engagement with literacy. Janine wants her students to develop the skills and strategies they need at the word level, but she recognizes that word-level knowledge, while necessary, is not sufficient preparation for success in literacy. She also understands the challenge of integrating skill instruction with the use of those skills in authentic literacy activities. Thus, Janine was searching for an instructional framework consistent with district and state requirements that also provided multiple opportunities for students to integrate their learning about reading, writing, and classroom talk. The Book Club *Plus* framework allowed her to guide successfully her curriculum design, instructional activities, and classroom assessment in literacy.

CLASSROOM VIEW

Before I began this unit, before I decided to *do* a unit based on the Book Club framework, I thought it would never work. How was I going to engage 21 six-year-olds in book clubs, and get them to keep a reading log? I thought it was going to be difficult to get first graders to behave so independently and to start thinking about reading and writing in such a different way. How was I going to get them to trust their own thinking? I had serious doubts that they would even be able to write indepen-

dently and understand some of the strategies I wanted them to learn and apply.

I have spent the last four weeks in my classroom, observing the growth and progress of 21 first graders. All of them have come to understand reading and writing in a new way. They have learned that reading is for a purpose; they have realized that reading means more than just being able to recite words on a page accurately; they have discovered how to use their thinking as an aid in writing and for understanding text.

—Janine Rodrigues

The purpose of this book is to introduce primary-grade teachers to Book Club *Plus.* The Book Club *Plus* framework is the result of research undertaken by Taffy Raphael and Susan Florio-Ruane with members of the Teachers Learning Collaborative (TLC), a network of teachers and teacher educators across southeastern Michigan (Florio-Ruane, Berne, & Raphael, 2001; Raphael, Florio-Ruane, Kehus, George, Hasty & Highfield, 2001). Using a broad theme, Our Storied Lives, to organize our research, we developed the Book Club *Plus* framework to address new problems of practice in contemporary classrooms. The original Book Club program addressed a specific problem of practice in literacy instruction: how can we ensure that all our students—regardless of decoding and fluency levels—have meaningful opportunities to engage with and respond to text that was written for their age level? In pursuit of this goal, Book Club has always focused on using high-quality, age-appropriate literature to promote students' critical thinking in response to what they are reading.

In most classrooms across the United States, many students' reading levels and their age levels differ. Therefore, it isn't enough for educators to use age-appropriate materials. We must also give students opportunities to work with texts at their instructional levels in settings such as guided reading. These are the *dual obligations* of all teachers who teach literacy. Our first obligation is to ensure that all students interact in meaningful ways with texts that are appropriate for their age levels—exploring ideas, learning to respond to the texts through written symbols (pictures, words, phrases, sentences) and orally in dyads, small groups, and whole-class settings. Our second, and equally important, obligation is to ensure that all students work with texts that are appropriate for their reading levels, so that they can learn the workings of our written symbol system.

Many Book Club teachers have resolved this dilemma by using Book Club in addition to a basal reader or other commercial program for guided reading. However, they also report that in doing this, they feel a lack of coherence in their literacy programs, a disconnect between the two settings, and a concern about how to allocate limited time effectively. Further, teachers face increasing pressure as they strive to respond to the letter and spirit of new national, state, and local standards for literacy achievement. We created Book Club *Plus* as a framework to organize the literacy curriculum in efficient, but also effective ways. Samples throughout this book from our work with the Our Storied Lives theme help illustrate how this framework can work in your classroom.

Simply put, the "plus" in Book Club *Plus* represents the literacy curriculum into which the Book Club program can be embedded. The original Book Club program takes its name from the small, student-led discussion groups called "book clubs." These discussion groups, along with the other three components of the Book Club program (reading, writing, and community share), remain central to the Book Club *Plus* framework. The original Book Club program, with its focus on age-appropriate materials, is an ideal site for teaching students comprehension strategies, questioning practices, critical thinking, and literary elements. It is the place for teachers to teach and for students to practice all those skills and strategies teachers would want them to learn regardless of their reading levels.

Building Blocks of the Book Club *Plus* Framework

In addition to the core Book Club context and its four components, we have created a Literacy Block, which is organized in terms of guided reading groups and literacy centers that are described and shown on the chart below.

Book Club *Plus*: A Complete Literacy System

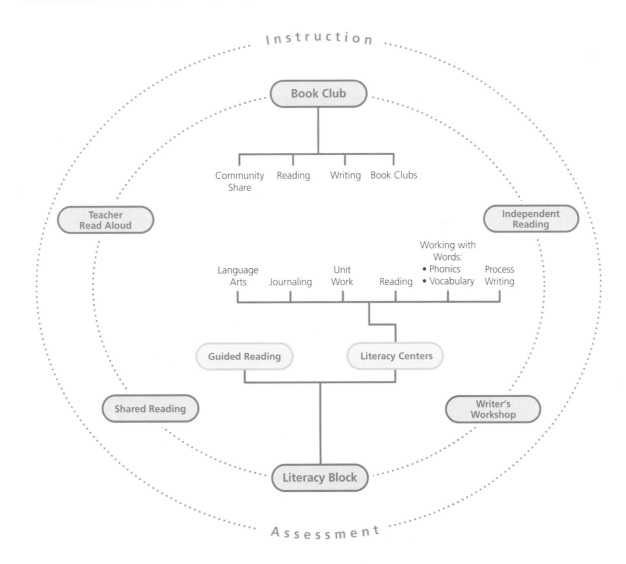

Literacy Block features guided reading, which allows teachers to work with students using texts appropriate to their reading level. Students not working with the teacher use their time for small group and independent practice including journaling, computer activities, spelling, process writing, etc. Literacy Block is the context in which teachers can explicitly teach, coach, and scaffold students' use of concepts, strategies, and skills tailored to their instructional level—including word-level work, vocabulary study, and sight word practice.

Writer's Workshop provides the site where teachers help students make important connections between reading and writing. Students study literary texts as models to enhance their own writing and engage in independent inquiry and sustained writing related to the themes they have been exploring in their texts.

Teacher Read Aloud is a crucial element in the *Plus.* It is always a potential source for encouraging intertextual connections—comparing information across a variety of texts. In many primary classrooms, it is the teacher read aloud that is used as the Book Club book, since young children usually are unable to read books with enough substance to warrant discussion.

Shared Reading is a modification of the teacher read aloud in which students follow along page-by-page in groups of three or four as the teacher reads aloud. Students can pore over the text and in some cases look at a book's rich illustrations as they hear the text of the book read aloud. Shared reading is often used as a companion to writer's workshop. The shared reading books serve as models to inform students' writing.

Independent Reading occurs when students are skilled enough to read books with substantive content that warrants discussion. As students mature and hone their reading skills, they are able to read texts independently or in pairs or small groups and then write and talk about what they've read.

Together, Book Club, Literacy Block, writer's workshop, independent reading, teacher read aloud, and shared reading support early success in literacy by providing contexts for learning that students find meaningful (as shown in the graphic on page 3). Coherence is preserved, although students may work, alternately, in heterogeneous and similar-ability groups. This design helps to create community and meaning by linking four parts of classroom activity which are usually disparate: (1) students of all reading abilities have opportunities to learn with age-peers and also in "by-ability" instructional groups; (2) all group work is linked thematically, with authentic text material on the unit's theme(s) used in the book clubs and in guided reading in the Literacy Block; (3) project work involving writing and oral language is also linked to the themes; and (4) all students share at least one age-appropriate text in book clubs to anchor response and discussion among all learners regardless of reading ability.

Research Support for Book Club *Plus*

Recent legislation places emphasis at K–3 levels on acquiring the code (e.g., phonics, phonetics, and phonemic awareness) and on recognizing words and reading them with fluency. Of course, being literate in a global society will take more than knowing the code. In a recent review of research, Au (2002) notes that in the United States, we have seen increasing expectations for literacy levels to meet minimal or basic standards of achievement. She points out that our society is no longer characterized by manufacturing and agriculture, but instead by knowledge and service. This, coupled with the global economy in which our children will live, suggests that literacy learning in school must fulfill not only the purposes of good citizenship and personal fulfillment, but must also teach our students to read and evaluate texts critically.

Research by Taylor, Pearson, and their associates, (e.g., Taylor, Pearson, Clark & Walpole, 2003) echoes Au's (2002) assertion that our society continues to raise the bar in terms of what it means to be a literate citizen. This research also finds that particular features inside classrooms optimize students' chances of attaining such literacy. Studying schools in which students perform at levels higher than those of students in schools of similar demographics and schools where socioeconomic conditions would predict low reading achievement, these researchers identified essential features of successful teaching. First, teachers used questions requiring complex reasoning rather than simple recall in discussing texts. Second, they used a coaching style, rather than a telling style, helping students see how skills and strategies are applied in the context of reading and writing rather than using isolated worksheets. Third, students had more time for independent reading. Follow-up research demonstrated a *negative* relationship between isolated instruction in comprehension strategies and skills and students' performance levels on standardized tests, in contrast to teaching such strategies in the context of reading and writing. Students were far more successful in classrooms that avoided passive response types, such as turn taking, in favor of active discussion of texts (Taylor, Pearson, Peterson, & Rodriguez, in press).

Au (2002) argues that the following conditions are needed to optimize literacy achievement:

- Student ownership, engagement, and active involvement are supported.

- Instruction is oriented toward engaging expressive tasks, thinking about complex ideas, and powerful communication.

- Literature and other thought-provoking texts form the basis for response, both written and oral, as well as substantive discussion of text among peers.

- Instruction in literacy strategies and skills is directed at their use in the contexts of communication, comprehension, critical thinking, and literary response, rather than taught as isolated content and process.

- Coaching rather than telling and active rather than passive student behaviors promote the independent application of literacy strategies and skills.

We believe that instruction in both our language system and in high levels of engagement and thinking using the language system must begin at the earliest levels of literacy instruction. However, it has been customary in our primary classrooms to teach reading, writing, vocabulary, and literature response as separate parts of the school day and curriculum. It has also been the custom to teach basic skills in advance of and outside the use of text language to communicate. These customs do not place youngsters' emergent literacy in the center of their learning and teachers' practice. Instead, formal education imposes a chronological, developmental order on literacy acquisition. Yet this order leaves teachers with unanswered questions. Among them are the following:

- How do I find all the time I need to teach all that is involved in literacy?

- When should we introduce our students to the various components that contribute to becoming literate?

These questions subsume many, many others, as reflected in Janine's comments as she considered her goals for her first grade students: What is the relationship (in terms of when to teach) between teaching basic skills (i.e., symbol and word knowledge) and introducing more critical aspects of literacy? What are appropriate contexts for teaching skills and strategies? How should I group my students? What kinds of texts should I use? Can young children be expected to write when they don't have formal letter knowledge and spelling skills? What if my students are just beginning to learn English? In early primary grades, what is the relationship between helping students "learn to read" and "read to learn"? In designing Book Club *Plus*, we wanted to answer some of these questions, building on what we have already learned and described in the Book Club program.

The Guiding Principles

In Book Club, students are encouraged to interact with text and other students through writing and conversations to explore important themes that emerge from age-appropriate books. Book Club strengthens the use of literacy for authentic purposes in engaging classroom contexts. We wanted to retain this quality of the Book Club program while transforming it in three ways. First, we wanted to integrate guided reading instruction and related skills and strategy practice. Second, we wanted to connect the Book Club activities—and related writing experiences such as students' reading logs and process writing—to learning about content in other areas of the curriculum such as social studies and/or science. Third, we wanted to offer teachers a framework for planning instruction that is locally adaptable to the diverse needs and demands of a primary classroom.

In this transformation, we were guided by three principles: (1) meaning-making through language and other symbol systems is fundamental to literacy learning, (2) literacy is a cultural practice, and (3) engagement, ownership, and voice in literacy learning are particularly important for young learners.

 PRINCIPLE #1: *Meaning-making through language and other symbol systems is fundamental to literacy learning.*

Book Club *Plus* recognizes the fundamental relationships among language, literacy, and thinking. Many scholars (e.g., Bahktin, 1981; Vygotsky, 1978) describe learning as inherently social. This means that what individuals learn and how learners construct meaning is a result of their interactions with a myriad of more knowledgeable others in formal and informal settings. More knowledgeable others can include adults, such as parents, teachers, and school resource personnel; and youngsters, such as siblings, friends, and classmates. The view of learning as being based in dialogue and social interaction stands in stark contrast to the conventional view of education as involving the transmission of information and values—which assumes that teaching is the same as telling. As curriculum researcher Douglas Barnes suggests,

> Our ability to talk and think is not simply our own invention, but has arisen from taking part in all the shared projects, collaborations, dialogues, and disputes that have constituted our lives. Anything we say is embedded in a history of meanings that preceded our lives, and is immensely more inclusive and varied than our experience can possibly be. It follows that we build up our ability to talk and think by participating in dialogue with others . . . . we must meet different voices, different modes of discourse, different values and attitudes . . . . To think that all that is needed is to tell students what they should know is to expect them to arrive without having traveled. (1995, p. 6)

Communication of ideas, both in written and oral language, is not only the primary purpose of literacy, but it is also one important medium through which interactions among learners and more knowledgeable others take place. This is especially important when we consider that students can engage in oral and written response to text and to one another's ideas within literate activities (e.g. thinking about, responding to, questioning text) even before they have a well-developed understanding of the written language system.

One of the primary-grade teacher's commitments is to ensure that students have access to interesting, engaging, and challenging texts through teacher read aloud and shared reading, listening centers, reading buddies from higher grade levels, and other similar sources. In such settings, primary children are encouraged to participate in the literacy activities surrounding these texts. If making meaning through language and other symbol systems is fundamental to thinking, as we believe, such activities around texts are important to the intellectual development of the young child. Our mandated national education goal is not simply to have all students decode successfully by the end of third grade. It is for all students to reach high levels of literacy by the end of third grade, and to use these literacy abilities in school and throughout their lives. Our programs must work to achieve that goal and to promote the literate thinking and learning of children throughout their school careers.

PRINCIPLE #2: *Literacy is a cultural practice.*

When we speak of communication as both the chief aim of literacy and the chief way in which literacy is learned, we are acknowledging that literacy is part of culture. When we watch a child or adult read silently, it is easy to think of literacy as reading, and of reading as a skilled, private activity. However, looking deeper, we see that the why, how, and wherefore of this apparently private activity are profoundly social. First, the text represents ideas an author has written for purposes of communication. Second, as he or she reads that text, the reader is making sense of the author's written expression in terms of experience. Moreover, the skilled practice that enables that reader to make sense of text is taught and learned by people who are in communication with one another. Finally, for literate societies, the text and the tools for making sense of it are an essential part of the social organization of the community. In short, as Barton (1994) has suggested, literacy is ecological in nature—far from pristinely practiced by readers or writers in isolation, it is messy and rich with the various elements that make up the life of the group and the lives of individuals within it.

To say that literacy is a cultural practice, however, is not to deny that culture itself has multiple faces in the lives of our students. We have in the United States a pupil population whose primary cultural experiences in the home and community differ widely in terms of heritage, language, and socioeconomic circumstance. Beyond this diversity, we are all multicultural in the sense that we participate simultaneously in a variety of cultural groups (e.g. families, workplaces, peer groups, churches), and we therefore learn and practice multiple literacies which we are able to use appropriately in the various cultural contexts of our lives.

Much of the knowledge required to achieve these complex activities is part of our inheritance both as human beings and as members of communities.

Yet the teaching and learning of written language and its application to complex reasoning is not likely to be accomplished independently of a person's participation in formal schooling—itself a very important cultural institution. To say that literacy is cultural means that it is learned, taught, and used in a myriad of contexts, for a myriad of purposes.

Young children's literacy experiences take many forms. They may include bedtime reading, a predominant literacy routine in many middle class families. However, they may also include early experiences in church, as one teacher in the TLC realized when she reflected on her own literacy learning. She had thought initially of her childhood as devoid of literacy experiences, since she had few books of her own. Then she realized how rich her literacy experiences had been as she learned psalms and prayers and shared these among peers in Sunday school and with her family at home and in church. Still other literate practices take the form of oral narratives, told across generations and shared as part of family histories. These narratives introduce children to concepts of story—characters, plot, sequence of events, and so forth.

The texts children hear also reflect cultural practice. As Birkerts (1994) and others have noted, literature represents the recorded history of humanity. Literature serves as a mirror and a window. It can reflect societies' values, practices, and our own beliefs about the world. It can provide a window into the values and practices of people, places, and times we will never encounter personally (Bishop, 1992; Galda, 1998). When we acknowledge the role that literature plays, it becomes clear that the literacy curriculum is a powerful tool. It can promote critical thinking about ourselves and about our society. It can help our young children, as well as their teachers, understand their own perspectives as limited by a cultural context and, in certain ways, different from the perspectives of others with whom we share the planet.

We want our children to be able to participate well in the diverse world. They must be able to reason well, think critically, and work with many different information sources. Even very young children are exposed to relatively uncensored information—from television and film to websites. And many children depend on school as the place where they will acquire critical thinking skills. Thus, a central goal of Book Club *Plus* is to help young children make meaningful connections between their earliest literacy experiences and school literacy; to provide meaningful contexts where they can see the big picture of their literacy learning while they learn the skills and strategies that will help them become independent readers and writers; and to understand that becoming literate means responding to literature from a personal, a creative, and a critical stance. Because the classroom is itself a powerful cultural context for our students, we teach in ways that provide opportunities for all students to access literacy. We work to optimize the power of shared understanding and purpose in supporting each student's efforts to learn new skills and knowledge.

PRINCIPLE #3: *Engagement, ownership, and voice in literacy learning are particularly important for young learners.*

Core to Book Club is the concept of student engagement. This concept has been around for decades, described in the 1960s in terms of "time on task" (Carroll, 1963). Engagement in this sense was a simple construct—learners were engaged, by definition, if they were spending time on the relevant task. But over the past 40 years, we have learned more about the nature of engagement. Engagement now implies motivation—the will to apply the skills and strategies learned, as Paris and his colleagues have noted (Paris, Lipson, & Wixson, 1983). Engagement is seen in classrooms with "lively discussions," as Gambrell and her colleagues have described (Gambrell, 1996). Most recently, engagement has been characterized in terms of students' ownership of literacy skills, strategies, and activities (Au, Carroll, & Scheu, 1997).

Au and her colleagues talk about ownership as students' valuing of literacy. We see ownership when students elect to read during free time, when they read outside the classroom, write (whether with words or symbols) for fun or to accomplish a goal, tell their friends about a story they've heard, or share a favorite author. They feel confident in their ability to read and write or in the potential to learn to read and write conventionally. When we speak of voice in a writer's craft, we are referring to his or her particular way of writing to express, persuade, argue, and so forth. Mastery of written language as readers and writers ultimately enables students to use literacy as a powerful expressive tool. Similarly, readers have voices. They respond to texts, understanding their content and learning to think about how texts work. Comprehension, critical thinking, and an awareness of how texts are made and interpreted combine to give readers powerful voices with which to respond to the written word.

The Book Club *Plus* Framework

It is at the level of the classroom activity setting that the Book Club *Plus* framework most visibly and dramatically transforms classroom instruction. In our explanations that follow, we focus primarily on Book Club and Literacy Block as the core contexts in which literacy instruction occurs. We bring in the teacher read aloud as a common site where students can hear the Book Club book, since books with enough substantive content for book club discussions are often written at a level that young children are unable to read independently. Thus, in the early primary grades, we must remember that, in the Book Club context, access to the content of the text is more important than is the ability to decode that text independently. Finally, we bring in writer's workshop as a site where students can engage in a range of writing opportunities connected thematically to their reading.

We turn now to a detailed description of the core contexts—Book Club and Literacy Block.

Book Club as a Context for Literacy Learning

Within Book Club, the four components—community share, reading, writing, and book clubs—interweave to support students' learning to read, respond to, and discuss literature in student-led groups (as shown in the diagram below). These components are implemented with flexible lengths of time for each, depending upon student needs and teacher goals. For early primary-grade children, the book club component can be embedded within the read-aloud context, the literacy instructional program, or students' content-area study.

Community Share

Opening community share is a teacher-led, whole-group activity. The teacher uses the activity as the site to (a) set the context for upcoming reading, writing, and talk about text, (b) review related text content such as the previous day's reading, and (c) teach skills and strategies appropriate to all students, no matter what their reading level (e.g., identifying what is important, comparing across texts). The teacher typically controls the topics of discussion and the turn taking that occurs during the opening community share.

Closing community share reconvenes the small groups to share ideas and issues that emerged in their book club discussions. This time the topics grow out of the students' discussion groups, though for organizational purposes, the teacher tends to manage the turn taking.

▶ **Components of Book Club**

All components of Book Club support students' small-group discussions. Explicit instruction in reading, writing, listening, and speaking skills helps students succeed in all areas of the curriculum.

Reading or Read Aloud

Writing

Book Club Discussion Groups

Opening Community Share

Closing Community Share

Instruction

Reading

The reading component can take different forms in primary grades, depending on the children's fluency with print. It involves students gaining access to the book to be discussed, regardless of their reading level. In kindergarten or first grade, the teacher typically reads the text to the children. Books that young children can read independently—wordless picture books, pattern books, decodable texts—generally do not have enough substance on which to build meaningful conversation. Thus, the teacher read aloud is the primary way for students to access the text. In the read-aloud program, the point is to use the context to help students develop their abilities to write in response to and to talk about texts that they hear.

A modification of the teacher read aloud is the shared reading format. For shared reading, the teacher still is the primary person reading, but enough copies exist for students to follow along page-by-page in groups of three or four. Books with rich illustrations are particularly relevant to the shared reading format so each child can pore over the text while hearing the words read. One particularly positive aspect of shared reading is its interactive nature. Shared reading invites student-to-student and teacher-to-student interaction. By third grade, children are more able to read text independently or in pairs and small groups, and the substantive content of the readable books can be worthy of being Book Club books. Thus, as children mature, the reading component moves into an independent reading format.

Writing

In Book Club *Plus,* students learn to see writing as a tool that can serve many functions, such as reflecting on reading, gathering and organizing information, practicing literary forms, and sharing ideas with others. The writing component involves response in students' reading logs. These responses help students prepare for and reflect upon book club discussions. Sustained writing occurs when writer's workshop activities connect thematically (e.g., similar genre, theme, content, author craft) to the Book Club books. For young children, writing can incorporate a range of symbol systems, including pictures to convey the "pictures in their heads" that the books prompt them to scribble and other forms of "pretend" writing. While intermediate-grade children often use writing as a way to prepare for their book club discussions, emergent and early readers often use writing as a way to extend their thinking *after* they have had a chance to talk about the book in small or whole-class settings (Grattan, 1997).

Student Book Clubs

A book club is a student-led discussion group for which the program was named. The class is divided into heterogeneous groups of four to five, varying in reading level, gender, classroom status, verbal abilities, and so forth. Students remain in their book clubs throughout a unit. On some occasions, all book clubs read and discuss the same book. At other times, they read different books encircling the shared theme. In all cases, the books are theme and age-appropriate and sufficiently complex to warrant and support in-depth discussion and a range of responses. Within book clubs, students discuss ideas that emerged from their reading and log responses, airing questions, confusions, and related personal experiences. Students learn norms for appropriate behavior such as listening with respect, building on others' ideas, debating and commenting on ideas, assuming leadership, and following another's lead. Thus, learning to read, write, and talk in Book Club embodies democratic processes and learning within community. In Chapter 5, Talk in the Classroom, and in Chapter 7, Classroom Management (pages 115–117), we describe ways in which very young children can be introduced to student-led discussion groups.

Literacy Block as a Context for Guided Reading Groups

Literacy Block forms the second core context within the Book Club *Plus* framework. Here teachers use texts and activities appropriate to students' reading levels, work with students directly in guided reading, and support them in related centers. In the guided reading groups (see Fountas & Pinnell, 1996), students are grouped by their instructional levels—usually assigned to work at, above, and below grade level. Occasionally a teacher may decide to have more than three groups, but we have found that having only three groups maximizes the teachers' opportunity to meet with the students in their reading groups. The texts that students use during guided reading—regardless of the reading group in which students are placed—are linked thematically to their Book Club book(s).

When not meeting with the teacher, students work independently in Literacy Block centers. Some teachers set up the centers as physical places where students engage in the work: process writing center, phonics center, vocabulary center, etc. Other teachers set up all these types of activities together in one area. Students pick up directions and necessary materials at the designated area but work at their seats. Still other teachers use a combination of these two approaches so that students can pick up and take back to their seats individual work, but meet in a specific physical space for paired and small group work (e.g., reading center).

Our research finds that interweaving Book Club and Literacy Block and their supporting components is an efficient way to integrate reading and the language arts. But perhaps more important, it is a way to teach all youngsters and, in so doing, engage and even accelerate the learning of those who are not achieving at grade level. By working within and across ability groups, within thematically linked texts at a variety of difficulty levels, with scaffolded instructional support, and with membership in an authentic literate community, students are able to learn both skills and their use. This experience and the social context in which it occurs create a synergy that can accelerate students' literacy development. (Florio-Ruane, Raphael, Highfield, & Berne, 2004). Finally, by linking the Book Club *Plus* activities to students' subject-area learning, the framework also supports early readers in applying literacy skills across the elementary school content areas. Students not only learn academic content; they also gain confidence in their ability to learn about complex ideas and subjects by using the tools of reading, writing, and oral language. It is one of the most important purposes of schooling in our society, and, as Au (2002) asserts, it is what we mean today when we say that a person is "literate."

Conclusion

We began creating the instructional context of Book Club *Plus* in primary-grade classrooms with our three guiding principles in mind: literacy instruction should keep meaning-making as its central focus, whether instruction is about word level knowledge or thinking critically about text; literacy is a cultural practice; and students' ownership and voice is central to their success. The ways that a teacher weaves the guiding principles and components of Book Club *Plus* together depends on his or her local situation. Elements of the local situation include class composition, the curriculum and materials being used, and the standards and benchmarks for which teacher and students are accountable. Across all adaptations of the framework, the teacher aims to honor the dual commitments of instructionally-appropriate and age-appropriate engagement with text. The students and the teacher work to create a coherent literate environment where efficiency and meaning are maximized by the weaving together of an array of literate practices in a thematic and balanced curriculum. In Janine Rodrigues's words, ". . . with so much focus on test scores, on bringing children to a certain level, at times it's hard to remember that we have to make all this meaningful." That is the goal of Book Club *Plus.*

In Chapter 2, we show how these key ideas, principles, and goals are realized in the content and curriculum of the Book Club *Plus* framework.

Content and Curriculum

Content in the Book Club *Plus* Framework

In Chapter 1, we describe how Book Club *Plus* in primary-grade class-rooms presents teachers with opportunities to teach their students important literacy skills, strategies, and attitudes. Here we discuss the elements of content and curriculum that we use when we decide to apply the Book Club *Plus* framework in our classrooms. Content refers to what our students will learn about reading, writing, and oral language as they participate in these settings and activities. Curriculum is how the learning of skills, strategies, and written-language concepts supports the learning of ideas—specifically those comprising the academic curriculum.

Within these instructional elements, we are committed to ensuring that all students have opportunity to learn four core curricular areas: (1) comprehension, (2) writing, (3) language conventions, and (4) literary aspects. The chart on the following two pages presents the four curricular areas of the core Book Club program described in *Book Club: A Literature-Based Curriculum,* 2nd Ed., (Raphael, et al., 2002). However, the content in each area reflects modifications that fit the goals of primary-grade teachers. We've worked to maintain our own vision of the literacy accomplishments of students who have completed elementary school. The four categories shown in the chart reflect the range of what we want our students to learn in each year of school, adapting the focus and content as required for each grade level.

Curricular Target Areas

Comprehension

Background Knowledge

- Understand concepts of print
- Make predictions
- Draw on prior knowledge
- Build knowledge as needed
- Use context clues (including picture clues)
- Make intertextual connections

Processing Text

- Understand story sequence
- Change predictions as appropriate
- Use imagery to build pictures of the story
- Recognize important ideas and information
- List key ideas
- Make inferences
- Build vocabulary

- Develop interest in words, their history, and their meanings
- Organize and use knowledge of text structure
- Describe aspects of characters, setting, plot sequence, and author's message

Monitor Own Reading

- Ask questions
- Clarify confusions

Writing

Foundations

- Represent ideas on a page (pictures, symbols)

Writer's Workshop

- Plan
- Draft
- Revise (adding or deleting ideas)
- Publish

Writing as a Tool for Thinking

- Reading logs
- Think sheets
- Share sheets

Writing from Sources

- Write ideas in own words
- Avoid simply copying others' writing
- Make connections (text to text, text to self, text to theme)

On-Demand Writing

- Write text appropriate to age level (e.g., complete a sentence, write a sentence, write multiple sentences related by topic or theme)
- Write on an assigned topic

Language Conventions

Words

- Know decoding strategies using knowledge of phonics (e.g., beginning and ending sounds), phonemic awareness (e.g., word families), and context (e.g., picture clues, sentence clues)
- Read words fluently
- Spell conventionally

Grammar

- Use appropriate language choices (verbs, syntax, punctuation) in oral reading, discussion, and writing
- Use basic punctuation to make sense of text and convey ideas in writing

Interaction

- Work with peers to set goals
- Work with peers to explore ideas (e.g., through inquiry projects)
- Interact with peers in literacy contexts (small group work, pair activity, center activity)
- Participate effectively in fish-bowls and/or book clubs

Literary Aspects

Literary Elements

Theme

- Construct author's "message"
- Make text-to-self connections

Point of View

- Understand characters' POV
- Describe author's POV

Genre/Structures

- Recognize and use narrative structure to retell a story, summarize a story, create a story
- Recognize and use basic informational text structures (e.g., explanation and description) to retell and to create informational texts
- Recognize stories/ articles from various genres (e.g., poetry and song, short story, picture book, informational text, informational story books, biographies)

Author's Craft

- Describe author's styles
- Identify text features specific to author (e.g., how can you tell this is a book by [insert author's name])
- Identify illustration features characteristic of illustrator

Response to Literature

Personal

- Share experiences
- Share personal feelings
- Place self in story situation
- Compare self to characters

Creative

- Ask "What if?" (change event in plot and explore impact)
- Dramatize events and characters' attitudes or actions
- Illustrate events and characters
- Apply ideas and issues in new ways or to new situations

Critical

- Explain changes in beliefs or feelings
- Use evidence from text to support ideas
- Discuss author's purposes
- Identify author's craft
- Use text as a mirror of own life and as a window into lives of others

The chart on pages 16–17 summarizes the scope and sequence lists and standards that exist across national to local levels. For example, in the comprehension component in the early primary grades, in addition to general background knowledge that we want students to acquire, we must include assessing students' knowledge about concepts of print (e.g., how to hold a book, directionality, information conveyed through print and pictures). In terms of literary aspects, just as older children develop an understanding of authors, we want primary students to be aware of the authors who write their books and to engage in the full variety of responses to literature. We also want them to learn to think in terms of story themes, as Au (1992) and Lehr (1991) have demonstrated young children can do. Regardless of the curricular area, instruction supports students' progress toward achieving standards that are required at the national, state, and local levels. The next section describes the ways Book Club *Plus* can address the goals of the wider curriculum.

Curriculum in the Book Club *Plus* Framework

At the primary-grade levels, Book Club can be brought into the literacy and school curricula using one of three models: (a) the teacher read-aloud program, (b) using Book Club *Plus* to integrate the Book Club and Literacy Block (i.e., guided reading) contexts, and (c) integrating Book Club activities and subject area learning in science and social studies. These models are not static. They can be used and combined in many different ways depending on your literacy requirements. In the following sections, we discuss key instructional decisions that teachers need to consider, and we illustrate these with two examples. We categorize these decisions in terms of:

- Decisions about themes and related literature selection

- Decisions about organizing for the week

- Decisions about grouping

Example 1. Teacher Read Aloud in a Kindergarten Classroom

The read-aloud model can be particularly useful with emergent and early readers, providing them with an understanding that reading is a meaning-making process inviting connections within and across books, and between books and their own lives. Students can learn fundamental concepts about print, such as directionality and word-picture relationships. They can learn about different genres, including folk tales (e.g., "Trickster" tales, *Just So Stories*); or different versions of classic stories (such as *Cinderella, Mufaro's Beautiful Daughters* by John Steptoe, and *The Rough-Face Girl* by Rafe Martin); poetry, realistic fiction, informational storybooks; and expository resource materials. Young children can begin to construct understandings at the thematic level while engaging in a range of personal, creative, and critical responses. In short, the teacher read aloud introduces students to substantive texts that they would be unable to read or experience on their own. At the same time, the teacher can teach literacy skills and strategies appropriate to all children at their age level (e.g., how to ask good questions, how to respond in a variety of ways), regardless of their reading level. This is *absolutely crucial* to students' success in literacy. Moreover, it provides struggling readers with access to texts appropriate to their age and interest levels and asks them to write in response to and talk about these texts with their peers (Grattan, 1997; Young, 2001).

In a unit designed for kindergarten students, Barbara Naess used the teacher read-aloud context to engage students in Book Club activities appropriate to young children. As she planned the unit, Barbara considered possible themes appropriate to her five-year-old students. She wanted to begin with a unit for which students would have extensive background and a high level of interest. She wanted a theme that had potential for using stories and other genres, including poetry and informational texts. And, like all Book Club unit themes, she wanted it to be "worthy" of the time she and her students would spend reading, writing, and talking about it.

For kindergarten students moving from home to school, learning about themselves and each other is always engaging. Thus, Barbara decided on the theme All About Me, and she developed related theme questions that she would ask her students to consider as they heard each text. The theme questions were:

- Who am I?

- In what ways am I different from other children?

- In what ways are we the same?

- What makes me special?

- What does it mean to be me?

Barbara planned to end each book discussion by returning to these questions, asking students to elaborate on their answers in terms of what they had learned from the texts.

There are many books written for five-year-olds that address this theme. Text selection was based on four criteria: (a) potential for children's engagement, (b) availability, (c) content accessibility, and (d) appropriateness. The engagement criterion required books that children would find interesting. The availability criterion required books that could be accessed in the classroom, school, or public library. When using the Book Club framework to create a read-aloud unit, the availability criterion is generally easy to meet since only one copy is critical. However, availability can be a factor when multiple copies of texts are needed (e.g., for guided reading and shared reading). The accessibility criterion dictates that students have sufficient background knowledge to understand the text, while the appropriateness criterion requires that this understandable content be one that parents would find reasonable for their children to read or hear. With these criteria in mind, Barbara created three book sets with content that she believed her students would find to be engaging, accessible, and appropriate to their age level. She hoped these books would prompt them to think about theme questions, make intertextual connections (within and across book sets), and connect these among the texts and their own lives.

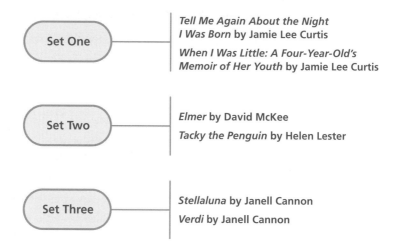

Set One

Tell Me Again About the Night I Was Born by Jamie Lee Curtis

When I Was Little: A Four-Year-Old's Memoir of Her Youth by Jamie Lee Curtis

Set Two

Elmer by David McKee

Tacky the Penguin by Helen Lester

Set Three

Stellaluna by Janell Cannon

Verdi by Janell Cannon

Many other books address this theme, from the classic story of the ugly duckling to *I Like Being Me: Poems for Children about Feeling Special, Appreciating Others, and Getting Along* by Judy Lalli. These can be made available in a classroom library and brought into the unit through book talks that encourage students to look at these books during independent reading or to check them out to be read at home.

With the theme and book sets identified, Barbara made decisions about organizing her unit. She considered factors such as time (e.g., how much time could she spend on Book Club relative to other classroom demands) and lesson flow (e.g., whether to complete a book in one reading or over several days). She decided that with the three book sets, it made sense to distribute them over a three-week period. Given the relatively short length of time it would take to read each story, she read one story each day and a poem from the *I Like Being Me* anthology on the third day, repeating this cycle each week. This allowed her to return to the stories for shared reading activities or follow-up activities related to vocabulary and word study.

Barbara spent approximately 40 minutes a day on the Book Club activities, based on her estimation of her students' ability to sustain their attention and interest. For opening community share, she did short literacy mini-lessons on knowledge appropriate to the children's age level and to her district curriculum. For example, she taught about authors and illustrators, parts of a book, how to make and check predictions about story content, how to make text-to-text and set-to-set connections, and how to connect the books they heard to the theme and to their own lives. She also taught vocabulary concepts relevant to the unit such as "same" and "different."

The reading component took the form of teacher read aloud. Children then wrote entries for their reading logs, often finishing a starter sentence (e.g., for *Verdi,* "When I am grown up, I still will . . ."). Unlike in intermediate grade settings, there is a great deal of chatter as primary-grade students write. They often talk aloud and interact with other children at their table.

Students then shifted from writing to discussion using fishbowls (see Chapter 7, pages 115–117 for a detailed description), in which a book club group volunteers (or is invited) to conduct their discussion at the table in the center of the room. The rest of the class observes and then critiques the discussion. This is where, even in the read-aloud model, teachers consider issues related to grouping students. In the read-aloud model, grouping students for their book clubs involves thinking about which students work well together and creating groups that are heterogeneous in terms of verbal ability, gender, ethnicity, and classroom status. Since all students are working from the same texts, it is easy to change groups should the need arise. Barbara invited each book club to have a student-led discussion while sitting in the fishbowl. There was usually time for two or three book clubs to meet each day, so that over the course of the week, each book club had a turn.

Following the book clubs, the students moved into closing community share where they discussed ideas from their book clubs under Barbara's leadership. Generally, this part of the lesson focused on linking to the theme of learning about themselves. Throughout the unit, in both formal instructional and informal interactive settings, students learned how to interact with one another in small group and whole class settings, using guidelines for discussion that included:

- Everybody talks.

- Talk one at a time.

- Listen to each other to get good ideas.

- Respect each other.

- Talk about the books.

For writing activities during the unit, Barbara used a few sentence starters such as "I am unique because . . ." and asked students to complete each sentence. Some students used a few letters they had learned to represent their ideas. Others imitated writing with scribbles. Still others drew small pictures. Students then "read" what they had written to Barbara, who wrote the conventional words for them on the page. All students illustrated their sentences. The students' work was made into a class book that was placed in the classroom library after a short time on display in the school library.

Through the All About Me unit, Barbara and her class learned about literacy through reading, writing, and talk. They also gained experience and knowledge in learning within a community and practicing many principles fundamental to a democratic society. (See Chapter 10 for an example of a complete read-aloud unit.)

Example 2. Book Club *Plus*

Our second example illustrates Book Club *Plus* in Janine Rodrigues's first-grade classroom. Her unit was a genre study of trickster tales that she created to introduce her students to Book Club *Plus.* Janine's district used a basal reading program as the primary source of instructional material, but her principal allowed teachers flexibility in when and how the basal reading program was implemented (in Chapter 11, we illustrate how Book Club *Plus* can be used when teachers are more constrained in how the basal must be used).

As with all teachers in her district, Janine must meet her district's new reading initiative, which dictates that teachers distribute their literacy instruction among four areas: fluency, word knowledge, comprehension, and writing. Moreover, Janine is aware of the recent research documenting the importance of ownership and engagement, teaching strategies and skills in context, authenticity of texts and tasks, and creating active learners. Because this unit occurred early in the school year, Janine decided that engaging her students and encouraging their ownership was of primary importance to set the tone for the school year while also introducing them to the Book Club *Plus* activities. She chose to focus on the genre of trickster tales to promote students' thinking about character at two levels. At the simplest level, she used the trickster to introduce the story element of character. At a more complex level, she used the trickster tales to help students think about the concept of character attributes, extending from their descriptions and discussions of the tricksters' attributes across stories to examining their own character traits—for example, what makes each of them a good person.

Having determined her theme, like Barbara, she applied the criteria of potential engagement, availability, appropriateness, and accessibility to select texts to support the instructional contexts. She also stocked the classroom library with a range of titles.

Selected Titles for Trickster Tale Unit

Contexts	Texts
Teacher Read Aloud/ Book Club Books	*Anansi and the Magic Stick* by Eric Kimmel *Anansi and the Talking Melon* by Eric Kimmel *Flossie and the Fox* by Patricia McKissack *Raven: A Trickster Tale from the Pacific Northwest* by Gerald McDermott *Tops & Bottoms* by Janet Stevens
Guided Reading	Selections from leveled readers and the first-grade basal reading program
Special Classroom Library	*Coyote Steals the Blanket: A Ute Tale* by Janet Stevens *The Gingerbread Boy* by Paul Galdone *How Rabbit Tricked Otter and Other Cherokee Trickster Stories* by Gayle Ross *Little Red Riding Hood* versions by Candice Ransom, Trina Schart Hyman, and Harriet Ziefert *Old Bag of Bones: A Coyote Tale* by Janet Stevens *Three Tales of Trickery* by Marilyn Helmer *The Tortoise and the Hare* by Janet Stevens

As is typical with early primary students, Janine's Book Club activities took place around the teacher read aloud. Guided reading occurred within the Literacy Block activities. The classroom library was used during independent reading. Writer's workshop took place daily. For both Book Club and independent reading, Janine needed only one copy of each book. For guided reading, each child in a reading group needed a text leveled by reading ability. For that reason, and to meet district policies about using the adopted basal reading program, Janine used trickster tales found in the basal anthology and the leveled reading books. If she worked in a district that did not require the use of the basal reader, and further, if her district had the resources for her to purchase books, Janine could have selected literature for her guided reading program as well, using criteria such as the percentage of decodable words.

With the theme and literature in place, Janine turned to organizing for instruction. Her first decision was how to divide her time between Book Club and Literacy Block activities. Ideally, in the early primary grades, there is time to include both activities each day. Teachers can establish a schedule with Book Club in the morning and the Literacy Block in the afternoon, or vice versa, for example. Or teachers can begin with Literacy Block and culminate the morning literacy activities with Book Club. One advantage of

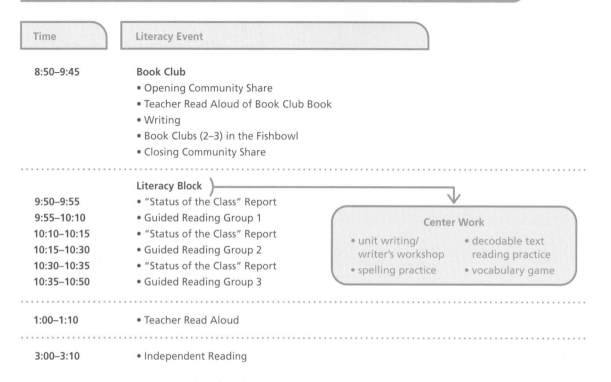

Possible First-Grade Book Club *Plus* Literacy Focus

Time	Literacy Event
8:50–9:45	**Book Club** • Opening Community Share • Teacher Read Aloud of Book Club Book • Writing • Book Clubs (2–3) in the Fishbowl • Closing Community Share
	Literacy Block
9:50–9:55	• "Status of the Class" Report
9:55–10:10	• Guided Reading Group 1
10:10–10:15	• "Status of the Class" Report
10:15–10:30	• Guided Reading Group 2
10:30–10:35	• "Status of the Class" Report
10:35–10:50	• Guided Reading Group 3
1:00–1:10	• Teacher Read Aloud
3:00–3:10	• Independent Reading

Center Work
• unit writing/ writer's workshop
• spelling practice
• decodable text reading practice
• vocabulary game

this schedule is that students are immersed in their theme work and partici-pate in multiple groups over the course of the day, lessening the possibility of any stigma from being viewed as a member of the "low group." A typical day in a first-grade classroom is represented in the table above.

Janine elected to use Book Club *Plus* to organize the two-hour block of time mandated by her district for literacy instruction, and to use two addi-tional short periods in her classroom. Right after recess, as a way to calm her children for the afternoon's academic work, she would do a read aloud not necessarily connected to the Book Club *Plus* unit theme. Independent read-ing occurred at the end of the day—a time that could be dedicated for this purpose throughout the school. She built writer's workshop into the center activities during Literacy Block, sometimes having her students work inde-pendently, and other times shortening her time with the reading groups to provide for a 20-minute whole-class lesson on writer's workshop.

Extensions to Upper Primary Grades

Book Club *Plus* has been used effectively from first through middle-school levels. The two examples in this chapter illustrate common ways in which teachers in the primary grades implement Book Club within the broader context of their literacy curriculum. There are differences, however, between early primary (i.e., kindergarten and first grade) and later primary (i.e., second and third grades). There may be differences in the allocation of time across curricular areas. For example, by third grade, more time is allocated to science and social studies. There are differences in the range of reading levels, of course, as students move up the grade levels. Throughout this book, we provide illustrations of several Book Club *Plus* classrooms.

Teachers' decisions, regardless of their specific situation, focus on literature selection, grouping, and organizing literacy routines. The latter is perhaps the most visible difference between early and later primary-grade classrooms. By second or third grade, time allocations across the curriculum may not permit both Book Club and Literacy Block activities to occur on the same day, as Janine was able to do. In such cases, teachers must decide how to allocate their time, and TLC members have found several effective possibilities. Some teachers prefer to alternate weekly between Book Club and Literacy Block. The advantages of this schedule include time to read three or four titles, and even to reread certain books for specific purposes related to learning literacy skills and strategies and to developing thematic content knowledge. For older children who are beginning to read chapter books, a week is usually enough time to finish their books. Further, the extended time gives students a week to engage in a sustained writing activity to support their reading and their talk in book clubs. One disadvantage can occur when students have chapter books that they cannot complete in a week. When they shift to Literacy Block, they may not return to their chapter books for a week. Thus, alternatives such as the two-day or three-day cycles may be preferable—giving students sufficient time with a single text and not too much time between "reads." As shown below, another organizational pattern

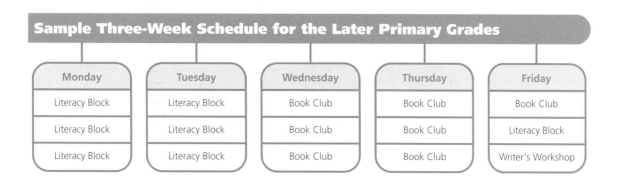

Sample Three-Week Schedule for the Later Primary Grades

Monday	Tuesday	Wednesday	Thursday	Friday
Literacy Block	Literacy Block	Book Club	Book Club	Book Club
Literacy Block	Literacy Block	Book Club	Book Club	Literacy Block
Literacy Block	Literacy Block	Book Club	Book Club	Writer's Workshop

is to use Monday and Tuesday for Book Club, Wednesday and Thursday for Literacy Block, and Friday to "swing" between the two, serving as the first day of a three-day Book Club cycle or the last day of a three-day Literacy Block cycle, or a day to focus on writer's workshop.

Conclusion

Regardless of the organization used to create a Book Club *Plus* literacy environment, students have multiple opportunities to engage with text through reading and talk and to use writing as a tool to respond to what they've read and create new texts. Through these activities, students learn literacy content—how to read, write, and talk about text—while, at the same time, they learn through the literature about themselves, their cultures, our histories as a society, and the content knowledge we have accumulated over the ages.

In this chapter, we have described the content that is taught within Book Club *Plus* and the curricular study that is possible through Book Club *Plus*. In the next chapters, we focus more closely on the content of the literacy curriculum that is central to the Book Club program: reading comprehension, writing, and classroom talk.

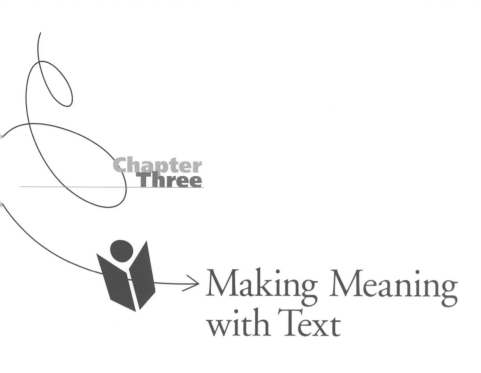

Chapter Three

Making Meaning with Text

Comprehension: What Will We Teach?

Think about the last text you read. Maybe you were sitting on a train or in a comfortable chair in your living room. As you lost yourself in the text, you were actively drawing on a variety of sources of information and using a range of strategies to make meaning. Giving our students the tools with which they can comprehend a variety of texts is one of our most important goals in teaching literacy. In this chapter, we will describe comprehension instruction. We will begin with what is taught and then discuss *how* it is taught. Then we will end with recommendations for opportunities to teach comprehension within the Book Club *Plus* framework.

In learning to read, our students learn and practice a variety of comprehension skills that experienced readers take for granted. For example, one of the authors of this book describes reading *Dreams of Trespass: Tales of a Harem Girlhood* by Fatima Mernissi for a book club discussion with a group of teachers. Despite her lack of experience with the country and time period in which the book is set, she used a variety of familiar strategies to access background knowledge before even starting the book. She drew from the title to think about books that might be similar. The word *tales* told her this was going to be a narrative. *Harem girlhood* brought back memories of the character Scheherazade from old Disney movies. The back cover told her the genre—memoir, so she thought about other memoirs she'd read. She also drew from quotes on the back cover and raised questions, such as whether "dreams of trespass" were metaphorical and what that might mean. Before even beginning the book, she was involved in accessing background knowledge, making intertextual connections, and predicting what the text might be about. Later, while reading the book, our reader identified key ideas in the narrative. She noticed themes and continued to make intertextual connections. She also defined unfamiliar words using context clues. In short, our skilled reader made meaning using a range of strategies that built on related background knowledge and experiences. In a Book Club *Plus* classroom such as the one described in the Classroom View below, students are regularly given authentic experiences that allow them to practice these strategies—the strategies of skilled readers.

All teachers know how crucial comprehension is to successful reading. While reading or listening to texts, readers of all ages and abilities use a wide variety of comprehension techniques. The third-graders in the Classroom View demonstrate how comprehension instruction is manifested in students' independent practice within a book club setting. They use comprehension strategies in authentic ways—multiple strategies at one time to answer their real questions. They do not require their teacher to tell them what to do, nor

CLASSROOM VIEW

Background Knowledge and Experiences

Six children, grouped hetero-geneously, from MariAnne George's third-grade classroom are in a book club talking about *Stone Fox* by John Reynolds Gardner. *Stone Fox* is the story of Little Willy and his dog, Searchlight, who must save Little Willy's grandfather's farm by coming up with the money to pay back taxes. They enter the annual dog sled race to try and win the money. The group is discussing the part of the book where a tax collector goes to the home of Little Willy and his grandfather demanding payment of back taxes.

This segment opens with Kendra's* statement that she is confused. Kendra raises two questions: (a) Did they harvest potatoes and have a lot of them to sell? and (b) Was the tax collector real? Kendra, Olivia, and Tegan lead the discussion with supporting comments

from Marika, Habib, and Eric. Together, they evidence co-construc-tion of meaning as they use different comprehension strategies that they have learned.

Kendra: I was kind of confused when they said, when he said, after Searchlight was plowing the field, I thought they had harvest-ed the potatoes, and they just they sold like a lot of them and got $200.

Olivia: Yeah I know, that's what I thought, but I guess they made half their debt.

Marika: And Little Willy said they was gonna grow more [potatoes.

??:** [more potatoes

Olivia: [more potatoes every year, but it'd be

??: Yeah

??: It's be more and more money

??: Yeah

Marika: Did he sell it, or?

Olivia: I'm not sure, I think he did, but I'm not really sure

Habib: He did say it.

Kendra: I think they did and they said something about $200.

Habib: Yeah, $200

Olivia: And all he needed was $300, but still.

Tegan: But, I . . .

Notice in this section that the students are working to clarify whether or not Little Willy and his grandfather need money to pay taxes. They are identifying impor-tant information in the story, does she expect them to demonstrate comprehension only on specific tasks, such as questions to be answered following reading. However, the development of their ability to participate effectively in a book club discussion group and to make sense of text was not left to chance, but cultivated through age- and grade-appropriate practices.

For example, Barbara Naess, whom we met in Chapter 2 (see page 19), introduced her kindergarten students to books she would be reading to them as part of the All About Me unit. She showed them Cannon's two books, *Verdi* and *Stellaluna* and encouraged them to access their appropriate prior knowledge. She also asked them to recall other books they had read by the same author or about the same ideas so that they could predict what the current book might be about.

As Barbara read the story to them, the kindergartners drew inferences (e.g., about why Verdi did not want to be like the others). They thought about literary elements (e.g., the important events in the story and the order

(e.g., there had been a good potato harvest) but that $200 is only part of the amount of taxes owed. They are asking clarifying questions (e.g., Did he sell the harvest?) They are also using their background knowledge about money—that $300 is a lot of money.

Having sorted this out to their satisfaction, they turn to Kendra's second question, whether the tax collector was a real person.

Kendra: Do you think the tax collector, at the beginning I thought the tax collector was a person trying to get money but when I read about Mis, the mis, the guy at the bank, I realized that he was real but I didn't know a tax collector could carry a gun.

Tegan: Yeah, and I thought he was just like, he was a like a stealer and he wanted the money.

Eric: [Yeah

Olivia: [Yeah and that's what I thought, with a gun, it's sort of like

Tegan: kinda obvious

??: Okaaay!

Olivia: A gun! Why would he want a <u>gun</u>?

Tegan: I think maybe he just, he wanted the money right, money right then,

Olivia: Instead of <u>later</u>, (using hand movements to the side as she says "later"),

Marika: [yeah

Olivia: [later

Again we see this group of students working together to make sense of the stranger with a gun who shows up at Little Willy's to collect the back taxes. And again, the students draw on background knowledge—they didn't know a tax collector would carry a gun; they knew (perhaps from television or movies) that there might be people who would lie to steal someone's money and that these people *do* carry guns. They thought about cause and effect—why would he want a gun to begin with? And they put together text evidence to draw a conclusion: The man at the bank would not vouch for the tax collector if he were not a real one.

* All students' names have been changed.
** *??* indicates that the speaker could not be identified
[indicates overlapping speach

TEACHING LITERARY ELEMENTS AND COMPREHENSION

Because Book Club *Plus* is a literature-based curriculum, we emphasize how helpful literary knowledge can be, and we believe in the importance of teaching students about response to literature. Thus, while not directly about comprehension, the categories related to literary elements interweave throughout our comprehension instruction activities. We think of these as:

• response strategies, or "How does what I have read make me feel, imagine, or believe?"

• literary elements, or "How does this story work?"

in which they occurred) and they engaged in other strategies to help them construct the meaning of the story. Barbara also prompted them to monitor their understanding (e.g., ask questions and adjust predictions to see if they are understanding the story). In these ways, Barbara's kindergartners were learning the foundations for comprehension that all skilled readers must have. This is critical because the foundations for mature engagement with text—the kind demonstrated by the reader of *Dreams of Trespass*—begin during children's earliest interactions with texts.

Three Principles of Comprehension Instruction

As you have read, children have many strategies at their disposal for improving comprehension. A child's ability to make meaning in individual, small-group, and whole-class settings greatly depends on the child's understanding and use of multiple strategies to aid comprehension. How effectively children learn to control this broad knowledge base depends on the teachers' consistent instruction of skills and strategies in the context of reading, writing, and talking about text. There are many instructional models for comprehension, and these models share some common elements. Comprehension instruction in Book Club *Plus* is built on three basic principles:

 PRINCIPLE #1: *Comprehension instruction should be explicit.*

Students need to know that reading text is a process of making meaning and that good readers use certain strategies or tools to help them make meaning. In Book Club *Plus,* we teach our students both what the strategy is and how it works. We give the strategy a name that makes it easy to recall, and we describe the strategy's benefits. This makes it more likely that students will add the strategy to their repertoires.

 PRINCIPLE #2: *Comprehension strategies must be modeled by more knowledgeable others, including teachers and peers.*

It's not enough simply to tell students about a strategy; they must see and hear it employed by a good reader. One method teachers use to model strategies is through thinking aloud. Teachers talk or think aloud about the application of a specific strategy, giving students a concrete model of how a good reader uses it. Likewise, many teachers provide written models of particular strategies in action. Students need multiple exposures to good models before they're able to adapt and internalize the use of a strategy.

PRINCIPLE #3: *Comprehension strategies must be scaffolded by the teacher until students are able to apply the strategies successfully during independent reading and response to reading.*

As students learn and practice comprehension strategies, they gradually become independent users of each strategy. During this process, the teacher begins to step back. He or she offers the occasional gentle reminder and gradually becomes a mere facilitator of meaning. When students have internalized a strategy and are able to apply it at the correct times and in correct ways, they are actively participating in making their own meaning. The continuum chart below illustrates the various roles the teacher plays during the instruction process.

This comprehension instruction model uses a four-phase structure to help students gain independence. The teacher begins by assuming responsibility and control over the activity and engaging in most of the thinking. With each phase and with the teacher's gradually-decreasing support, students assume greater and greater responsibility for the intellectual work.

In the first phase of a typical lesson, the teacher explicitly teaches the concept. For example, when Nina Hasty introduced her students to the two over-arching Question Answer Relationships, or QAR (Raphael, 1986; Raphael & Au, 2002)—*In My Head* and *In the Book*—she began by explicitly naming the concept and describing the two categories to her students with the aid of

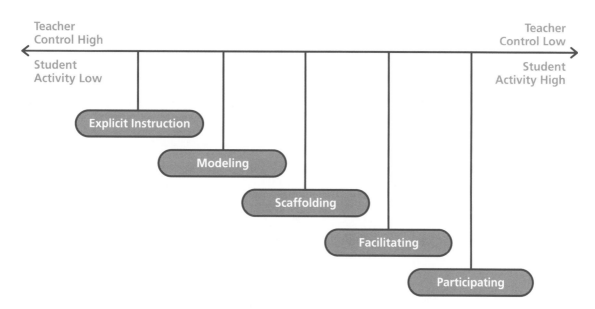

Teacher's Roles in Instruction

Teacher Control High

Teacher Control Low

Student Activity Low

Student Activity High

Explicit Instruction

Modeling

Scaffolding

Facilitating

Participating

Chart adapted from Kathryn H. Au and Taffy E. Raphael (eds), *Literature-Based Instruction: Reshaping the Curriculum* (Christopher-Gordon Publishers, 1998).

a chart. She then read a few paragraphs of a book to them, followed by two questions. By reading portions of the text from a transparency and thinking aloud, Nina led her class through the process of answering the questions and determining if the answers were *In My Head* or *In the Book.* This modeling shows students how to go through the process. (See page 42 for more discussion of the QAR strategy.)

In the second phase of the lesson, the teacher and students work together to identify the QAR and the appropriate answer information. Thus, the teacher still does much of the intellectual activity, but the students are now helping. Continuing with Nina's lesson, we can see how this plays out. Nina again read aloud from a transparency as her students listened. After reading, Nina helped students through the process by providing scaffolding with questions that led students to determine where the answer information came from. Students helped and learned to identify information sources.

In the third phase, the students take more responsibility. Nina set up the next section of the story, then gave students a paragraph to read with a partner, followed by two questions. Partners worked together to both answer the question and think about where the answer information came from. Nina roamed the classroom, listening to the children read and talk about the questions, and noting where they might be confused. In this phase, students are doing most of the work but the teacher scaffolds and facilitates as necessary.

In the fourth phase of the lesson, students assume full responsibility. Nina set up the last part of the story, and then gave each child a paragraph followed by two questions. Each child completed the work independently and turned it in. It served as an assessment of individual performance. Based on this work, Nina was able to determine whether to continue working on this in a large group setting, within guided reading groups, or within flexible groups pulled together across reading levels for students who appeared to need more help.

Comprehension Strategies

In Book Club *Plus,* teachers explicitly teach students comprehension strategies grouped within three categories that grow out of research in comprehension and text understanding (e.g., Dole, Duffy, Roehler, & Pearson, 1991; Langer, 1995; Paris, Lipson & Wixson, 1983):

- background knowledge strategies— "What do I already know that helps me step into the world created by this text?"

- text processing strategies— "What can I do to make sense of the text as I move through this text world?"

- monitoring strategies— "How do I know if the meanings I've created make sense?"

Examples of strategies in each category appear in the chart below. Each strategy is described in detail in the following sections of this chapter.

Background Knowledge Strategies

Background knowledge is information that readers possess before encountering a text. Readers connect new information to their background knowledge in order to make sense of the text. The strategies described in this section help emergent and early readers as well as those entering second and third grade become adept at using their background knowledge effectively.

Concepts of Print

Teaching children concepts about print is crucial, particularly for emergent and early readers. As you have read, students in Barbara Naess's kindergarten class (see Chapter 2), and some of Janine Rodrigues's students (see Chapter 1) needed instruction in basic strategies for following along as the teacher reads. These included how to hold a book, directionality of print, how meaning is carried through pictures and words, the difference between words

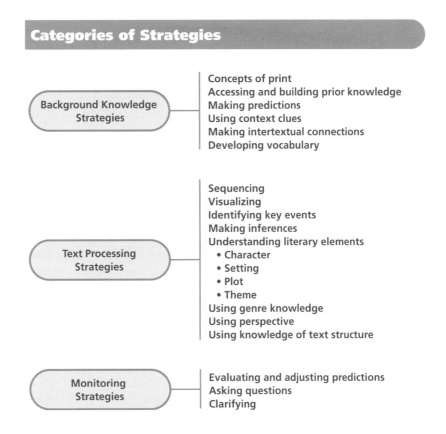

Categories of Strategies

Background Knowledge Strategies
- Concepts of print
- Accessing and building prior knowledge
- Making predictions
- Using context clues
- Making intertextual connections
- Developing vocabulary

Text Processing Strategies
- Sequencing
- Visualizing
- Identifying key events
- Making inferences
- Understanding literary elements
  - Character
  - Setting
  - Plot
  - Theme
- Using genre knowledge
- Using perspective
- Using knowledge of text structure

Monitoring Strategies
- Evaluating and adjusting predictions
- Asking questions
- Clarifying

and sentences, and so forth. Clearly, readers must know how books are held and read before they can learn more complex aspects of books such as literary elements. In Book Club *Plus,* guided reading, shared reading, and read aloud all provide good opportunities for teaching concepts of print.

Accessing and Building Prior Knowledge

Accessing prior knowledge is a useful strategy because it helps readers place stories and informational texts in a familiar context. The trick for most students is to know what background knowledge might be relevant. Teachers introduce young readers to what is valid background knowledge through teaching routines such as modeling and thinking aloud. Ultimately, Book Club *Plus* teachers want their students to understand that useful background knowledge includes their own experiences, vicarious experiences learned through listening to peers' stories, reading books, watching movies, and so forth. They want students to learn that it isn't enough to think about this

CLASSROOM VIEW
Accessing Prior Knowledge

This routine was used in MariAnne George's third grade classroom as part of an autobiography-based unit called Stories of Self. One of the stories MariAnne chose for her unit was "Chicken Coop Monster," by Patricia McKissack. This story takes place on a farm owned by the main character Melissa's grandparents. Melissa has been sent to live on this farm for the summer because of her parents' impending divorce. Melissa had been president of the Monster Club at home and firmly believes that monsters exist. She becomes convinced there is a monster in her grandparents' chicken coop. Her grandfather helps her learn to face the monster, suggesting that this is the only way to make her fear go away.

In MariAnne's classroom, accessing students' prior knowledge was

important to their entering Melissa's world. It helped them think about what her story reveals about facing our fears, both literal (the chicken coop monster) and metaphorical (fear of the changes happening to her family). To help students activate prior knowledge, MariAnne created two pairs of questions for students to talk about prior to listening to or reading the story:

1a. Have you ever had something that made you afraid?

1b. In the story we are going to read today, Melissa goes to visit her grandparents for a summer on their farm. While she's there, something makes her very afraid. What do you think it might be?

2a. When you were afraid, what did you do to overcome your fears?

2b. In the story we are reading today, Melissa's grandfather gives her some important advice about how to overcome her fear. What do you think he might have told her?

MariAnne knew her students were unlikely to answer the questions accurately because they had not yet read the text. Yet she knew the questions would help highlight key ideas that would emerge as the students read or listened to the story. They would help students draw on their own and each others' experiences to make sense of what Melissa did in the story.

background knowledge; they must think about how they can use it to make sense of what is happening in the texts they are reading or hearing.

A typical routine to make such connections explicit is a modification of Jane Hansen's (1981) approach, in which teachers create pairs of questions designed to elicit background knowledge. Readers are then guided to consider how they can use that knowledge to interpret their text. This routine is illustrated by the Classroom View on the previous page.

Other ways of building knowledge include engaging in inquiry prior to reading a story, watching videos with stories that take place in similar settings, or looking at pictures. For example, *Sarah, Plain and Tall* by Patricia MacLachlan, is a chapter book that young children enjoy, but it requires background knowledge about prairie life in the 1800s and the challenges of being a single parent with a farm to run. Building background by displaying pictures from that era and having students draw comparisons between their lives and those of children in the pictures can make it more likely students will understand the issues in the story. By third grade, students might do short-term, small group inquiry projects to examine life in the 1800s. Sharing what they learn with each other prior to beginning the book creates a pool of knowledge that they can draw upon. There are many ways for teachers to help students individually or as a group activate and/or organize background knowledge. In Book Club *Plus,* opening community share, Literacy Block, and guided reading can provide the opportunity for such inquiry. Graphic organizers, concept webs, time lines, and event tables are useful for organizing information generated through background building activities.

Making Predictions

Good readers continually make predictions as they read, monitoring and adjusting them as new information is unveiled. Good readers also realize that reading should make sense as they progress through a text. Predicting helps students make sense as they read, rather than waiting until the story is finished to see if it made sense. Students can make predictions about what will happen in a story based on the book's title, illustrations, and what they know about content. To make good predictions, students need some background knowledge, which should be developed before they engage with a text. Students can also use their knowledge of story structure to predict the outcome of a story. If they recognize that most stories have a problem that is resolved by the end, they have a clue about where events in a particular story might be leading.

Predictions play a role in entering the text world as well as moving through it. Revisiting one's predictions as more information is acquired helps a reader continually engage with the content and events in the text. It also foreshadows strategies for monitoring comprehension—particularly when readers' predictions are frequently incorrect. Sometimes the reader is not expected to make accurate predictions, such as when the point of the text is surprise. But if the author is not trying to trick the reader, lack of appropriate predictions may signal comprehension problems.

Teachers can help students include time for predicting in each opening community share. During a read aloud, modeling or thinking aloud can demonstrate how good readers use predicting throughout the story, not just at the beginning. Prediction is also one of the choices for written log responses, which encourages students to practice using the strategy throughout a book. Teachers can also model or encourage predicting during guided reading.

Using Context Clues

Context clues can help students at the word, sentence, text, and thematic levels, so there is a large return if students understand how context clues work. Young readers often have picture books as their core texts. Thus, learning how to use pictures and words as sources of information is helpful. In Book Club *Plus,* we emphasize the role of context clues in helping readers make accurate guesses when guesses are necessary. We teach students to use pictures as sources of information about where the story takes place, who is in the story, key events in the story, and characters' feelings. We teach students to use their knowledge of letter sounds—especially beginning and ending letters—in concert with other words they know in the sentence to make an educated guess about any unfamiliar words. A big part of using context clues is having strong monitoring skills as well. Readers must always ask themselves, "Does this guess make sense?" The more background knowledge they have, the more accurate their guesses will be.

Making Intertextual Connections

Helping students make intertextual connections is another way teachers help build and activate prior knowledge. Barbara's unit is a classic illustration. Students examine the idea of All About Me—who they are and what makes them unique—by reading sets of books that prompt such thinking and comparisons. Both Tacky the penguin and Elmer the elephant learn to value what makes them different from others. Stellaluna and Verdi illustrate how all living creatures change as they grow up. The two picture books by Curtis—*Tell Me Again About the Night I Was Born* and *When I Was Little*—develop children's understanding of the memoir genre.

Effective teachers help students sort through the information they recall from other sources, recording and validating what is accurate, clearing up misconceptions, and helping children begin to distinguish fact from fiction. Whatever method you use to help students make intertextual connections, remember that the content of the story must be familiar to students in order for them to connect new information to what they already know.

Developing Vocabulary

An important aspect of building background knowledge involves vocabulary development. Graves & Watts-Taffe (2002) identify four components necessary for a balanced vocabulary instructional program:

- wide reading

- teaching individual words

- teaching word-learning strategies

- fostering word consciousness

Book Club *Plus* units are designed to include a wide variety of genres in the read aloud, shared reading, guided reading, and independent reading contexts. Drawing upon this wide range of texts promotes interest and engagement in reading. Having students read as much and as widely as possible is one of the most powerful ways to build vocabulary.

Combining the teaching of individual words along with other sorts of instruction and activities promotes vocabulary growth and development. In the Book Club *Plus* framework described in Chapter 9, students are introduced to key words before reading to help remove some of the most obvious obstacles to comprehension. They learn to understand and appropriately use vocabulary related to autobiography, including *artifact, heritage, ancestors,* and the word *autobiography* itself. Similarly, in the Trickster Tale unit (see Chapter 2, page 22), Janine Rodrigues's students learned what a trickster was, as well as how tricksters are represented as *stereotypes* in *folk tales* from different cultures. They learned those terms as well as terms related to literary elements in the trickster tales such as *characters* and *story moral.*

Book Club *Plus* teachers skillfully weave the use of new vocabulary words into background-building activities so that students will be able to understand the words in context during the story. While much vocabulary development takes place during the reading of a story, it often makes sense to introduce key terms prior to reading. This helps build word consciousness— the awareness of and interest in words and their meanings. Allowing students to comment and ask questions about words helps clarify and enrich the meanings. Also, hearing the words repeatedly in classroom discussions is another natural way for students to learn their meanings.

Word-learning strategy instruction is ongoing in Book Club *Plus* units. Students may be working on using context clues to figure out new words during shared reading, practicing a dictionary-use skill during Literacy Block, completing an activity at a phonics center, or even working with the whole class during community share to learn how to use word parts to figure out the meanings of unknown words. Building knowledge of how words work is an important part of helping students build background knowledge.

Text Processing Strategies

Good readers draw on a range of strategies to move through a text. The strategies listed in the chart on page 33 are some of the most commonly used and taught strategies in elementary schools.

Sequencing, Visualizing, Identifying Key Events

Good readers often use familiar strategies, such as sequencing, visualizing and describing key events. Pausing to think about what has happened during the last chapter or section of a book requires readers to identify key events (i.e., summarizing). Breaking a summary into smaller, chronologically ordered chunks is known as sequencing. And creating mental images or pictures of what the author describes is visualizing.

These activities assume that students can distinguish key ideas from information that is less important. In fact, distinguishing important from less important information is a sophisticated strategy for young children to apply. By third grade, students can and should begin developing it. Readers who fail to do so give every textual detail equal weight, which becomes overwhelming in longer texts.

Keene and Zimmerman (1997) explain that

> there are three levels at which proficient readers make decisions about what is most important in any text: They decide what is important at the whole-text level, the sentence level, and the word level. After we read, we make rational judgments about what was essential, but even as we read, we make continual decisions about what sentences or phrases are most essential in a paragraph and even which words are most important in any given sentence.

Teachers can help their students identify important information by thinking aloud during read alouds and community share, and also during guided reading. As students offer their ideas, the teacher can help students think about the importance of each idea to an understanding of the book as a whole. As students become more aware of how the teacher does this, they will begin to think aloud in their book clubs.

As readers engage in such activities, they provide the basis for revising earlier predictions and creating new ones. The reading log is a useful resource for having students archive their thinking and strategy use throughout their interactions with a book.

Making Inferences, or Reading Between the Lines

Making inferences involves using clues in the text to figure out what is happening in a story and to gain a deeper understanding of the story's elements. Throughout a story, readers must often make subtle inferences to understand events, relationships between characters, and details about setting.

If students are not making inferences during reading, often they'll misunderstand a story. For example, in Jamie Lee Curtis's *Tell Me Again About the Night I Was Born,* it sometimes takes students a while to understand that the person telling the story is the same one asking to be told the story by her parents. The reading between the lines occurs when the students understand that the child in the book already knows this story and asks to be told the story again and again. Students recognize this behavior because they also like to hear the same story repeated by their parents. Identifying the narrator can be a confusing part of *Tell Me Again About the Night I Was Born,* but once students understand this nuance, the whole story makes perfect sense to them.

The importance of metacognition becomes especially clear with respect to making inferences. If a student's comprehension breaks down, he or she must be able to apply an appropriate strategy to get back on track. Students who have experienced explicit instruction, repeated modeling, and scaffolding in how to make inferences will know what to do when they realize they're confused. They'll know they can look for clues in the text from which they might infer answers to their questions.

▶ **Possible Classroom Chart**
Students are given room to add thoughts on inferring at the bottom of the chart.

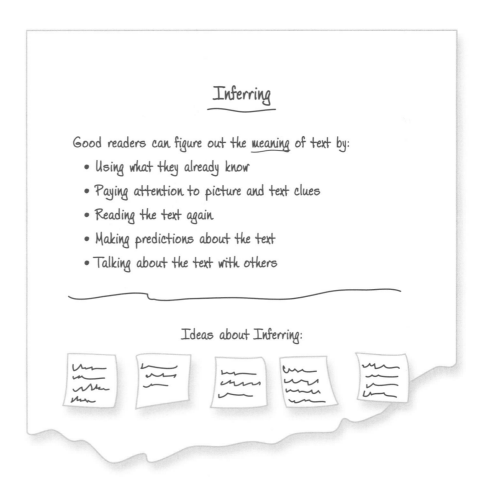

Inferring

Good readers can figure out the meaning of text by:
- Using what they already know
- Paying attention to picture and text clues
- Reading the text again
- Making predictions about the text
- Talking about the text with others

Ideas about Inferring:

Understanding Literary Elements

For narrative texts, literary elements such as character, setting, plot, and theme are the components of discussion. Emergent and early readers benefit from learning about these elements and how to use this knowledge to talk about stories. Character is often the most salient element for young readers and can be a useful entry point for talking about a story. For example, in Barbara Naess's All About Me unit (see Chapter 2, page 19), Elmer, Stellaluna, Verdi, and other characters became the focal points of think alouds and student discussions. The class thought together about characters' motives (e.g., why Elmer didn't like being different colors at first, and why Verdi didn't want to change), as well as their appearance, habits, decisions and so forth.

Setting can also generate good discussion. For example, students can discuss what constitutes the setting for a story and whether the setting is central to where the story takes place (e.g., Could this same story happen on a farm or in a city?).

Researchers (e.g., Sipe, 2000, 2002; Sipe & Bauer, 2001; Lehr, 1991; Au, 1992) have shown that very young children can think about stories not only in terms of literal descriptions of content but in terms of the ideas a story represents. For example, MariAnne George's third graders understood that *Stone Fox* illustrated the importance of taking responsibilities, trying our best, and standing up for what we believe. Barbara Naess's students understood that the books they read illustrated the power of difference and the importance of valuing each others' unique traits. Janine Rodrigues's students learned to think about how to treat one another through the stories of the trickster and the impact of his tricks on his friends.

Using Genre Knowledge

Another aspect of analyzing literary elements is genre study. In Book Club *Plus,* children hear and, when able, read a variety of genres—folk tales, fantasy, poetry and song, informational texts, and contemporary fiction. Teachers can support students by describing each genre and then helping students unpack the elements that make each genre unique. During opening community share, Literacy Block, and guided reading, readers can be introduced to other examples and features of a particular genre. Janine's Trickster Tales unit illustrates quite clearly how an entire unit may be devoted to exploring a genre within a set of other instructional goals (e.g., developing students' writing-reading connections; learning how to be a good friend). In other units, the genre may not be a primary focus. Instead, the theme is explored through a variety of genres. For example, the sample frameworks detailed in Chapters 9–11 illustrate how a range of genres—poems, contemporary realistic fiction, autobiography—can be studied in the service of a theme.

Using Perspective

As students listen to and read powerful texts, they begin to understand different perspectives. The children may encounter viewpoints that are different from their own. In these cases, teachers can ask the students to put themselves in the character's shoes to make sense of the character's actions and feelings. Readers draw on their own background knowledge and make connections to other texts to help them do this. During student-led discussions, students may find that their classmates have unique perspectives on the story. During guided reading, teachers can help students understand that being able to take various perspectives can help them make meaning. Closing community share is another good context for this teaching, as small groups and individual students share various ideas and interpretations of the text. Students may also think about perspective by assuming the point of view of a whole group of people.

Using Knowledge of Text Structure

Typically, Book Club *Plus* units center on narrative texts. However, we believe it is crucial to provide ample opportunities for students to engage with informational texts. This makes possible the teaching of comprehension skills unique to such texts. At upper elementary-grade levels, such opportunities occur when students engage in inquiry prior to or following their work with the core Book Club book. Similar opportunities can be a part of Book Club for primary-grade children. In fact, recent research (e.g., Duke, 2003) indicates that this is particularly important, since less than ten percent of first graders' school days—often less than one percent!—is spent working with informational texts.

Text structures are used to organize whole books and also paragraphs or sections of a text. Text structures include enumeration, sequential order, explanation, description, cause/effect, compare/contrast, and problem/solution. When students learn to recognize these text structures, a book or a section of text makes more sense because it's not just an undifferentiated mass of sentences. Students see connections between ideas and understand why authors organized their texts as they did.

During book club, students may read nonfiction or informational text in the research phase of a unit. This provides an excellent context for instruction about text structures and their role in comprehension. Guided reading and Literacy Block can also provide exposure to informational texts. In addition, sometimes fiction is organized so that text structures are evident. For example, when MariAnne taught a Stories of Culture unit, students read many autobiographies that represented different cultural groups and varying immigrant experiences. To these autobiographical texts and related fiction she linked informational texts that helped students unpack concepts such as culture, cultural contact and change, and essential elements of culture. The informational texts provided opportunities to talk about how such books are organized. For example, students can learn about such features as the table of contents and index. They can see how information can be conveyed through illustration, graphs, and charts, and how to identify information that is relevant to the stories they read.

Monitoring Strategies

Good readers are successful in large part because they have learned to monitor their own understanding. Here we discuss strategies that younger students can learn to help them monitor their comprehension.

Evaluating and Adjusting Predictions

We've already discussed the importance of making predictions as a background knowledge and text-processing strategy. We noted that predictions become useful tools for monitoring comprehension during reading. As teachers read aloud, they often model how to evaluate and adjust earlier predictions. Pausing to think aloud, a teacher might recall a prediction and note that new information in the text has proven the prediction to be correct or incorrect. If a prediction turns out to be wrong, the teacher might analyze how he or she went astray or remark that the plot has simply taken an unexpected turn. Then the teacher would make a new prediction based on the most recent information from the text.

Students can also use their response logs to monitor and adjust predictions. One common format is a three-column chart in which students make predictions, revisit their predictions at a later point, and then record new predictions. This format reminds students that predicting is a continuous process and that they can become better readers by reviewing and evaluating their earlier predictions. Monitoring and adjusting predictions can also take place during guided reading.

Asking Questions

Asking questions is another effective monitoring strategy. Teachers can model this strategy while reading aloud. They can also teach students explicitly about different kinds of questions and when they might be asked. Some teachers use Question-Answer Relationships, or QAR (Raphael, 1986; Raphael & Au, 2002), to help students think about how questioning can improve text comprehension. QAR helps students understand that answers come from one of two sources. As shown in the chart on page 43, they are either based on prior knowledge (*In My Head)* or found in the text (*In the Book*). Within these two categories, further distinctions can be made. *In My Head* answers can be either all prior knowledge (*On My Own*) or something

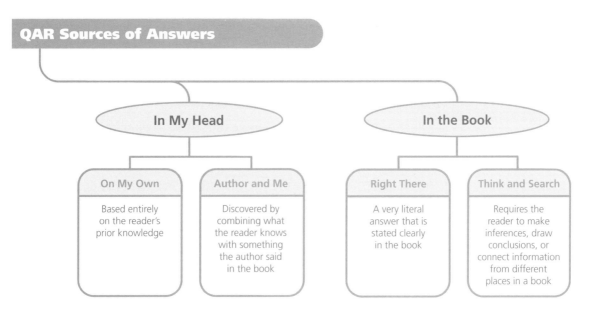

QAR Sources of Answers

In My Head

On My Own

Based entirely on the reader's prior knowledge

Author and Me

Discovered by combining what the reader knows with something the author said in the book

In the Book

Right There

A very literal answer that is stated clearly in the book

Think and Search

Requires the reader to make inferences, draw conclusions, or connect information from different places in a book

(Based on *Super QAR for the Testwise Student*, Raphael & Au, 2002)

in the text combined with what the student already knows (*Author and Me*). *In the Book* answers can be either literal answers (*Right There*), or not explicitly stated but determined by drawing conclusions, making inferences, or looking in several places throughout the text (*Think and Search*).

Developmentally, teachers can build students' QAR knowledge across grade levels. Raphael and Au (2002) suggest that for emergent and early readers (kindergarten and first grade), the emphasis be on simply distinguishing between information from our heads and information from the books we hear. By second grade, many students are able to distinguish between the two *In the Book* QAR strategies and by third grade many are able to understand the two *In My Head* strategies.

When students recognize the relationships between questions and answers, they're able to use this knowledge to help make meaning. Students ask questions in community share, in book clubs, and in response logs. They answer questions in community share and in book clubs. Students also ask and answer questions in guided reading. Using QAR and other strategies encourages students not only to ask good questions as part of comprehension, but also to think about big ideas and themes within a story.

Clarifying

Good readers realize when something they've read doesn't make sense, and they work to clarify their misunderstanding. There are several ways to do this. The reader can reread the section that doesn't make sense. Or, the reader can simply continue reading. Context clues in the next few lines may help clarify the misconception. If these two strategies don't work, the reader can ask someone else. In Book Club *Plus* this is likely to happen in one of several ways. When reading with a partner or small group, the reader can stop and ask someone else what a certain section of text means. When reading independently, the reader can use his or her reading log to write down a question. Then, during the next book club discussion, the group can work together to answer the question, using the text for support as needed. When the text is read during guided reading, the student can work with the teacher to find an answer.

Primary-grade teachers can help students develop their clarifying skills by presenting explicit instruction, modeling through think alouds and during guided reading, and encouraging repeated practice. Simply pausing during a read aloud or guided reading to have children signal thumbs up or thumbs down is a first step toward emphasizing that reading is supposed to make sense. If thumbs are down, the teacher can prompt the students to share what they *do* understand and then to articulate a question. This can be an important step toward emphasizing the importance of seeking help and for understanding that peers can be as important a resource as the teacher.

Conclusion

A central goal of any reading program is to help students learn to construct meaning from text. Using Book Club *Plus* is an effective way to accomplish this goal. Comprehension strategies can be taught and practiced by students in several settings. Opening community share is one important context for teaching comprehension strategies from which all students would benefit having in their repertoire. In this setting, teachers explicitly teach and model strategies that students can use to prepare for reading, to record ideas and responses in their reading logs, to make meaning as they read, and to monitor their progress. Strategies needed by smaller sets of students are more appropriately taught within flexible groups focused on specific needs, or within guided reading groups when needs seem to be associated with reading levels. All students can practice comprehension strategies as they read and listen to literature in book clubs or in the fishbowl setting described in Chapter 7, pages 115–117, as well as through their reading log entries. With Book Club *Plus* as a framework for the language arts curriculum, there are also multiple opportunities for instruction within students' guided reading groups, center activities, and independent reading. In addition, by modeling and thinking aloud during oral reading and closing community share, teachers can continue to reinforce and build upon students' use of these strategies. Through reading, writing in their logs, and discussing text in book clubs, students have many opportunities to practice and fine-tune their application and understanding of a variety of comprehension strategies.

Writing in
Book Club *Plus*

Writing in the Classroom

When it comes to young students' writing, there are two different positions on what to emphasize during literacy instruction. The traditional view of writing instruction placed such a high priority on the accuracy of spelling and letter formation that children were not encouraged—sometimes not allowed—to write until they had gained mastery in these areas. For the past few decades, an alternative philosophy has promoted writing as early as possible. This emergent literacy view links children's earliest experimentation with writing tools—large crayons and pencils, finger painting—with the development of positive attitudes toward writing, creativity, and envisioning themselves as writers.

As teachers, we firmly believe in the importance of writing and in helping students understand the value of writing for a variety of purposes. This is important for primary-grade children who vary widely in their ability to manipulate the written symbols of our language system, and in their letter-sound knowledge, vocabulary, spelling capabilities, and understanding of the forms and functions of writing. Even without the large body of research that exists, primary-grade teachers recognize that students' writing abilities emerge over time with practice and with opportunities to write in authentic situations. In this chapter, we will examine several teachers' approaches to writing, and we will illustrate the ways in which writing supports Book Club *Plus*.

CLASSROOM VIEW
Writing: Friendship Unit, Grade 1

Chris Cimino wanted to introduce Book Club *Plus* into her first-grade classroom. She believed that Book Club *Plus* would work well as an instructional framework to integrate reading and writing instruction. The unit she developed for this introduction focused on friendship and became a vehicle for a variety of writing activities—activities that served to enhance students' literacy skills, extend their comprehension of the texts, and apply ideas taken from their reading to their own lives.

Chris had several reasons for focusing her unit on friendship. She knew that there was a variety of good literature on the topic. She felt that the theme provided multiple opportunities for writing and discussion. She also hoped that the unit would develop her students' understanding of friendship and strengthen their interpersonal skills. She was motivated to build this unit after observing the struggles of her students to resolve social issues with their peers. As Chris reflected in her journal, "I hear terms like 'You're not my friend,' or 'I don't want to be friends anymore,' and then I have to address my students' hurt feelings. I want my class to understand that it's okay to have negative feelings and emotions toward a friend because of a particular incident, but that they can still remain friends and care about that person."

Once she had established her theme, Chris selected literature that would foster students' thinking about the complexities of friendship. Through their reading, she wanted students to examine what it takes to make and to be good friends, how the path to good friendships can sometimes be rocky, and how to handle these ups and downs. To accomplish her instructional objectives, Chris devised activities for students to *write into, write through,* and *write out of* the unit and texts. These concepts are explored in detail starting on the next page.

The class *wrote into* the unit theme by writing their thoughts about the qualities of a good friend. Other prompts asked them to *write into* specific texts by making connections and thinking about key ideas. By responding in their reading logs and answering questions, students *wrote through* the unit. Chris wanted the *writing through* activities to help her students think deeply about the literature and make connections to their own lives as well as to other texts. Students *wrote out of* the unit by engaging in more structured writing assignments, such as sending postcards to friends, creating simple essays on topics that relate to friendship, and eventually developing their own problem-solution friendship stories.

These writing activities allowed Chris to evaluate students' learning throughout the unit. She was able to measure their ability to organize their thoughts, stay on topic, make connections across texts, and make text-to-self connections. Through fishbowl (see page 115) discussions, students showed how they could use what they had written to inform their talk about the books. Students' writing was also instrumental in supporting and extending their comprehension. Conversely, the texts they read served as models of excellent writing, which helped to develop their writing skills.

Reading and Writing Stances

In Book Club *Plus,* we draw on three relationships between reading and writing that support each other and are consistent with the categories of comprehension strategies described in Chapter 3, pages 32–44. When readers read or hear text, they create what Judith Langer (1995) calls an "envisionment" of the text world. Initially, readers must enter this text world, bringing with them their own experiences, whether from previous texts or from their own lives. Thus, readers use background-knowledge strategies, many of which involve writing, as they create meaning from the texts. Readers and writers move through the world of the text, using the comprehension and response strategies and skills they have learned to build their understanding of the text world. When they leave the text, they analyze how the text worked, drawing on their knowledge of literary elements and response.

In Book Club *Plus,* we help students to use writing as a tool to support these different stances and, further, to see the texts they read and hear as models for the writing they create. Through writing, students engage in critical thinking and analysis of the texts they are reading or hearing, as well as learn to manipulate written language symbols. To achieve these goals, writing takes three forms (see also Raphael, Kehus, & Damphousse, 2001). The chart below summarizes the objectives within each of these forms.

- *Writing into* a unit helps students get ready to think about the big ideas and content in the units and the texts that they are reading and hearing.

- *Writing through* a unit supports students' meaning-making as they read and listen—from exploring words to making text-to-self connections.

- *Writing out of* a unit promotes reflection about concepts and ideas students encountered during reading, extends their understandings to new situations and connects their reading and life experiences to the theme(s) they have been exploring.

Writing Objectives Within Book Club *Plus*

Writing Into	Writing Through	Writing Out
• Set the stage • Access or highlight relevant background knowledge • Raise questions, set purposes, and create guiding questions • Foster word consciousness • Connect to self and connect self to texts	• Chart information • Identify important information • Identify supporting details • Identify plot points • Explore characters, setting	• Reflect and respond – Personal – Creative – Critical • Make text-to-self, text-to-text, text-to-theme connections • Extend text concepts

◆ FUNCTIONS OF WRITING

As students write *into, through,* and *out* of their texts, they are learning to see writing as a tool that can serve many functions. These functions include:

- reflecting on reading.
- gathering and organizing information.
- practicing literary forms.
- sharing ideas with others.

Writing into, through, and *out* are independent of the chronology of the unit. In other words, *writing into* activities can take place at any time during the unit. The same is true of *writing through* and *writing out* exercises. Readers or listeners may be in the middle of a chapter book but may *write into* the text as they begin each new chapter or set of chapters. Readers and listeners may engage in *writing out* although they may be in the middle of a story. For example, after reading several pages, students might consider characters' motivations and relationships. By the middle of the book, students might have acquired enough information to be able to compare characters' actions to those of characters in other stories or to themselves or to people in their lives. In Book Club *Plus* classrooms, writing supports students' text understandings and prepares them to engage in conversations about the books by encouraging them to *write into, through,* and *out of* their reading and listening experiences.

Writing Into a Unit or Text

Teachers use a range of activities to prepare their students for making sense of texts they listen to or read on their own. *Writing into* occurs at the opening of a unit, the beginning of a book, and when students return to a text after leaving it to engage in other activities. *Writing into* prepares students for understanding big ideas and ensures that they have the relevant background knowledge to make sense of the text(s). We present examples below to illustrate the broad array of opportunities for *writing into* a literary selection.

Access and Develop Background Knowledge

Asking students to think about their own experiences as they relate to topics or events in a book has become common practice for enhancing comprehension (Au, 1979; Hansen & Pearson, 1983; Block & Pressley, 2003). Typically, teachers such as Chris Cimino identify important concepts in a text or a unit. Then they create activities that prompt their students to think about events or experiences in their own lives that might help them understand the text.

For example, at the beginning of her unit, Chris wanted students to define the concept of friendship in terms of their own experiences. She led a discussion about friends, giving each student a planning chart. Students were expected to write ideas about friendship, even if their ability level meant they did not have many ideas or could not express their thoughts legibly. One student filled in the details shown on the next page. Note: original spelling, symbols, and format are preserved in all students' writing samples.

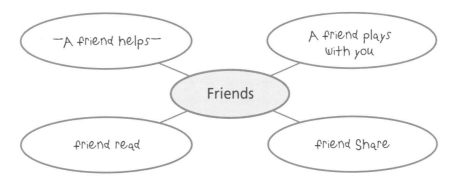

Other students captured similar thoughts, but their ideas were not necessarily as complete or as easily read. After a brief discussion, pairs of students shared with each other and the class what they had listed on their individual charts. Chris then asked each student to write a short definition of what makes a good friend. She emphasized that they should write about the general idea of a good friend. Based on his chart and the class discussion, one student wrote the following:

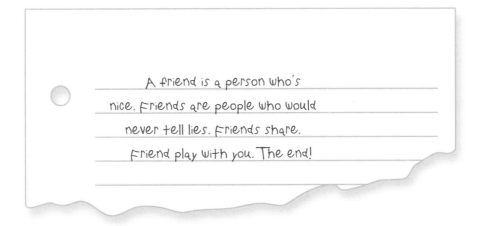

During community share, all of the students read what they had written. Students whose writing was not conventional were asked to mimic reading their responses. Chris recorded their ideas on chart paper. This gave all students the chance to contribute to the chart, even if their writing did not reflect standard language conventions. It also gave Chris information she could use to evaluate what her students learned about the concepts in the unit. As Chris had expected, students wrote about how positive it is to have friends. They did not, however, offer much about the effort it takes to be a good friend, which would be a major focus in the unit.

Raise Questions and Set Purposes

Writing into can be used to engage readers in thinking about their own experiences, as well as to set purposes and raise questions for their reading. Donna Ogle's (1986) KWL framework is designed specifically to help students set their own purposes for reading and listening (see Think Sheet 13, KWL Chart). This framework guides students to consider what they know ("K"), what they want to learn, ("W"), and then to examine what they have learned ("L") after reading. For example, Jeni Ness, a third-grade teacher, used three theme questions for a unit focused on family relationships.

In what ways are families similar and different?

What makes your family special?

What are some cultural traditions that your family celebrates?

Because Jeni wanted to track what students learned about these three concepts, she briefly talked about the new unit and the three questions before giving her students a think sheet. This think sheet had a table with three columns. The theme questions appeared in the first column, and the other two had the headings "What I know today" and "What I learned" followed by blank space. Students were asked to write the date above "What I know today" and then jot down what they already knew for each of the questions. The third column was to be completed at the end of the unit.

Following this information gathering, Jeni began the first of the unit books. To prompt students' thinking about relevant experiences from their own families, she used *Family Pictures: Cuadros de Familia* by Carmen Lomas Garza, which uses brilliant illustrations, as well as text in Spanish and English, to describe Garza's community. Jeni modeled how she connected the Garza book to her own life using a family photograph. From this modeling, she and her students generated a list of the things they knew about their families and what, in addition, they wanted to learn. This discussion gave many of the students ideas about questions to ask family members, such as "Who is in the family?", "What do they do together?", and "What makes the family special?" A chart was begun with these three questions to remind students what they might learn and write about their family conversations.

Word Consciousness

Writing into is also an opportunity to foster students' word consciousness (Graves & Watts-Taffe, 2002). Recall that word consciousness (see Chapter 3, page 37) promotes students' awareness of and interest in words and their meanings. During Black History Month, second-grade teacher Cammy Anderson taught a unit emphasizing informational texts by reading and writing about heroes. In the unit, she emphasized the heroic behavior of

THINK SHEETS

A think sheet is a handout that prompts a particular type of written response to literature or to a unit theme. The think sheets section following page 295 contains a variety of examples of think sheets you might use. You can copy and distribute the think sheets we've provided, or you can create your own.

historical figures such as Harriet Tubman and Martin Luther King, Jr. One of her goals was to heighten her students' awareness of words—specifically words that describe heroes in all walks of life. Initially, the class discussed heroes and students listed heroes based on their background knowledge and experiences. Somewhat predictably, the students listed the names of super-heroes. Cammy wanted her class to think more deeply. She invited her students to listen for words in the texts they were hearing and reading that were about being heroic or that described heroes. Cammy asked students to keep lists of words that they noticed and told them the words would then be mapped onto classroom charts. *Writing into,* in this case, became a tool for writing about words and their meanings, and for developing an interest in shades of meaning.

Reentering a Text

While the preceding examples illustrate the importance of *writing into* activities prior to beginning a unit or a book, *writing into* is also relevant as students reenter a text world after leaving it (e.g., not enough time to complete a picture book in a day; the design of a chapter book to be read across multiple sittings). Janine Rodrigues taught her first graders how important it is to engage in prediction throughout their reading. In one activity, Janine gave the students a think sheet to guide them in two phases of prediction. On the left side of the sheet were the words *I predict,* followed by several blank lines for students to write their predictions. An area below the lines provided an opportunity to illustrate what they thought might happen. On the right side of the page was the question *What's your thinking behind your prediction?,* followed by blank lines for students to explain their reasoning.

In her entry about *My Grandmother Is a Singing Yaya* by Karen Scourby D'Arc, a student wrote, "I predict that lulu will not tel yaya to stop singing." Her picture shows the two characters smiling at each other and a sun brightly shining over them. Her reasoning was "because lulu will hurt yayas feelings. And if lulu tells yaya to stop singing yaya will be sad." In contrast, another student predicted that "Lulu should tell her yaya to stop singing because its inbersing her and its giving her a head ack." Her reasoning was that "I think that she is going to hurt yayas felling and she will stop singing." Janine was pleased to see a debate about the various positions ensue during community share. Students were highly motivated to continue reading the story to find out what happened, and they did so with a deeper understanding of the consequences of Lulu's actions. They learned the importance of not simply stating a prediction, but explaining the underlying rationale.

As students became more adept at identifying reasons for their predictions, Janine's writing activities provided less formal support. For example, a *writing into* activity for Tomie dePaola's autobiography, *Nana Upstairs & Nana Downstairs,* involved using illustrations to prompt students' thinking about what was happening in the story and why. To reenter the text, Janine high-lighted the illustrations on two pages (depicting Tomie and his ninety-some-thing great-grandmother sitting next to each other tied into their respective chairs) and wrote the question on the board, "Why was Tomie tied into his chair?" Students were asked to write their predictions and their reasons before reading further. One student's response is shown below.

This writing helped students focus on an important event in the story and what that event revealed about the relationship between Tomie and his great-grandmother, while continuing to practice the strategy of predicting and providing supporting reasons. Students had a chance to talk with partners about what they predicted; then they took out their response logs and rewrote their prediction. The student's log entry (below right) shows how ideas were extended as a result of the discussion.

Clearly, writing, then talking, then writing again enhanced the student's original thinking and provided important "wonderings" to guide further reading. This pattern also required that all students remember to explain their thinking. As the unit progressed, Janine offered increasingly open-ended *writing into* activities. The students were simply reminded of the importance of predictions for getting back into their story.

▶ **Writing Into Prediction**

> Tommy said
> he wnted
> to be tied
> in the chair.
> Because maybe
> Tommy would
> like to talk with his
> grandma.

▼ **Rewritten Prediction**

> I predict that
> maybe they will play a
> lot together. Maybe
> they will go back to
> their chairs and have
> some more candy
> together. May be
> Tommy will   will
> grow up and still visit
> his grandma.
> Maybe tommy would
> have a lot of candy
> with his grandma.

Writing into a text can occur prior to reading anything in a unit. These activities share an emphasis on helping students access and develop personal perspectives, ideas, and information that will enrich their understandings of future reading. Students in kindergarten and first grade are encouraged to record their ideas using existing knowledge of symbol systems that will help them remember their points and "read" them later. Greater expectations of students' use of conventional language are put into place as students progress through first, second, and third grades. In every grade, writing is used functionally to engage students in thinking about relevant ideas, recording ideas related to upcoming reading, and providing a base for sharing their ideas with each other and their teacher.

Writing Through a Unit or Text

Writing through an individual text or a unit of study involves making ongoing reader-text connections, charting information so that it is more easily recalled for discussions, and tracking what has been learned. These strategies are useful as students read and think about narrative and informational texts. By participating in *writing through* activities to make sense of stories, students identify plot points, consider why they are important, and explore literary elements such as character development. Similarly, *writing through* activities for informational text can be used to help students understand basic ways that informational texts are organized—to compare and contrast important ideas; to explain or describe a place, person, or event; to lay out a problem and potential solutions. The process of *writing through* continues to help young readers focus on vocabulary terms, emphasizing the word consciousness that Graves and Watts-Taffe (2002) have identified as important to students' literacy development. Many of the entries listed on Think Sheet 5, Things to Do in Your Reading Log, guide students to *write through* texts. *Writing through* also invites students to practice the comprehension strategies discussed in Chapter 3.

Tools for *Writing Through*

When students have *written into* a text or unit, their questions about theme and about texts set goals for their reading and listening. The *writing through* process helps them chart and organize information related to their goals and express ideas for later use in small group and whole class discussions. Many Book Club *Plus* teachers have had success in explicitly teaching *writing through* strategies—such as sequencing, visualizing, and describing events—that are designed to enhance students' comprehension and engage them in responding to texts.

For example, Janine uses a Beginning-Middle-End think sheet to bring together sequencing, visualizing, and describing strategies. Her think sheet is divided horizontally into three sections. As a text unfolds, students record

INTRODUCING
BEGINNING-
MIDDLE-END
ACTIVITY

**If your students are
not familiar with this
activity . . .**

- Model your thinking
  about what to write for
  the beginning section.

- Work together to create
  the sentence(s) for the
  middle section.

- Have students work in
  pairs to write their sen-
  tence(s) for the ending
  section. Invite students
  to share their think
  sheets with the class.

SHARE SHEETS

A share sheet is a blank
sheet of paper that stu-
dents use to respond to
literature as they see fit.
Share sheets allow stu-
dents to combine several
response types on a single
page. This is helpful during book clubs because
they won't need to flip
though their logs looking
for entries written or
drawn on different pages.
Many teachers introduce
share sheets only after
students have learned a
wide variety of response
types. This might not
occur during the first few
units you teach.

events and illustrate them. In the end, students have a complete record of
events in the text, the order in which they happened, and the images they
created in the mind of the reader or listener.

Maps and webs are other valuable *writing through* tools once they have
been explained and modeled for the students. Several teachers have used
charts similar to the web that Chris used in the Friendship unit (see pages
48–49). Cammy Anderson adapted this web design for her unit. During the
unit, her students read informational texts about black history and biographies of related famous figures such as Harriet Tubman, Rosa Parks, and
Martin Luther King, Jr. Her unit emphasized inquiry and research processes
to learn about these people and to draw conclusions that would answer the
following questions: "What makes a hero?" "How are Tubman, Parks, and
King heroic?" "What are things each of us can do in our everyday lives to be
more like a hero?" Students created a web for each person they studied. As
they read or listened to different texts, they jotted down what they learned
related to the person's motivations (e.g., "When he was a little boy he saw
white only sign. He was sad."), insights into who each was as a person (e.g.,
"When he was Yong he sang in a coir."), and actions that made them heroic
(e.g., "he helped change the law. He made a speech I have a dreem." "used
powerful words not wopions [weapons]"). Cammy's *writing through* activities
prompted note taking of important ideas, which is what skilled readers do
when reading informational text.

Janine used a version of the web to introduce students to engaging in
multiple responses while reading and listening to stories. During her Book
Club *Plus* unit on trickster tales, she acquainted students with several
response strategies and literary elements, modeling each one and supporting
students' use of a newly-learned response strategy through coaching. Students
used the individual responses and comprehension strategies when they were
introduced and with her support, but Janine's goal was to have her students
be able to use more than one strategy. In this way, students would demonstrate independence, and they would respond as mature readers and listeners
who typically have more than one way of responding to a given section of
text. To support her students' use of multiple response strategies, Janine
introduced them to share sheets (see sidebar on this page). This activity
encouraged students to record more than one response to a single selection
or text section.

Students learned to think in extended ways about text as they used the
share sheet, or web, format for different purposes. For example, students'
webs were set up so they could record events and literary elements, and then
use their web to summarize the story. Thus, in the center, they described the
story problem. In one box they detailed the main characters, in a second
they described the setting, in the third they listed the main events, and in the
fourth they described the resolution. Share sheets are an important tool for

helping students learn to write extended responses. A common concern of early primary teachers is that most of their students will write only a single sentence. Introducing multiple response strategies and modeling ways for recording several related ideas is an important early step in developing strategies for sustained writing.

Questions that focus students' attention, or driving questions, are useful in more ways than one. Inspired by teaching strategies outlined by Debbie Miller in her book *Reading with Meaning: Teaching Comprehension in the Primary Grades,* Janine used a driving question in an earlier example as part of the prediction activities for *writing into* a text. Driving questions are also relevant to *writing through* a text. Janine's method is to write a driving question on the board, calling students' attention to it and encouraging them to think about the question and possible answers as they read or listen. The questions may be about the story theme, ideas in an informational text, interesting words, and so forth. She then distributes a think sheet on which students can write the question and possible answers.

Another invaluable tool in helping students to *write through* a unit is a strategy we call **speedwriting.** Referred to as freewriting by Peter Elbow in *Writing Without Teachers* and used in various ways by many educators, this strategy is essentially a way to free our young writers of rules and restrictions so they can develop their ideas and practice writing with fluency. Whether it is known as speedwriting, freewriting, or by another name, its features are:

- writing without stopping for a period of time.

- focusing on ideas and meaning, not language conventions.

- creating text for future use, not as a final product.

In our Book Club *Plus* classrooms, we call our speedwriting sessions Speedwriting Parties (Florio-Ruane, Hasty, Beasley, 2000) in order to capture the fun and exciting aspects of writing and make the parties events that our students look forward to throughout each unit. Our name for this activity emphasizes speed in order to encourage students to get many ideas down on paper rather than work diligently to get one idea down with correct spelling and punctuation. Speedwriting is a powerful tool, especially among students who lack confidence in their writing abilities. Students are able to express on paper ideas that they never knew they had. Additionally, this activity encourages the idea of creating drafts, enables students to generate text for oral sharing, and allows students to create thoughtful responses to their own reading and to read-aloud books.

Using the activities and strategies we've described to *write through* a text, students learn how to use writing as a tool to organize, synthesize, and remember important ideas, questions they have, words they find interesting or confusing, and their own personal response to the texts they have read.

TEACHING TIP

Many primary-grade teachers find sticky notes useful in helping students *write through* a unit. Sticky notes provide an easy way for students to indicate specific places in a text to which they want to return and to keep track of their ideas as they read.

SPEEDWRITING

Speedwriting in connection with Book Club *Plus* was originally discussed at a research meeting. Susan Florio-Ruane then mentioned it to Nina Hasty, who fully developed the idea in her Grade 1/2 classroom. You can read about Nina's speedwriting activities in Chapter 11, starting on page 227.

Such activities focus their attention both on the ideas in a narrative or informational text and on how the text itself works. Just as the *writing into* exercises help students enter the text world, these *writing through* activities support students as they step out of the text world to apply what they have learned to new situations.

Writing Out of a Unit or Text

Writing out of a text or a unit gives students a chance to think about what they have read and consider its meaning in their lives. Students need the opportunity to reflect on what they've read—responding to it personally, creatively, or critically as we describe in Chapter 2. It is through *writing out* that students often share experiences and personal feeling, as well as what they have learned from units with informational texts as their focus. They respond creatively when they speculate on "What if . . .," changing events or characters in ways that affect story outcomes or historical events, or when they apply what they have learned to new situations. They respond critically when they describe changes in their beliefs or feelings, drawing on text evidence, as well as when they examine an author's craft. The chart on pages 16–17 in Chapter 2 identifies a broad range of curricular areas that *writing out of* texts and units can support. In the next section, we illustrate how different kinds of writing (e.g., on demand, writing from different sources, sustained writing) can be used in authentic ways to achieve goals in the literacy curriculum.

Thinking About Theme

Whether the goal is to prompt students to reflect, to synthesize, or to extend their thinking after reading a particular story or engaging in a particular unit, *writing out* often helps students make links among the stories they have just read, their own lives, and the theme of the unit. For example, Chris's Friendship unit emphasized the energy and effort it takes to be a friend. By bringing these issues to the surface with each book, she believed she could help students develop the life-long skills and strategies they need in order to sustain meaningful friendships. She introduced *A Color of His Own* by Leo Lionni, in which a chameleon wants to be one color, like the other animals, so that they will be his friends. She wanted students to make connections to their own lives and to the theme. For this *writing out* activity, she asked students to respond to the question, "Have you ever felt like you didn't fit in or belong, like Leo, because you were different from your friends? Write about this in your journal." One student still working on his writing skills wrote the following response.

HOW TO KEEP STUDENTS WRITING

We have used the following methods to help students expand their ideas and continue writing:

- Invite students to share writing with a partner. What does the partner want to know more about?

- Have students revisit unit questions (big theme questions) periodically.

- Encourage students to add details and evidence from the text to support their ideas.

- Conduct a whole-class mini lesson during which you share student writing (with students' permission) using the overhead projector. Talk about what is good about a piece of writing and what can make it even better.

Threr sad yoy lek different. And I did Wok a Waay.

"They said, 'You look different.' And I did walk away."

Another student, with more developed literacy skills, responded in this way.

When Lana was born everybody cared about her.
I thought I didn't feel like I belonged. But then
after she got older my family started caring about
all of us

These students and their peers shared their written ideas in fishbowls and in closing community share. With Chris's scaffolding, they explained how their writing related to the story they had read and to their own lives. They further discussed what they'd learned about friendship, bringing out such ideas as "You can be friends with kids who are not like you" and "We should show others that we care about them because they might not know it otherwise." Their observations reflected the important connections they were making through reading and writing within the theme.

While Chris emphasized the idea of making feelings visible to friends through *writing into* and *writing through* activities, she developed end-of-unit *writing out* activities to help students make connections across the books they had read and heard. As a culminating, sustained writing event, Chris required each of her first graders to plan and write a problem-solution story about friendship, again emphasizing the theme, their own knowledge, and the many examples they had read and heard throughout the unit. Students were asked to build on what they had learned about the theme from all the books they heard and were to create their own story based on an event from their own lives. She scaffolded their writing in three ways. First, the whole class generated a list of all they had learned about friendship. The list emphasized how friends behaved, problems friends might have, and how friends solved different problems. Second, she gave students problem-solution webs, similar to the one pictured below, to help them map out their own friendship problems and the way they were solved.

▶ Student Web
  Sample

Chris displayed a blank chart and brainstormed a few different problems that she had with her friends. Then, she thought aloud about which one she would most like to write about (e.g., it would make an interesting story; she thought it was a problem others might find helpful to think about) and circled her choice. She jotted down notes for describing characters, setting, problem, and solution in the four circles surrounding the central circle. Students then planned their own problem-solution friendship stories. Third, when students had finished their planning webs, they "rehearsed" their stories before writing their "sloppy copy." They could rehearse them with Chris or with a student of their choice. Students then created their "sloppy copies" for editing and wrote their final drafts accompanied by illustrations. These were compiled into a class book, and each student received a photocopy of the final product.

Students' stories revealed their understanding of ideas developed throughout the unit, both about friendship and about how friends address misunderstandings, as well as their comprehension of the problem-solution structure in text. The student's story that follows exceeded grade-level expectations. Her characters and situation reflect both the down and the up sides to friendship. Her title sets the stage for the story, and she even includes dialogue appropriately punctuated. The problem is clearly stated, as are the solution and the lesson.

▶ **Student Samples: Problem-solution stories**

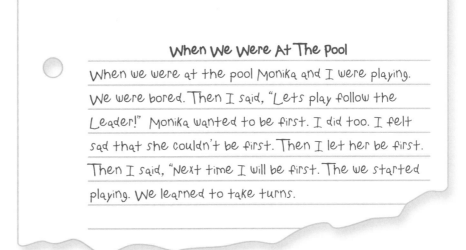

When We Were At The Pool

When we were at the pool Monika and I were playing. We were bored. Then I said, "Lets play follow the Leader!" Monika wanted to be first. I did too. I felt sad that she couldn't be first. Then I let her be first. Then I said, "Next time I will be first. The we started playing. We learned to take turns.

Somewhat less sophisticated, but capturing the essence of what Chris had hoped her students would learn is this story.

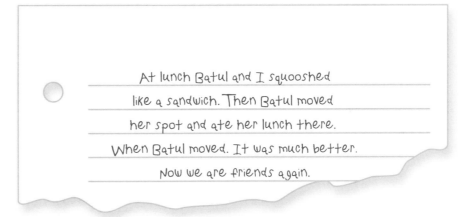

At lunch Batul and I squooshed like a sandwich. Then Batul moved her spot and ate her lunch there. When Batul moved. It was much better. Now we are friends again.

The third sample is somewhat less clear on the cause(s) of the problem with a friend or how it was solved, but reflects grade-level performance.

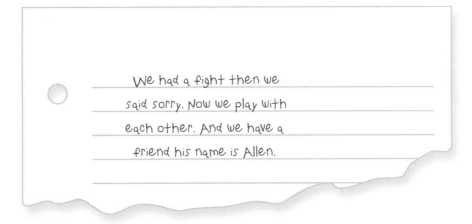

We had a fight then we said sorry. Now we play with each other. And we have a friend his name is Allen.

These three texts not only show the range of students' understandings about story, they provide a window into students' sustained writing and use of conventional spelling and provide an opportunity for teachers to assess students' progress. (Refer to Chapter 6 for ways to use students' work to make visible the progress they are making on important standards and benchmarks required by the school, district, and state.)

Not all *writing out* activities are as elaborate as the examples above. Teachers can encourage students to make text-to-self as well as the text-to-theme connections described above by having them draft essays after a single text or at the end of unit. For example, Janine used Valerie Flournoy's *The Patchwork Quilt* for making text-to-text connections. One student compared Flournoy's story, which shows a granddaughter learning to appreciate the stories told by the patches of fabric in her grandmother's quilt, to *The Rag Coat* by Lauren A. Mills. In the Mills story, a young girl wears a rag coat to school. Her classmates tease her for wearing rags until she points out to them that each scrap of fabric in her coat tells a story. The student's first-draft essay shows the impact of the continual modeling, scaffolding, and practice she has had in responding to literature. In addition to her focus on a deep theme, she takes risks with regard to spelling so that she can use the words she feels are best, rather than limit herself to ones she can accurately spell (e.g., writing "beuteful" for *beautiful,* "master pecite" for *masterpiece*), using action verbs ("cherd" for *cheered*), and experimenting with punctuation, both periods and an exclamation point.

Deeper thinking about texts begins with smaller steps toward extended writing as students *write out of* a text or a unit. For example, in the beginning-of-the-year unit that Janine taught about tricksters (see Chapter 2, page 22), one of the outcomes she expected was that students would develop an understanding of the characteristics of a trickster tale. She used two *writing out* activities to evaluate

▶ **Student Sample: Essay**

I was thinking about a story and a other story the patchwork quilt and the rag coat and I'm thinking that. In both storys they both wanted to make. Something beuteful that has love and that rermebers life stoys because a Quilt or a coat Does never forget a Life story. And if You make it has Love and it is a Master pecite. If I Would hoped and Cherd and scream To do it trest me I would loved it!

▶ **Student Sample:**
Trickster Letter Poem

They are good at telling lies
Rabbits are clevr.
I like tricksters tricks
Coyote is not very clever.
Kid of slik.
Som tricksters are tricky
They are smart
Every trick is not funny
Rabbits like to trick coyotes.

their knowledge. In the first, she asked them to define *trickster*. Students' responses, such as "Tricksters are almost always animals that get into trudl. They trick people," provided a quick window into whether they understood that the tricksters took animal forms in the stories and that their goal was to trick others. Then she asked students to write a "Trickster Letter Poem," each line beginning with a letter that vertically spells the word *trickster*. From these activities, Janine could see that the students had learned the genre.

They knew that tricksters were slick, smart, and not always funny. They were seeing the use of animals as stereotypes. They recognized that tricksters lie. Most important, Janine's first graders were expressing themselves in writing.

Writing to Extend

Beyond learning about the theme and related content, we want students to extend their literacy experiences to their own lives. One of our favorite examples is from first-grade teacher Julia Stern's unit, Learning to Be a Good Friend, in which she read several books illustrating the complexities of friendship. For a *writing out* activity, Julia and the class talked about the concept of random acts of kindness. Students were encouraged to identify "Random Acts of Friendship" in their own setting. Julia positioned stacks of Random Act forms, which were folded 3 x 5 inch notepapers, all around the room. On the front flap was a yellow smiley face, with *Random Acts of Friendship* written below in large letters. Each day, students completed a form when they saw a random act of friendship and dropped their form(s) in a large jar. At the close of the school day, Julia read aloud those acts to the class. Two examples follow on page 62.

Date: 4 – 14 - 03

_____Jordan,_____ you were a good friend

when you ___when you Helpt Sammy put his___

___cot in his Backpack By Holding His Backpack___

From: ___Mark___

Date: 4 – 23 - 03

_____Eliza,_____ you were a good friend

when you _____you were a good friend when you_____

___were playing with me outside___

From: _____Amy_____

▶ **Student Samples:
Random Acts of
Friendship**

Conclusion

Primary-grade students in Book Club *Plus* classrooms show that even very young children can be introduced to fairly complex themes and issues in their reading and can use writing to work through these complexities as they enter, move through, and leave the text worlds. Moreover, this relationship is reciprocal. The more they use writing as a tool to explore the complexities in texts, the more their own writing begins to reflect the complexities of ideas, sentence structure, and word choices. Becoming deeper thinkers about the books they experience and having ways to record these thoughts provide the foundation students need to engage in interesting and exciting classroom talk in their fishbowls, book clubs, and whole-class settings.

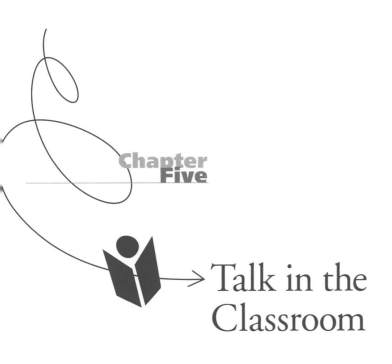

Chapter Five

Talk in the Classroom

Oral Language and Constructing Meaning

As we have already seen, the thematic, integrative nature of Book Club *Plus* gives students a sense of common purpose and community as they learn and use literacy. Thus, reading, writing, and discussion in Book Club *Plus* are not practice for eventual communication. Instead, they are authentic practice of the communication essential to learning. This move toward meaning and authenticity promotes engagement, ownership, agency, and comprehension of complex ideas. In this chapter, we continue our focus on meaning-making within the contexts of the Book Club *Plus* framework. We pay special attention to the role of oral language to support students' construction of meaning from text.

In a society as diverse as that of the United States, the richness of oral language practice provided for in the Book Club *Plus* framework is particularly valuable. It enables students of varied first languages and levels of proficiency in English to hear and use English in genuine, supportive contexts. This fosters increased oral fluency and serves as a bridge to fluency in reading and writing in English. To achieve this kind of oral language practice in a literacy curriculum, we encourage you to think with us about how conversation becomes an explicit instructional tool at all grade levels—particularly in the early grades.

Toward a Pedagogy of Talk for Early Literacy Learning

Discussion plays an important role in literacy learning. We can expand print-based learning by talking about text in a variety of ways. Talk strengthens our ability to read and our ability to use reading as a tool to learn about ideas. We explicitly use talk in our teaching when, for example, we explain a concept or assess students by listening to them answer questions. The importance of talk, however, extends far beyond these uses. In the Book Club *Plus* framework, conversation (both teacher-led and among peers) plays a key role in literacy learning.

Conversation can be a slippery medium for instruction. Many of us have learned that school talk consists not of conversational give and take, but of a relatively closed system of teacher initiation, student response, and teacher evaluation recycled many times within lessons. Part of a literacy teacher's work is to be reflective about talk—to be able to seize its educative potential as the classroom's chief speaker/listener. In this way, the teacher can provide systematically rich contexts for students to learn by means of conversation and can also speak and listen in ways that foster and assess learning in authentic spoken and written communication.

It is hard to think about how talk works in teaching, learning, and assessing because it is so much a part of our lives that it is taken for granted—usually as a means, rarely as an end. As youngsters learn to read and to take meaning from print, however, text-based conversation is a primary way they acquire and practice comprehension skills and strategies. We seem to know this intuitively as parents and caregivers of young children. In the family, adults and older children talk to youngsters about all types of texts—picture books, environmental print, visual texts, and oral narratives. This informal socialization teaches youngsters that language—its sounds and the symbols standing for those sounds—is powerful. To master the spoken and written language systems is to be able to wield the power of language as a tool for communication, self-expression, creativity, and thought.

As children enter school, greater emphasis is placed on the written language system and the use of language to ask questions, investigate concepts, and reflect on what they know. With this shift in emphasis, it is easy to become preoccupied with the written language system to the point of overlooking its connection (beyond the phonemic level) to spoken language. Talk is a part of literacy and the comprehension process. It is also the cultural glue that holds communities together and sustains their literate practices.

Talk About Text in Book Club *Plus*

If talk is to be a key tool for teaching and learning of the literacy curriculum, then the teacher must plan for and enact talk about text in thoughtful ways. When oral language is an explicit part of a literacy curriculum, it is usually taught, practiced, and assessed in a formalized way (e.g., learning to speak before a group, learning to make a topically relevant response). However, proficiency extends beyond these forms and functions and is an essential part of learning to understand, create, and think textually. Nowhere is this process more evident than in the talk about text that occurs within thematic units in Book Club *Plus*.

SAMPLE "I CAN" STATEMENTS

- *I can* stay on topic when I talk.
- *I can* share my feelings and ideas.
- *I can* contribute to a good book club discussion.

In Chapter 6, in our examination of assessment, we introduce the idea of "I Can" statements (Au, 2001) framing the goals toward which students reach in their practice of book club discussions. In Chapter 7 we discuss the oral language settings the Book Club *Plus* framework offers. We describe them in terms of the management and operation of classroom literacy activities (e.g., setting up fishbowls and student-led book clubs). If we take a closer look at both the activities of the Book Club *Plus* framework and at the "I Can" statements for successful book club participation, we can see that it is not only the amount of talk but the kinds of talk that matter when conversation supports literacy learning. The "I Can" statements, for example, describe the forms and functions of conversation that is used within book clubs. This conversation reflects learning that is collaborative, engaged, and critical as well as courteous. In these activity settings, how students manage conversation is important not only to etiquette but to investigating and learning about the complex texts and concepts under discussion (Florio-Ruane with deTar, 2001).

Book Club *Plus* offers several ways in which students can practice using spoken language to learn from text—teacher-scaffolded instruction in the whole-group setting called community share, teacher-guided (coached) peer-led discussions in fishbowl settings, independent peer-led book discussions, and writing in response logs, which serve as a place to plan ideas for discussion and to reflect in writing upon recent discussions. The Book Club *Plus* framework suggests that teachers mobilize a great deal of conversational activity to foster learning and to practice higher-order reasoning, concept development, skill and strategy development, and comprehension of both age-appropriate literature and literature at the students' instructional level.

Three Key Instructional Purposes

Talk about text within Book Club *Plus* is intended to teach, support the development of, and assess three kinds of thinking:

- Talk to *surface* knowledge related to a text and its theme

- Talk to *inquire* into the text and its theme

- Talk to *reflect* upon what has been learned about the text and its theme

Teaching these skills, concepts, and strategies requires that spoken language exceed the incidental talk we do in classrooms. Book talk is not limited to discussion of the written language simply at the phoneme level, or used solely to provide answers to factual recall questions. As the chart on page 66 shows, there are many different activities within Book Club *Plus* that support the key instructional purposes. In subsequent portions of the chapter, we examine talk within the classroom of MariAnne George, one of this book's authors, during her yearlong exploration of the theme Our Storied Lives. We discuss the talk in teacher-led discussions during community share, in the teacher-

TRANSFER OF CONTROL

The teacher's role in classroom talk can vary from a great deal of control to giving students the opportunity to direct their own discussions as shown on the chart on page 31.

Talk About Text Within Book Club *Plus*

Instructional Purpose	Function	Form	Activity Within Book Club *Plus*
Surface knowledge	• Access or obtain background knowledge prior to reading	• Declarative – discussing – brainstorming – researching	• Read-aloud discussion • Opening community share
Inquire into text	• Inquire to gather information by and during reading	• Interrogative – asking questions – researching	• Book club conversation • Guided reading session • Writer's workshop
Reflect upon text	• Ownership and reflection on what has been learned from text	• Explanatory – summarizing – synthesizing	• Closing community share • Unit project

coaching setting of fishbowl, and in the independent, peer-led book club discussions. Note that some of the examples in this chapter were adapted from research reported in George, Raphael, and Florio-Ruane, 2002; and Au, Raphael, Florio-Ruane, and Spiro, 2002.

Teacher-Led Talk About Text

Recently, educators and researchers have recognized literacy not only as a set of skills, but also as a cultural practice. This has led those of us in literacy education to reconsider the content of the literacy curriculum as well as our instructional methods and assessment practices. Examples of this refocusing include examining the nature and potential of home-school-community relationships as resources for literacy education (e.g., Moll, 1992) and rethinking how to facilitate teachers' understandings of the relationships among culture, the literacy curriculum, and the oral and written texts used in teaching.

As described earlier, we formed the Teachers Learning Collaborative (TLC) to develop and study a literacy curriculum framework that could help teachers accomplish this work, even with the youngest students—and, importantly, with students who are struggling to learn to read and write. We found one part of the solution in the structure of literacy activities, and we found the other in their thematic content. Our research showed that the structure and the content work together, creating a synergy that fosters engagement and practice to accelerate learning (Florio-Ruane, Raphael, Highfield, & Berne,

2004). The overarching theme we designed for the curriculum was Our Storied Lives. This yearlong theme contains three six- to eight-week units: Stories of Self, Stories of Family, and Stories of Culture. Each unit draws upon a set of books that supports the particular focus developed with the Book Club books, the books for guided reading or short stories, the teacher read aloud, the books for shared reading that are often the basis for mini-lessons during writer's workshop, and the special classroom library, which sustains students' independent reading. Further, each unit includes a culminating project that requires students to apply and integrate language arts skills and strategies along with ideas related to the overarching theme.

We found that reading, speaking, and writing about their lives and the lives of people different from themselves provided a meaningful context for linking students' reading, writing, and talking about texts. As the examples in this chapter illustrate, MariAnne George's students explored the content of Our Storied Lives using conversation to *surface* knowledge, to *inquire* into text and theme, and to *reflect*.

Setting the Scene

During the period of this project (1999–2001), MariAnne taught third grade in a suburban school that serves as a center for teaching English as a second language to students from throughout the district. Located in a relatively prosperous suburb, it is home to families from many parts of the world. Thus, her classroom was both multicultural and multilingual, and many of her students struggled to learn to read and write in English.

MariAnne hoped that a focus on culture would turn the diversity of backgrounds and first languages in her room into resources rather than obstacles to literacy learning. She encouraged students to find ways to engage personally with the stories they read and told, thus making reading and response to literature more meaningful, engaging work. In emphasizing the substantive content of culture in her Storied Lives curriculum, MariAnne began to shape how students would use conversation to *surface* knowledge related to culture, to *inquire* into the various aspects of culture in their own lives and the lives of others, and to *reflect* upon what they were learning.

Stories and Lives

MariAnne traced the children's understanding of culture in a variety of activities that allowed her access to their thinking over the course of the school year. She used the whole-class context of community share to introduce her students to both content ideas (e.g., learning about culture) and process (e.g., how to ask questions, to use the text for supporting ideas, and to make intertextual connections). Students learned ways to talk about texts and ideas through explicit instruction, modeling, and scaffolding in this setting. Later, they applied what they had learned as they took increasing responsibilities for their own discussions. To fit her theme, the texts MariAnne chose for the teacher read aloud, the Book Club discussion books, and the students' guided reading were autobiographical. They featured high quality, authentic multicultural literature. She hoped to help children make connections—through talk and through writing—to their own personal experiences, expand their horizons, and to expose them to ethnic groups, cultures, and experiences different from their own.

Book Club *Plus* is based on the theory that language and literacy skills are learned through socially interactive settings that allow children to play with language and take risks. The Book Club *Plus* framework provides an instructional format of discussion-based learning: some teacher-led, some student-led, some whole-class, some small-group. Thus, MariAnne's students who were learning English had many opportunities to try out the new language in small-group situations such as book clubs, guided reading groups, and collaborative projects. For example, during one guided reading group, a student became very excited when he initially opened the book *Family Pictures: Cuadros de Familia* by Carmen Lomas Garza. The text is written in both English and Spanish. "Would you like me to read it in Spanish?" he excitedly asked the small group. He proceeded to read each page trying to explain the relationship of words to the illustrations. He then followed along as the class read the English text, interrupting at key points to say the word in Spanish for the other students. This was the beginning of this student becoming an engaged reader—he seemed to value reading, and he, as well as his peers, began to see his home language as an asset that enabled him to make meaningful contributions to his teacher's and his peers' literacy learning and meaning-making.

Oral and written narrative played a vital role in helping with this transition. The use of narrative has been written about extensively as a means by which students come to understand their world. Helping children transform these cultural products (stories) into cultural resources enables them to explore and express cultural differences in the classroom social network. It is in experiencing these differences that students discover themselves as I's and you's (Friere, 1998). In MariAnne's classroom, after students studied themselves as individuals in Stories of Self, they moved to considering their histories in terms of Stories of Family. To make the concept of family stories visible, the unit featured books by Patricia Polacco. Her books were chosen for several reasons: (a) she is a prolific author from Michigan, the home state of MariAnne and her students; (b) Polacco's stories are based on family events; and (c) she possesses a representative family history. These family stories and histories are grounded in cultural stories and histories, which support not only children's literacy learning but their deepening understanding of culture. Polacco's books provide fertile ground for children to make personal connections between text and their own lives and to involve their families in this journey.

FAMILY STORIES

One way to help students connect personally through talk and through content, is to have them share stories from their grandparents' generation. Students gather the stories by talking with their family. They write these stories, and then they share them orally with the class.

Personal connections both to the autobiographical form of Polacco's literature and to its content connections emerged in students' book club discussions. In a discussion of *Chicken Sunday*, for example, a student remarked, "My dad travels to lots of different places. He brings back eggs like that for us. But he just calls them 'P' eggs because he can't remember the word *Pysansky*." In a subsequent whole-group discussion that day, students began to share other family events they were reminded of by the book, with some students making explicit links to the traditions of their native countries. Throughout the study of family stories, students drew connections between the family activities in the stories and those in their own lives. From these connections, we can see the beginnings of their attention to similarities and differences in personal and family activities and settings. Their work in the Stories of Family unit established a firm base for the explicit study of culture through the exploration of how their own and their family stories grow out of their cultural heritage and how literature represents many such stories of culture.

Stories of Culture: KWL

In one of the first community share settings for the Stories of Culture unit, MariAnne began using talk to *surface* knowledge by asking the question she had raised earlier in the year, "What is culture?" Using the context of a KWL lesson, she pointed out a large sheet of paper covering the front board. Students, familiar with the format, responded to her question by brainstorming ideas and categories of concepts that they believed related to culture. The first responses described their own backgrounds, perhaps because of their ongoing focus on self and family. (Note: All students' names have been changed.)

For the next five minutes, students each described their heritage in terms of their ethnic histories. Students then identified many of the features of culture often described in social studies texts, including dress, hair, language, and foods. As the transcript excerpt below illustrates, if we were to listen to this part of the discussion out of context, in person or on video, we might find it repetitive and dull.

MariAnne George [MAG]:	I want to know what you know, what you know about culture. Who can tell me something they know about culture?
Oscar:	Like my culture is Mexican.
MAG:	OK so Oscar thinks his culture is Mexican. How is it *Mexican*? Tell us how it is? What, were you born there?
Oscar:	Shakes head [3 seconds inaudible, answering question]
MAG:	His family was born there. Mom or Dad?
Oscar:	Uh no my grandparents.

MAG:	Grandparents, okay, so his grandparents were there, were born in Mexico. Okay, Angela?
Angela:	My culture is Italian.
MAG:	Your culture is Italian. Why is that?
Angela:	My grandma was born in Italy.
MAG:	Italy. Okay, how about you, John?
John:	German
MAG:	Okay, because . . .
John:	My grandma she was born in Germany, and my grandpa was born in somewhere in Europe.

Yet, as we look further, both at the unfolding speech activity and at the teacher's plans for the unit, we can see that an essential function of oral language is occurring here. What knowledge is *surfacing* in this classroom talk? Students are activating relevant background knowledge, trying out the idea of ethnicity as related to family and self (and eventually as related to culture), cycling back to books and ideas already read and discussed, and preparing for new occasions for reading, writing, and speaking. Moreover, as a literate community, students are giving voice to their own backgrounds and hearing those of others—they are embodying and also discovering a very important dimension of culture in the United States. We are all from somewhere and we are continually learning to live and work together as a democracy. This is a powerful theme for literacy learning.

From Self and Family to Culture

Over the course of *surfacing* knowledge about culture, the children in MariAnne's classroom began to use talk to *inquire,* to raise questions that conveyed their grappling with more abstract ideas (e.g., culture as both dynamic and complex, culture as built on traditions, culture as a reflection of values, cultures as coming into contact with one another, cultures other than those based in ethnic traditions). In the next phase of the KWL lesson, MariAnne asked them to formulate questions to guide their upcoming study. As the example from the lesson transcript below illustrates, students generated questions that illustrated the depth of their thinking. These questions and ideas stood in marked contrast to their understandings of culture as a set of physical features and limited to ethnic heritage.

Oscar:	How are different cultures made?
MAG:	Oh, how are cultures made? Making into what . . .
S1:	I know, how do you get off of a culture?
S2:	How do you get rid of a culture?
S3:	How do you quit a culture?
MAG:	Like maybe "can a culture stop?"
S1:	Yeah
MAG:	Okay so culture stops.
	[11 seconds inaudible, students talking quietly while teacher writes on board]
MAG:	Oscar?
Oscar:	[3 seconds inaudible, asking a question]
MAG:	You guys are thinking of some really good questions. Rita?
Rita:	How is culture started?
MAG:	How is culture started? That's a good one.
Lisa:	Can a new culture be started?
MAG:	Can a new culture be started?
John:	No, how can a new culture be started?
MAG:	Okay, John, what I will do is after I put "can a new culture be started," I will put how? Okay Caitlin.
Caitlin:	If you join a culture and you didn't like it [2 seconds inaudible, answering question].
S1:	That is kind of like quitting cultures.
MAG:	Well, I think that maybe goes along with here, some of these. I know what you mean, but I think when we work on these ones that will lead up to that question. I think that is part of these ones.
Samantha:	Sometimes we can have more than one culture, like my mom is from China and my dad is from Mexico.
MAG:	So, Samantha just brought up a really good point: that sometimes we might have a lot of different cultures that make us up.
MAG:	How many of you have, because Samantha said you might have more than one cultural background. How many of you have more than one cultural background?

Here the talk shifts from assertion to inquiry. Modeling a kind of talk essential to good book club discussions as well as to complex learning, MariAnne encourages students to offer questions, not answers. As part of this activity, they are also called upon to listen to and remember what has

BOOK DISCUSSIONS

Susan Florio-Ruane with Julie deTar (2001) found inquiry-oriented talk among teachers within adult book discussions. Labeling it "joint inquiry," they claim that this type of talk permits exploration of a complex text or topic, advancement of comprehension by means of questioning, and also retention of a sense of group cooperation. This type of talk pushes learning in preparation for reading as well as in discussion of books already read by the participants, while strengthening the conversational bonds of the developing literate community.

already been offered by other speakers, mapping their turns at talk onto what has been said either to build upon or to deviate from it. They wait quietly as MariAnne writes what has been said on a chart at the front of the room—under "W", the "What I want to learn" part of the KWL activity. Unlike the uninterrupted flood of parallel declarations in the opening phase of talk, this phase of talk is slower, more collaborative, and interrogative. Participants are speaking, listening, and recording ideas in order to wonder, and the reading they are preparing for will help them explore these wonderings more deeply.

What Have We Learned?

Of course, the "L" column in MariAnne's chart remained to be filled gradually throughout the Stories of Culture unit and would be returned to as part of a final oral assessment, as students used talk to *reflect* on what they had learned about the texts they read as well as the theme of learning about culture. In both writing and discussion in the Stories of Culture unit, students revealed a deepening concept of culture as reflected in their own lives and as it affects others' behavior. A culminating activity involved each student in designing a quilt square that conveyed that student's cultural heritage. This square was to become part of a classroom community quilt. The quilt would convey the multiple representations and intersections of culture and its dynamic nature as it evolves through contact and conflict.

The quilt squares were assembled and hung in the classroom to honor not only each student's culture but each other's cultural heritages. Students had come to understand core principles about culture. Students described these important concepts in oral presentations that showed their literacy learning and cultural artifacts as well as their mastery of the idea of culture and the role of language and literacy in shaping and sharing cultural identity.

Drawing on children's cultural knowledge, prior experiences, and frames of reference helped create a classroom environment in which teaching, learning, and culture became inseparable. The discussions, types of questions, and teacher scaffolding gave MariAnne the opportunity to build bridges between the cultural experiences of her ethnically diverse students, mainstream students, and the curriculum content. The literature read and the types of activities carried out made learning encounters more relevant and effective for MariAnne's English language learning (ELL) students. As students developed a personal connection with their teacher and the stories told and read, they felt empowered by knowing their voice was legitimized. They began to take risks to push their literacy development.

Student-Led Talk About Text

The experiences MariAnne created for talk to *surface* knowledge, *inquire*, and *reflect* helped students internalize these functions and use talk among themselves to explore the texts they read. Whether the texts were part of the formal study of Our Storied Lives or were texts from other literacy activities in the classroom (e.g., assessment cycles, books read in common during independent reading), evidence of students' growing facility to use talk productively became apparent. Perhaps most telling was students' increasing use of their fishbowl and book club discussions to make meaning through collaborative knowledge-construction, through inquiry, and through reflection.

Getting Started

MariAnne's students' early fishbowls and book clubs illustrate the unevenness of students' initial attempts at self-direction. It is important to be realistic about what you might expect from your students early on in their conversations and realize that a free-flowing discussion is not typical in the students' early Book Club days. Rather, MariAnne provided a great deal of support, through the kinds of prompts students responded to prior to their student-led discussions to explicit discussion of expectations to on-the-spot scaffolding as she observed fishbowls and book club discussions. (Note: For a complete discussion of organizing and supporting fishbowls, turn to Chapter 7, pages 115–117.)

Talk for reflection was encouraged by teaching students several specific response prompts, including "Me & the Book" (how is this text affecting your own thinking and beliefs?), "Self-in-Situation" (what would you do if you faced a similar situation to that of one of the characters?), and "In the Character's Shoes" (if you were that character, how would you handle a given situation?). Students read *Chicken Sunday* by Patricia Polacco, and in the following transcript, they discuss the part of the story in which the children save up money to buy their grandmother a special hat. Notice how students draw explicitly on the "Self-in-Situation" prompt as they both identify with the character, and then try to predict what might happen next in the story. They *surface* knowledge from their own experiences, and from what is said in the story. (Note: The bracket [symbol indicates overlapping talk. ?? indicates an unknown speaker.)

Becky:	Maybe if like you were in the story, wouldn't that be cool, if your grandmother or your friend's grandmother really wanted a hat? And then you like pitched in and stuff? I don't get why he pulled the band-aid off of himself.
Steve:	[Wait. My—I think that the money in the j . . .
Becky:	[Eric, what's your prediction?
Eric:	Um, my prediction was they'll get the hat before Easter.

Steve:	I, I think that all the money that they've been saving is go, is to buy their grandmother a new hat, that the hat that she's always wanted at the hat store.
Becky:	(nodding her head). That's what they said in the story.
??:	By why didn't they, but why . . . [end of clip]

In our next segment, we illustrate one of the initial fishbowl discussions MariAnne's students engaged in. They talked about the story "Chicken Coop Monster," an autobiographical essay by Patricia McKissack in which she describes how, as a young girl, she was sent to live with her grandparents following her parents' divorce. A monster in the chicken coop serves as a metaphor for the fears she had to face and overcome. We see an excellent example of students engaging in talk that combines *inquiry* and *surfacing* knowledge as they try to figure out various confusing parts of the text and offer different opinions about the nature of the monster in the coop. At the same time, we see students struggle with having a voice in the discussion.

The students know that Melissa, the main character, has just talked with her grandfather, Daddy James. He had explained how he had to face his monsters to make them go away, and Melissa understands that she has to do this too. She is going out to the chicken coop. The children think Melissa's grandmother, Ma Franky, is out there—perhaps because as the story ends all three (Ma Franky, Daddy James, and Melissa) are together. Notice how Jacob raises the first *inquiry* question about this segment, then draws information from the text to sort out details, especially once John wonders how Ma Franky could be outside in the first place when the author states that everyone is asleep.

Jacob:	How can Ma Franky—
Sean:	(inaudible)
Jacob:	I know, but,
John:	[How can Ma Franky be outside?
Jacob:	[How can Ma Franky be outside?
John:	When she was inside like 2 [minutes ago?
Jacob:	[I know, I know, there's a part when she said everyone was asleep.

As part of *surfacing* relevant knowledge, the students summarize key story events (underlined below). Jacob begins by using QAR knowledge. John elaborates by describing the relevant text information, while Jacob continues summarizing.

Sonya:	No.
John:	Yes.
Jacob:	Yes, yes she was. In the book, there was
John:	No, no, wait, <u>everyone was asleep</u>. They were, it was, like, after dinner and then <u>everyone else went to bed</u> and then <u>she went up</u>—
Jacob:	I know, she—
John:	And she went to bed, and then she went outside.
Holly:	No, after Daddy Frank, he talked to her about the monster, then she went inside.
John:	Yeah, but then how could Ma Franky be out there <u>before</u> her? It's in the back yard.
Holly:	Like 2 minutes, . . .
Jacob:	Yeah.
Holly:	She's there and . . .

Drawing on what they know, the students suggest that it's an "old story," meaning a story that took place a long time ago, so would the author have had characters use a tape recorder when they didn't have that kind of technology? Also notice how Jacob reiterates Sean's question. He puts the question back on the floor, with the added commentary that this was a farm and a long time ago.

Jacob:	Yeah, and then Sean's question is she could have recorded herself or something, but I mean on a farm back then, you think (laugh).
John:	They had . . .
Jacob:	They had mechanicals, stuff like that?
Sean:	Ohhhh. I have . . .
John:	That's an old story.

Students have internalized much of what was modeled during community share, focusing on key ideas and important questions, *surfacing* knowledge that they find relevant. However, most of the discussion involves Jacob, Sean, and John, with an occasional comment by Holly. As the conversation continues, Holly reinforces that this story took place a long time ago, before there were TVs, but there is no acknowledgement of her contribution by any of her peers—neither the other girl in the group, nor the boys who were dominating thus far. As in the early segment, Holly's responses are interrupted by one of the boys in the group. In this case, Sean offers up an opinion of who the monster might be.

Holly:	I mean, how would there be, I mean, there wasn't even a TV!
Sean:	I just got, I just got a great opinion. Maayybee, uh, I forgot her name, but—
Jacob:	Might be Ma Franky?
Sean:	No, the girl who got her arms cut?
Jacob:	Oh, uh

At this point, the other girl in the group, Sonya, tries to enter the conversation by providing the elusive name. What is interesting is that this is the first time the boys in the group have acknowledged either of the girls' attempts to add to the conversation. Inviting all participants into the conversation is a skill these students are still acquiring.

Sonya:	May Elizabeth?
John:	Yeah, May Elizabeth.
Sean:	May Elizabeth, well, I think maybe when she was in there, she might of accidentally kicked the can.

The students in this and the next segment create an argument against the inference on the table, raising the question of where in the text the incident had occurred.

Jacob:	(shaking his head no) And how could . . .
Sean:	And May Elizabeth was inside there. The rooster was like laying down or something, and he hit his leg and got stuck in there.
Jacob:	Yeah but, that May Elizabeth, was in the <u>middle</u> [of the story], and now we're talking about the <u>end</u> so that's two different sections, I mean,
Holly:	Well, yeah . . .

At this point, the students have begun to sort out that the event couldn't have happened as Sean suggested since the two events occurred on different days. Holly has the floor briefly, summarizing the boys' suggestion that Ma Franky was in the coop, and suggesting she may have gone there upon hearing May Elizabeth.

Jacob:	That doesn't make sense, does it?
	[simultaneous speaking]
Holly:	You guys were saying that Ma Franky could have been in the chicken coop . . .

Sean: It wasn't the same, it wasn't the same <u>day</u> . . .

Holly: She would have heard May Elizabeth.

Although these children were just beginning to develop their abilities to engage in student-led discussion, this example is a powerful illustration of not only how well the small, heterogeneous groups can function to promote substantive talk about text, but also how challenging it can be to give all students a voice. One of the functions of fishbowl is to provide opportunity for all students to hear the same small-group discussion and, upon its completion, analyze it for both substantive ideas and for the process participants used. After this fishbowl, during closing community share, MariAnne focused on two areas of critique, asking students to think about:

- What did you learn today?

- What was hard in today's fishbowl discussion?

- What new ideas do we have about our theme?

These questions served two functions: using talk to *surface* understandings and using talk to *reflect* and analyze on the quality of their peer discussions.

In response to MariAnne's question about what they learned, several students from outside the fishbowl identified hypotheses for who was in the chicken coop and whether or not there was a monster. Others reiterated who the important characters were in the story, and some said they had been confused by some of the same things as the fishbowl group.

When asked to *reflect* upon what might have been hard for the discussants that day, one girl asked the question, "Why didn't the boys let the girls talk?" This was a key insight into one of the group's biggest challenges—the domination of discussion by the boys. It led to an interesting debate. Jacob first said that it was not true, that they had let the girls talk (Notice his use of the word *let.*). Holly heatedly stated that this was not true, that she had been cut off several times. Jacob then said that it was okay that he and Sean talked the most because it was Sean's question that started the discussion. He used the phrase, "it was our group"—suggesting a bit of ownership over how the conversation flowed. John and Holly both said, "No one owns the group!" MariAnne used these points to talk about what makes a good book club discussion. They had been developing a list of features that would later become a rubric. Today, they added two features: (1) the discussion belongs to everyone, no matter who asks the question, and (2) all participants have a chance to say what they want to say.

The fishbowl provides an important place for students to learn to engage in talk about text. It is a setting that provides many advantages for this early learning. Students are all focused on a single conversation. The teacher has the opportunity to listen to the full conversation and lead a discussion about both substantive ideas and process. Students are not distracted by other groups talking at the same time that they are. The teacher can step in if a conversation is flagging or if it seems opportune to model a particular conversation strategy. In addition, the closing community share can be framed to elicit both the good ideas and the strengths of the group's discussion, as well as those areas where more practice is needed.

In our next example of early student-led discussion, students are talking about *Roxaboxen* by Alice McLerran, in which the narrator tells about an imaginary town that she and her friends created when they were children. Their horses were stick horses, and their houses were made of clay. Two features emerge in this illustration: students use talk to *reflect* on the story, sharing what they liked about the story (e.g., favorite parts), and students demonstrate their growing sensitivity to the idea that the discussion belongs to everyone. Notice how they are beginning to explicitly invite each other into the conversation. Sean opens this segment by observing something he thought was funny (i.e., unusual, as opposed to humorous). The other students build on Sean's opening by describing what they liked and building on what he had begun (e.g., with the same topic, horses; with the same response, favorite part).

Sean:	It was kinda funny how, um, Anna May? She always got caught for speeding. I wonder why she never got a horse? So she never had to get caught, unless she liked getting caught, but . . .
Eva:	Um, I like how they had sticks as horses and, um, sticks carved as wheels to sports cars.
Lisa:	I liked how they all used their imagination, and I'm hoping that the author of the book writes another book to come after that.
Sean:	Joe, what was your favorite part?
Joe:	(speaking very softly) Fav, my favorite part? Um, I liked when they pretended that the sticks were horses. I do that sometimes.
Sean:	The only part that I really didn't like of the story was the one when they grew out of Roxaboxen. I got kinda sad that they didn't go back and even, but finally Francis went back after fifty years.
Eva:	Lisa, what was your favorite part?
Lisa:	My favorite part was the war? And where they had, where they were galloping around on the horses.
Joe:	I bet that the boys really liked that.

| Lisa: | I wonder if they ever had, like a parade and they dressed up their horses in certain type of flowers and some vines, um, and . . . |
| Sean: | Maybeee. |

The students' reflection spanned their own opinions (e.g., favorite parts, what they like to do that is similar to the characters in the story, the power of the characters' imaginations), stepped into another's perspective (e.g., Joe imagining what "the boys" might like), and expressed emotion (e.g., Sean's sense that it was sad that the characters didn't return to Roxaboxen and that the one that did return didn't do so for fifty years). Looking at these samples, we can see how important it is for the teacher to focus attention on students' talk about text through explicit discussion about talk, through instruction in a range of responses, through modeling and scaffolding during community share, and through providing opportunities for students to engage in self-directed talk about text among their peers.

As students become more proficient at substantive talk, reasonable turn-taking, and peer support in the fishbowl settings, you can consider moving students into the book club setting for their discussions. An example of an end-of-the-year discussion among students from MariAnne's classroom is in the Classroom View on pages 28–29. In that conversation, the students weave skillfully among the three key instructional purposes for classroom talk about text. Of course, the key differences between fishbowl and book club discussions are the greater responsibility the students have to assume for discussion, hearing talk from other groups that is potentially distracting, and less attention from the teacher who must give time to all the discussion groups. Some early primary teachers have maintained fishbowls throughout the year. Others move from fishbowls to book clubs in mid to late spring. Others move to book clubs once a week as a special opportunity after excellent fishbowls. You will need to make your own decision based on your students' needs and capabilities.

Regardless of when the transition occurs from fishbowl to book clubs, it is important to review classroom charts and "I Can" statements about what it means to be a good contributor to a discussion and how to make meaningful contributions. It is helpful to remind students to think about other settings where they have conversation—the playground, the dinner table—and to keep natural conversation behaviors in mind. For example, students in school often fault each other for overlapping talk. Yet, on the playground or in the cafeteria, they often talk at the same time, collaboratively constructing a story. Helping students keep real conversations in mind and extending this knowledge to meaningful talk about text is as important as observing the rubrics or rules for book club conversations.

Conclusion

An opportunity for all students to actively engage and participate plays a significant role both as content (i.e., the stories we read, hear, and tell about culture) and as a way of thinking and representing knowledge to oneself and others (Bruner, 1996). There are many powerful themes (such as Our Storied Lives) that can accomplish the goals of Book Club *Plus.* What is key to a successful Book Club *Plus* unit, in addition to a rich stock of literature for book club discussions and guided readings, is a theme of significance to youngsters and a well-planned curriculum within which spoken and written language are interwoven to engage learners, support and extend their literacy development, and foster community in the classroom.

Not all classrooms invite conversation. Literacy is taught without much regard for the richness of children's oral-culture background. With this in mind, the educational task becomes a matter of not ignoring or even suppressing those oral tools but of stimulating and developing them, and then of introducing literacy and its associated intellectual tools in coordination with the oral (Egan, 1997). This is a process of integrating and connecting who we are and what we know with what we will come to know as a function of literacy. Many opportunities must be provided in the classroom for students to construct their own knowledge. As part of creating those opportunities, teachers should recognize those funds of knowledge (Moll, 1992) in students' homes and communities and make them valuable to learning inside the classroom (Nieto, 1999). There is gathering research evidence that when conversation in the classroom reflects student diversity and is mobilized in literacy-related classroom practices, student enthusiasm increases and school achievement improves (Au, 1980; Au & Jordan, 1981).

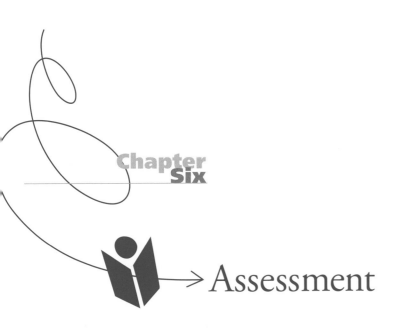

Chapter Six

Assessment

Goals of Book Club *Plus* Assessment

An important part of successfully implementing Book Club *Plus* in your classroom is assessing students' progress as they read, write, and talk in the different learning contexts. The Book Club *Plus* assessment approach is based on the mutual importance of maintaining visible and high performance standards while promoting teacher and student ownership of those standards. Within Book Club *Plus,* we want standards to become part of the everyday conversation in the classroom, and we want teachers and students to see these standards as meaningful to literacy learning. To achieve our goals for assessment, we track student learning throughout a typical Book Club *Plus* unit in several ways, using a variety of tools. These tools may include work samples collected in portfolios, reading logs and journals, standardized tests, running records and teacher observations, student self-evaluation sheets, evaluations of student-led book clubs, language and fluency skills checklists, and project evaluation sheets. Assessment is ongoing and aligned with instruction, and it covers the following areas of learning: reading, writing, discussion, self-evaluation, and content knowledge.

In this chapter, we discuss our vision for the Book Club *Plus* assessment system. Then we talk about identifying target standards and benchmarks and adapting these standards to make them more meaningful to you and your students—giving examples that show how we adapted standards for our classrooms. These examples will guide you as you create an assessment system for your own Book Club *Plus* classroom, with your own state and district standards and guidelines. We also describe tools you might use to monitor progress in the various Book Club *Plus* contexts and ways to select, organize, and report the data you collect. Finally, we discuss making wise instructional decisions based on your assessments of your students' strengths and needs.

Developing an Assessment System

Since 1990, when we began developing Book Club, formal assessment has become increasingly emphasized. Students' literacy performance levels are the focus of both politicians and the media and continue to be of fundamental concern to primary-grade teachers. To help students meet standards and benchmarks at national, state, and local levels, teachers need to identify tools useful in monitoring students' progress to ensure that instructional time is spent effectively. But these tools will make sense only when (a) teachers have a clear sense of their curricular goals and (b) both teachers and students have ownership of the assessment process. That is, assessment needs to align with

CLASSROOM VIEW
Assessment: Grade 3

Amy Heitman was active in TLC throughout the development of Book Club *Plus.* This glimpse into her classroom illustrates the alignment of instructional content and assessment practices in a Book Club *Plus* classroom.

During Amy's third year of teaching, she built her literacy instruction around Book Club *Plus.* Like many teachers, Amy believes that assessing students' entering reading and writing proficiency is critical to teaching literacy skills and strategies effectively. She wants to ensure that her third-grade students gain the skills they need. In addition, she wishes to encourage their love of all aspects of literacy. Amy believes that writing has a fundamental role in the achievement of these goals because it serves to both support and extend students' reading activities and their talk about text.

Within the first week of school, Amy gave her students the writing prompt "Tell me about yourself." For comparison purposes, she planned to repeat the prompt with her students in the spring. In response to the prompt, Shaila, one of Amy's third graders, wrote the letter below.

In analyzing her students' writing, Amy first focused on the degree to which students were able to communicate ideas clearly using the forms and structures of English.

For example, Amy noted that Shaila used temporary spellings to convey her ideas. Further, Shaila seemed to reflect logical sound-symbol correspondence in her temporary spellings. Amy decided that she needed to support Shaila and her classmates' efforts by encouraging them to continue experimenting while providing lessons about word patterns and other aspects of spelling. Shaila's writing also

> Dear Mir. Hetman
> I've had a greaet time with you latly I love
> it at this school I like the kides haer to
> When I go home I go outside to play with
> my friends

standards and benchmarks the district has deemed critical, and both teachers and students need to be able to use the assessment activities to guide their literacy work over the school year. To create the Book Club *Plus* assessment system, we identified key curricular areas that are taught within the Book Club program (see Chapter 2, pages 16–17). We used Kathryn Au's (2001) Standards-Based Change Process to guide us in targeting those standards and benchmarks that serve as a map for monitoring students' progress.

The Book Club *Plus* model, articulated by the teachers in the Teachers Learning Collaborative (TLC), involves four phases. First, teachers articulate their vision of the readers/writers they hope to see when these students graduate from their school. Second, teachers think about what, at their grade level, they are contributing toward helping students achieve this vision. In this second phase, teachers identify key standards and benchmarks that serve

informed Amy about Shaila's knowledge of spelling rules (e.g., "latly" and "I'v" both are missing the silent e, while "greaet" and "kides" include a silent e where none belongs), understanding of sentence structure (e.g., she created a series of simple sentences), and understanding of text structure (e.g., she created a topic sentence—"I'v had a greaet time with you lately"—supported by details that indicated she loves the school and the children that attend it). As Amy looked at the class writing samples, she identified specific spelling, handwriting, grammar, and reading lessons she could teach to support her students' efforts to communicate ideas clearly.

Amy also examined her students' responses in terms of writing for a purpose and an audience. In Shaila's sample, Amy noted the letter format, which was not suggested in the directions. Amy interpreted this as evidence of Shaila's awareness that the sole audience for this text was her teacher and that letters are designed for an individual to read.

Amy used the information she gathered from the class writing samples to identify aspects of audience and purpose she needed to emphasize in her instruction. This information also helped her identify concepts about genres she wanted to introduce through literature, informational reading and writing activities, and oral presentations.

Finally, Amy focused on her students' use of expressive abilities to engage their audience—to draw on personal voice and awareness of audience. Shaila's example was not very engaging. She conveyed two ideas using a list format typical of many of her peers' early writing: she liked the school and her teacher, and she played with friends after school. In addition, Amy noticed ambiguity in Shaila's text. Was she having a great time only lately, meaning it was less than great in the past? Why? Was her sentence "I love it at this school" an indication that she had been in a less appealing school? Who were the friends that she was playing with

after school? Were they from her school? Amy also looked at what was not included in Shaila's sample, such as any reference to her heritage, cultural background, values and dreams, or relationships to her friends and family. In short, there was little of Shaila in the sample.

In comparing Shaila's letter and her peers' writing with what she expected from graduating third graders, Amy was able to make important instructional decisions about what to emphasize in her writing curriculum within the Book Club *Plus* framework. She felt confident that she would be able to meet the needs of her students during the school year using teachable moments across the curriculum as well as specific instructional activities within reading, writing, and other subject areas.

as the foundation of their teaching. In the third phase, teachers create an assessment plan to provide the evidence they will need to know how their students are performing on the benchmarks they have targeted. Knowing the students' performance levels, in turn, helps teachers in the fourth phase—developing a strong literacy instruction plan to help students build needed skills and strategies in the targeted areas.

The Vision and the Curriculum

Determining what to assess began with a discussion of the skills students should master by the end of elementary school. We believe that reading-writing connections are mutually supportive: reading supports students' development as writers and writing supports students' development as readers. Both activities support students' ability to engage in meaningful talk about text. There are also core comprehension strategies that students must develop, literary elements that they must understand, ways of responding to literature meaningfully that they need to master, and knowledge of the workings of our language system that they must internalize. Further, students should feel ownership over this knowledge and engage in literate activities for their own purposes. The TLC articulated the vision of an excellent Book Club *Plus* student in the following way:

> *All Book Club students will feel enthusiasm for books and ideas; will be avid and successful in reading, writing, and talking about different genres of text; and will engage in literacy for a variety of purposes in and out of school.*

With this in mind, you can think about what to include in the instructional curriculum across a grade level to help students achieve these goals. For example, in the curricular area of comprehension students need help to work on standards related to background knowledge, processing text, and monitoring their own reading. The curriculum chart, which was introduced and discussed in Chapter 2 on pages 16–17, summarizes the broad content included in the Book Club *Plus* teachers' curriculum.

As discussed on page 18, the four major curricular target areas—comprehension, writing, language conventions, and literary aspects—reflect the range of what we want our students to learn about in each year of school, adapting the focus and content as required for each grade level. For example, in addition to general knowledge that we want students to acquire and to use, we must include assessing students' knowledge about concepts of print—holding a book, reading from left to right, using both print and pictures to acquire information. In terms of literary aspects, we want primary students to be aware of the authors who write their books and to engage in the full variety of response to literature that researchers, such as Sipe (1998), have demonstrated they are able to do. We also want them to learn to think in terms of story themes, as Au (1992) and Lehr (1991) have shown young students can do.

Regardless of the curricular target area, Book Club *Plus* instruction supports students' progress toward achieving standards that are required by the national, state, and local institutions relevant to their educational context and that are appropriate in format to the age levels being taught.

Identifying Target Standards and Benchmarks

Once you have determined what you hope to accomplish and have identified core curricular areas, you can work from your state and local benchmarks to evaluate your students' needs and potential areas of instruction. For example, in the Chicago Reading Initiative, teachers are expected to spend a two-hour block of time distributed among comprehension, word knowledge, fluency, and writing. The Illinois state standards provide further details for what a teacher might focus on in these four areas, (e.g., Students are expected to "comprehend a broad range of reading materials."). Specific related standards include making comparisons across reading selections and identifying important themes and topics.

Au (2001) suggests that standards be reworded to become as visible as possible to guide classroom activities effectively and to make their purposes apparent to students and parents. Converting the standards to "I Can" statements emphasizes students' ownership and control. The table on pages 86–87 provides a sample of how standards statements and "I Can" statements written to match the Book Club *Plus* core curricular areas relate to national standards developed by professional educational organizations. These organizations include the National Council of Teachers of English (NCTE), the International Reading Association (IRA), and the National Council for the Social Studies (NCSS). For a complete listing of these standards, please refer to pages 136–137.

To create our sample chart, we thought about the core areas on which we wanted to focus (reading, writing, discussion, self-evaluation, and content-area work) and then created one or two "I Can" statements for each of these areas. Creating a table such as this with your own state standards can help you guide instruction and evaluation in your own classroom.

Teachers in some Book Club *Plus* classrooms posted their "I Can" statements as clear reminders of the standards that they wanted to guide their classroom discussion, writing, and reading. For both students and teachers, this prominent display functioned as a quick way to reference the goals they were all working toward.

ASSESSMENT TIP

The "I Can" statements are versatile enough to reflect the content of specific units as well as the relevant standards and benchmarks. Janine Rodrigues created "I Can" statements for her Trickster unit. By translating general standards into objectives tied to her particular unit, she developed a tangible set of guidelines to help her students focus as they worked with trickster tales. For example, *I can* write about my thinking all by myself in my reading log, in a sorting map, and in my own trickster story; *I can* make a prediction and prove why it might happen.

Sample Correlation Chart

Sample Book Club *Plus* Standards	National Standards (NCTE/IRA Reading/Language Arts; NCSS Social Studies)	Insert Your State Standards and Goals	Sample "I Can" Statements for Classroom Conversations
Reading 1: Students can retell a story in their own words.	**NCTE/IRA Standard 4.** Students adjust their use of spoken, written, and visual language (e.g., conventions, style, and vocabulary) to communicate effectively with a variety of audiences. **NCTE/IRA Standard 12.** Students use spoken, written, and visual language to accomplish their own purposes (e.g., for learning, enjoyment, persuasion, and the exchange of information).		I can retell a story in my own words.
Reading 2: Students can make meaning from a variety of texts.	**NCTE/IRA Standard 2.** Students read a wide range of literature from many periods in many genres to build an understanding of the many dimensions (e.g., philosophical, ethical, aesthetic) of human experience. **NCTE/IRA Standard 3.** Students apply a wide range of strategies to comprehend, interpret, evaluate, and appreciate texts. They draw on their prior experience, their interactions with other readers and writers, their knowledge of word meaning and of other texts, their word identification strategies, and their understanding of textual features (e.g., sound-letter correspondence, sentence structure, context, graphics).		I can make meaning when I read a variety of texts.
Writing 1: Students can use writing to communicate ideas.	**NCTE/IRA Standard 4.** **NCTE/IRA Standard 5.** Students employ a wide range of strategies as they write and use different writing process elements appropriate to communicate with different audiences for a variety of purposes. **NCTE/IRA Standard 8.** Students use a variety of technological and information resources (e.g., libraries, databases, computer networks, video) to gather and synthesize information and to create and communicate knowledge.		I can write to communicate my ideas.
Writing 2: Students can write for different purposes and audiences.	**NCTE/IRA Standard 4.** **NCTE/IRA Standard 5.** **NCTE/IRA Standard 8.** **NCTE/IRA Standard 12.**		I can use writing for different purposes and audiences.

Sample Correlation Chart, *continued*

Sample Book Club *Plus* Standards	National Standards (NCTE/IRA Reading/Language Arts; NCSS Social Studies)	Insert Your State Standards and Goals	Sample "I Can" Statements for Classroom Conversations
Writing 3: Students can demonstrate their expressive abilities by creating texts that engage an audience.	**NCTE/IRA Standard 12.**		I can show "me" in my writing.
Culture 1: Students can understand their own culture and that of others.	**NCSS Standard 1.** Social studies programs should include experiences that provide for the study of culture and cultural diversity. **NCSS Standard 2.** Social studies programs should include experiences that provide for the study of the ways human beings view themselves in and over time. **NCSS Standard 4.** Social studies programs should include experiences that provide for the study of individual development and identity.		I can use artifacts to describe: my own cultural heritage, others' cultures, and similarities and differences across cultures.
Culture 2: Students can define culture in a way that reflects its rich, complex, and dynamic nature.	**NCSS Standard 3.** Social studies programs should include experiences that provide for the study of people, places, and environments. **NCSS Standard 5.** Social studies programs should include experiences that provide for the study of interactions among individuals, groups, and institutions.		I can define culture and how cultures change.
Discussion 1: Students can participate and contribute to a good book club discussion.	**NCTE/IRA Standard 4.** **NCTE/IRA Standard 6.** Students apply knowledge of language structure, language conventions (e.g., spelling and punctuation), media techniques, figurative language, and genre to create, critique, and discuss print and nonprint texts. **NCTE/IRA Standard 12.**		I can contribute to a good book club discussion.
Evaluation 1: Students can draw on evidence to reflect on and evaluate their own learning.	**NCTE/IRA Standard 1.** **NCTE/IRA Standard 12.**		I can show and/ or tell what I learned and how I learned it.

Tools for Assessment

Standards, benchmarks, and "I Cans" make it possible to monitor students' progress and make wise instructional decisions (Au, 2001). In addition to the "I Can" statements, there are many tools that Book Club *Plus* teachers use to gather evidence to monitor their students' progress. Each teacher uses a variety of assessments to determine if students are meeting goals and to report this information to interested participants (students, parents, administrators). The chart below gives an overview of possible assessment sites. Following the chart, we give several examples of how Book Club *Plus* teachers have gathered evidence and monitored their students' progress.

Book Club *Plus* Assessment Sites

Initial Assessments

- Grouping
  - Book clubs: heterogeneous groups with respect to ability
  - Guided reading groups: Informal reading inventories and word lists (see page 112), district assessments, basal reader pretests
- Writing samples to identify areas for instruction
- Favorite book lists to assess students' knowledge of literary texts and authors

Ongoing Assessments/ Sources of Evidence
(Connected to "I Can" statements)

- Evaluation and think sheets
- Fluency assessments
- Teacher observations and anecdotal notes
- Comprehension checks using reading log entries
- Strategy work during guided reading
- Literacy center work
- Student self-evaluations
- Writer's workshop
- Portfolios
- Informal reading inventories and word lists

Summative Assessments
(Connected to "I Can" statements)

- End of book/unit summaries and essays
- Student self-evaluations
- Repetition of initial writing samples
- Unit projects
- Portfolios
- Standardized tests

Selecting and Organizing Data

The assessment sites given in the chart are possibilities. It is up to you to choose the best assessments to gather data in your classroom. For example, Barbara Naess, working at the kindergarten level, identified appropriate standards for her students and created "I Can" statements to make these standards accessible to her five-year-olds, e.g., I can compare one book to another. I can connect what I read to my own life and share my thoughts. Barbara then identified specific evidence that she could use to measure her students' progress on these standards. She evaluated their ability to compare across reading selections using different sources of information. For one source, she examined their contributions to whole group and book club or fishbowl discussions comparing sets of book pairs. For another source, she recorded their contributions to a class Venn diagram that compared the paired books and made comparisons across sets of books. Barbara also developed a rubric for evaluating students' progress in exceeding the benchmark (working at a level more typical of students above the student's current grade level), meeting the benchmark (working at the level one would expect at the end of the current grade level), or still working on the benchmark (not yet having achieved end-of-year level of success):

Exceeding the Benchmark: Makes multiple comparisons between books, or extends comparisons to more than two books (e.g., across sets of books, to read alouds, poetry, and other texts).

Meeting the Benchmark: Makes simple comparisons between book pairs or book sets, prompted or unprompted.

Working on the Benchmark: Does not make comparisons, or comparisons are not accurate.

The TLC colleagues also created simple forms that allowed them to record data about each student's performance. The sample shown on page 90 illustrates how the group defined features of successful writing to communicate ideas. To develop this rubric, TLC members each brought three samples of their students' writing to a meeting. Each sample represented a student who exceeded, met, or was still working on the standard. Through their discussion, the teachers identified essential features that distinguished the work at each level. They then compared what they had seen in their students' work to nationally normed rubrics such as the popular "six-trait writing system." Teachers across the company initiated the six-trait writing system in the 1980s. One source of information about the six-trait writing system is *Creating Writers Through 6-Trait Writing Assessment and Instruction* by Vicki Spandel. While the TLC teachers could have begun with the already-established system, they believed that for their professional development, they needed to start with their own samples and develop their own rubrics. Comparing their work to existing assessment instruments provided an important check on the expectations they had for their students' achievement levels.

Notice that the rubric captures a range of features that relate to communicating ideas in writing, including the number and depth of ideas that are included, the scope of sources the writer draws upon (e.g., background knowledge, Internet sources, movies, books, magazines), and the style in which the ideas are communicated—at the sentence level as well as in terms of skills such as grammar and spelling. This chart is typical of TLC's scoring tools—easy to use for both a holistic score (Did the overall paper appear to meet, exceed, or fall short of the standard?) and for the specific areas of strengths or concerns that influence teachers' instructional decisions.

▼ **Sample rubric for recording data about student performance**

Standard	Rubric Features	Working On	Met	Exceeds
Writing to communicate ideas	Appropriate number of ideas to convey topic			
	Some depth to the ideas included			
	Ideas cohere			
	Ideas are from more than one source			
	Sentences vary in complexity			
	Conventional spelling, grammar, and punctuation			

In another example of gathering evidence, you might find that a typical set of state standards requires that students be able to use correct grammar, punctuation, spelling, capitalization, and structure; create organized and coherent writing for specific purposes and audiences; and deliver ideas in writing for a variety of purposes. In this case, the application of conventional language rules can be evaluated in final drafts as students practice different literary forms and in final drafts of products students have created to share with others. In addition, you can examine students' informal writing (e.g., reading log entries, first drafts, such as Shaila's letter, note cards for inquiry project reports) for a measure of the degree to which students are able to automatically apply such rules in their day-to-day writing. You may notice students who are adept at conventional spelling, grammar, and mechanics in all kinds of writings; students who are able to apply the rules of usage to final drafts but have less control in their day-to-day writing; and students who struggle with these conventions in all settings. Clearly, different instructional decisions are needed for each of these students.

Composing well-organized and coherent writing for specific purposes and audiences can be evaluated within and across classroom writing activities and assignments. Two key questions guide assessment of this goal:

- Are students comfortable engaging in writing to accomplish different tasks?

- Do students have command of the various aspects of the writing process appropriate to their age level (e.g., prewriting strategies, organizational strategies, editing, and revising)?

Teachers evaluate students' facilities in planning, drafting, and revising the texts they create in their day-to-day activities and in those writing activities that involve interactions with their family and community.

The students' ability to communicate in writing to accomplish different goals can be evaluated by looking at the ways in which writing serves as a tool for reflecting, gathering and organizing information, practicing literary forms, and sharing ideas with others. Teachers can evaluate the degree to which students' voices are maintained across types of writing, while their sensitivity to audience needs varies. For example, there should be clear differences in the amount and form of information included in a reflection page in a student's reading log and the amount and form in a report that will be heard or read by others. In first drafts, students' writing—such as Shaila's—would reflect their attention to developing ideas and making their stories engaging (and thus, might contain errors in spelling, punctuation, and/or grammar), while later drafts would maintain the students' engaging text while correcting earlier errors. Students' selection of ways to convey ideas would vary between genres associated with stories and poetry and those associated with conveying information through essays or reports. These include writing to persuade someone toward social action (e.g., creating a neighborhood park or making a change in school cafeteria rules), conveying one's opinion through a critical essay (e.g., how to be a good friend, or how one can contribute to family in meaningful ways), or even selecting an appropriate genre, as Shaila did in choosing to write a letter. In short, to evaluate this goal, teachers use multiple writing samples that function in various ways in classroom activities and subject areas, as well as in students' learning across school subjects.

Similar processes of analysis are necessary to evaluate students' progress on each of the standards required in the setting in which any Book Club *Plus* teacher works. The table shown here provides an example of how colleagues in TLC thought about evidence in relation to certain standards. Notice that each standard has a least one source of evidence associated with it for examining students' progress.

Possible Assessment Sites

Reading 1: Students can retell a story in their own words.	Opening/Closing Community Share, Class Presentation, Guided Reading Groups, Literacy Center Work, Pre/Post Writing Prompt
Reading 2: Students can make meaning from a variety of texts.	Opening/Closing Community Share, Book Club Discussion Groups, Guided Reading Groups, Literacy Center Work, Standardized Tests, Pre/Post Writing Prompt,
Writing 1: Students can use writing to communicate ideas.	Pre/Post Writing Prompt, Reading Log, Process Writing, Literacy Center Work, Standardized Tests
Writing 2: Students can write for different purposes and audiences.	Pre/Post Writing Prompt, Process Writing, Speedwriting, Class Presentation
Writing 3: Students can demonstrate their expressive abilities by creating texts that engage an audience.	Pre/Post Writing Prompt, Essay, Class Presentation
Culture 1: Students can understand their own culture and that of others.	Unit Project, Essay About Unit Theme, Opening/ Closing Community Share
Culture 2: Students can define culture in a way that reflects its rich, complex, and dynamic nature.	Opening/Closing Community Share or a KWL Lesson, Essay About Unit Theme
Discussion 1: Students can participate and contribute to a good book club discussion.	Fishbowl, Book Club Observation Sheet, Book Club Self-Assessment
Evaluation 1: Students can draw on evidence to reflect on and evaluate their own learning.	Review of Portfolio, Self-Evaluation Sheets, Opening/Closing Community Share

Chris Cimino, teaching a first-grade unit on friendship (see Chapter 4), developed this chart that correlated her "I Can" statements with specific pieces of evidence and a rubric.

▼ Grade 1 Rubrics

"I Can" Statement	Rubric Focus	Criteria
I can compare one book to another.	I will evaluate and assess students' progress through our whole group discussions during community share, through response journals and students' ability to answer prompts relating to text and character comparison, and through fishbowl discussions.	3: (exceeds grade level expectations): Student is able to make many connections between books in terms of characters, themes, etc. 2: (meets): Student is able to make some connections between at least two books in terms of theme, character, etc. 1: (in progress): Student is not able to make connections between books in any way or connections are very limited.
I can connect what I read to my own life and share my thoughts through writing and talk.	I will evaluate and assess students' ability to make personal connections to text through journal responses, fishbowls, and structured writing assignments. Students are expected to make contributions using all three modes.	3: Student is able to make several connections between self and what is read. Connections are relevant. In written responses, student uses conventional spelling. 2: Student makes at least one connection that is relevant and uses conventional or developmentally-appropriate spelling. 1: Student makes no connections or the connections are not relevant. Written work is hard to read.
I can stay on topic when I write.	I will evaluate and assess through response logs and structured writing assignments.	3: Student writes several complete sentences relating to a single specific topic. Sentences are clear and in sequential order. Uses conventional spelling. 2: Student is able to write a few complete sentences, which are clearly ordered and make sense. Uses conventional or developmental spelling. 1: Student is not able to do the assignment or what the student has written is hard to read.

In addition to standards-specific scoring systems, it is useful to have summary charts that can be used in measuring students' progress in the contexts specific to Book Club *Plus*. For example, while many local and state standards have yet to emphasize discussion as a site for evaluating students' achievement, such a rubric was fundamental to tracking Book Club *Plus* students' success. Similarly, since the ability to use reading logs effectively is specific to success in using book clubs, a rubric can be used to examine students' progress in this area. The charts on pages 94–95 articulate levels of accomplishment related to students' discussion and reading log abilities. Evaluation sheets that appear after page 315 offer ways to evaluate students in a variety of areas. You will find two "I Can" self-evaluation sheets, a Checklist for Language Arts Skills, a Fluency Checklist, various sheets for assessing reading log and book discussion performance, and rubrics for assessing unit work.

Rubric for Book Club Discussions

Score	Criteria
5	• Stays focused on topic, theme(s), questions, or characters • Uses evidence from the text and/or personal experience to support ideas • Appropriately introduces new ideas • Builds/expands on others' ideas • Respects others' ideas • Talks for a clear purpose • Appropriately supports less active members of the group
4	• Focuses on some major themes, issues, questions, or characters • Effectively uses some evidence from text, content area, and/or personal experience to support ideas • Occasionally introduces new ideas appropriately • Occasionally builds/expands on others' ideas • Respects others' ideas • Purpose for speaking is usually clear • Sometimes supports less active members of the group
3	• Focuses on secondary themes, issues, questions, or characters OR lacks detailed discussion of major themes • Uses little evidence from text and/or personal experience to support ideas OR use of evidence is only somewhat effective • Less than effective at introducing new ideas • Builds some on others' ideas but may resort to round-robin turn taking • Demonstrates some sense of purpose for speaking • Demonstrates some respect for others' ideas
2	• Makes few references to important themes, issues, questions, or characters OR lacks detailed discussion of any themes • Uses little evidence from text and/or personal experience to support ideas OR use of evidence is ineffective • Purpose for speaking is unclear or lacking • Seldom builds on others' ideas and may resort to round-robin turn taking • Demonstrates little respect for or attention to others' ideas • Seldom introduces new ideas • Speaks infrequently
1	• Superficial response with minimal reference to the text or personal experiences • Uses trivial textual details or irrelevant personal experiences to support ideas • Perseverates on ideas—does not build on them • Does not introduce new ideas • Demonstrates no clear purpose for speaking • Speaks very infrequently • Raises hand before speaking and/or resorts to round-robin turn taking

Rubric for Book Club Reading Log Entries

Score	Criteria
5	• Focuses on major themes, issues, questions, or characters • Effectively uses evidence from text, content area, and/or personal experience to support ideas • Produces multiple, related, and well-developed responses • Writes for a clear purpose • Generates a well-focused, connected, and coherent response
4	• Focuses on some major themes, issues, questions, or characters • Effectively uses some evidence from text, content area, and/or personal experience to support ideas • Produces several related responses • Purpose for writing is fairly clear • Generates a focused, connected, and generally coherent response
3	• Focuses on secondary themes, issues, questions, or characters OR lacks detailed discussion of major themes • Uses little evidence from text and/or personal experience to support ideas OR use of evidence is less than effective • Demonstrates some sense of purpose for writing • Generates a somewhat focused, connected, and coherent response
2	• Makes few references to important themes, issues, questions, or characters OR lacks detailed discussion of any themes • Uses little evidence from text and/or personal experience to support ideas OR use of evidence is ineffective • Purpose for writing is unclear or lacking • Response has inadequate focus, connection between ideas, and overall coherence
1	• Superficial response with minimal reference to the text or personal experiences • Writing is a string of trivial textual details • Demonstrates no clear purpose for writing • Generates an unfocused, unconnected, and incoherent response

Engaging Students in Self-Evaluation

The teacher tools for monitoring and evaluating progress described above provide the basis for teachers to know where their students stand in their literacy progress. Moreover, they provide a foundation for making wise instructional decisions throughout the school year. Yet it is also important for students to understand how to self-evaluate and monitor their progress; they must have a sense of ownership of their own learning to be active themselves in noting where they need help and how to get it.

Teachers have found it helpful to engage students in the process of developing rubrics to guide their reading, writing, and talk. For example, Karen Eisele's third-graders created the self-evaluation rubric shown below. They listed features of a good discussion as being worth four points while one point signaled features that were detrimental.

▶ **Grade 3 Self-Evaluation Rubric**

A "4" means	A "1" means
- There would be discussion	- Ignoring the people in your group
- Look at who is talking	- Not paying attention
- Ask questions	- Throwing paper airplanes
- Share your ideas	- Being nasty
- Stay on topic	- Fooling around
- Sitting at your seat	- Not staying on topic
- Stay with your group	- Not sitting in your seat
- Listen	
- Use a smaller voice	

In another example, Amy Heitman's students decided they needed a list that reminded them of the "Do's" of a good discussion, as shown on the next page. With Amy's help, each group generated a list of goals based on their "Do" list that they might choose to focus on during a specific time period (e.g., a week, a book club meeting, a grading period).

With their goal chart posted in the room, students referred to the list and made their own "I Can" statements to convey what they needed to improve upon when they engaged in talk about text. Their "Personal I Cans" became part of their portfolio documenting process. They tracked ways in which they worked to improve their abilities and provided specific documentation. During parent-teacher conferences, Amy invited her students to participate as well, and many took their parents through their portfolios to explain what they were doing in school, how close they were to achieving their goals, and what they were planning to do to ultimately meet the goals they had established. The "I Can Self-Evaluation" on page 98 (see also Evaluation Sheet 13 following page 315) illustrates one format Amy used to help her students organize this part of their portfolio. Notice that Amy taught her students to identify the specific book, event, and/or date, as well as describe the example that illustrated their progress on the "I Can."

The phase of assessment that focuses on identifying standards and benchmarks is crucial to students' success. A combination of national/state/district standards and benchmarks, teacher-generated rubrics, student-generated rubrics, and various tracking formats provide the information that teachers need to make wise instructional decisions and that students need to assume shared responsibility for their progress in literacy learning.

Be a good listener as well as a speaker.

Ask questions that will lead to more ideas.

It's okay to disagree with someone in an agreeable way.

As more ideas are shared, more people will add or join the discussion.

Include everyone in the discussion. Ask a question to pull someone into the conversation.

Stay on topic.

◄ Sample from Amy Heitman's Class: The "Do's" of a good discussion.

Everyone participates and shares in discussion.

Everyone supports each other.

The group will be friendly.

The group members can ask each other questions and help clear up anything they don't understand.

The group stays on topic or on ideas that are close to the topic.

Consider everyone's point of view and talk about different points of view

► Sample goals based on the "Do" list.

▶ "I Can"
Self-Evaluation

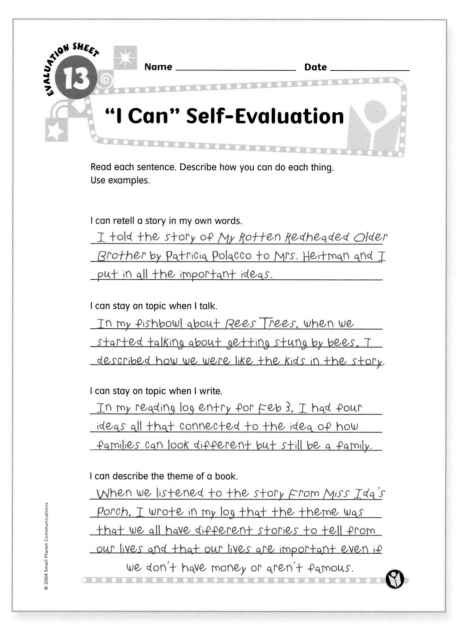

EVALUATION SHEET
13

Name _____   Date _____

"I Can" Self-Evaluation

Read each sentence. Describe how you can do each thing.
Use examples.

I can retell a story in my own words.

I told the story of My Rotten Redheaded Older
Brother by Patricia Polacco to Mrs. Heitman and I
put in all the important ideas.

I can stay on topic when I talk.

In my fishbowl about Bees Trees, when we
started talking about getting stung by bees, I
described how we were like the kids in the story.

I can stay on topic when I write.

In my reading log entry for Feb 3, I had four
ideas all that connected to the idea of how
families can look different but still be a family.

I can describe the theme of a book.

When we listened to the story From Miss Ida's
Porch, I wrote in my log that the theme was
that we all have different stories to tell from
our lives and that our lives are important even if
we don't have money or aren't famous.

© 2004 Small Planet Communications

Tools for Reporting Student Progress

Another important aspect of assessment is reporting progress to students, to parents, and to administrators. It is important to report the breadth and depth of students' learning with details that go beyond simple letter grades. Some of these reporting methods apply to the daily activities in the classroom: reading, log writing, book club discussions, guided reading for comprehension and fluency. For example, Evaluation Sheet 9 is a Book Club Observation Sheet that we've used to report assessment data to our students. The form lists several criteria for book clubs. Other tools are specific to the projects that students complete during a unit. Evaluation Sheet 17, Quilt Writing

I can figure out a theme from my reading.

3 (Exceeds)	**2** (Meets)	**1** (Working On)
	Ethan	
	Carlos	
	Maria	
	Kim	
	Liz	
	Marc	
	Danielle	
	Lian	
	Maggie	
	Sean	
Bella	Oscar	
Jackson	Christina	Edwin
Sarah	Damian	Jesse
Dreese	Rhiannon	Grayson
Evelyn	Derek	Dalton
20%	63%	17%

Project Student Assessment, allows teachers to report their assessment of students' work on a project during the unit described in Chapter 11. We work with students to help them respond to the evaluations, thus engaging them in a dialogue about their progress toward meeting specific "I Can" statements and encouraging their ownership of the standards.

Other tools, such as report cards, give parents and students periodic updates on progress. Standard report cards don't always reflect the many skills and strategies that students are learning. You may want to incorporate additional assessment information into the report cards used by your school system. For example, you may want to attach Evaluation Sheet 5, Checklist for Language Arts Skills, to your district report card. The checklist focuses on some of the specific skills that students practice in Book Club and Literacy Block. You might adapt this checklist or create a similar attachment that reflects what you and your students are accomplishing through Book Club *Plus*.

Administrators are also an important audience. Of course, district and state tests are one source of information for administrators. However, you may want to report progress on "I Can" (standard) statements. One method of reporting this information is to create a bar graph using information from your rubrics that show which students have exceeded (3), met (2), or are working on (1) particular standards. An example of such a bar graph is shown to the left. During the year, you can use these kinds of bar graphs to show progress to administrators and to inform your instruction.

Making Wise Instructional Decisions

When teaching within the Book Club *Plus* framework, there are multiple opportunities to make instructional decisions about what to emphasize based on initial assessments of students' strengths and needs. For example, over the course of their school year, students in Amy's classroom engaged in reading, writing, and talk about their own lives. Students read literature that highlighted the genres of autobiography and autobiographical fiction, and they studied authors known for writing from their own life experiences and their craft. Instructional activities in writing, for example, focused on "I Can" statements that were based on the national, state, and district standards. Students maintained portfolios of their work that they believed had the potential to show their progress on the "I Cans." Each sample in the portfolio held a sticky note, written by the student, explaining why the sample was included and what progress it showed for a specific "I Can." Students wrote extensively in reading logs, during writer's workshop, and within social studies instruction so that they learned to use writing as a tool for reflecting, gathering and organizing information, practicing literary forms, and sharing ideas with others.

The writing tools developed through TLC were important for making instructional decisions over the course of the school year and for summative evaluation of students' progress in writing. For example, TLC members used a post-test writing prompt, repeating the same directions (that students write in response to "Tell me about yourself") that they gave in the fall.

Shaila's post-test writing sample is shown on the next page. It is, like the pretest, a first draft, but even as a first draft, much information can be obtained about her progress. Amy felt that Shaila's pretest indicated she was still working on each of the three standards in writing (see page 93). Amy used the post test to both compare performance and to identify whether Shaila had met each of the standards, exceeded expectations, or was still working on one, two, or all three.

In terms of using correct grammar, spelling, punctuation, capitalization, and structure to communicate ideas, Shaila's post test reveals effectiveness in many aspects. She continues to have excellent control over sounds and symbols, using temporary spellings for more complex vocabulary (e.g., an ear "infekshen," "scrapt"). Her spelling has improved, showing only minor mistakes (e.g., "cept" rather than kept) that can be easily corrected in a next draft. Thus, her command over spelling and sounds is becoming more automatic, reflected in few spelling errors and appropriate temporary spellings on a first draft. She has begun to use punctuation marks more easily—to end sentences, as well as attempted to signal dialogue (My mom said "whats so funny Don . . . any better than this" he said). Her punctuation does not appear to be completely automatic. She may need more instruction, or perhaps she has not attended to it, knowing this is a first draft. She still has work to do on paragraph structure, though her overall story structure shows more sophistication than her pretest response. Moreover, she has adopted some of the craft used by authors such as Polacco, using capital letters and exclamation points for emphasis and using large print to convey a story character's loud voice. She appears to meet the standard for her grade level on communicating her ideas through command of the language conventions.

While this is only one sample, it can be used to examine her ability to write a well-organized and coherent piece of writing for specific purposes and audiences. She has narrated a family story, indicating that she no longer sees

Shaila 4/12/00

A long tinme ago I hade a dog named Boomer. When I was about 2 or 3 we went to PA. Well we were in the car and Boomer had to go to the bathroom but my mom didn't know. Like a minute later he started to wake up and cry out then he went poop in the car. Well here is what happened. I started scdreaming because of the smell and my sister was ten and she had an ear infekshen so she started crying and then my mom slamed on the brakes and yelled WHAT,S GOING ON BACK THERE but we didn't answer and cept on screaming. She got out of the car opend the back door and first thing she saw was a pile of, of, POOP!!!   She calmed down, scrapt out the poop and picked me up. The first thing I did was throw up. My Mom put me down and I started screaming again. My dad got out of the car and burst out in laughter. My mom said "whats so funny Don. I mean our kids are in the car screaming - Boomer pooped inside the car and Shaila threw up on me. "I don't think anything is going to get any better than this" he said. Then she got in the car and so did my dad and drove away. An hour later I was sound asleep and my dad was reading a news paper wile my sister was reading Hiedie.

THE END

Your friend,

Shaila

▲ Shaila's Post-Test
   Writing Sample

herself in terms of discrete details, but rather as having a storied past, one worth writing about in ways that engage her audience. She uses story conventions, such as the opening "A long time ago." She has a cast of characters with personalities she conveys through their words and actions. She uses story structure effectively and draws on her knowledge of story craft appropriately. When this writing is juxtaposed against her reading logs and informational writing, it will further inform Amy about Shaila's ability to adjust her writing for different purposes. Standing alone, it certainly conveys her knowledge of story. Moreover, she ends her narrative by signing off as she would with a letter—just as she did on the pretest. This conveys an awareness that this story will have an audience. She shows good progress in meeting the standard related to writing for different audiences and purposes.

In terms of the third standard, reflected in the statement "I can show me in my writing," there is tremendous growth when compared to her initial writing sample shown on page 82. This is a personal story, and we learn much about Shaila and her relationship to her family members. She conveys an impression of her older sister, her father's sense of humor and ability to remain calm, the role of literacy in the family (father reading newspaper, sister reading *Heidi* as the mom drives along), and Boomer the dog. She has clearly met, if not exceeded, the standard for third grade related to voice.

Conclusion

What have we learned through our work in developing an assessment system within the Teachers Learning Collaborative? We are committed to the close linking of assessment, instruction, and curriculum. As Valencia (2000, p. 248) has written, classroom assessment "provides timely, concrete evidence of students' learning that can support or refute high-stakes assessments. More importantly, it provides evidence behind the grades." Teachers in the collaborative who worked through the process of developing their assessment system felt they had much greater knowledge of individual students' progress and a better understanding of the progress of their class. They had more control over instructional decisions; better ways to communicate to students, parents, and administrators their methods of instruction and information about students' progress; and more confidence in making instructional decisions. The standards, rather than being dictated from external sources, became a force for taking control of their teaching. Members of the TLC believe, as Valencia (2000, p. 248) suggests, "Teachers who understand and focus on content standards, and who make links between instruction and classroom assessment, are more likely to be effective."

Chapter Seven

Classroom Management

Getting Started

Getting the Book Club *Plus* program started in your classroom means making many important decisions. You will need to think about your level of implementation, your curriculum, standards, themes, literature selection, the grouping of students, daily instruction, reading aloud, developing a classroom library, and how to work with children who are learning to speak, read, and write in English. In this chapter, those of us who have successfully used Book Club *Plus* in our primary-grade classrooms offer some suggestions and strategies that have worked for us. We provide practical guidance to primary-grade teachers using Book Club *Plus* for the first time.

Level of Implementation

As we discussed in Chapters 1 and 2, teaching literacy in the primary grades carries many responsibilities. Some of you are working with students with virtually no knowledge of the written symbol system. Others have students who are unable to move from one area of the room to another without adult guidance. Some children have wide experience with story listening and have well-developed concepts of print, while other children have extensive experiences in story telling. As described in Chapter 1, the cultural heritages of children and their prior experiences in school influence their use of and understandings about literacy.

Therefore, it is important to analyze how you want to implement Book Club *Plus* for the first time. You need to consider your students, your comfort level with the Book Club *Plus* concepts, and the purpose you want this work to serve in your classroom. To help you think about the approach that you will use in your classroom, we've put together the following questions:

- How much experience do I have with integrating literacy and content-area instruction?

- How much experience do I have involving my students in inquiry?

- What age are my students, physically, intellectually, socially, and emotionally?

- How comfortable do I feel asking my early literacy students to produce something in writing—using pictures, letters, and other forms of representation?

- How often have I asked my students to talk about the books I read to them?

- Do my students sit in rows when they work, or do I group them at tables?

- Do I create a strong sense of the classroom as a community of learners?

- Do I expect my students to work in pairs or small groups, independent of me or other adults in my room?

- Do I let my students talk about the books they have been exploring during independent reading—in pairs, small groups, or a whole class setting?

Your answers to these questions can help you determine whether you will start using Book Club alone or move immediately into teaching and creating Book Club *Plus* units. For example, you might want to use Book Club alone as a way to make your read alouds a substantive literacy experience for students (see Chapter 10). By combining your read-aloud program with the Book Club cycle, your students can learn how to engage with texts in meaningful ways. They can make personal and intertextual connections, critique the authors' style, engage in language play, construct story understandings, observe characters in terms of their development and their role in the story, and so forth. As we've learned from decades of research, e.g., Applebee (1978), Au (1992), Lehr (1991), and Sipe (2000, 2002), Sipe & Bauer, (2001), children's abilities to understand narrative, respond to literature, and identify story theme begin to develop at a very young age. Book Club activities linked to read alouds are one important school context that support this learning.

In another situation, your goal may be to provide a bridge between what students are studying in school subjects (e.g., understanding family and community in social studies or learning about how to care for the environment in science). You might want to select books to read aloud that are thematically linked to the social studies or science curriculum. This approach can provide an important first step in integrating the curriculum and can help your students understand literature as a source for learning not only about themselves, but also about the world that surrounds them.

Finally, you may choose to use the Book Club *Plus* framework to organize your literacy curriculum, including guided reading, writer's workshop, and book clubs (see Chapters 9 and 11). As discussed in Chapter 6, you will want to consider your state standards and benchmarks as you determine the level of implementation in your classroom. In the next sections, we feature information and ideas pertaining to managing a Book Club *Plus* classroom. Use any information that you find relevant to the Book Club context you're creating for your students.

Choosing a Relevant and Engaging Theme

Choosing a theme is an important aspect of developing a Book Club *Plus* unit. A good classroom theme explores big ideas that are appropriate to the age level of the students. Themes are not arbitrary or superficial; they invite real discussion. Above all, you want your themes to show students how reading can help them better understand their lives, one another, and the world around them.

You can use a single topic to create several different themes, so it is important to think about *why* you are selecting a set of books. For example, the topic "friendship" is relevant to primary students, since they are learning a lot about the roles and responsibilities related to being and having a friend. This topic can be developed into several relevant themes, as shown in the examples in earlier chapters. While the examples focus on the same topics, their themes and related theme questions differ. Thus, the selected texts that focus on the topic of friendship will be introduced and talked about differently depending on their chosen themes. To illustrate, *Frog and Toad Are Friends* by Arnold Lobel and *Ira Sleeps Over* by Bernard Waber can be framed as talking about what it means to be a friend, as well as about challenges to friendship. For Book Club, themes drive our text selection. These themes should (a) explore something meaningful to primary-grade children, (b) be specific enough to provide an umbrella for questions to direct discussions, and (c) be reflected in the content of the texts that are chosen.

It's helpful to frame your themes as open-ended questions. These "big theme questions" inform students that the class is thinking about certain ideas. We suggest that you post the "big theme questions" in your classroom for the duration of the unit. Return to the theme questions frequently with your class, adding to and revising answers and possibly adding new questions. Your role is to model how reading related texts and participating in the activities can inform or change how you answer the theme questions.

Qualities of a Strong Theme

**A strong theme
at the primary grades . . .**

- is meaningful and worthy of exploration by kids at a grade level.
- can be supported by a variety of literature below, at, and above grade level.
- invites discussion.
- helps students connect to the literature.
- motivates students in their reading.
- is open-ended and has no single right answer.
- is relevant to people of all ages.
- takes time to sort through.
- allows for explicit teaching of ideas and comprehension strategies.
- allows students to take and defend their viewpoints with examples from literature.

Whenever possible, try to select themes that allow you to make connections to several curriculum areas. If you share teaching responsibilities for certain curricular areas with your colleagues, talk to them about themes the entire group may want to teach. By making explicit connections to other curriculum areas, you can encourage students to look at every theme from more than one angle. For example, a unit about how to be a good friend can combine reading and discussing theme-related literature with a social studies unit on how countries can cooperate and be "friends." Students can also participate in a project that compares the different ways that people demonstrate that they know how to be good friends, as Julia Stern's students did when they recorded the "Random Acts of Friendship" they observed among their classmates (see page 62 in Chapter 4).

Selecting Literature

Literature has the potential to do so much for your students. Quality literature touches the aesthetic, cultural, social-emotional, intellectual, and imaginative abilities of young children. Selecting quality literature is of utmost importance for a successful Book Club *Plus* unit, whether students are reading independently or listening to books read aloud. When we've developed Book Club *Plus* units, we've found that we work back and forth between choosing the quality literature that helps elaborate on our selected theme and ensuring that the literature we've chosen supports the curricular goals we want to achieve throughout the unit.

We've found many resources to help us in our literature selection. The most obvious is our own experience with particular books and the recommendations of colleagues. We find the annotations in sources such as *The Horn Book* and *Book Links* to be invaluable for locating books that fit particular themes and grade levels. Also, the Internet can be a useful tool for researching selections. Locally, we have talked with the managers of children's bookstores and children's librarians. Columns in *The Reading Teacher* and in *Language Arts* often contain wonderful recommendations

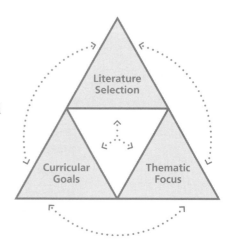

for new books. From these and other sources, such as lists of Caldecott, Newbery, and Coretta Scott King award winners, you'll want to choose high-quality literature to support your theme. Your specific selections will be based on a combination of factors.

Potential for Discussion Primary-grade children have the ability to sustain interest in stories with plot and character development and to enjoy stories that explore basic concepts, human emotions, and relationships. They also have the need to distinguish between real/make-believe or good/bad behavior (Lamme et al., 1980). Therefore, look for books that students can talk about, whether they read or listen to them being read. Choose books with problems to which children can relate and that will inspire them to talk and form opinions. Characters in the midst of dilemmas or endings that leave the reader wondering have the greatest potential for discussion. Issues such as the treatment of animals, care for the environment, family, and friendships are all good starting points for developing themes to which students can respond with opinions and experiences. At the same time, consider your students' reading levels and maturity levels. Some issues and topics won't be appropriate for primary-grade students even if they are theme-related.

Developmental Level A book should be developmentally appropriate. Some picture books, while relatively easy to read, can present very complex and mature issues. Some primary students may be able to independently read books such as *Hiroshima No Pika* by Toshi Maruki, *Pink and Say* by Patricia Pollaco, *Smoky Night* by Eve Bunting, and *Golem* by David Wisniewski, but these books deal with topics that many primary-grade students might not be ready to handle. On the other hand, a book whose main character is much younger than your students may present issues that no longer interest your class. Use your discretion to select developmentally appropriate material for your students.

Content Choose books with subject matter with which your students can connect by way of prior knowledge. You can give your students a knowledge base by talking to them about the content while examining the pictures, by having them participate in a project or writing piece that introduces the ideas, or by reading aloud other books related to the content. Other sources or ways to develop prior knowledge include videos, Web sites, pictures, or personal stories. When your students have an adequate knowledge base to make connections to the book, their written responses and book club discussions will benefit. Look for stories that students can relate to their own lives and that will appeal to both girls and boys. Over the course of the year, most Book Club teachers strive for a balance between male and female main characters.

Text Difficulty Books written at the kindergarten, first-grade, and early second-grade levels rarely have enough substantive content to provide a basis for a book club discussion. Thus, book club discussions are usually based on a text that you have read aloud to your students. As students move through the primary-grade levels, they can assume more responsibility for reading the text independently. However, it is likely that you will always have students in your room who do not have the reading skills needed to read independently. Thus, Book Club teachers use many different ways to ensure that their students have access to the text before the book club discussions occur. They may use commercial versions of books on tape or, if these aren't available, create their own through family and community volunteers and volunteers from older grade levels. They may allow their students to read in partners or small groups. They may send a book to the resource room to be read in advance of the Book Club activities.

Selecting texts for use in guided reading during Literacy Block is just as important. These texts must relate to the overall theme as well as meet criteria for text difficulty at the instructional level of the students. If you have leveled readers or use a commercial (basal) reading program, you can go through the stories and re-group them to fit your overarching theme. For example, when we created a unit for Nina Hasty's students who were in first and second grade, we looked through the basal reader and identified the stories that focused on describing a child's life. We used the materials in the basals, though not necessarily in the order presented in the manual. If you are not constrained to a single program, you can choose from a range of texts.

We suggest that you first choose the books that students will read (or listen to) and discuss in their book clubs. Then build your collection of leveled materials for guided reading, as well as books for read aloud, shared reading, and books for your classroom library that students can use for independent reading. Before finalizing your choices, make sure that the books provide the opportunity to teach the skills and strategies that you have identified as important to your curriculum goals.

Relevance to Curriculum Goals Most teachers are required by their state or school districts to meet specific curriculum standards. Most are also under considerable pressure to have students perform well on various standardized tests. As you plan your daily lessons for Book Club and Literacy Block, you will create and use a variety of opportunities to teach your required benchmarks and standards.

Many language arts skills and comprehension strategies will flow naturally from your teaching of the Book Club books and guided reading materials. These strategies include genre, author's craft, plot, making inferences, predicting, questioning, important ideas, activating prior knowledge, and making intertextual connections. The literature you choose will provide a context from which you can extract activities that focus on language conventions, such as phonics, word study, or comprehension skills such as cause and effect. As students interact in various contexts, you'll find opportunities for direct instruction in speaking and listening skills. The writing that students

---

● **GOOD LITERATURE FIRST**

It isn't necessary to teach all skills within the structure of a single Book Club *Plus* unit. You'll lose the focus on getting students engaged in the literature. You can abuse good literature by trying to force it to accomplish too many narrow goals. Let it be good literature first, a teaching tool second.

do during a Book Club *Plus* unit allows you to teach the writing process and specific writing, spelling, and punctuation skills.

Understanding your curricular goals for the term or year will help you choose a theme and literature appropriate for your class. On page 143 in the Stories of Self sample unit, you can see a model of how to correlate a Book Club *Plus* unit to a set of language arts standards. (Further discussion about curriculum goals is in Chapter 6.)

▼ **Setting Curricular Goals**

Nina Hasty used this set of goals to guide her in teaching and assessing speaking and listening skills.

Goals for Listening and Speaking

- Students will be able to listen effectively to speakers by using good listening skills.

  Listening Skills
    - Eye contact with speaker
    - Sitting position to show that they are attentive
    - Movement is minimal
    - Answers questions about what the speaker read
    - Knows when to clap, because they were paying attention

- Students will be able to speak to an audience by using good speaking skills.

  Speaking Skills
    - Position of hands at side or holding paper
    - Eye contact with audience at least once
    - Voice loud enough for everyone to hear
    - Paper is positioned so that audience can see the speaker's face
    - Movement is minimal

- Students will be able to hold an age-appropriate conversation about books that displays good speaking and listening skills.

  Discussion Skills
    - Takes turns talking
    - Makes eye contact with speaker
    - Summarizes what a speaker said
    - Disagrees without an argument
    - Explains opinions/thoughts/ beliefs clearly

Cross-Curricular Connections One advantage of Book Club *Plus* is its ability to integrate various areas of your curriculum. Using literature that draws upon social studies or science topics can help you build a unit focusing on specific content in a literature environment. Students' book club discussions will add depth and relevance to their content-area studies. For example, within Kathy Highfield's Stories of Self framework (pages 139–200), you will find activities that ask students to collect and present artifacts. Collecting, examining, and presenting these artifacts is one step in students' understanding of their own cultural heritage and the concept of primary-source data. This, in turn, relates to the two National Council for the Social Studies (NCSS) thematic strands—Culture and Individual Development and Identity. Within the unit, students are also reading autobiographies and, through these pieces of literature, are studying people, places, and environments that will better help them understand other people's cultures and the similarities and differences across cultures.

Tips for Selecting Books

- Choose a theme to focus your selection of books.
- Consult reviews and book lists in journals and magazines.
- Ask other teachers about books they've enjoyed using.
- Keep your curriculum goals and theme in mind as you look through books.
- Ask your school librarian which books children in your class are borrowing.
- Talk with representatives in the children's section of your local bookstores.
- Pick something you like. Your enthusiasm will rub off on your students.

Choosing a Great Read-Aloud Book

Ask yourself these questions:
- Will the class/child enjoy hearing this book?
- Could the book spark lots of discussion?
- Can the child read the book alone? (You want to choose books a little above a child's independent reading level for read aloud.)
- Will the class need some background information to understand the book? (It is perfectly acceptable to provide this information for students and to stop at any time during a reading to fill in gaps in understanding.)

Availability There are practical considerations that enter into literature selection. You will want to make sure that all students have their own copies of the books they'll be reading in their book clubs. Having access to a copy of the book increases a student's sense of ownership in reading. In other reading contexts, you will not need class sets of books (e.g., in shared reading, one book for every three or four students is sufficient).

As you choose books for your unit, think about the following: What book sets are available? What financial resources are available for purchasing books if you wish to round out a set or obtain new titles? What chapter and picture books can you find in libraries to accompany any commercial materials the district has adopted? Do your students have any preferences for particular authors, genres, topics, or themes, and can you respond to these preferences with available or obtainable texts?

In our quest to acquire books, we've found that some districts or county offices have classroom sets for loan. We've also purchased books with money from our instructional funds, saved bonus points from commercial book clubs to purchase books, put together sets borrowed from various libraries, found colleagues who were willing to share book sets, and occasionally bought books ourselves.

Your Own "Thumbs Up" Remember that your own experience with a book will affect your success in using it in your classroom in any reading context (e.g. book club, guided reading, read aloud, shared reading). When you use a book that you've enjoyed reading or teaching in the past, you transmit your passion for the book. In return, students will approach reading or listening to the book with a positive attitude. As you gain experience with Book Club *Plus,* you will learn which issues and which books students may find interesting, disturbing, or challenging.

Grouping Students

Grouping is key to successful Book Club *Plus* classrooms. Student-led book groups and groups within Literacy Block are formed using different criteria in different contexts.

Grouping for Book Clubs

Group dynamics can impact how a book club functions, and we have found size, diversity, attitudes and general social skills, and students' own choices to be key factors in creating successful groups. Don't be afraid to try different combinations for book clubs. Grouping quiet children together can help them open up. A group of highly-verbal children can also work. Many factors influence how well a group works.

Size Size is the first consideration. We recommend four to five students per book club group because it creates opportunities for different opinions to emerge, it can easily continue if one or even two students are absent, and it is small enough to manage (e.g., sit at the same table or in a small circle on the floor). The book club membership remains constant throughout a unit, regrouping for the next unit.

Diversity We recommend mixing students across gender, ethnicity, interests, reading abilities, verbal abilities, and personalities. Our reasons for encouraging diverse membership include creating opportunities for students to hear a number of different perspectives and stretching students' social skills as they interact with students outside their immediate circle of friends. Good book club discussions occur when students bring different strengths and experiences to the table.

Attitudes and Social Skills Students' attitudes and their social skills clearly contribute to the success of a group. Observe your students' attitudes toward other children in group work and on the playground. Who seems shy? Who has a strong, outgoing personality? Who seems to take care of peers? Who seems to take school activities seriously? There is no one way to balance attitudes and dispositions and to cut across friendship circles. For example, two strong, outgoing personalities might dominate a group. On the other

WHEN TO REGROUP BOOK CLUBS

We like to keep book clubs stable throughout an entire unit. However, if you discover midway through a unit that your groups are not working out, don't feel that you're stuck with them. You can regroup students at any time to create better-functioning book clubs.

hand, four strong personalities might create lively talk. We've also found that close friends and students who strongly dislike each other challenge the smooth dynamics of a group.

Primary-grade children do have social or friendship circles, though they tend to be more fluid than those in the upper grades. Through book club discussions, students get to know each other more deeply than they might in other settings. Students learn the value of stepping outside the familiar to meet new people and make new friends. It also helps students learn that they can work across many settings without becoming close friends with everyone.

Students' Choice Many teachers have asked us if it is necessary to allow students to choose their own books which, in turn, means choosing their book club members. We believe firmly in encouraging student ownership of literacy, but we do not believe that choice in grouping is necessary to achieve their sense of ownership. We recommend, at the end of each Book Club unit, asking students to engage in self-evaluation: (a) How did their group work during book club discussions? (b) What and how did their own participation contribute? and (c) What do they plan to work on next time? We end this activity by asking them to list two or three peers they think would help them work on their goals next time. Teachers then can take into account the students' recommendations and try to place at least one of the peers they name in their next book club group.

Grouping for Literacy Block

Central to Literacy Block is guided reading, where students meet with the teacher for literacy work at their instructional level. In this setting, groups of six to nine students are relatively homogeneous with respect to reading ability (e.g., three groups: students working mostly at grade level, students working generally above grade level, students who are struggling with grade level texts). These groups are not permanently fixed—clearly we hope that our struggling students 'catch up' and that students at grade level begin to surpass grade level expectations. However, the group membership tends to remain fairly stable, at least within a grading period.

To group students appropriately, particularly at the beginning of the year, you will need to gather information with formal and informal assessments to inform your decisions. The information you gather should provide insights into both their general understanding of literacy, as well as specific information about their knowledge of conventional print, vocabulary, and comprehension strategies. To become familiar with your students' literacy

AUTHOR'S COMMENT

"I group students homogeneously for guided reading, but I don't group them at all for centers. Some teachers do, some don't. I have choice time where students move between centers as they see fit. Other teachers have centers rotate after a given time. You will need to choose what works for you."

—Kathy Highfield

Possible Assessments

- *Developmental Reading Assessment,* by Joetta Beaver (Celebration Press, Pearson Learning Group, 1997)
- *Qualitative Reading Inventory-3,* by Lauren Leslie and Joanne Caldwell (Pearson Allyn & Bacon, 2000)
- *Basic Reading Inventory,* by Jerry L. Johns (Kendall Hunt, 2001)
- *Orbit W.R.A.P. An Informal Writing and Reading Assessment Profile* (Learning Media, 2001)
- *Dolch Basic Word List* (Preprimer to Third Grade)
- Comprehension pretests and vocabulary assessments from a basal reading program

understanding informally, ask them the following questions either orally or in writing: What is reading? What do you think a good reader does? What do you do when you are reading and you come to a word you don't know? The answers to these questions give you a window into your students' thinking, strategy use, and self-esteem as readers.

To assess students' knowledge of concepts, skills, and strategies, you may want to gather information using the district-recommended assessments, such as an informal reading inventory. Your district may also have assessed at the end of the previous year. If you are unsure which assessment to use, check with your principal or curriculum director. You may want to use one or more of the reading and vocabulary assessments listed on page 112.

Reading and Vocabulary Assessments At the beginning of the year, it can take a week or two to administer assessments to all of your students. We have found it useful to create a short unit focused on getting to know each other that includes opportunities to read, write, and talk about books as a whole class, in small groups, in pairs, and independently. This gives you an opportunity to observe your students' interactions in an variety of settings: Who can work independently? How does each student write (e.g., conventional spelling, temporary spelling, good sound-symbol correspondence)? What kinds of questions do students ask as you read or when given a chance to talk with a partner? How strong are each student's word-recognition skills?

Writing Assessments To assess students' writing ability early in the year, a writing assessment can be tied to the introductory unit activities. We have found it useful to gather information on students' writing in three contexts: (a) in response to reading, (b) in a sustained writing activity, and (c) in a dictation or copy format, which simply illustrates students' control over letter and word formation, as well as punctuation. Together, these writing samples provide baseline information about basic writing skills, voice and expression, ability to organize ideas—areas that most state learning standards indicate are important to literacy instruction. The early samples can be used to illustrate students' growth if similar information is gathered mid-year and at the end of the year.

Pulling It Together With information from the reading and writing assessments, you can group students for guided reading with confidence. The writing assessments also provide insights into instructional needs in that area. Areas the whole group needs to work on can be addressed through mini-lessons during writer's workshop, or if particular skills can be related to the texts they are reading, through mini-lessons during opening community share in Book Club. Areas of need that are related to reading levels can be addressed during guided reading. Areas of need that cut across ability levels but are not needed by the entire class can be covered in small, flexible groups that meet during writer's workshop or at other times when students are engaged in independent work.

 **TEACHING TIP**

When using a reading inventory, keep the following in mind:

- Review directions for administering the assessment.
- Look for a reading assessment that has both reading passages and comprehension questions.
- Emphasize comprehension when deciding between levels of success.
- Organize your class so that students are not distracted.

Daily Instruction

Although the flexibility built in to Book Club *Plus* allows individual teachers to design a unit that fits their scheduling constraints, the following model has worked well in many classrooms.

The instructional core of Book Club *Plus* is formed by lessons in opening community share, guided reading groups, and literacy centers. Opening community share is the whole-class setting in which the teacher clarifies the text and the topics of the day for her students. These community share lessons may take place before or after students do their reading, writing, and discussing in book clubs or fishbowls, but they always relate to the day's reading assignment and to the writing students do in their logs. Because of Book Club's focus on comprehension and interpretation, explicit instruction in these related areas is important in the daily lessons. From opening community share, the teacher segues easily from setting the stage to the reading or read-aloud portion of the day.

After students read, the writing component of Book Club occurs in several ways. First, students are encouraged to "jot down" notes on sticky notes. If each students has a copy of a Book Club book, or students are sharing copies, they may put the sticky notes right on their books. If not, teachers can put chart paper in an accessible place, marking the relevant page numbers so students can place their notes on a communal wall chart. Students also keep individual response logs or journals for each unit. They can record their ideas in their journals prior to talking about the books with their peers. Finally, after their discussion, students can add to or change their response logs.

Primary-grade students can engage in student-led discussion groups, but they tend to participate in these discussions in the fishbowl setting described in specific detail in the next section. After student discussions, some teachers have students return to write once again in their reading logs. Others move directly to closing community share—a whole-class discussion during which the teacher guides the students to think about what they have learned about the theme, the content, and any focus lessons (e.g., genres, questioning practices, vocabulary).

The focus on comprehension and on fluency continues in guided reading groups. Several times a week, students meet in these groups to read instructional-level texts and receive direct instruction in reading strategies. At the same time, students are introduced to and practice important language arts skills in the literacy centers. Many Book Club *Plus* teachers conduct whole-class mini-lessons on the skills and activities that are featured in their literacy centers.

Book Club and Literacy Block lessons focus on four main curricular areas: comprehension, writing, language conventions, and literary aspects. We developed this curriculum based on the guidelines for our school districts, current reading research, and our experience with a wide range of commercial programs. As you compare your own curriculum statements, objectives, and standards with our lessons, you can add skills and strategies accordingly. For more information about teaching comprehension strategies in Book Club and guided reading, see Chapter 3.

Fishbowl

One of the challenges of Book Club involves teaching young children how to have a good conversation about a book—conversation that is not only fun and interesting but also educative and to the point. Talking about books requires knowledge about literature, about various kinds of responses to literature, and about strategies for comprehension and interpretation. A participant in a conversation also needs knowledge of conversational strategies, such as listening well, building on another's ideas, inviting silent participants into the conversation, and so forth. These are all skills that students at the primary grades are in the process of acquiring. Thus, students require time and modeling to learn how to hold thoughtful discussions about books.

Fishbowl is an important site for modeling and practice. As shown in the model below, by watching a book club in action and then discussing what took place, the whole class learns to recognize specific behaviors that contribute to successful conversations. To introduce primary-grade students to book club discussions using fishbowl, teachers have used various groups to model what a book club discussion looks like. Some teachers create an adult book club group consisting of the teacher and two or three other adults

The Fishbowl Model

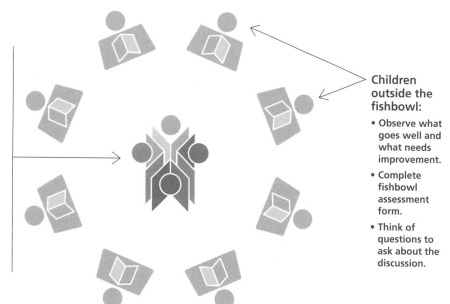

Children within the fishbowl:

- Construct meaning from a text.
- Work together to make connections.
- Practice literate talk.
- Develop personal response skills.
- Actively listen to others.

Children outside the fishbowl:

- Observe what goes well and what needs improvement.
- Complete fishbowl assessment form.
- Think of questions to ask about the discussion.

(parent volunteers, school administrators, resource room teachers, cafeteria helpers, and so forth). The adult group models a discussion about a book the children know well—perhaps a recent read aloud. Other teachers have enlisted upper-grade students with experience in book club discussions to be in the first fishbowl. After students see a book club modeled once or twice, you can then select book clubs from your class to be in the fishbowl. Here are some ways you can use fishbowl in your class:

- Arrange the desks or tables in your classroom so that one book club sits in the center and all other students have a clear view. You might want to create a permanent fishbowl area, or make the area very easy to create by moving just a few desks. Students may also sit on the floor. Leave one chair or one space empty so that a fishbowl can have a "visitor." Students may want to bring their books to the fishbowl to refer to as they talk.

- In the first part of the fishbowl, have the group in the center engage in a brief book club discussion. We recommend three to four minutes for young students. (You may sometimes want to extend the conversation and use it as an opportunity to discuss how to keep a group on task without an adult.)

- Encourage students observing the fishbowl to think about ideas they'd like to contribute to the discussion (i.e., substantive content focus) and what they think the fishbowl discussants did well (i.e., process focus).

- After the discussion, ask the students on the outside if anyone has something to share with the fishbowl group. Have a volunteer sit in the visitor chair and make a comment or ask a question of the group. After the group interacts around the visitor, another visitor can participate.

- Following the discussion, ask students on the outside if they have any other ideas they would like to share with the whole class (keeping the focus on the substantive content). Then, shift the focus to process: "What did the group do well today?" Finally, ask those in the fishbowl, "What was hard for you today?" to elicit any problems and to talk about what they might do in the future if such problems arise.

- When the first fishbowl is completed for the day, a second and even a third group may be called up, depending on your time and the students' attention span. Over the course of a week, each book club group should have at least one opportunity to be in the fishbowl, and of course, many opportunities to observe and comment on book club discussions in the fishbowl.

- Fishbowls are useful throughout the year. You may want to return to fishbowls when there are specific issue(s) occurring in your book clubs. The fishbowl provides an opportunity for direct instruction about the issue(s).

The fishbowl pattern, then is to begin with a discussion group in the fish-bowl, move to observer participation in the form of a visitor to the fishbowl, then turn to whole-class discussion. At first focus on content and on the positives, then on the problems that can be addressed for future improvements. You might create a chart listing these behaviors and display it in the class for future reference. The list can serve as the basis for a rubric to evaluate students' individual participation. If your students are having trouble commenting on the fishbowl, consider handing out Learning From the Fishbowl, Evaluation Sheet 3, to help students think about what they are observing.

Fishbowl is a wonderful context for improving students' discussion strategies. It provides a convenient site for teachers to scaffold their students' early book club discussions. For very young children—kindergarten and first grade—fishbowl may be your primary means of student-led discussions for most of the year, preparing the students well for participating in individual book clubs later.

Reading Aloud

Reading aloud is an integral part of all Book Club *Plus* units, though its role varies across the grade levels. In the early primary grades—kindergarten and first grade, and for some students, into second grade—the Book Club book *is* a teacher read aloud. This is because at these early grade levels, the texts students can read independently rarely have the substantive content to lead to interesting discussions.

By the middle of second grade and beyond, the read aloud complements the other Book Club books, linked thematically in meaningful ways. The read aloud may occur prior to the day's Book Club or Literacy Block activities, after lunch or recess, or at the end of the day. The read aloud creates important opportunities for intertextual connections and opportunities to expose students to texts they might not otherwise read independently. For example, students in Cammy Anderson's second-grade class were studying the idea of freedom for all people. One of the important figures they had learned about in social studies was Martin Luther King, Jr. For Book Club, Cammy had selected a book about Martin Luther King, Jr., that she felt was appropriate to their independent reading level, but she used excerpts from his *I Have A Dream* speech for her read aloud over a few days.

Book Club teachers of all grade levels spend 10–20 minutes a day reading aloud to their students. This is in addition to the students' formal Book Club book that the teacher may read to them as part of specific Book Club activities, such as reading logs and fishbowls. Read alouds provide the perfect arena for the instructional demonstrations of think alouds (Davey, 1983) that are central to comprehension strategy instruction. The think aloud gives children the opportunity to see our thinking when we read: the connections we make, the questions we ask, our inferences, and our predictions. Reading aloud and showing what thoughtful readers do is central to comprehension strategy instruction.

How do we go about creating a read-aloud unit that best suits the needs of our young students? Hoffman, Roser, and Battle (1993) suggest a model of what factors contribute to a good read-aloud experience:

- Designating a legitimate time and place in the daily curriculum for read aloud

- Selecting quality literature—stories with enduring themes, age-appropriate text

- Sharing literature related to other literature allows children to explore interrelationships among books, discover patterns, think more deeply, and respond more fully

- Discussing literature in lively, invitational, thought-provoking ways to encourage personal responses as well as the exploration of connections to self, between text, and linkages within and among texts

- Grouping children to maximize opportunities to respond

- Offering a variety of responses and extension opportunities—journal writing, drawing, or paired sharing—prior to small- or large-group discussion

- Rereading selected pieces

Advantages of Reading Aloud

- Reading aloud gives the whole class a context within which to make intertextual connections.
- It provides an opportunity to model ways that we make connections between literature and real life.

- Listening to a read-aloud book helps students develop fluency and increases their language use in writing and speaking.
- Hearing the teacher read aloud with good intonation, inflection, and emotion lets children understand what good readers sound like.

- Reading aloud introduces students to beautiful language that they might not be aware of in their silent reading. We notice that our students' vocabularies and language use expand to include words from our read-aloud books.

Shared Reading

Shared reading is an important part of many classrooms using Book Club *Plus*. It offers a highly interactive reading experience. The teacher reads aloud and brings features of the text (e.g., ways illustrations are used, poetry, style, genre, author's craft) to the attention of the students. Shared reading takes place with both fiction and nonfiction. It might even include newspapers and magazines for children. The class discusses ideas from the text and makes connections to the theme, other books, and relevant personal experiences. These discussions are linked to writer's workshop—helping students see that the texts they read provide useful models for specific forms and functions of their own writing.

For shared reading, we use books that are appropriate to our students' age levels, even though some of the students in our classrooms may not be able to read them independently. We obtain a set of about ten books for the class. Small groups share one text and follow along as we read. In this way, we can introduce students to many interesting books while avoiding the cost of buying or obtaining a class set of each book.

Shared reading occurs once or twice a week during a unit, often in connection to writer's workshop or as a way to introduce a new concept for Book Club. For some teachers shared reading can be done on Literacy Block days before students move through the centers, particularly if students will also be participating in writer's workshop. Other teachers might spend several days or even a week just doing shared reading to facilitate in-depth work with one author or genre that they will be featuring in the upcoming Book Club activities.

Special Classroom Library

To support our units, we gather books for a special classroom library. These books relate by genre, theme, topic, or author to the Book Club, guided reading, read-aloud, and shared reading books. We try to select books that reflect our students' diverse interests and reading abilities. Special classroom libraries provide options for the independent reading that we expect our students to do every day. We encourage students to select from this library. Even if students are not able to read these books independently, they benefit from examining the pictures and text in a variety of books. Arranging the books by topic or genre helps students learn about different kinds of books and identify books they like.

We also maintain a regular classroom library of books and magazines of all types, from which students can choose materials for independent reading. Our special classroom library is separate from the regular library, and it usually exists on a table or special shelf. It changes over the course of the year as our curricular topics and units change. We always include one copy of each of the books used in the unit—including those read during guided reading, shared reading, and the teacher read alouds. Students enjoy rereading books they have heard; and having the guided reading texts available takes the mystery out of reading group membership. Students who struggle as readers often ask more able readers to read to them from their age-appropriate guided reading books. Students who are reading at grade level often have fun exploring the picture books that thematically link to their other reading, creating opportunities for additional intertextual connections. As the year progresses and your students have more experience with Book Club, you can expect to see students turn to the special classroom library to help answer a question or prove a point during a book club discussion. Early in the year, you may want to model this behavior for students. This can help students begin to see the practical value of reading. You may notice that students even bring in their own additions from their trips to the local library or from their home collections. Thus, the special classroom library helps students fulfill the basic goal of becoming self-motivated readers.

Inclusion

Book Club *Plus* is a framework designed to support differentiated instruction and to build a classroom literacy community. Thus, Book Club teachers have found it helpful to include all students in their literacy instruction, drawing on "push in" resource teachers to support students with special needs during Book Club and on "pull out" programs to help prepare students for Book Club participation. Students who require additional support include those who have been diagnosed with particular learning problems and those for whom English is not their home language.

The Concept of Inclusion

Today's schools strive to place each student in an environment that is minimally restrictive—that is, an environment that suits the student's unique educational, social, emotional, and developmental needs. At one end of the continuum of services, students are placed full time into the general education classroom with support from teacher consultants and specialists who team teach with the regular classroom teacher. At the other end of the continuum, students are placed entirely outside the public school system in private programs.

Over the years, we've taught many students who in the past would have been excluded from "regular education" classrooms. Some of these students had been diagnosed with learning problems in a particular subject area. Some had been diagnosed with problems with attention or behavior (e.g., ADHD, ADD, emotional impairments). Some students were developmentally different from their peers because of physical challenges. With few exceptions, children facing these challenges have successfully participated in all the activities of Book Club *Plus,* with the appropriate help. We detail the nature of this support in the following sections.

Reading Support

One benefit we've discovered with inclusion in Book Club *Plus* is an increased desire and motivation to become better readers. Students in Book Club *Plus* feel better about themselves because they're reading harder books—books with plots and real ideas—and because they're being challenged to think and make meaning from text appropriate to their age and grade level. Their social and developmental needs are met because the books appeal to their interests. They're also set on an equal footing with their peers, something which often does not happen for some children. Through Book Club, struggling readers can begin to understand *why* they are learning the skills and strategies taught in their guided reading groups and reinforced in their resource room classes.

Struggling readers clearly require support to read the Book Club text, since it is written for their age, rather than their reading level. These students may take their books home and pre-read (independently or with an adult) a portion of the book. Then, in class, they reread as much as they can, knowing they've already read or heard it once. Through repeated readings, students grasp more details that they can discuss in book clubs. Shared reading can help all students become more able readers. Paired reading can also be effective—a child sits with a more able reader and follows along as the text is read aloud. The child might also read to the more able reader, who becomes a tutor and guide.

A similar idea is to record the book. Since Book Club began in the early 1990s, we have seen dramatic increase in the availability of commercially prepared—and relatively inexpensive—books on tape. In fact, we have found that the stigma associated with going to the listening center to hear the book is all but removed, given the popularity and visibility of books on tape at bookstores. Creating a classroom library of tapes or CDs can help provide meaningful contexts for teaching fluency.

We have used the concept of creating a classroom library of books on tape as a vehicle for encouraging repeated readings, something advocated by researchers, but with practical limitations (i.e., Why would anyone want to read the same text over and over?). By asking volunteers to create books on tapes for earlier grade levels, we engage second, third, upper elementary, and middle school students in rehearsing to record a picture book, or a chapter from a chapter book. By engaging in repeated readings to prepare for upcoming audio recording, the older struggling reader reads more materials at his or her reading level. Students "audition" to record a book or chapter that will become part of the classroom audio library. Students then rehearse their readings, sign up for recording, and record their sections. (Note that if each student reads only part of a book, the recording sessions must take place in chronological order if you wish to avoid editing the tape for sequence.) Teachers or parent volunteers may also create books on tape for the classroom library. This is especially valuable if you have adults or older students who speak the native language of some of your students who are English Language Learners (ELL). Recording their books in their native languages provides opportunities for students to hear the books as they were intended to be heard—not in the stilted English they may hear from each other. Moreover, it gives them the substantive knowledge base to think about how they might respond to the text they have heard, rather than using all their energy in decoding and translating.

At times we have the resource-room teacher pre-read or reread sections of the book aloud for one or more students. This reinforces concepts and helps students get the flavor of the language. At the primary grades, we frequently read aloud part or sometimes all of the Book Club book for the whole class. This sparks interest, allows students to hear the language of the book, and reinforces the ideas presented in the story. Special-education teachers can provide a wealth of information and ideas. If you are working with a special-education teacher, ask that teacher to sit in on book clubs and to suggest adaptations to meet individual students' needs.

By providing reading support for our inclusion students, we've been able to create interest and continued motivation, not just for Book Club, but for reading in general. Such motivation is important when students are asked to practice reading skills at other times during the day. Book Club helps them understand why the development of these skills is so important. Students are inspired to practice skills that will allow them to participate in meaningful book club conversations with their peers.

Developing Social Skills

You probably know from your own experience that many students struggle when placed in small groups, especially when no teacher is present. Even if students have sufficient knowledge about comprehension strategies, they may lack the social skills necessary for working in a group, and inclusion

CLASSROOM VIEW
Inclusion: One Example

Henry was a first-grade student who was a pre-primary writer. He had a limited understanding of letters, sounds, and printed material. During speedwriting, he was allowed to draw pictures based on the story to help him figure out what he wanted to say. Then one of the teachers would write down his dictation. The teacher and Henry would read the words on his paper. This helped him see the letters that made up each word, hear the sounds that went with the words, and eventually share his writing during community share.

students are no exception. We've been able to address this issue in several ways. First, our early lessons focus on how to talk in book clubs. While some primary-grade students are able to work in task-oriented groups (i.e., cooperative learning groups), the focus of a student-led response group (or a fishbowl) is different. Therefore, instruction in very specific social skills—how to ask good questions, how to build on another student's comments, how to engage a classmate who is not talking, and so on—is crucial for the entire class. During these lessons, you should pay particular attention to inclusion students to monitor their understanding.

Second, we've asked special-education teachers to provide small-group instruction that follows up on the lessons we teach in opening community share. Inclusion students can practice the elements of good group discussion in a small group, which is less risky than speaking up in front of the whole class. This has helped students become more confident and more able to meld easily into the classroom community. Through this kind of instruction, we've experienced success with emotionally troubled and learning impaired students who might have struggled to adjust socially in a classroom setting.

We've seen students reap real benefits through their participation in Book Club *Plus*. They are exposed to language learning in a social and cooperative setting. They must learn how to cope in these situations and practice appropriate coping strategies. They learn through experience how students are expected to behave in social situations. Developing students' social skills requires patience, time, training, and some trial and error on the part of the teacher, but the benefits are well worth the effort.

Instructional Aides In some schools, instructional aides accompany special-education students into the classroom. The instructional aide might help a student read the assigned Book Club or guided reading text, or the child might dictate his or her journal entry to the aide. Often the aide's role is to provide appropriate language-learning support for the student (i.e., sign language). We've found the presence of an instructional aide to be comforting to the inclusion student and not at all a disturbance or hindrance to the dynamics of a small group.

Frequently Asked Questions

The following section addresses some specific questions that teachers have asked us about Book Club *Plus.* Many are questions that teachers of any grade would ask; however, we have answered each one with the particular needs of primary-grade students in mind. We've divided the questions into three categories: curriculum, management, and student diversity. Use this section as a quick reference guide to find the practical information you need to get your own Book Club *Plus* program under way.

Curriculum

How can I help students make text and content connections?

- Select books, both fiction and nonfiction, that are age-appropriate and deal with the theme of your unit and content-area material.

- Use read-aloud books to create opportunities for text-to-text and text-to-self and text-to-world connections. Identify one or two places in the read aloud where it would not be too disruptive to pause and point out connections between the text and Book Club and guided reading books. Examine ideas from the text that relate to your life or to the lives of your students, and/or show students how ideas from the book(s) link to content-area discussions or texts.

- Point out cross-curricular connections in shared reading books. Choose shared reading materials to support cross-curricular links and intertextual connections. Use the interactive nature of shared reading to allow students to practice verbalizing connections that they notice.

- Build a special classroom library with books in the content areas that are also related to your Book Club *Plus* literature.

- Use community share as an opportunity to point out cross-curricular connections and to model intertextual links. Model how to make explicit links between ideas—for example, by saying, "I'm responding to what Caitlin said about. . . ."

- Create thematic units that involve content-area studies and related Book Club *Plus* readings.

How can I integrate my district's curriculum requirements in the Book Club Plus program?

- Obtain a current copy of your state, district, or school curriculum guide prior to developing a Book Club *Plus* unit. For example, many state board of education Web sites list specific learning goals or standards for each grade level in literacy and content areas. Referring to such guidelines can help ensure that you are teaching what is valued within your district. In Book Club *Plus,* we use the general categories of comprehension, writing, language conventions, and literary aspects because they are the easiest to correlate to the varied language used across the fifty states and the even more diverse district and school language of standards.

- Pre-read Book Club and guided reading literature and highlight or mark sections that lend themselves to instruction related to the district curriculum.

- As you read through the sample frameworks in this guide, consider which of your district-provided materials you could use to supplement or replace materials in one of our units. In addition, look for books and other district materials that can help you pull together your own thematic Book Club *Plus* units.

- As you examine your district curriculum requirements, consider other parts of your day when you address areas listed in the guide. Because reading and writing are skills that apply to all areas of the curriculum, Book Club *Plus* need not be the sole site for language and literacy instruction in your classroom.

Management

What guidelines for book club discussions should I share with my students?

- Help students generate their own list of guidelines for talking about literature. Ask them about conversations they've had in various contexts (at home, on the playground, in the classroom) and about various topics (television programs, sports, personal experiences). Discuss what makes a conversation interesting, the kinds of interactions students enjoy, and various ways of participating.

- Share some guidelines that students have generated in previous years or in other classrooms. For example, students in one of our classrooms generated the list below:

  — Tell what you like or don't like about the book.

  — Everyone should talk. If someone isn't talking, ask her or him a question.

  — Ask questions about ideas in the book.

  — Listen to others and then talk. Take turns speaking.

  — Talk about parts of the book that remind you of something in your life.

  — Don't argue with people who disagree with you. Talk about their ideas instead.

  — Explain your opinions, thoughts, views, and/or beliefs about the book.

How do I get my students to talk in their book clubs, especially when they're just starting the program?

- Refer to Chapter 5, Talk in the Classroom, on pages 63–80. Talking about your expectations will help students overcome their hesitations.

- Use the fishbowl technique to model book club discussions. See pages 115–117 for a complete description of the fishbowl technique.

- Talk to students about the book before they read, write, and participate in book clubs.

- Have students listen to an audiotape or view a videotape of book club discussions.

- Use short transcripts of book club discussions as "plays" that students can enact. Use the play to elicit how it felt to participate in different ways—someone who had little to contribute, someone who dominated, someone who argued, etc.

- Keep the discussions short, especially if students have little experience or history with discussion.

⬥ CRITERIA FOR A GOOD READING LOG ENTRY

- Develops connections
- Answers prompt(s)
- Expands on ideas
- Connects text to student's life
- Shows evidence from text
- Uses log as resource

- Give students specific suggestions for "how to get started." Suggestions can include: (a) finding a sentence from the story that seems to be very important or that might give a clue about upcoming story events, (b) sharing a picture or an entry from their logs and asking for others to make comments, (c) developing a good question (if they know Question Answer Relationships, Author and Me, or Think and Search) to get the conversation started, (d) posing a "what if?" where a key event or character in the story is changed and students consider how the text might have played out differently.

- Tell students that it is natural to have pauses in their conversation.

- Remind students that overlapping speech will happen and is okay as long as everyone understands each other.

- Introduce or model strategies that can help the conversation get back on track, e.g., asking someone to restate an idea or to stop for a minute to allow everyone to think.

- Enlist students who are more confident speaking in groups to support the more reticent group members by directing questions to them and listening respectfully to their responses.

What support can I give my students in creating good reading log entries?

- Share examples of high-quality reading log entries with students. If your students are willing to share their own entries, you can have the class add to, expand upon, and analyze them. Discuss what's good about each entry and then talk about how it could be improved.

- Some teachers encourage students to write without stopping. This strategy helps students use writing as a thinking tool.

- Develop a chart of suggestions for good log entries. Remember to include free writing as an option so students don't feel constrained by the choices.

- Model each response type, and then have students practice it in their logs the same day.

How much time should I allocate to Book Club and Literacy Block?

- If you can allocate 120 minutes a day to Book Club *Plus,* you can easily fit in both Book Club and Literacy Block each day. This can include time from the language arts as well as the content-area curriculum when exploring a thematic unit.

- For example, in the chart below, Mondays and Tuesdays allow 75 minutes for Book Club and 45 minutes for Literacy Block; Wednesdays and Thursdays simply reverse the time allocation, allowing 75 minutes for Literacy Block and 45 minutes for Book Club. You'll notice that the key differences in the two-day sequences are the number of groups you can reasonably meet with during Literacy Block. You can meet daily with the students who are having the most difficulty (Group #1 in the chart), and meet with the other two reading groups 3–4 days a week.

- If you have less than 120 minutes each day, you can modify the schedule. Many teachers who have 75 minutes a day simply use Monday and Tuesday for Book Club, Wednesday and Thursday for Literacy Block, and Friday as the "swing" day, based on their students' needs.

- Friday can be used for writer's workshop, giving you an opportunity to work with individual students while everyone else engages in their own writing projects, or you can work with students in small, flexible groups on skills and strategies that cut across reading groups but are not appropriate for the whole class. Friday can also be used as a third day in the Wednesday–Thursday sequence or a first day in the Monday–Tuesday sequence. Shared reading activities are often linked to students' writing instruction, so it often makes sense to include shared reading during writer's workshop.

- For more scheduling options, see pages 24–25 and see the sample Book Club *Plus* frameworks in Chapters 9 and 11.

Scheduling a Week: 75–120 Minutes/Day

Monday	Tuesday
Book Club [75 minutes]	
• Opening community share	
• Reading	
• Writing	
• Fishbowl or book clubs	
• Closing community share	
Literacy Block [45 minutes]*	
Group #1	Group #1
Group #2	Group #3

Wednesday	Thursday
Literacy Block [75 minutes]*	
Group #1	Group #1
Group #2	Group #2
Group #3	Group #3
Book Club [45 minutes]	
• Opening community share	
• Reading	
• Writing	
• Fishbowl or book clubs	
• Closing community share	

Friday
"Swing" Day
• Writer's workshop with flexible groups
• First day of Monday/Tuesday sequence
• Third day of Wednesday/Thursday sequence

*Independent work (centers): journals, skill work, independent reading, unit project work, writer's workshop

What can I do to help familiarize students with Book Club Plus routines?

- Students at the primary grades need guidance and support when participating in Book Club *Plus* units for the first time, and to a lesser extent during subsequent units. Be explicit when you discuss Book Club and your Literacy Block routines.

- Some teachers spend the first months of the school year practicing both the Book Club and Literacy Block routines. Others like to limit the number of choices for several weeks while students become more familiar with routines. Still others teach an entire Book Club unit at the beginning of the year, but don't do Literacy Block or centers during the unit. Instead, they teach their curriculum to the entire class and ease students into working independently or at centers while one group of students is being led by the teacher in guided reading. You will need to find a combination of methods that works best for you. The following suggestions may help:

  — Use fishbowl to demonstrate discussions.

  — Have students brainstorm discussion rules and behavior.

  — Be specific about ways to respond in reading logs.

  — Give students the option of responding to their reading with drawings and labels.

  — Use community share to discuss and solve problems with book clubs.

  — Practice rotating among centers.

  — Limit the number of centers at first.

  — Review choices and deadlines for work done at centers.

  — Have a center with a quiet activity for students who are having trouble participating on a particular day.

- Ask parent volunteers to supervise centers occasionally. For example, you might ask parent volunteers to help students at the writing center. Parents can act as reviewers and can also help students publish their work.

- Give students more than one day to complete assignments. Some of us found it helpful to give students until Friday to hand in the assigned work. Your students may need extra time because your periods are short.

- Post charts in the classroom that students can use as guides. Use text and graphics to convey meaning. For example, you might create charts entitled "The Big Theme Questions," "Center Work," "Rules for Book Club Discussions," "The Writing Process," "Fishbowl Manners." Allow students to contribute their ideas to these charts, particularly during community-share discussions.

- Review past lessons and plan activities that reinforce what has already been learned. If you feel students are getting off-track in their book groups, you might review the criteria for book club discussion in community share.

- To give students ownership, refer to their ideas (in their words) and use their work as examples.

How can I show what my students are learning if the mandated report card doesn't provide room to record observations of classroom talk and log entries?

- See the evaluation sheets in the section following page 315. Review the rubrics introduced in Chapter 6. These checklists and rubrics can be used to augment a mandated report card. You may use or adapt these checklists to help parents and administrators understand the kinds of learning taking place in your classroom.

- Have students gather small samples of writing to show what they have been learning. Interpret the data for parents by writing notes or putting self-adhesive notes on the writing samples.

- Use your own "I Can" statements which are correlated to your district curriculum to record evidence of students' progress. (See Evaluation Sheets 1 and 13.)

- Ask students to identify their best log responses and explain verbally why they're the best.

- Let students borrow audiotapes of their own book club discussions. Send home the tape and a small tape recorder (if available) so that parents can listen to it. You might also write a letter giving a summary of the book and telling parents how reading the book and discussing it in book clubs support the class curriculum goals.

Student Diversity

What do I do if my students do not get along during their fishbowl or book club discussions?

- If you see unproductive book club interactions, it may mean that
  — students need more experience in fishbowls where you can support them.
  — students in the group have a personal problem with each other that stems from another event in the school day.
  — students are testing the boundaries of what they can do when the teacher is not immediately supervising them.

- Consider the potential source of the problem and then take action.
  — If students need more experience learning to build on each others' ideas or share their own thinking, have them get into pairs facing each other. Have them practice a specific form of interacting (e.g., asking a question or sharing an opinion then responding and following up; looking at a problem from two different perspectives and finding what is similar and different).
  — If the cause seems to be socially based, look at the rubrics of a good discussion that the class has generated. Think aloud about what might happen if there is an argument on the playground between two book club members before they come to book club. Elicit ways of "leaving this behind" when you enter a book club discussion.

- If the socially-based causes do not appear remediable within the class context, separate the problem students. It might help to have them observe a successful book club or fishbowl and make a list of what they observe as being good. Then, make a list of what they can do to make a book club work.

- Don't be reluctant to move students from unproductive settings, but do hold them accountable (e.g., they should not be rewarded for inappropriate behavior by simply being able to participate in another group).

- Ask students to name other students they would like to have in their book clubs. (Note: Friends don't always work well together.)

- Have students who haven't been getting along work on a specific, finite task. Working together in a controlled situation may allow the pair to discover areas of mutual interest and give them practice in working toward a common goal.

What should I do if a student refuses to participate?

- Talk to the student individually. Try to pinpoint what is preventing the student from participating. Ask: Do you feel shy about talking in front of the group? Do you find the writing difficult? Is the book too hard or too easy for you? Do you find the subject of the book boring? Are you having problems with a particular classmate? The answers to such questions can give you ideas about how to motivate the student.

- If one student refuses to participate, encourage others to keep going. Sometimes having the option of sitting quietly for a few minutes gives a reluctant student a sense of control, and that student will eventually decide to join in.

- Students with behavioral problems may respond to the following ideas:
  — Create a behavioral contract or point chart for a certain period of time. Give the student specific goals, such as asking one question per book club meeting, using at least one response type in the reading log, not interrupting when someone else is speaking, etc. Review successes and discuss how to improve in areas that remain problematic.
  — Give the student responsibility for an organizational aspect of Book Club or Literacy Block. Ask the student to collect reading logs or organize books—anything to get the student involved.
  — Allow the student to move to a "time out" space if he or she feels out of control.

How can I engage students for whom English is a second or third language?

- Refer to pages 120–123 for a detailed discussion of inclusion.

- Consider using a theme that builds the value of the experiences of students who have come from other countries and speak different languages. Emphasizing the value of different experiences is an important way to bring students into the classroom community.

- Make sure that the classroom library contains books written in the child's primary language.

- Seek district assistance for a classroom bilingual aide if available in your district. Where multiple languages are spoken in your school but specific bilingual support isn't available, see if children with greater English experience from your students' native countries are in the school and can serve as interpreters.

- Look for translations of Book Club and guided reading books in the student's primary language.

- Allow students who speak the same language to hold book club discussions in their home languages. Then, ask them to summarize in English (collectively). One Book Club teacher who taught 100% ELL had one book club group speaking Urdu, one speaking Spanish, and the rest using English, English was not the home language for any of the students. The Urdu and Spanish speaking groups included a few students who had a relatively good command of English and a few who were just beginning to learn English. This way, all students could participate in the discussions and those learning English were able to work collectively to translate what they had talked about so that others could understand.

- Emphasize key vocabulary concepts before reading the text—pulling out actual sentences from the text, reading them aloud, talking about the meaning, and having the students use the concept/vocabulary to share something about their own lives.

- Communicate with a bilingual/ELL teacher about your Book Club *Plus* plans. Ask the teacher to help you write a letter to a student's parents or guardians (in their home language, if necessary) about what kinds of learning experiences the student will encounter in class.

- Find books in the student's primary language that have thematic connections to the unit theme. Invite the student to share (by drawing, writing, or speaking) how these books are similar to or different from the Book Club and guided reading literature.

- Describe log response choices in a student's primary language. Post these descriptions in the classroom. For very young students you may want to use pictures or samples to show different types of log responses. Allow them to write in their native languages first if they have already developed some written language skills.

- Translate vocabulary terms. Ask student "experts" to teach the class how to pronounce words in the respective first language. Other students can demonstrate how to pronounce the English terms.

- Coach the class in how to help a student learning English. If the student makes a one-word response, encourage others in the group to demonstrate how to put that word into a sentence.

What are some techniques and ideas that I can use to make my units run smoothly?

- Annotate your books with "crib notes" as you are reading, particularly since many picture books don't have page numbers. These notes will be valuable during community share and guided reading when you're trying to formulate questions or writing activities for your students. Mark pages you want to highlight for students—parts of the book that reveal something about a character or the theme, show a genre, exemplify a skill, seem to require additional support, or illustrate why you enjoy the book.

- Include videos, songs, news articles, Web sites, and magazines that relate to your unit.

- Expand your unit with creative activities and writing. During your unit, students will write informally in their reading logs as a tool for thinking. Throughout the unit, they should also work on other writing assignments. The writing can include log entries, pieces in a specific genre, responses to specific ideas found in the literature, etc. Projects that involve writing are detailed in the sample units.

- Writing opportunities and projects at the primary grades often engage students' individual learning styles with other forms of creative expression. Think about artistic and musical links you and your students can make to pieces of literature. As you build your units, try to include activities in which students can draw, color, paint, glue, build, and perform. Ideas for these activities should spring from the specific literature and theme(s) in your units.

- Integrate speaking and listening activities into your unit. Students can practice listening and speaking in book club and fishbowl discussions. You can teach specific lessons about how to speak to a group and how to listen carefully when they are in the audience. Students can write and read aloud sentences and paragraphs about ideas that come up during the unit.

- For Book Club *Plus* to succeed, students must feel comfortable sharing their ideas in small-group discussions and in front of the class. Reading aloud and shared reading of theme-related books can help turn a class into a community in which students feel safe, included, and valued as individuals. The class builds content knowledge, forms opinions, expresses beliefs and feelings, and grows as a community of readers and writers.

- Show students how literate persons approach a book and share their ideas with other readers. During read-aloud and shared reading sessions, bring up your own ideas, model how to make intertextual connections, and write notes on the board or on chart paper.

Introduction to the Sample Frameworks

Preparing to Teach a Book Club *Plus* Unit

In Chapters 1–7, we present the research and experiences that shape different aspects of Book Club *Plus*. The chapters about comprehension, writing, talk, assessment, and classroom management lay the groundwork for you to begin thinking about how you might use the Book Club *Plus* framework for literacy instruction in your own classroom. The next three chapters show you how three primary-grade teachers integrated elements of the Book Club program with their literacy curriculum requirements. Below is an introduction to the sample frameworks described in Chapters 9, 10, and 11 and an explanation of ways in which Book Club can help you to meet specific educational standards.

Understanding the Sample Frameworks

Kathy Highfield taught literacy in a third-grade classroom, and she had relative freedom to choose her own literature and shape her own literacy program. MariAnne George taught literacy in a primary-grade classroom with many children who did not speak English as their first language. Nina Hasty taught literacy in a split-grade-level classroom of first and second graders. Her district mandated the use of a basal reading program. Can Book Club work for these teachers in their varied circumstances? The answer is yes. One of the true assets of Book Club is that it is adaptable to unique classroom circumstances. Each sample framework contains ideas and routines that you may want to incorporate in your units.

In Chapter 9, which focuses on Kathy Highfield's third-graders, we illustrate what we consider to be the "full expression" of Book Club *Plus*. This is the model you might follow if you have the freedom to build your literacy curriculum completely around Book Club using trade books of your own choosing, and if your students are able to participate fully in aspects of Book Club such as peer-led discussion groups, independent reading, and various writing activities. In addition to the Book Club lessons, students participate in Literacy Block for direct skills instruction and guided reading—using literature chosen by you.

Chapter 10, Framework for a Read-Aloud Unit, is a unit that MariAnne George developed to show how to supplement a literacy curriculum with elements of the Book Club program through a thematic read-aloud unit. You will notice that in this chapter, there is no Literacy Block. Literacy skill instruction occurs within the Book Club lessons, in whole-class contexts such as opening and closing community share. Guided reading occurs outside the Book Club lesson plans provided—during another part of the day. This read-aloud framework can help prepare early primary students—both pre-readers and beginning readers—to participate in all the contexts of Book Club *Plus*. Of course, read-aloud units are adaptable for use with all primary-grade students. Through this unit, students have the opportunity to learn and practice a variety of reading, writing, and discussion skills.

Chapter 11 illustrates how the Book Club *Plus* framework can be created in classrooms where teachers are mandated to use a basal reading program. In these classrooms students listen to and read literature at their grade levels, write in response to the literature in their logs and other formats, talk about books in fishbowls and book clubs, read literature that is thematically connected and explore "big ideas," and participate in guided reading and writer's workshop. However, the specific guided reading, vocabulary, and phonics skills taught within the unit derive from the basal reading program's scope and sequence and teacher's guide. Nina Hasty was able to adapt the Book Club *Plus* framework by making relatively easy modifications of text selections and by drawing on suggestions from the basal reader. Her version of Book Club *Plus* allowed her to meet the dual obligations of literacy instruction, reengage her students in literacy, and respond to the requirement that the basal remain core to her reading program.

In the upcoming chapters, you will have the chance to examine more detailed descriptions of the frameworks described above. These samples demonstrate how Book Club can work effectively in a variety of classrooms.

Meeting Standards Within the Frameworks

As teachers, we understand the need for assessment within the classroom to comply with specific curriculum standards of states and school systems. To help teachers in a wide spectrum of schools and districts meet their curriculum requirements, we've correlated our activities to national language arts and social studies standards. Chapter 6, Assessment, provides a complete discussion of assessment and meeting standards within a framework and includes sample rubrics and student and teacher samples. In the sections below, we present the national standards that inform the sample Book Club *Plus* frameworks in the next three chapters. We also include a brief overview of the ways in which these standards shape Book Club's major curricular areas and an explanation of how you can promote teacher and student ownership of national, state, and local standards in the classroom.

Curriculum Standards

The lesson frameworks in this book correspond to four major curricular target areas—comprehension, writing, language conventions, and literary aspects. These target areas are based on national, state, and district standards and on the scope and sequence charts of widely-used commercial programs. These curricular areas are described more fully in Chapter 2 and detailed in the chart on pages 16–17.

National Language Arts Standards

The chart on page 136 presents the Standards for the English Language Arts as defined by the National Council of Teachers of English (NCTE) and the International Reading Association (IRA). To show how you can use each framework to meet a specific set of standards, we correlate the lessons and activities within each of our samples to these standards. You can look for these correlations in the Curriculum Correlation Charts and the Unit Overview Charts provided with the sample frameworks.

Social Studies Standards

In many cases, a Book Club *Plus* framework creates an ideal structure for integrating instruction. Book Club teachers can select literature related to science and social studies content and then make cross-curricular links that enrich all areas of the curriculum. To clarify the links between these units and social studies content, we've correlated unit activities and lessons in our samples to standards established by the National Council for the Social Studies (NCSS). The NCSS has identified ten thematic strands in the social studies curriculum, shown on page 137.

NCTE/IRA Standards for the English Language Arts

1. Students read a wide range of print and nonprint texts to build an understanding of texts, of themselves, and of the cultures of the United States and the world; to acquire new information; to respond to the needs and demands of society and the workplace; and for personal fulfillment. Among these texts are fiction and nonfiction, classic and contemporary works.

2. Students read a wide range of literature from many periods in many genres to build an understanding of the many dimensions (e.g., philosophical, ethical, aesthetic) of human experience.

3. Students apply a wide range of strategies to comprehend, interpret, evaluate, and appreciate texts. They draw on their prior experience, their interactions with other readers and writers, their knowledge of word meaning and of other texts, their word identification strategies, and their understanding of textual features (e.g., sound-letter correspondence, sentence structure, context, graphics).

4. Students adjust their use of spoken, written, and visual language (e.g., conventions, style, and vocabulary) to communicate effectively with a variety of audiences and for different purposes.

5. Students employ a wide range of strategies as they write and use different writing process elements appropriately to communicate with different audiences for a variety of purposes.

6. Students apply knowledge of language structure, language conventions (e.g., spelling and punctuation), media techniques, figurative language, and genre to create, critique, and discuss print and nonprint texts.

7. Students conduct research on issues and interests by generating ideas and questions and by posing problems. They gather, evaluate, and synthesize data from a variety of sources (e.g., print and nonprint texts, artifacts, and people) to communicate their discoveries in ways that suit their purpose and audience.

8. Students use a variety of technological and information resources (e.g., libraries, databases, computer networks, video) to gather and synthesize information and to create and communicate knowledge.

9. Students develop an understanding of and respect for diversity in language use, patterns, and dialects across cultures, ethnic groups, geographic regions, and social roles.

10. Students whose first language is not English make use of their first language to develop competency in the English language arts and to develop understanding of content across the curriculum.

11. Students participate as knowledgeable, reflective, creative, and critical members of a variety of literacy communities.

12. Students use spoken, written, and visual language to accomplish their own purposes (e.g., for learning, enjoyment, persuasion, and the exchange of information).

NCSS Thematic Strands

1. **Culture**
    Social studies programs should include experiences that provide for the study of culture and cultural diversity.

2. **Time, Continuity, and Change**
    Social studies programs should include experiences that provide for the study of the ways human beings view themselves in and over time.

3. **People, Places, and Environments**
    Social studies programs should include experiences that provide for the study of people, places, and environments.

4. **Individual Development and Identity**
    Social studies programs should include experiences that provide for the study of individual development and identity.

5. **Individuals, Groups, and Institutions**
    Social studies programs should include experiences that provide for the study of interactions among individuals, groups, and institutions.

6. **Power, Authority, and Governance**
    Social studies programs should include experiences that provide for the study of how people create and change structures of power, authority, and governance.

7. **Production, Distribution, and Consumption**
    Social studies programs should include experiences that provide for the study of how people organize for the production, distribution, and consumption of goods and services.

8. **Science, Technology, and Society**
    Social studies programs should include experiences that provide for the study of relationships among science, technology, and society.

9. **Global Connections**
    Social studies programs should include experiences that provide for the study of global connections and interdependence.

10. **Civic Ideals and Practices**
    Social studies programs should include experiences that provide for the study of the ideals, principles, and practices of citizenship in a democratic republic.

Standards-Based Assessment and "I Can" Statements

As discussed in Chapter 6, the Book Club *Plus* assessment approach promotes maintaining high performance standards while encouraging teacher and student ownership of those standards. The goal is for standards to become part of the conversation in the classroom. Au (2001) suggests that standards be reworded to become as visible as possible. Therefore, it is advantageous to look at your state and district standards and convert them to "I Can" statements. These "I Can" statements can be posted to be used with your students. Evaluation Sheets 1 and 13 provide examples of "I Can" statements. More examples and rubrics can be found in Chapter 6.

The lessons in each sample framework reflect decisions that the teacher made regarding the instruction that students needed in order to make progress toward achieving the standards or "I Cans." As you review each sample framework, you will notice Assessment Tips that will help you think about how you can integrate the use of "I Can" statements into your classroom and monitor your students' progress.

Getting the Most from the Sample Frameworks

As you read the next three chapters, you'll notice that while these frameworks share many common elements, each one is also unique and reflective of the needs of a particular teacher and group of students. In presenting these varied samples, we show how the Book Club *Plus* framework gives teachers the flexibility to integrate the elements of the Book Club program with their own specific curriculum needs and requirements. We hope that these sample frameworks will inspire you to create units that reflect the needs and interests of your own students while also meeting your specific curriculum objectives, district guidelines, and goals for literacy instruction.

Framework for
Book Club *Plus*

Why Conduct a Book Club *Plus* Unit?

Book Club *Plus* units immerse primary-grade students in literature and provide opportunities for them to relate literary works to their own lives and to other literature. This is a framework for a Stories of Self unit. It fits under the overarching yearlong theme, Our Storied Lives, as mentioned at several points in this book. The unit achieves its goals through two primary contexts for literacy instruction, Book Club and Literacy Block. These two contexts help literacy teachers meet the dual obligations described in Chapter 1—to ensure that students have the opportunity to engage with materials at both their reading levels and their age levels. In Book Club, teachers work with students to improve their comprehension and critical thinking skills with texts that are appropriate to their students' ages and grade levels. In Literacy Block and related center activities, teachers use texts appropriate to students' reading levels to work with students on skills and strategies they need to become more facile at decoding and related basic skills. By participating in these two contexts, students can meet and even exceed literacy and social studies standards mandated by their district and state education systems.

Structure and Schedule

In this chapter, we describe how one third-grade teacher, Kathy Highfield, taught a unit using only trade books. In Kathy's district, teachers were encouraged to use trade books for instruction while the organization of their literacy instruction was left open. Teachers also had clear state and district standards and benchmarks that they needed to address in their teaching. Kathy used Book Club *Plus* to frame her teaching. This helped her create a coherent yearlong literacy curriculum that linked in meaningful ways to other school subjects—social studies in this particular unit. Her students reflected a range of reading levels, so she provided instruction at both their reading levels (through guided reading and individual work during Literacy Block) and at their age levels (through Book Club activities).

This combination of contexts supported and challenged all the students in Kathy's classroom. Assessment occurred throughout the unit. Kathy used the assessment information to guide instructional decisions and to help students make progress toward their goals. To inform your decisions, you can use the suggestions for assessment found in the planning charts and in the Book Club and Literacy Block lessons, "I Can" statements (see Chapter 6 and Evaluation Sheets 1 and 13), and your own assessments. You might also use information from literacy center activities for additional assessment opportunities each week.

To create the schedule for this unit, Kathy drew from the generic scheduling plan shown on page 127 of Chapter 7. Kathy included the core contexts of community share, reading, writing, and book clubs/fishbowls within the Book Club days. Guided reading and literacy centers were used within the

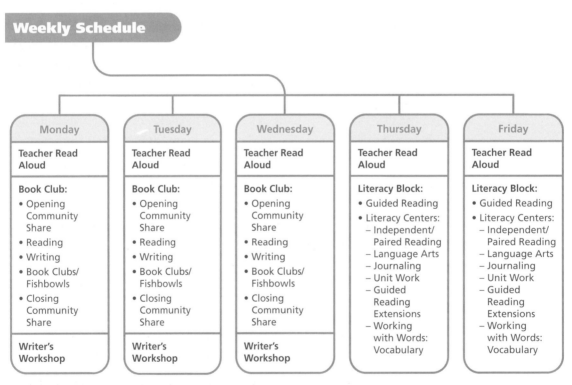

Weekly Schedule

Monday	Tuesday	Wednesday	Thursday	Friday
Teacher Read Aloud	**Teacher Read Aloud**	**Teacher Read Aloud**	**Teacher Read Aloud**	**Teacher Read Aloud**

Book Club:
• Opening Community Share
• Reading
• Writing
• Book Clubs/ Fishbowls
• Closing Community Share
	Book Club:
	• Opening Community Share
	• Reading
	• Writing
	• Book Clubs/ Fishbowls
	• Closing Community Share
		Book Club:
		• Opening Community Share
		• Reading
		• Writing
		• Book Clubs/ Fishbowls
		• Closing Community Share
			Literacy Block:
			• Guided Reading
			• Literacy Centers:
			  – Independent/ Paired Reading
			  – Language Arts
			  – Journaling
			  – Unit Work
			  – Guided Reading Extensions
			  – Working with Words: Vocabulary
				Literacy Block:
				• Guided Reading
				• Literacy Centers:
				  – Independent/ Paired Reading
				  – Language Arts
				  – Journaling
				  – Unit Work
				  – Guided Reading Extensions
				  – Working with Words: Vocabulary

Writer's Workshop	**Writer's Workshop**	**Writer's Workshop**		

*Shared reading is done two times a week. Independent reading occurs daily.
Unit Work is completed throughout each week.

Literacy Block days. Teacher read aloud and shared reading occurred within both Book Club and writer's workshop. Because Kathy had approximately 90 minutes per day to allocate to the Stories of Self unit work, she incorporated key contexts of Book Club *Plus* every day.

This chapter illustrates how a Book Club *Plus* unit is organized and taught using trade books. Within the unit, we not only describe in detail what Kathy did, but we also note ways in which the unit can be customized for your classroom.

Why Explore Stories of Self?

In this chapter, we illustrate one thematic unit—Stories of Self. Stories of Self focuses on students' understanding of themselves and their role within the world. The exploration of this theme through literature, discussion, and literacy activities supports students as they continue to broaden their perspectives about the world. The theme helps students understand the role of culture in understanding oneself and others.

Creating a Trade Book Model for Book Club *Plus*

Trade books are a wonderful resource for teaching literacy within a theme. In our research, we've seen repeatedly how important it is to have thematic content that invites students into literacy. Both younger students as well as struggling readers become engaged when reading about topics of interest to them. The stories used in this Stories of Self unit bring the voices and experiences of children, families, and their communities into the school curriculum. In short, our students become captivated by literacy because they see themselves in the texts they read.

Unit Themes

In this unit, students explore who they are and their changing roles within a variety of contexts, such as their family, their classroom, and their many communities outside the classroom. Questions that lend themselves to exploration in this unit include, Who am I? Why do I think, believe, and act as I do? Who and what have influenced me? How these questions are framed will vary, of course, depending on the age level of the students with whom you are working. The themes we work to develop in this unit include the following:

—Many different people have helped me become who I am today, including my family, my friends, and the people in my community.

—My classmates and I are alike in many ways, but we are also different in important ways too, and I am a unique person.

—It is as important to value how we are different as it is to find ways we are the same.

—There are many ways to show others how much we care about them.

—Our lives can be represented through different means, including stories, artifacts, time lines, poetry, autobiographies, and illustrations.

In addition to the "big ideas" of the theme, we also develop students' knowledge of the autobiography genre and of social studies concepts that connect to the study of self, such as culture. You may want to display key theme questions, such as the ones below, over the course of the unit. The first two relate to the concepts within the theme, the third relates to the autobiography genre, and the fourth emphasizes an important social studies concept.

—How is my life like a story?

—What do I learn from studying my own life and the lives of my classmates?

—What is autobiography?

—What is culture?

Literacy Skill Instruction

The chart that follows correlates the Book Club and Literacy Block curriculum areas to individual lessons in the Stories of Self unit. For additional information about each curriculum area, refer to the chart in Chapter 2, pages 16–17. Lessons are also correlated to the language arts standards established by the National Council of Teachers of English and the International Reading Association. Numbers in parentheses refer to specific NCTE/IRA standards (see page 136).

Curriculum Correlation Chart

Curriculum Area	Lessons in Stories of Self
Comprehension	**Week 1** Getting Started (3, 4, 5, 6, 11) **Weeks 2–6** Literacy Centers (3, 4, 5, 6) **Lesson 3** Sequence (3, 4) **Lesson 4** Literacy Block: Stepping Into the Text (3, 6) **Lesson 5** Literacy Block: Moving Through/Stepping Out of Text (3, 6) **Lesson 7** Compare and Contrast (3, 4, 5, 6) **Lesson 8** Character Map (3, 6) **Lesson 9** Literacy Block: Questioning (3, 6, 7) **Lesson 10** Literacy Block: Questioning, Intertextual Connections (3, 6, 7) **Lesson 12** Questioning (3, 7, 11) **Lessons 14–15** Literacy Block: Intertextual Connections, Looking for Information, Author's Craft and Visualizing (3, 6, 11) **Lesson 18** Summary, Interpretation (3, 4, 6, 11) **Lessons 19–20** Literacy Block: Summarizing, Author's Craft, Finding Important Details (3, 6, 9, 10)
Writing	**Week 1** Getting Started (3, 4, 5, 6, 11) **Weeks 2–6** Writer's Workshop (4, 5, 6, 12) **Lessons 1–20** Daily Log Writing (3, 5, 6, 12) **Lesson 2** The Tripod Log Format (3, 4, 5, 6, 11) **Lesson 18** Summary, Interpretation (3, 4, 6, 11)
Language Conventions	**Week 1** Getting Started (3, 4, 5, 6, 11) **Weeks 2–6** Literacy Centers (3, 4, 5, 6) **Lesson 1** Introduction to Book Club (1, 2, 3, 4, 11, 12) **Lesson 2** The Tripod Log Format (3, 4, 5, 6, 11) **Lesson 3** Sequence (3, 4) **Lesson 4** Literacy Block: Synonyms, Connotations (3, 6) **Lesson 5** Literacy Block: Word Choice, Fluency (3, 6) **Lesson 9** Literacy Block: Word Phrases, Word Sightings (3, 6) **Lesson 10** Literacy Block: Word Phrase Charts (3, 6) **Lessons 14–15** Literacy Block: Context Clues, Word Parts (3, 6) **Lesson 18** Summary, Interpretation (3, 4, 6, 11) **Lessons 19–20** Literacy Block: Synonyms, Antonyms (3, 6, 9, 10)
Literary Aspects	**Week 1** Getting Started (3, 4, 5, 6, 11) **Lesson 2** The Tripod Log Format (3, 4, 5, 6, 11) **Lesson 6** Me & the Book (3) **Lesson 11** Author's Craft (3, 6) **Lesson 13** Characterization, Critique (3, 4, 5, 6, 11) **Lessons 14–15** Literacy Block, Author's Craft (3, 6) **Lesson 16** Feelings (3, 11) **Lesson 17** Character Relationships (3, 5, 11) **Lessons 19–20** Literacy Block: Author's Craft (3, 6, 9, 10)

Integrating Instruction

The Stories of Self unit provides many opportunities for cross-curricular connections, particularly with social studies. For your convenience, we've identified links with social studies content based on the ten thematic strands defined by the National Council for the Social Studies (NCSS). A complete listing of the NCSS strands is available on page 137. The chart that follows highlights the five strands that relate closely to the Stories of Self unit.

Correlation to Social Studies Thematic Strands

NCSS Thematic Strands	Lessons and Activities
1. **Culture** Social studies programs should include experiences that provide for the study of culture and cultural diversity.	Weeks 1–6, Lessons, Unit Work, and Writer's Workshop
2. **Time, Continuity, and Change** Social studies programs should include experiences that provide for the study of the ways human beings view themselves in and over time.	Lessons 1, 16, 17, 18; Weeks 2–6, Unit Work; Weeks 2–6, Writer's Workshop
3. **People, Places, and Environments** Social studies programs should include experiences that provide for the study of people, places, and environments.	Lessons 1, 2, 4, 6, 7, 8, 17, 18
4. **Individual Development and Identity** Social studies programs should include experiences that provide for the study of individual development and identity.	Lessons 1, 2, 4, 6, 7, 8, 16. 17, 18; Weeks 2–6, Unit Work; Weeks 2–6, Writer's Workshop
5. **Individuals, Groups, and Institutions** Social studies programs should include experiences that provide for the study of interactions among individuals, groups, and institutions.	Lessons 2, 3, 17, 18

Unit Overview

This chart outlines the complete six-week Stories of Self unit. Book synopses, weekly planning charts, and general procedures for the weeks of the unit are given on pages 146–169.

Six-Week Unit Overview

This unit has been correlated with the NCTE/IRA Standards for the English Language Arts (see page 136). Numbers in parentheses refer to specific standards.

Week 1: Getting Started

- Class discusses themes of autobiography and culture. (2, 11)

- Teacher Read Aloud: Roald Dahl selections (2, 3, 11)

- Unit Work: Teacher starts projects and introduces Life History Portfolio. (3, 5, 8)

- Assessment: See Week 1 planning guide.

Week 2: Book Club and Literacy Block Begin

- Book Club and Literacy Block: See individual lessons for details. (3, 4, 5, 6)

- Teacher Read Aloud: Roald Dahl selections (2, 3, 11)

- Shared Reading: William Joyce selections (2, 3, 11)

- Writer's Workshop: Snapshot of Me writing project (4, 5, 7)

- Unit Work: Students bring in personal artifacts and share them with the class. (4, 5, 11, 12)

- Assessment: See Week 2 planning guide.

Week 3: Book Club and Literacy Block

- Book Club and Literacy Block: See individual lessons for details. (3, 4, 5, 6)

- Teacher Read Aloud: Dahl books and some William Joyce picture books (3, 11)

- Shared Reading: *The World of William Joyce Scrapbook* (2, 3, 11)

- Writer's Workshop: Students write about themselves as babies. (5, 7, 12)

- Unit Work: Each student gathers three personal artifacts and shares them with the class. (4, 7, 12)

- Assessment: See Week 3 planning guide.

Week 4: Book Club and Literacy Block

- Book Club and Literacy Block: See individual lessons for details. (3, 4, 5, 6)

- Teacher Read Aloud: *Judy Moody* (2, 3, 11)

- Shared Reading: Continue *The World of William Joyce Scrapbook* (2, 3, 11)

- Writer's Workshop: Each student tells the story behind his or her first name. (5, 7, 9)

- Unit Work: Students make an All About Me collage. (3, 4, 5, 11, 12)

- Assessment: See Week 4 planning guide.

Week 5: Book Club and Literacy Block

- Book Club and Literacy Block: See individual lessons for details. (3, 4, 5, 6)

- Teacher Read Aloud: End Dahl books and *Judy Moody.* Start *Flora and Tiger: 19 Very Short Stories from My Life* by Eric Carle. (2, 3, 11)

- Shared Reading: *Glorious Angels, Angel to Angel,* and *Brown Angels* by Walter Dean Myers (2, 3, 11)

- Writer's Workshop: Students write about a photograph of a mystery person. (5, 7, 11, 12)

- Unit Work: Students start a new activity centered around scrapbooks. Students also continue work on previous weeks' artifact activities. (4, 7, 11, 12)

- Assessment: See Week 5 planning guide.

Week 6: Wrap-Up Options

- Book Club and Literacy Block: Book clubs/fishbowls; comprehension and vocabulary strategy reviews (3, 4, 5, 6, 12)

- Unit Work: Students wrap up and evaluate unit projects. Students respond to unit theme questions. (3, 4, 5, 11)

- Assessment: See Week 6 Wrap Up.

Synopses of the Featured Books

Book Club Literature

Roxaboxen **by Alice McLerran**

During her childhood in Yuma, Arizona, the author's mother played in a "town" called Roxaboxen that she and other children in her neighborhood invented. The children made houses, streets, and shops for Roxaboxen out of rocks, glass, and wooden boxes, and they created "money" from pebbles strewn across the hill. This semi-autobiographical book draws the reader into Roxaboxen to enjoy the idea of an invented town where children have made the rules.

26 Fairmount Avenue **by Tomie dePaola**

In this autobiographical book, the author recalls an important year in his life—when he was four years old and his family began building a new house at 26 Fairmount Avenue in Meriden, Connecticut. Throughout the book, he describes adventures and memorable moments that include his neighborhood friends and his colorful and loving extended family. The book ends when dePaola and his family finally move from their apartment to their brand new house.

The Canada Geese Quilt **by Natalie Kinsey-Warnock**

Ten-year-old Ariel must deal with the impending arrival of a new sibling, which has her feeling left out. Then her grandmother suggests they work together on a quilt for the baby, and Ariel begins to feel part of things. But when her grandmother suffers a stroke and faces a difficult recovery, Ariel no longer knows how to relate to her. At first, she avoids her. When she realizes her grandmother has given up hope, she begins to work on the quilt again, hoping to inspire her grandmother to get better. Together they complete the baby's quilt, and then Ariel's grandmother surprises her with a very special gift.

Guided Reading Literature

Below Grade Level

The Baby Sister by Tomie dePaola

Another in dePaola's autobiographical series, this tells the story of his excited anticipation of the birth of his new sibling. Young Tommy happily wishes for a baby sister with a red ribbon in her hair, and he looks forward to seeing his Aunt Nell, who is scheduled to care for him when his parents go to the hospital. However, when his mother finally does go to the hospital he is stuck with strict Nana. And then he can't visit his mother in the hospital because chicken pox is going around. However, he feels better about everything when he is finally able to hold his new baby sister.

George Shrinks by William Joyce

A young boy awakens one morning to find that he is about three inches high. He's smaller than his toy soldiers, but he still tries to complete his daily chores the best he can. To take out the garbage, he harnesses a wagon to his baby brother; to feed the goldfish, he dives into their water; to wash the dishes, he turns sponges into skis. Readers see how his life turns into one big adventure.

When I Was Little: A Four-Year-Old's Memoir of Her Youth by Jamie Lee Curtis

A four-year-old girl compares the skills she has now to those she had as a baby. Students will like comparing the four-year-old's perceptions to the reality shown in the pictures. The topic of the book is also one that students will recognize. They, too, are proud of their accomplishments even if they are not quite up to the standards of the adults around them.

When I Was Young in the Mountains by Cynthia Rylant

This award-winning picture book describes moments of one young girl's childhood in the Appalachian Mountains. She recalls seeing her grandfather come home in the evenings covered with the black dust of the coal mines, going to the swimming hole, taking baths in the kitchen, and sharing special times with her family.

At Grade Level

Family Pictures: Cuadros de Familia by Carmen Lomas Garza

Written in both English and Spanish, this book depicts scenes from the author's childhood in a Hispanic community. The text and the paintings show a family that supports each other and the people around them.

The Popcorn Book by Tomie dePaola

Colorful illustrations and text present a variety of interesting facts about the history of popcorn. Readers get information about various periods in history, as well as two popcorn recipes.

Tell Me Again About the Night I Was Born by Jamie Lee Curtis

Jamie Lee Curtis describes with a twist a familiar request from young children. The child who is asking about the night she was born was adopted from another country. In this case, the child herself actually ends up telling the story of her parents receiving the call, traveling to the hospital, and taking the baby girl to a loving family home.

Above Grade Level

The Tarantula in My Purse: And 172 Other Wild Pets by Jean Craighead George

Jean Craighead George allows the reader a glimpse into her life and tells how she and her children lived with and created homes for many wild animals. Readers learn about pet crows, owls, fish, and a tarantula. They also learn about animal behavior. Note: Many of these events happened before permits to house wild animals were necessary.

Read-Aloud Literature

When you read aloud, you create a common literary context for the whole class. You increase opportunities for intertextual connections while you model fluent reading. The theme-related selections below work particularly well with this unit.

The BFG by Roald Dahl

In this novel, BFG stands for "Big Friendly Giant." BFG is a giant who, unlike the evil giants he lives with, is friendly and lovable. One night he kidnaps a little girl named Sophie, and the two of them become friends and work together to end the cruel activities of the other giants.

Boy: Tales of Childhood by Roald Dahl

Dahl presents stories and vignettes from his youth, which he spent in Wales and in Norway. The humorously written autobiography includes stories about his family, his experiences at boarding school, and his mischievous antics with his friends. Readers can see how the experiences of his youth shaped his sense of humor and his writing style in adulthood.

Charlie and the Chocolate Factory by **Roald Dahl**

In this classic novel, reclusive chocolate maker Willy Wonka opens his chocolate factory to five lucky members of the public for the first time in years. The finders of five golden tickets hidden in candy bars get a tour of the factory by Wonka himself. Charlie Bucket becomes one of the five when he finds a dollar bill in a gutter and buys a candy bar that has a golden ticket. The experience changes his life forever.

Flora and Tiger: 19 Very Short Stories from My Life by **Eric Carle**

Each illustrated vignette, which is no more than three pages long, presents different moments in the author's life. He introduces readers to his grandparents; reflects on the influence his father had on his love for drawing, storytelling, and animals; and describes such incidents as finding a wasp trapped in his trousers.

It's Great to Be Eight by **Beverly Cleary, et al**

This collection of stories and excerpts about being eight years old includes pieces by Beverly Cleary, Roald Dahl, Paula Danziger, Patricia Maclachlan, E.B. White, Judy Blume, A.A. Milne, Syd Hoff, and others.

It's Terrific to Be Ten by **Beverly Cleary, et al**

This collection of twelve stories and excerpts includes pieces by Paula Danziger, Barbara Clark, Katherine Paterson, Lois Lowry, Beverly Cleary, Christopher Paul Curtis, and others.

Judy Moody by **Megan McDonald**

It's the first day of third grade, and Judy Moody is in a bad mood. She doesn't want to go to a new classroom with a new desk, and she's afraid she'll have to sit next to a boy who eats paste or listen to kids who had better summer vacations than hers. However, her bad mood doesn't last long, and over the next few weeks she throws herself into an interesting class assignment—creating a "Me collage."

My Life in Dog Years by **Gary Paulsen**

This autobiographical book reveals interesting details of the author's life through his experiences with eight of his dogs. Readers meet Cookie, a sled dog who saves Paulsen's life; Snowball, the puppy he gets when he is seven years old and living in the Philippines; Josh, a border collie who most recently has shared his home; and others.

Tom by **Tomie dePaola**

Another in dePaola's series of autobiographical picture books, *Tom* focuses on the special relationship the author enjoyed with his grandfather, after whom he is named. He and his grandfather share many special experiences. They read the comics, tell each other stories, and work together in the butcher section of his grandfather's store.

What a Year! by Tomie dePaola

This autobiographical picture book, set in 1940, depicts Tomie at six years old and starting first grade. Readers see Tomie trick-or-treating with his brother, dealing with a case of chicken pox, getting to stay up past midnight on New Year's Eve, and enjoying radio shows, movies, and good times with his friends and family.

When I Was Nine by James Stevenson

With watercolors and few words, the author describes one special summer he experienced as a child in the 1930s. He climbs trees, plays ball, listens to the radio, and even publishes his own newspaper. Then he and his family take a trip and he has the chance to expand his world and see many new sights.

Shared Reading Literature

In shared reading, children sit in groups and read one book together. Often the teacher will read the book aloud as the students follow along. This provides an interactive reading experience in which students can pause to discuss, share, and address questions. Shared reading provides the teacher with a context in which she can direct students' attention to key features of the author's craft, often as part of explicit instruction leading to an extended writing activity during writer's workshop or during one of the literacy center activities. The following titles work well with the unit theme:

Angel to Angel: A Mother's Gift of Love by Walter Dean Myers

Photographs and verse focus on relationships between mothers and their children. The book features ten poems that accompany a series of old photographs of African-American mothers, grandmothers, and children. Each poem gives a different perspective on motherhood.

Bently & egg by William Joyce

Bently Hopperton, a frog, is asked by his best friend Kack Kack, a duck, to watch her newly-laid egg so she can go visit her sister. Bently agrees but becomes bored and decides to paint the plain white egg with beautiful colors. Unfortunately, a young boy then takes it, believing he's found an Easter egg. What follows is a humorous adventure as Bently tries desperately to save his friend's egg.

Brown Angels: An Album of Pictures and Verse by Walter Dean Myers

This book celebrates childhood through poetry and early twentieth-century photographs of African-American children of different ages. The verses that accompany the photographs focus on a variety of aspects of childhood.

Dinosaur Bob and His Adventures With the Family Lazardo
by William Joyce

Bob the dinosaur is a friendly pet that guards the family home and plays baseball and the trumpet. He runs into trouble one day when he is arrested for chasing cars with his dog friends and disturbing the peace, but by the end of the book he is forgiven and enjoys a celebration with his family.

Glorious Angels: A Celebration of Children **by Walter Dean Myers**

This follow-up to *Brown Angels: An Album of Pictures and Verse* celebrates childhood in different cultures. Poems accompany a variety of images, from Asian youngsters in traditional dress to American children celebrating the Fourth of July.

The Leaf Men and the Brave Good Bugs **by William Joyce**

In this picture book an elderly woman loves her garden but no longer senses the magic it held for her when she was a child. She becomes ill, and her garden falls into frightening disarray. The insect inhabitants worry and call on the mythical Leaf Men to drive out the evil Spider Queen, restore order to the garden, and bring some childhood magic back to the elderly woman.

Rolie Polie Olie **by William Joyce**

Rolie Polie Olie, a small robot, lives on a distant planet with his mom and pop, his sister Zowie, and his dog Spot. The details of their ordinary but happy day of family life include playing, working, eating, and getting ready for bed.

The World of William Joyce Scrapbook **by William Joyce**

This colorful autobiography, which Joyce calls a scrapbook, tells the story of Joyce's life through snapshots, stories, excerpts from his books, and previews of books to come. He allows readers into his world to see his home, family life, work life, childhood, and elaborate holiday celebrations.

Special Classroom Library

During a thematic unit, it is important to stock your classroom with theme-related literature at a variety of reading levels and, if possible, representing a number of cultural backgrounds and even first languages. The goal is a print-rich, themed, multi-ability print environment to support the Book Club *Plus* unit and the class sense of a learning community. We suggest the following titles:

The Art Lesson **by Tomie dePaola**

Young Tommy discovers that he loves to draw. An art teacher gives him a chance to follow his own individual style and direction.

Author Talk **compiled and edited by Leonard S. Marcus**

Through interviews, photographs, early writings, and memorabilia, this collection gives readers a glimpse into the early lives of fifteen authors of books for young adults. Featured authors include Laurence Yep, Judy Blume, and Russell Freedman.

Fly High! The Story of Bessie Coleman **by Louise Borden and Mary Kay Kroeger**

This picture book tells the story of the first African American woman to earn a pilot's license. Readers learn about how hard she worked to realize her dreams and how she inspired others to pursue their own dreams.

Goin' Someplace Special **by Patricia McKissack**

This award-winning picture book tells the story of Tricia Ann, a young African-American girl who lives in racially segregated Nashville, Tennessee, in the 1950s.

Margaret Knight: Girl Inventor **by Marlene Targ Brill**

At the age of twelve, Margaret Knight invented a safer loom for mill workers. After witnessing many accidents, she wanted to improve the working conditions of mill workers.

My Chinatown: One Year in Poems **by Kam Mak**

Through realistic paintings and free-verse poems, Kam Mak tells the story of a young immigrant from Hong Kong trying to adjust to his first year in New York City's Chinatown.

The Other Side **by Jacqueline Woodson**

A young white girl and a young African-American girl become close friends, despite the fact that they live in a racially segregated world with a fence between them.

There's an Owl in the Shower **by Jean Craighead George**

Through the story of one owl and one family, George shows a conflict between loggers and environmentalists in a small logging town in California. The main character gains a new perspective on owls when he ends up caring for an owlet that has fallen from its nest.

Other Media

A Visit with Tomie dePaola. (Videocassette, 25 Minutes).

In this video, Tomie dePaola, author and illustrator of several books featured in this sample framework, gives a tour of his home and his studio and talks about how he creates his books and artwork.

Week 1: Getting Started

Week 1 Planning Guide

Book Club and Literacy Block

• Introduce Book Club and Literacy Block	One 30-minute session

Read Aloud

• Roald Dahl's *Boy*, selected chapters	Daily 20–40 minutes

Unit Work

• Introduce unit and themes.	One 20-minute session
• Make chart "What is autobiography?".	One 20-minute session
• Make chart "What is culture?".	One 20-minute session
• Introduce life history portfolios.	

Writer's Workshop

• *When I was Nine* by James Stevenson and life milestone activity	Two 45-minute sessions

Assessment

• Assess students' reading levels.	Ongoing
• Writing Prompt: Tell Me About Yourself	Three 45-minute sessions

Book Club and Literacy Block

- You may want to preview the components of a typical Book Club lesson during this week (see also Lesson 1, page 170). Tell students that they will be reading or listening to books, writing about texts, meeting in groups to discuss their ideas, and meeting as a class to talk about the books. Review the terms, *Book Club, Opening/Closing Community Share,* and *Fishbowl.* Talk about fishbowls and if possible, gather some adults or more experienced Book Club students to demonstrate fishbowl. Explain how participating in book club groups will help students think and talk about what they are reading.

- Briefly discuss that students will also be working with you in guided reading groups. Explain that in guided reading students will be learning strategies that will help them understand what they are reading. Finally, mention the types of literacy centers or activities that you intend to use.

- Introduce any procedures you would like the class to follow during Book Club and Literacy Block. Discuss how you would like students to organize their work.

Read Aloud

- Read aloud from *Boy* by Roald Dahl. Dahl's autobiographical sketches tie in well with the unit theme. Preview the book in order to locate the sketches that seem most appropriate for your students. Other Read-Aloud options appear in the list on pages 148–150.

Unit Work

- Introduce students to the theme Stories of Self. Start a class discussion about *autobiography* and *culture.* To help students see how their ideas change over time, make class charts for the following questions: What is autobiography? What is culture? To begin, write *What is autobiography?,* on the top of a chart or transparency. Ask students to share ideas about autobiography. Since this is a brainstorming session, accept all responses. For example, some students might say that autobiography has to do with stories or books. Others might wonder if it has to do with cars. Write down the ideas to determine the extent of classroom knowledge about the genre. Some teachers like to date the entries because they add and change ideas during the course of the unit.

- Tell students that some of the work they create during this unit will be put into a life history portfolio. Tie the idea of the portfolio to the theme of autobiography. Tell students that this portfolio will build a picture of them as students and as people. They can add to the portfolio throughout the unit and even the year. Discuss the format the portfolio will take. You may want to use folders, binders, or boxes to hold items.

- Give students the opportunity to discuss any of their ideas before hanging the charts in the classroom for use throughout the unit.

Writer's Workshop

- Introduce a theme project by telling students they are going to make a time line of significant events in their lives, such as the one on page 155. Discuss such common milestones as learning to walk or talk, riding a bike, or sleeping over at a friend's house. Read aloud *When I Was Nine* by James Stevenson. Encourage students to think about milestones in their own lives. Then give each student a large piece of construction paper to fold into eight squares. Have students write, *"When I was one . . ., When I was two . . ."* and so on in each square. Tell students to complete each sentence

▲ Student Sample
This student created eight illustrations with sentences to represent each year of her life.

and draw a picture or attach a photograph to illustrate the "year." Have them complete the project at home and bring it back by the beginning of the next week. This time line can be put in students' life history portfolios.

Assessment

NOTE: This sample framework was developed for the beginning of the school year. Kathy Highfield worked with a list of "I Can" statements to help guide her decisions about instruction and assessment (see Evaluation Sheet 1). The following assessments provided information that she used in her decision-making.

- Assess your students' instructional reading levels to help you place them in guided reading groups. There are many different ways to descibe homogeneous groupings. For the purposes of this unit, we have used the following terms: Above Grade Level, At Grade Level, Below Grade Level, and Struggling Readers. You may want to conduct an informal assessment by asking students about reading to determine their attitude and their use of comprehension strategies, or you may choose an assessment tool. Most school districts recommend a particular reading inventory. Your district may also give tests at the end of the previous year. If you are unsure of which assessment tool you should use, check with your principal or district curriculum director. If there is no recommended assessment, refer to the chart on page 112 for some suggestions.

- To assess writing skills, begin a three-day exercise using the writing prompt, "Tell Me About Yourself." This assessment also allows you to study the way students think. As students encounter different authors, they will learn about author's craft and begin to incorporate some of that craft into their own writing. This writing assessment will help you gauge students' progress in writing throughout this unit and throughout the year.

  To begin, tell students that you would like to know them better and that you would like them to write about their lives. Ask them to keep in mind the topic, "Tell Me About Yourself," as they write.

  Remind students of the discussion about milestones. Explain that while people experience many of the same things, everyone experiences them differently. Let students spend about five minutes thinking of significant events from their lives. Each student should make a list of these ideas to save. Give students time to use their lists to write a draft description of themselves. At the end of your class time, collect all of their papers.

- On day two of the writing assessment, return the papers and give students twenty minutes to read and revise their drafts. Next, tell students that they are now going to help each other. Model ways to give and receive comments. Remind students to give positive comments along with suggestions for improvement. (You might use the fishbowl method to show students how peers can help each other edit and revise.) Then group students in pairs and have them spend about fifteen minutes conducting peer reviews. Some pairs of students may need more time to revise their descriptions. Finally, collect all students' writing.

- On the final day of the writing assessment, distribute students' writing and talk to them about final drafts. Emphasize that students should try to revise and edit their writing so you will understand what they are trying to say and so the writing tells you something about them. Remind them to think about their grammar, spelling, and punctuation because these are all part of helping the reader understand the writing. Give students about twenty minutes to complete their work.

  After the students have completed the writing assessment, have them explain how making the time line was the same or different from writing their "Tell Me About Yourself" descriptions. Was it easier or harder to make the time line? Why?

Week 2: Book Club and Literacy Block Begin

Week 2 Planning Guide

Book Club

• *Roxaboxen* by Alice McLerran	Three 40–60 minute sessions

Guided Reading and Literacy Centers

• *When I Was Little* by Jamie Lee Curtis • *Tell Me Again About the Night I Was Born* by Jamie Lee Curtis • *The Tarantula in My Purse* by Jean Craighead George	Two 40–60 minute sessions

Read Aloud

• Roald Dahl books	Daily 20–40 minutes

Shared Reading

• William Joyce's books	Two 20-minute sessions

Unit Work

• Artifact Activity	One 10-minute session to introduce; two 20-minute sessions to share

Writer's Workshop

• Snapshot of Me	Three 30-minute sessions

Independent Reading

	Daily 10–20 minutes

Assessment Suggestions

• Review "I Can" statements with students. • Observe students in fishbowl setting. Record examples of talk that leads to good discussion. • Evaluate artifact activity.	Ongoing

Book Club

Students will read, respond to, and discuss Alice McLerran's *Roxaboxen*. Refer to pages 170–174 for Lessons 1–3.

Guided Reading

Students will meet in small groups at their instructional level to read the following books: Jamie Lee Curtis's *When I Was Little: A Four-Year-Old's Memoir of Her Youth* and *Tell Me Again About the Night I Was Born,* and Jean Craighead George's *The Tarantula in My Purse.* Each guided reading lesson includes one comprehension and one vocabulary focus. Students will focus their comprehension strategy learning on stepping into, moving through, and stepping out of texts and their vocabulary learning on fostering word consciousness. Refer to pages 175–178 for Lessons 4–5.

Read Aloud

Read passages from Roald Dahl books such as *Boy, The BFG,* or *Charlie and the Chocolate Factory.* Begin talking about how these passages relate to the unit theme.

Shared Reading

On two days for periods of twenty minutes, have students read from a William Joyce picture book such as *Bently & egg, Dinosaur Bob, The Leaf Men,* or *Rolie Polie Olie.*

Unit Work

- Conduct an artifact activity that will encourage students to think about their own storied lives. Discuss the term *artifact.* Help students make the connection between artifacts and their stories of self. We suggest you have students complete one artifact activity during each week of the unit. You might assign one specific activity for each week, or give students a list of possible activities to choose from. In this sample framework, we've assigned one artifact activity per week. During this week, have each student bring from home an artifact that tells something about him or her. Invite them to show and explain their objects to the class.

- We suggest you have students make a pictorial representation of each activity (a drawing or digital picture) for their life history portfolios. You may want to complete Evaluation Sheet 2, Artifact Activity, for some or all artifact activities.

- As an ongoing unit project, add to the class "What is autobiography?" chart and revisit the unit theme questions. Students' responses to these questions will undoubtedly change with each week.

ASSESSMENT TIP

This is a good place to introduce "I Can" statements. Evaluation Sheet 1 gives a list of "I Can" statements developed for the Stories of Self framework. Discuss the concept of standards with your students. For example, you can discuss your expectations for how students will participate in book club discussions or talk about how you expect them to show what they are learning about the theme through their writing. Remind students that the reading and activities in this unit are all related to the Stories of Self theme.

Writer's Workshop

- Tell students that they are going to write a piece called Snapshot of Me. Explain what a snapshot is and how students can convey information about themselves in this way. Students may think of physical attributes, skills, or other character traits that they can describe to create a vivid picture of themselves. Give students time to plan the information they would like to include and to start their rough drafts. Ask students to bring in a photo from home to put on their snapshots, or have them do a drawing to go along with their writing.

  Tell students to continue working on their Snapshot of Me throughout the week, finishing their rough draft and beginning to revise their work. Let students work in pairs to help each other edit and revise. Think Sheet 3, Writing Process Checklist, can help students with their editing. (Remind students to bring in a photograph, take a photograph at school, or use school pictures.)

  At the end of the week, hand out Think Sheet 4, Snapshot of Me, for students to use for their final piece. Some students may need more time to complete their work. You can display the Snapshot of Me pieces on a bulletin board or place them in students' life history portfolios. A student sample of this project is shown below.

▶ **Snapshot of Me**
This student's snapshot includes details about what she wants to do when she grows up, her pets, her family, and her favorite author.

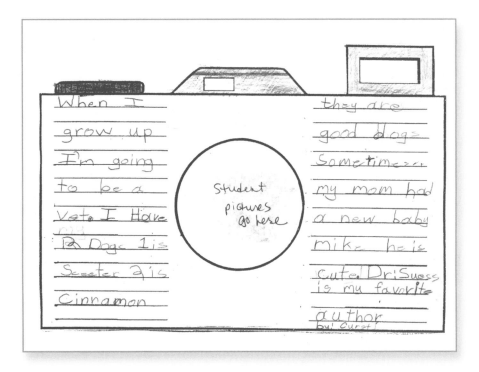

TEACHING OPTION

If you choose to have a spelling activity or center during Literacy Block, you may want to consider adding words from the Book Club or Read-Aloud books to your students' spelling list. These words might either be theme-related, e.g., *culture, family*, or related to the spelling pattern students are currently studying.

Literacy Center Options

NOTE: In Kathy Highfield's classroom, students are given a list of choices for their centers. She calls one group over at a time to guided reading, while other students work on their literacy choices independently. Your preference and your students' ability to work independently will dictate whether you use literacy choices or create more structured centers. (See pages 240–243 for ideas about structured centers.)

- Students do independent or paired reading of William Joyce's books.

- Have students complete Snapshot of Me writing.

- Guided Reading Extensions: silent (rereading) time and vocabulary. (See Lessons 4 and 5, pages 175–178, for detailed descriptions.)

- Give students a lesson from the district spelling program.

- Have students write a journal entry to the prompt, "More About Me."

- Present other literacy activities required by the district curriculum.

Independent Reading

In this week and in subsequent weeks, each student should spend 10–20 minutes a day reading a book he or she selects. You might have students choose a book from the special classroom library, school library, or home.

Week 3: Book Club and Literacy Block

TEACHING OPTION

You can help students develop the monitoring strategy of questioning. Have each student read a short selection from one of the Read-Aloud books or from the Special Classroom Library list (You may need to choose more than one passage depending on the reading levels of your students). Have each student write three questions that they would use to help themselves understand the selection. Then have them reread the passage and answer the questions. Some students may gain more from this activity if they work with a partner.

Book Club

Students will read, respond to, and discuss Tomie dePaola's *26 Fairmount Avenue.* Refer to pages 179–182 for Lessons 6–8.

Guided Reading

Students will meet in small groups at their instructional level to read the following books: William Joyce's *George Shrinks* and *Dinosaur Bob,* and Jean Craighead George's *The Tarantula in My Purse.* Each guided reading lesson includes one comprehension and one vocabulary focus. This week, students will focus their comprehension strategy learning on questioning and their vocabulary learning on finding word phrases that express author values, their values, and their family values. Refer to pages 182–185 for Lessons 9–10.

Read Aloud

Continue reading aloud from the Dahl books you began in previous weeks. You might also want to read aloud any of the Joyce picture books suggested in week two, such as *Bently & egg, Dinosaur Bob, The Leaf Men,* or *Rolie Polie Olie.* This will complement the shared reading selection suggested below.

Shared Reading

With students, read *The World of William Joyce Scrapbook* for 20 minutes a day for two or three days. Encourage students to connect information in the book to the William Joyce picture books they have read. Help students make

Week 3 Planning Guide

Book Club	
• *26 Fairmount Avenue* by Tomie dePaola	Three 40–60 minute sessions

Guided Reading and Literacy Centers	
• *George Shrinks* by William Joyce • *Dinosaur Bob* by William Joyce • *The Tarantula in My Purse* by Jean Craighead George	Two 40–60 minute sessions

Read Aloud	
• Roald Dahl books • William Joyce's books	Daily 20–40 minutes

Shared Reading	
• *The World of William Joyce Scrapbook* by William Joyce	Two or three 20-minute sessions

Unit Work	
• Artifact Activity • Revisit charts "What is autobiography?" and "What is culture?".	One 10-minute session to introduce; two 20-minute sessions to share One 10-minute session

Writer's Workshop	
• Baby Story	Three 30-minute sessions; time to share stories

Independent Reading	
	Daily 10–20 minutes

Assessment Suggestions	
• Observe students' ability to make meaning when reading. • Collect students' logs and use rubric to review progress in writing and making theme connections.	Ongoing

the link between writing their own autobiographies from artifacts to what they are learning from their reading. Mention to students that they are learning the way in which writers' ideas come from their own experiences. Note that artifacts can jog memories of an experience and that the things that we keep reveal something about us as people.

Unit Work

• Ask each student to bring in a small brown lunch sack with three small artifacts that will tell the class something about him or her. As you discuss the activity with students, make the connection to their shared reading of *The World of William Joyce Scrapbook.* Lunch bags are useful because they encourage students to bring in small items that are easily transported.

• Invite students to share their artifacts and answer questions about them. As with all unit projects, have students save some type some type of pictorial representation of this artifact activity for their life history portfolios.

Writer's Workshop

• Discuss with students how much they have already learned about how people represent their lives. Ask them to talk about this concept using examples from their own artifact stories or books they have been reading, e.g. *Boy: Tales of Childhood, The World of William Joyce Scrapbook.*

• Send a letter home with each student asking for an interesting/funny/cute baby story. Caregivers should convey the story to the children, and then the children can put the story down on paper. You might encourage caregivers to give students copies of baby pictures to include with their final story drafts.

• Give students time throughout the week to work on their stories. Talk to students about how these kinds of stories are part of their heritage. Think Sheet 3, Writing Process Checklist, will help students edit their work.

• Encourage students to present their final stories, complete with photographs and/or illustrations, to the rest of the class. Talk about why it is interesting to think about and write about a story from one's past.

Literacy Center Options

• Students do independent or paired reading of books by William Joyce and Tomie dePaola, or Roald Dahl.

• Have students complete their baby stories.

• Guided Reading Extensions: silent (rereading) time and vocabulary. (See Lessons 9 and 10, pages 182–185, for detailed descriptions.)

- Give a lesson from the district spelling program.

- Have students write a journal entry for the prompt, "Other baby stories I'd like to share."

- Provide other literacy activities required by the district curriculum.

Week 4: Book Club and Literacy Block

Week 4 Planning Guide

Book Club

• *26 Fairmount Avenue* by Tomie dePaola	Three 40–60 minute sessions

Guided Reading and Literacy Centers

• *The Baby Sister* by Tomie dePaola • *The Popcorn Book* by Tomie dePaola • *The Tarantula in My Purse* by Jean Craighead George	Two 40–60 minute sessions

Read Aloud

• *Judy Moody* by Megan McDonald	Daily 20–40 minutes

Shared Reading

• *The World of William Joyce Scrapbook* by William Joyce	Two or three 20-minute sessions

Unit Work

• All About Me Collages • Revisit charts "What is autobiography?" and "What is culture?".	One 10-minute session to introduce; time at home to work, and two 30-minute sessions to share One 10-minute session

Writer's Workshop

• First-name Stories	Three 30-minute sessions; time to share stories

Independent Reading

	Daily 10–20 minutes

Assessment Suggestions

• Collect life history portfolios to evaluate progress in unit work. • Use rubric to monitor students' book clubs.	Ongoing

Book Club

Students will read, respond to, and discuss Tomie dePaola's *26 Fairmount Avenue.* Refer to pages 185–188 for Lessons 11–13.

Guided Reading

Students will meet in small groups at their instructional level to read the following books: *The Baby Sister* and *The Popcorn Book* by Tomie dePaola and *The Tarantula in My Purse* by Jean Craighead George. Each guided reading lesson includes one comprehension and one vocabulary focus. Students reading *The Baby Sister* will focus on the comprehension strategy of making intertextual connections; students reading *The Popcorn Book* will focus on the comprehension strategy of looking for information; and students reading *The Tarantula in My Purse* will focus on the comprehension strategy of author's craft. Vocabulary lessons in each guided reading group will focus on fostering word consciousness by using definitions and context information to learn and understand words. Refer to pages 188–192 for Lessons 14–15.

Read Aloud

Read aloud *Judy Moody* by Megan McDonald. In this book, the main character is asked to create a Me Collage for school. Tell students that this week they will create a similar collage.

Shared Reading

Have students continue to read and discuss *The World of William Joyce Scrapbook* twenty minutes a day for two or three days.

Unit Work

- Talk to students about how making a collage is another way of expressing ideas about themselves. In a collage, they can convey ideas about themselves in a very creative, even three-dimensional manner. Ask students what other means they have used to express their ideas, e.g. writing, drawing. You may want to chart students' responses about the different ways to represent stories of self.

- Tell students that using a questioning strategy can help them create their All About Me collages. They can ask themselves what they want to know when they meet someone for the first time. They can use their collages to try to answer questions that people might have about them.

- Ask students to create an All About Me collage similar to the one in *Judy Moody.* Encourage students to fill their collages with pictures from magazines that reflect their likes and dislikes. Have them select photographs and other images that signify something about their lives and personal histories.

Review the meaning of *heritage* and discuss the term *ancestors*. Talk about how the collage represents students' lives and what effect ancestors have on people living today.

- Invite students to share their collages with the class. Connect the students' collages back to your read aloud of *Judy Moody*. Discuss how each student's collage represents that student. This would be a good time to revisit the unit theme questions and add to the class chart about autobiography. Discuss how students' responses to the questions have changed.

Writer's Workshop

- Send letters home with students asking them to learn the stories of how they got their names. Encourage students to discuss the stories with their family and then put the stories down on paper. Give students time throughout the week to revise their stories. Think Sheet 3, Writing Process Checklist, can help students with their editing.

- If you have time during the week, read *The Name Jar* by Yangsook Choi. It ties in well with students' stories. Unhei has just moved from Korea to America and is concerned about how her classmates will react to her name. She decides to tell her classmates that she will choose a name at the end of a week. Her classmates decide to help her choose by placing names in a jar. In the end, Unhei chooses her own name.

- Encourage students to read their final stories to the class. Discuss how these stories are expressions of stories of self. Reflect on how our names show how different people help us become who we are.

Literacy Center Options

- Students do independent or paired reading of William Joyce's books, Tomie dePaola's books, Roald Dahl's books, and/or Megan McDonald's books.

- Have students complete their first-name stories.

- Guided Reading Extensions: silent (rereading) time and vocabulary. (See Lessons 14 and 15, pages 188–192, for detailed descriptions.)

- Distribute a lesson from the district spelling program.

- Have students write a journal entry for the prompt, "What are other name stories I know?"

- Provide other literacy activities required by the district curriculum.

Week 5: Book Club and Literacy Block

Week 5 Planning Guide

Book Club

• *The Canada Geese Quilt* by Natalie Kinsey-Warnock	Three 40–60 minute sessions

Guided Reading and Literacy Centers

• *When I Was Young in the Mountains* by Cynthia Rylant • *Family Pictures* by Carmen Lomas Garza • *The Tarantula in My Purse* by Jean Craighead George	Two 40–60 minute sessions

Read Aloud

• *Judy Moody* by Megan McDonald, Roald Dahl's books	Daily 20–40 minutes

Shared Reading

• *Glorious Angels, Angel to Angel,* and *Brown Angels* by Walter Dean Myers	Two or three 20-minute sessions

Unit Work

• Scrapbook Activity • Revisit charts "What is autobiography?" and "What is culture?".	Two 20-minute sessions One 10-minute session

Writer's Workshop

• Mystery-person Writing Activity	Three 40-minute sessions

Independent Reading

	Daily 10–20 minutes

Assessment Strategies

• Observe students' understanding of the unit themes. • Evaluate students' ability to apply comprehension and vocabulary strategies.	Ongoing

Book Club

Students will read, respond to, and discuss *The Canada Geese Quilt* by Natalie Kinsey-Warnock. Refer to pages 193–196 for Lessons 16–18.

Guided Reading

Students will meet in small groups at their instructional level to read the following books: *When I Was Young in the Mountains* by Cynthia Rylant,

Family Pictures by Carmen Lomas Garza, and *The Tarantula in My Purse* by Jean Craighead George. Each guided reading lesson includes one comprehension and one vocabulary focus. Students reading *When I Was Young in the Mountains* will focus on the comprehension strategy of summarizing; students reading *Family Pictures* will focus on using text and illustration to understand the story and author's craft; and students reading *The Tarantula in My Purse* will focus on finding important details. Vocabulary lessons in each guided reading group will focus on fostering word consciousness by promoting word play to learn new words. Refer to pages 197–200 for Lessons 19–20.

Read Aloud

- Finish reading aloud *Judy Moody* by Megan McDonald.

- Spend more time reading aloud from the Dahl books or read aloud from *Flora and Tiger: 19 Very Short Stories from My Life* by Eric Carle.

Shared Reading

Have students read *Glorious Angels, Angel to Angel,* and *Brown Angels*—all by Walter Dean Myers—for 15–20 minutes a day for two to three days.

Unit Work

- Introduce a scrapbook activity. Point out the connection to Stories of Self by discussing how a scrapbook is an expression of self over time. Compare a scrapbook to a collage. A collage shows something about a person at a specific point in time, while a scrapbook can be completed over a longer period of time. Bring in your own scrapbook if you have one and/or refer back to William Joyce's scrapbook for additional ideas.

- Tell students that they will help create a class scrapbook. Discuss what kinds of items to include. You will want to provide a three-ring binder or other means to hold the scrapbook. Encourage students to think about how their school and classroom affects them as people as they put together contributions for the scrapbook.

Writer's Workshop

- Collect childhood photographs from someone in the building, such as a teacher, a librarian, or the principal. To the students, this will be a mystery person—don't tell them that the person in the pictures is someone they know. Divide the class into groups of four students. Give a different photograph to each group of students. You might want to scan or make photocopies of the photos so you do not have to worry about losing or damaging the originals.

- Have each group write a story about a picture. After they've finished, invite each mystery person into the room to reveal his or her identity. Students can share their thoughts and stories about the photographs. Then each mystery person can share the real story(ies) behind each photograph.

Literacy Center Options

- Students do independent or paired reading of all the books used in the unit.

- Have students complete the mystery-person writing activity.

- Guided Reading Extensions: silent (rereading) time and vocabulary. (See Lessons 19 and 20, pages 197–200, for detailed descriptions.)

- Complete a lesson from the district spelling curriculum.

- Have students write a journal entry to the prompt, "My storied life."

- Present other literacy activities required by the district curriculum.

Week 6: Wrap-Up Options

NOTE: Week 6 of the Stories of Self unit is a period of time that you can use to provide closure. You may want to begin your closure activities earlier in the unit or you may extend the unit into only part of Week 6. Kathy Highfield preferred to spend Week 6 with theme-related discussions, activities, assessments, and reviews.

- **Book Club** Conduct a final book club/fishbowl session. Have students reread portions of *The Canada Geese Quilt* and write a paragraph about how the book supports the unit themes. You can give them a prompt such as: How is this a story an expression of self? What does this book show about families? If there is time, have several of the book club groups discuss their paragraphs in fishbowls. Collect students' paragraphs to use as a measure of their progress in writing and thinking about the themes.

- **Guided Reading** As needed, continue with the Week 5 guided reading activities. Set aside time for more guided reading with *When I Was Young in the Mountains, Family Pictures,* and *The Tarantula in My Purse.*

NOTE: At this point, students reading The Tarantula in My Purse *will have read twelve of the twenty-one chapters. When Kathy Highfield taught this unit, she continued to use the book with her above-grade-level guided reading group for several weeks after the Stories of Self unit ended. The* Tarantula in My Purse *lends itself equally well to the themes in the Stories of Family unit that was next in the Our Storied Lives yearlong theme.*

- **Strategy Review** As appropriate, review comprehension and vocabulary strategies (as a whole class or in guided reading groups). Look back at students' center work and/or your informal assessments to decide if students need additional instruction in any areas.

- **Unit Work** Give students time to wrap up unit projects that they began during each week of the unit, including the time line and artifact activities. Evaluate how well each student seems to have grasped the concepts of the unit. You may find Evaluation Sheet 2, Artifact Activity, helpful.

- **Theme Thoughts** Revisit the theme questions introduced at the beginning of the unit: How is my life like a story? What do I learn from studying my own life and the lives of my classmates? What is autobiography? What is culture? Have students focus on one of the questions and use it as a writing prompt to which they can respond over the course of 2–3 days.

  Ask students what they have learned from the reading and discussions during the unit. Revisit the charts that the class created throughout the unit. Discuss how students' ideas about the theme questions have changed over the course of the unit.

- **Assessment** Throughout the unit, you have assessed your students' progress with informal assessments, checklists, writing assignments, unit work, and reviews of center activities. The materials in your students' life history portfolios are an excellent source of information about your students' progress. Review your "I Can" statements and use the data that you have collected throughout the unit to evaluate student progress. You may want to have students complete Evaluation Sheet 1, "I Can" Self-Evaluation to inform your assessments. For additional assessment options refer to the evaluation sheets following page 315.

Lesson 1

Language Conventions:
Introduction to Book Club

Objectives:
- Introduce students to the language and procedures of Book Club.
- Introduce students to *Roxaboxen.*
- Ask students to make predictions.

Vocabulary:
ford
greased
ocotillo
special

Assigned Reading:
(Since the book has no page numbers, we have used phrases from the book to indicate daily reading.)

From the beginning of the book to the end of the page that starts "When Marian dug up a tin box . . ."

Writing Prompts:
- Roxaboxen is . . .
- What and where is Roxaboxen?
- How do you pretend?

NOTES:
- Reproducible think sheets and evaluation sheets, referred to throughout this unit, are provided in the back of the book following page 295. They can help students respond to their reading and they provide assessment options.
- All writing prompts for the Book Club lesson plans in this unit appear on Think Sheet 1. Pass out copies of this sheet so that students can refer to it as they complete each reading assignment.

- **Opening Community Share** Open this lesson by reminding students about activities they completed during the first week related to the theme Stories of Self. Tell students that throughout this unit they will be learning more about themselves and others. If this is your students' first experience with Book Club, introduce them to the program's structure and special language. Explain that during this week of the unit they will read a book by Alice McLerran called *Roxaboxen.* In coming weeks they will read *26 Fairmount Avenue* by Tomie dePaola and *The Canada Geese Quilt* by Natalie Kinsey-Warnock. Depending on your students' reading levels, you may choose to read one or more of the books aloud.

Explain that each day they will read. Sometimes they will listen as you read. They will think about the reading and write in their logs. Then they will meet in book clubs to discuss their ideas with other students. Sometimes they will gather in a fishbowl and watch one group of students hold a book club. They will also have the opportunity to exchange ideas with the entire class in community share.

- **Reading** To help students get into the book, preview the cover, tell a bit of the story, and examine the illustrations as a class. Show students how much you expect them to read. Use what you know about your students to place them in reading situations. Some students will be able to read the book independently, others may do better if they are paired with another student, or have the book read to them.

Before students write in their logs, talk about any vocabulary they found difficult. *Ford* is one example, but your students may have others to talk about.

- **Writing** Write the prompts for this lesson on the board or on chart paper. Have students copy the prompts into their reading log. You might discuss the prompts with the class before asking students to address them in their logs.

- **Book Club/Fishbowl** Instead of having students conduct their own book clubs today, you might gather a small group of adults to model discussion

VOCABULARY NOTE

Vocabulary can be included in many ways in Book Club *Plus.* In this sample framework, you will see vocabulary introduced in the Book Club context where all students are reading the same book. Examples are also given for vocabulary taught during guided reading and to the whole class in Literacy Block lessons. As you would do in your classroom, Kathy Highfield taught vocabulary and vocabulary strategies mindful of the needs of her students.

techniques in a fishbowl setting. (For more information on fishbowls, see Chapter 7, pages 115–117.) Your students will benefit from observing more experienced readers discussing a book. If you are unable to gather a group of adults, sit with a small group of your students to conduct the fishbowl discussion.

The goal of fishbowl is to show your students what a thoughtful conversation about text looks like. It's important for them to see how readers use text, prior knowledge, and personal experience to make connections. It's also important for them to know that in a book group, everyone gets an opportunity to share ideas. The students who are observing the fishbowl might be invited to participate in the discussion by sitting in a "visitor chair" within the group. You may want to distribute Evaluation Sheet 3, Learning From the Fishbowl, to help students evaluate fishbowls.

ASSESSMENT TIP

Take a moment to help students make the connection between working in the fishbowl setting and the "I Can" statements that you have for discussion. Review the "I Can" statements and how you will be observing students' fishbowl discussions.

- **Closing Community Share** First, invite students to share their responses to the book. Ask them what they think will happen next in the book. Encourage them to make predictions. Show them that they can look back at what they have read to get ideas about what might happen next. Next, ask students what they thought about the fishbowl discussion. What might be interesting about talking about books in small groups?

Lesson 2

Response to Literature: The Tripod Log Format

Objectives:
- Have students think about how the author helps the reader learn about characters in the book.
- Link students' reading to the theme.
- Introduce tripod reading log page. (See Think Sheet 2.)

Vocabulary:
plain
desert glass
amber
amethyst
bridle
raid

- **Opening Community Share** Ask students to think about the ways authors show readers what the characters in a book are like. Lead them to understand that authors reveal characters by describing their thoughts, actions, and words. Ask students to talk about how what they have read in *Roxaboxen* connects to the theme of the unit. How does *Roxaboxen* represent a story of self? For example, the reader knows the character names and the pictures show what the characters look like. Some students may mention that Marian is creative or a leader of the group because she discovered Roxaboxen.

- **Reading** After students read, talk about vocabulary that they found difficult. Some words are listed to the left. Discuss the words and determine their meanings, using context clues or a dictionary. You may want to add

Assigned Reading:
From "A town of Roxaboxen began to grow, . . ." to "Each year when the cactus bloomed, they decorated the grave. . . ."

Writing Prompts:
- Why do you think the author wrote about Roxaboxen?
- If you were a character in *Roxaboxen,* who would you be and what would you do?
- Who built Roxaboxen?
- Draw a picture of the house you would build in Roxaboxen.

some of the words to a class word wall. These vocabulary lists contain words that are challenging and/or important to students' understanding of the book. Encourage students to keep a list of words as they read. Have them include words that they find hard, interesting, or funny.

- **Writing** Before students write, encourage them to think about how they want to respond to their reading. Review the writing prompts and remind students to think about what they have learned about the characters in the story. Explain that there are many ways to respond to a piece of writing. Hand out Think Sheet 2 and read aloud the information.

 **LOG RESPONSES**

As students become more comfortable with the Book Club format, they will certainly have ideas and questions that go beyond the writing prompt suggestions given. You may want to consider giving students "free choice" as a log option. Think Sheets 2 and 5 give students a variety of suggestions for response. Encourage students to think about and respond to their reading creatively. For example, the tripod on Think Sheet 2 helps students strengthen their comprehension of the text, examine the author's craft, and connect to the book on a personal level. Encourage students to try responding from all three angles.

Discuss how parts of the tripod focus on students' understanding of the story: on a personal and creative response, or connecting the book to their lives; and on critical response, or analyzing the text and the author's craft. Show students how to draw their own tripod on a blank sheet of paper. Tell students that they can always look at Think Sheet 5 for ideas on what to write in their logs. It might help to post a copy of this think sheet in a prominent location in your classroom.

- **Book Club/Fishbowl** Have students move into their book clubs (or gather for fishbowl). During students' discussions, walk from group to group, helping students become familiar with the format. In the beginning, you'll want to visit each group daily to facilitate their conversations. You will need to model how to refer to a log for discussion ideas. Tell students that reading from their logs is not the same as holding a conversation. Encourage them to listen carefully to what others say and to respond thoughtfully. Remind them that using their log for discussion ideas can help them meet expectations for good book club discussions.

- **Closing Community Share** Ask each book club group to share something interesting they talked about with the class. Build on the students' comments to discuss the characters. Have they learned anything more about Marian? What about Charles? How does his being the oldest connect to the fact that he uses the biggest stones? Who is Frances? How do the characters behave as a group? Then turn the discussion to using a tripod format to write. Ask students how the tripod format worked for them. (The original research conducted on Book Club indicated that the

Comprehension:
Sequence

Objectives:
- Link students' reading to the theme of Stories of Self.
- Help students use sequencing as a strategy for checking their comprehension.

Vocabulary:
cemetery
grave
jeweled
seasons
remembering

Assigned Reading:
From "Roxaboxen had a cemetery, . . ." to the end of the book, not including the last page.

Writing Prompts:
- Roxaboxen is . . .
- How does this book make you feel?
- How is *Roxaboxen* like an autobiography?
- Write the important events of the story in sequence.

- **Opening Community Share** Have students think about their first day of school or another experience they have all shared. Ask the class to help you list three events from the experience. Help students understand the difference between an event and a detail. Then ask the class to arrange the events in the order in which they occurred. Tell students that this is called a sequence of events which shows the order in which events occurred.

  Explain the importance of sequencing. Ask students how they use sequencing. Point out that knowing the sequence of events not only helps them understand a story, but that it also helps them write and tell better stories. This is a good place to mention that when students are writing or telling their own stories of self, they should pay attention to the sequence of events. Remind students that sequence plays a part in how they represent their lives to others.

  Write a list of sequence words on the board: *after, always, as, before, during, earlier, later, next, then, when,* and *while.* You may also want to review the seasons of the year.

- **Reading** Have students look for clues about sequence as they read the last section of the book. If some students encounter difficulty with the text, pair them for shared reading or read the section aloud, pointing out clues to sequence that the author has included. Before students begin writing in their logs, read the last page of the book aloud to the class.

- **Writing** Encourage students to use details from the story to help them respond to the writing prompts. Tell them that they can also create their own response types to the book. Some students might enjoy making a numbered list of events in the book to help them remember the story.

- **Book Club/Fishbowl** Before students join their book clubs, remind them to think about what went well in their last discussion and what their group could do better. You

ASSESSMENT TIP

Carry a clipboard during book club discussions. Write down positive examples of talk that will lend itself to good discussion and share these with the class during closing community share.

may want to review some basic rules for book club discussions, such as being a good listener and not interrupting, letting everyone in the group speak, and not reading directly from a log.

If possible, observe each group. (You may want to make an audiotape of any group that you can't observe.) Assess how students communicate in the groups. Do they rely too heavily on their reading logs? Does everyone get a turn to talk? Join the discussion if you think some modeling might improve the conversation.

- **Closing Community Share** Give students a short time to talk about this Book Club lesson. Did they enjoy writing in their logs and meeting in book clubs? Use the information to adjust the way you conduct the book clubs.

Return briefly to the book's sequence of events. Note that in this section, the author moves from when the characters are children to many years later when they are adults. Ask students if they understand the sequence, even though the author does not provide details about the characters' lives as they grow up. You might point out the following phrases: "Each year," "Sometimes in the winter," "And by." Help students understand that these phrases signal sequence of events and the passage of time.

Discuss the last page of the book and relate the information to the genre of autobiography. Ask students to help you add to the "What is autobiography?" chart using what they learned by reading *Roxaboxen.*

PROJECT OPTION

Have students design their own Roxaboxens. First, each student draws a sketch of Roxaboxen. Then take the class outside to collect small rocks. On desk-sized pieces of cardboard let students build their own Roxaboxens using stones and materials they've brought from home. Students can also write descriptions of their imaginary pretending spaces on 3 x 5 index cards. Display the "Roxaboxens" in the library.

This project was originally used by Pam Griffith with her special-education students who were having trouble with the real and pretend aspects of *Roxaboxen.* However, this is a project that would work well with all students.

Lesson 4 Literacy Block

Objectives:

- **Guided Reading**
  - Students read instructional-level texts.
  - Comprehension Strategy: Students learn/practice stepping into the text and moving through the text.
  - Vocabulary: Foster word consciousness by teaching synonyms and discussing connotations.
- **Literacy Centers**
  Students participate in strategy, skill, and theme-extension activities.

Vocabulary:

When I Was Little:
handful
nursery
cubbies
floaties
torture

Tell Me Again . . . :
snoring
birth mother
adopt
nursery
potential
opera
lullaby

The Tarantula . . . :
contemplate
nurture
entomologist
ingenuity
primordial
maestro
talons

• Guided Reading

Before Reading Discuss that students will be learning a comprehension strategy called stepping into the text. Explain how looking at illustrations, the front and back cover, and reading clues from the overall impression of the book can help them understand the book. Have students follow along in their texts as you model "stepping into the text."

— *When I Was Little* Details to mention include the author and illustrator's name, the watercolor style, and the vibrant palette that the illustrator uses. Point out in particular the information about the author on the inside back cover.

— *Tell Me Again About the Night I Was Born* Discuss the terms *birth mom* and *birth dad*. Point them out in the family tree. If appropriate, have any adopted children in your group talk about adoption.

— *The Tarantula in My Purse* Tell students that they will be reading from a chapter book. Have students make predictions about the content based on your book talk and the title and table of contents of the book. You may find that students reading above grade level have never been explicitly taught how to use comprehension strategies effectively. Strategy instruction is important for this group so that they have the tools they need to be effective problem-solving readers.

During Reading Read the text aloud. Tell students to follow along in their books. Remind students that they stepped into the text and are now beginning to move through the text. As they move through the text, the students' most important job is to make sure the story makes sense to them.

— *When I Was Little* Encourage students to read the text aloud quietly with you, explaining that they should try to keep together. Ask students to listen for interesting words the author uses.

🛡 GUIDED READING NOTE

Throughout the Literacy Block lessons, we have made recommendations for comprehension strategies and vocabulary to be used during guided reading. It is easier to manage guided reading if you begin your unit teaching the same objectives to all groups and move toward individualized objectives once you know your readers better. Therefore, in this lesson and in subsequent Literacy Block lessons, we have provided one set of comprehension strategy instructions (with book-specific notes) for all your guided reading groups. Once you teach some core comprehension strategies to all your groups, then you are ready to use different strategies with the groups. Beginning with Lesson 14 of this unit, we show how teaching individualized objectives looks in the Book Club *Plus* classroom.

—*Tell Me Again About the Night I Was Born* Choral read the text with students following along in their copies. They should say each word as you read together.

—*The Tarantula in My Purse* Send students to read The Genesis and Chapter 1 by themselves. You may opt to read the introduction together. Students can choose to read silently or aloud. Give students sticky notes on which to write interesting words.

ASSESSMENT TIP

Evaluation Sheets 4 and 5, Quick Assessment Checklist, and Checklist for Language Arts Skills can help you keep track of student progress. You can adapt these checklists to match your "I Can" statements and district requirements.

After Reading Discuss the story. Ask students if they have any questions about what is happening in the story. Remind students that they stepped into the text and moved through the text today. Ask students to name some interesting words they read or heard. Discuss the meanings of the words and the author's craft in choosing particular words to create pictures in readers' minds.

—*When I Was Little* Provide examples of words that mean the same thing and talk about how specific words give readers different pictures in their minds, e.g., *handful:* some, a couple—what picture does *handful* give a reader compared to *some* or *a couple*?

—*Tell Me Again About the Night I Was Born* Give examples of words that mean the same thing and talk about the connotations of the words, e.g. *snoring—sleeping, breathing, exhaling, rumbling.*

—*The Tarantula in My Purse* Discuss connotations and give an example from the text, e.g. *contemplate—think, decide, choose, want.*

• **Literacy Centers**

—Choose from the Literacy Center Options for this week on page 160.

—**Guided Reading Extensions** In each Literacy Block lesson, we give additional support for extending the goals of your guided reading groups through center activities. For Lessons 4 and 5, all groups can participate in a similar fostering word consciousness activity. In subsequent weeks, the guided reading extensions will vary.

—**Vocabulary (all groups)** Hand out Think Sheet 6, _____ Map. Tell students to write the word *vocabulary* on the blank line. Instruct students to reread their books or texts twice. Tell them to write five interesting words, one in each circle on Think Sheet 6. If they can't find enough words, have them use some of the words listed in the sidebar of this lesson. Then, for each word, have students write synonyms that the author could have used. Have dictionaries and thesauri available. If students are unfamiliar with these resources, you may need to model how to use them. Think Sheet 6 will also be used in Lesson 5. Some students may need to take the think sheet home as homework.

🔖 **LITERACY CENTER TIP**

Rereading is an integral part of guided reading at the primary grades, particularly in third grade. Tell students that they will be rereading texts on a regular basis. Rereading increases fluency, develops vocabulary, and helps struggling readers meet grade-level expectations.

Lesson 5

Literacy Block

Objectives:

- **Guided Reading**
  - Students read instructional-level texts.
  - Comprehension Strategy: Students learn/practice moving through the text and stepping out of the text.
  - Vocabulary: Students use new vocabulary words in writing.

- **Literacy Centers**
  Students participate in strategy, skill, and theme-extension activities.

Vocabulary:

The Tarantula . . . :
orient
ply
precarious
plaintive
skeptics
exquisite
pablum
obstreperous

• **Guided Reading**

Before Reading Remind all students to bring Think Sheet 6 with them to guided reading. After students have gathered, help them step back into the book and discuss what happened in the story. Remind them that they will continue moving through the book and that they will step out of the book with a writing activity in a literacy center.

— *When I Was Little* Help students remember what they read yesterday and discuss any words that they found interesting.

— *Tell Me Again About the Night I Was Born* Discuss the narrator of this book. Discuss that the child asks the parents to "tell me again about the night I was born," but that it is the child who tells the story to the parents—in some parts directly to the mother and the father. What words does the author use to convey that the child is telling the story? (e.g. *me, I, you, Daddy*)

— *The Tarantula in My Purse* Discuss the words students found during Lesson 4. Talk about how important it is for authors to choose words that create vivid pictures for their readers.

During Reading With each group, make time to model fluent reading before asking students to read aloud.

— *When I Was Little* and *Tell Me Again About the Night I Was Born* With each group, choral read the book. Take time during the choral reading to listen for fluency and self-correction in each reader. It is not important for students to read every word together since they read at different speeds. However, you will want to keep them at about the same place without turning it into a chanting session. Evaluation Sheet 6, Fluency Checklist, can help you record information about students' fluency.

— *The Tarantula in My Purse* Assign students to read Chapters 2–4 aloud by themselves or with a partner. Take a moment to read the first few pages of Chapter 2 to model fluency. Ask students to pay particular attention to how their reading sounds to them as they read. However, remind students to focus on making sense of the text and then on fluency. Encourage them to note the words that Jean Craighead George uses.

After Reading (**all groups**) With each group, discuss the words students wrote on their think sheets. Explain how students are authors when they write and that they need to choose words that will make the best pictures in the minds of their readers. Tell students that as they step out of their stories, they will be rereading the books twice and that they will be doing a writing activity using words from their think sheets.

- **Literacy Centers**

  —Choose from the Literacy Center Options for this week on page 160.

  —**Guided Reading Extensions** Have students reread *When I Was Little* and *Tell Me Again About the Night I Was Born* two or more times. Have students in all groups write a paragraph using words from their think sheets. The paragraph should relate to the books they are reading or to the theme Stories of Self. Since word choice is the focus of this writing assignment, remind students to choose their words carefully. They should focus on words that will make the best pictures in the minds of their readers. To help you assess students' efforts, ask them to circle the words from their think sheet in their paragraphs and to underline any other special words they use.

TEACHING TIP

During choral reading, remind students not to provide a word for a student struggling with a difficult word. Students need time to apply strategies. It is better to wait at the end of a page for readers to catch up before moving on.

Lesson 6

Response to Literature:
Me & the Book

Objectives:
- Connect to the Stories of Self theme.
- Introduce students to *26 Fairmount Avenue*.
- Have students practice the Me & the Book response type.

Vocabulary:
Wizard of Oz
hurricane
foundation
gust
Mary Poppins

Assigned Reading:
26 Fairmount Avenue:
Chapter 1; pp. 1–8

Writing Prompts:
- Have you every felt like Tomie?
- What is the worst storm you have ever experienced?
- What do you think Tomie's family will find when they go to the new house?

- **Opening Community Share** Remind students that they are learning about themselves and other people through stories of self. Introduce students to *26 Fairmount Avenue.* Encourage them to examine the cover and flip through its pages. Explain that the author writes about a special year in his life—when his family was building a new home.

  Explain that the stories we read often remind us of people, events, and places in own lives. Ask if dePaola's descriptions of his family and the games he plays reminds students of people they know and things they do with their friends. Introduce the response type Me & the Book. (See Think Sheet 5, Things to Do in Your Reading Log.) Tell students that they can make connections to their own lives as they read, and then write about these connections in their reading logs. Explain that this can help them understand characters and events in their reading.

  Model how to write a Me & the Book response by thinking aloud and writing on the board how your own life connects to Roxaboxen. For example, "When I was a little girl, I couldn't wait for the snow to fall. Every year when the snow fell, snowplows would come and scoop the snow into mountains. We would dig tunnels into these mountains and would create a whole world, just like Roxaboxen." Tell students that they will practice connecting their lives to a book using Tomie dePaola's story.

- **Reading** As students read these first pages, have them concentrate on getting to know the author and his family. Ask them to write two or three details that tell them something about the family. Ask students to look for details that remind them of their own family and friends.

- **Writing** Explain that the first two writing prompts will help them to connect parts of the book to their own lives. Students may also want to make other connections.

   **ASSESSMENT TIP**

  Hand out Evaluation Sheets 7 and 8 to have students begin recording their thoughts about their reading logs and book clubs.

- **Book Club/Fishbowl** Have students gather in their book clubs or in a fishbowl to share their ideas about the book so far. Students might mention the details that stood out to them and what they understand about the people in the book.

- **Closing Community Share** Have students share their log responses and their reactions to the Me & the Book response type. Invite students to share the personal connections they made as they read. Make a connection to the artifact activity that students completed in Week 2 of the unit. Ask students to think about what kinds of artifacts dePaola might have collected from his own childhood for an artifact activity.

Lesson 7

Comprehension: Compare and Contrast

Objectives:
- Connect to the Stories of Self theme.
- Have students compare and contrast to improve their understanding of what they read and hear.

Vocabulary:
cellar
pestered

Assigned Reading:
26 Fairmount Avenue:
Chapter 2; pp. 9–15

Writing Prompts:
- Compare and contrast Tomie's relationship with his grandparents to your relationship with your grandparents.
- Describe your grandparents and great-grandparents.

- **Opening Community Share** Connect students to the theme of Stories of Self. Revisit the theme questions and ask students if they have any new observations to add to the class charts. Explain to students that to compare is to look at the similarities in two or more things, and that to contrast is to look at the differences. Tell students that comparing and contrasting helps readers make sense of characters and situations in stories as they read. Model how to compare and contrast on an overhead projector. Think aloud about two familiar characters such as Miriam in *Roxaboxen* and Roald Dahl as a boy. Through your modeling, demonstrate to students higher levels of thinking about characters.

  Explain that students will be using a Venn diagram to compare and contrast two people or things in their reading. Show students how to draw a Venn diagram on a sheet of paper. Demonstrate how the Venn diagram works using an example from the book or a simple everyday example, such as the similarities and differences in two animals.

- **Reading** Before students begin, point out the writing prompt that asks students to compare and contrast Tomie's grandparents to their own grandparents. Encourage students to note details about Tomie's grandparents as they read.

- **Writing** Encourage students to use details from the story to help them respond to the writing prompts. Students can respond in their own way to the reading, but encourage everyone respond to the compare and contrast prompt. Students can use the Venn diagram to organize their thoughts.

- **Book Club/Fishbowl** Let students discuss the writing prompts, their Venn diagrams, and any other issues that came up as they read. Continue to observe each book club group (or fishbowl), offering assistance and modeling good discussion skills whenever necessary.

 ASSESSMENT TIP

Collect students' logs. Use the rubric on page 95 to determine if they are working on, meeting, or exceeding expectations for writing, and making theme connections defined by your "I Can" statements.

- **Closing Community Share** Invite students to share their responses to the writing prompt. Ask them ways in which comparison and contrast could be a useful skill. Help students make intertextual connections by asking them to compare and contrast some of dePaola's adventures with some of Dahl's adventures in *Boy.* How are these two young boys and their lives similar, and how are they different?

Lesson 8

Comprehension:
Character Map

Objectives:
- Connect to the Stories of Self theme.
- Ask students to create a character map.
- Have students compare and contrast.

Vocabulary:
animated
bother
true story

Assigned Reading:
26 Fairmount Avenue:
Chapter 3; pp. 16–23

Writing Prompts:
- Make a character map of Tomie.
- List the characters in the book.
- Have you every experienced what Tomie did at the theater? How did it make you feel? Compare your experience with his.

- **Opening Community Share** Talk about the ways authors help readers understand characters in their books. Discuss how authors reveal aspects of themselves—their stories of self—through their characters. Ask students to explain how they get to know people in their own lives. Students might say they watch the way people treat others, listen to the things people say, and observe their actions. Explain that readers must do the same things to figure out characters. Spend time talking about what they know already about Tomie and other characters in *26 Fairmount Avenue.*

- **Reading** Before students begin reading, hand out Think Sheet 6, _____ Map. Instruct students to write the title word *Character* on the blank line. Tell students that this character map will help them respond to one of the writing prompts. It provides space for them to record details about the character Tomie as they read.

- **Writing** You might want to provide instruction for using the character map. Tell students to write the name *Tomie* in the center circle and then surround his name with details and quotations that help them understand Tomie. You might ask all students to respond to the character map prompt, along with another prompt of their own choosing. Model a character map on the board using a character from a familiar book, such as a book by William Joyce or a portion of a Roald Dahl selection.

TEACHING OPTION

Read aloud passages from Gary Paulsen's *My Life in Dog Years,* which is another twist on the autobiography genre. While dePaola uses the story of building a house as a way to share the details of his life, Paulsen shares details of his life by talking about the many dogs he has owned.

- **Book Club/Fishbowl** Encourage students to compare and contrast their character maps in their book club groups. They can also share their responses to the other prompts.

- **Closing Community Share** Continue the discussion of the writing prompts. What details about Tomie did most students record in their character maps? Encourage students to recall the Snapshot of Me activity and work with them to create a snapshot of Tomie and other characters in the book. Take a moment to return to the "What is autobiography?" chart. Have students' ideas about autobiography changed?

Lesson 9

Literacy Block

Objectives:

- **Guided Reading**
  – Students read instructional-level texts.
  – Comprehension Strategy: Questioning
  – Vocabulary: Students find words and phrases they value.

- **Literacy Centers**
  Students participate in strategy, skill, and theme-extension activities.

Vocabulary:

George Shrinks:
forget
fresh

Dinosaur Bob:
bodyguard
trumpet
globe
nibble

The Tarantula . . . :
hemlocks
winterized
attributes
vindictiveness
asunder

- **Guided Reading**

George Shrinks and *Dinosaur Bob*

—**Before Reading** Help students in each group use clues in the title and on the front and back covers to infer the content of the book. Next, go through the book examining the pictures. Have students do the majority of the talking. Model for students how to ask questions about pictures in the book. Encourage students to ask about pictures as the book progresses. Tell students to pay attention to interesting word phrases that William Joyce uses. These could be word phrases that students have never heard or they could be word phrases that students know well.

—**During Reading** Read the book once as a group. You may choose to stop and talk with students about how some of their questions are being answered and how new questions arise as a book is read. Encourage students to look for word phrases that they value or ones they think William Joyce values. Students can write these on sticky notes or on a piece of paper.

—**After Reading** Instruct students to look for answers to questions raised during the picture walk. Give students in each group time to discuss the reasons why they find certain words and phrases interesting.

The Tarantula in My Purse

—**Before Reading** Review Chapters 2–4 and introduce questioning as a comprehension strategy. Tell students that good readers ask questions as they read. Read a page from last week's reading and model how to ask questions to improve comprehension of the book. Tell students that

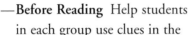

GUIDED READING NOTE

In Lesson 9, the procedures for *George Shrinks* and *Dinosaur Bob* are combined, while the procedures for *The Tarantula in My Purse* are presented separately.

there are some questions that we ask that the author doesn't answer and some questions that will be answered later in the book. Also tell students that good readers adjust their questions to use information from the book. Explain to students that as they read Chapter 5, they should be paying attention to word phrases they value. For example, you can tell them that the phrase *on time* is one that you value.

—**During Reading** Students will read Chapter 5 independently. Give students some sticky notes. Ask them to pay special attention to questions they are asking and to record them on sticky notes. If they don't notice themselves asking questions, tell them to focus on stopping at the end of each page and asking themselves three questions before they go on. Encourage students to look for word phrases they value or word phrases they think the author values.

 TEACHING OPTION

To challenge students to use word phrases and to notice word phrases being used, incorporate word sightings into your classroom. For word sightings, students observe someone else using a new vocabulary word or phrase and they report it to the class. Small slips of paper can be tacked on to charts to report a word or phrase "sighting."

—**After Reading** Have students organize the questions and word phrases they recorded on sticky notes. If students' questions have been answered, they should cross them off. Questions that haven't been answered can be discussed with the group in the next lesson. Encourage students to write word phrases they found interesting on sticky notes.

- **Literacy Centers**

—Choose from the Literacy Center Options for this week on page 162.

—**Guided Reading Extensions** Have students reading *George Shrinks* and *Dinosaur Bob* reread the books twice on their own or with a partner. Have all students work in their groups to make a list of questions on chart paper to discuss during Lesson 10. An important part of the activity is to have students discuss the questions as they write them. This is an opportunity for students to help each other answer questions about their reading. Only questions that can't be answered should be written on the chart paper. Students should also write any word phrases they value or they think the author values on a separate chart.

Lesson 10

Literacy Block

Objectives:

• Guided Reading
– Students continue to read instructional-level texts.
– Comprehension Strategy: Questioning
– Vocabulary: Students find words and phrases they value.

• Literacy Centers
Students participate in strategy, skill, and theme-extension activities.

Vocabulary:

The Tarantula . . . :
gluttonous
aggressive
alit
menagerie
invertebrate
pyramid

• Guided Reading

George Shrinks, Dinosaur Bob, and *The Tarantula in My Purse*

—**Before Reading** In each group, discuss the questions that students have. Reiterate that some questions are answered in a book and some are not. Ask students why they think this happens. Encourage students to cite examples of questions answered and not answered in their books. Then ask students if there were any questions that they needed to adjust as they read new information in the story. Spend some time answering questions and making sense of the text using a combination of illustrations and text.

—**During Reading** Students reading *George Shrinks* and *Dinosaur Bob* should reread their books. Students should read for fluency and comprehension. Students reading *The Tarantula in My Purse* should read Chapters 6–7. Remind all students to look for word phrases they value.

—**After Reading** Return to the charts that each group created in Lesson 9 of word phrases that they value and that they think the author values. Have students suggest word phrases for you to write on the charts that are used by parents, family members, and other people in their school community. Hang the charts in an accessible area in your classroom. Talk about why the word phrases are used and why they are valued. Help students understand that a word phrase can be valuable because of the meaning it helps an author convey to readers. Tell students that they might want to collect interesting word phrases to use in their writing. This activity will improve students' word consciousness and their vocabularies. As an extension of this activity, ask students to collect additional word phrases to write on stickies and put on the charts.

• Literacy Centers

—Choose from the Literacy Center Options for this week on page 162.

—**Guided Reading Extensions** Challenge the students in each group to choose three word phrases from their charts to incorporate into a

> **TEACHING TIP**
>
> The charts that each group has created in Lesson 9 can be used to help students make inter-textual connections between the books and to make further connections to the theme. With the whole class, examine the charts, noting any repetitions of word phrases. Discuss what kinds of phrases are valuable to writers. Ask students to talk about how the word phrases are used in their texts and how the phrases help the author tell his or her story of self.

sentence. Extend the activity by asking students to work with partners to incorporate additional word phrases into a conversation. You may want to have students write some of their dialogue on sheets of paper to share with other small groups.

Lesson 11 Literary Elements: Author's Craft

Objectives:
- Connect to the Stories of Self theme.
- Help students understand the meaning of author's craft.
- Guide students in identifying the distinct characteristics of one author's work.

Vocabulary:
builder
beret
plasterers

Assigned Reading:
26 Fairmount Avenue:
Chapter 4; pp. 24–31

Writing Prompts:
- How is the time of Tomie's childhood different from our present time?
- What style of writing and art does Tomie dePaola use in his story?

- **Opening Community Share** Discuss how all the stories students are reading are stories of self. Tell students that today they will focus on learning about an author's craft. Tell them that an author's craft is his or her special way of writing. Explain that an author often has a particular way of writing about people or places. A good way to help students clearly understand author's craft is to ask them how they would know a book or story is written by a particular author if they only focused on the author's words and couldn't read the entire book.

Ask students to think about Tomie dePaola's style, based on their reading of *26 Fairmount Avenue*. Read aloud pages 3 and 4 from *26 Fairmount Avenue* as students follow along in their books.

Ask students to look for similarities in the way that Tomie dePaola talks about how frightening it was to drive homeward through the hurricane and how the author describes Mrs. Crane. Students might notice the use of parentheses in each passage, in which dePaola is trying to squeeze in lots of information. Suggest that the author is having a conversation with the reader. Students might also say that he describes his family and friends with great detail—that people are definitely the focus.

- **Reading** As students read, encourage them to look for more examples of dePaola's special style. They can record page numbers so that they can refer to specific passages or illustrations in later discussions. Remind students to think about how Tomie dePaola's way of writing and describing his life can help them as they write their own stories of self.

◗ TEACHING OPTION

To extend students' study of author's craft, have them look at a few Tomie dePaola books next to one another. For example, read aloud the picture books *Tom* and *What a Year!* and ask students to identify examples of the author's craft.

Students can also discuss author's craft in the books by William Joyce, Roald Dahl, and Walter Dean Myers that they read throughout this unit.

- **Writing** Students should try to respond to both writing prompts and be prepared to share their responses in their book clubs and in closing community share.

- **Book Club/Fishbowl** Students might enjoy discussing the first writing prompt—comparing dePaola's era with their own. Students should think of specific ways in which their lives are different. They can also try to guess what in their lives might seem odd or different to children living years in the future.

- **Closing Community Share** Give students time to talk about the issues that were raised in this book club. Did they enjoy writing in their logs and meeting in book clubs or fishbowls? Use the information to make adjustments in the way you are conducting the Book Club lessons.

Lesson 12

Comprehension:
Questioning

Objectives:
- Connect to the Stories of Self theme.
- Guide students in creating good questions for book club discussions.

Vocabulary:
reserved
superintendent
faucet
contraption

Assigned Reading:
26 Fairmount Avenue:
Chapters 5–6; pp. 32–41

Writing Prompts:
- What do you remember about kindergarten?
- Write some good questions about the book that you can discuss in your book club.

▶ **Sample chart generated by Kathy Highfield's third-grade class**

- **Opening Community Share** Remind students that they are involved in learning about the theme Stories of Self. Ask students to tell you how what they are reading in Book Club and Literacy Block ties into the theme. Remind students that good readers often ask questions as they read. Readers ask *Who?, What?, When?, Where?,* and *Why?* in order to find meaning in what they read, to stimulate conversations about a particular book, and to make ties to a theme. Make a class chart that helps guide students in asking questions. The chart should list qualities of questions that make them helpful in book club as shown in the sample chart below. Work with students to generate some questions about the chapters they have already read.

> **Good Questions**
> Can't be answered with a yes or no
> Can't be answered with one word
> Generate discussion
> Make group members think
> Help keep the group on task

- **Reading** Give students time to read. Encourage them to think about questions that come up as they read. For example, they might wonder why a character might be behaving in a certain way, what they would feel if they were in a similar situation, and where the action of the story might be going.

- **Writing** Give students plenty of time to write good questions that will promote discussion in their book clubs. Encourage each student to write at least two questions.

- **Book Club/Fishbowl** Students can ask each other the questions they generated. If time allows, students might share with each other their first memories of school.

- **Closing Community Share** Continue the discussion of the writing prompts. Ask students why they think Tomie "never really liked kindergarten." Ask them to think about a new experience that was difficult. Do they think the author did a good job of showing how he felt at the time?

  Discuss the questions that came up in students' book clubs. Ask students if they practiced good questioning behavior. Encourage them to share examples of questions that generated discussion in their book clubs.

Lesson 13

Response to Literature:
Characterization, Critique

Objectives:
- Revisit the Stories of Self theme.
- Have students revisit and revise their character maps.
- Encourage students to identify their favorite parts of the book and practice explaining their reasoning for their choices.

Vocabulary:
disappointed
rescue
authentic
tuxedo
makeshift

- **Opening Community Share** Begin by making the connection to the theme. How does this book reflect a story of self? Ask students what they have learned about themselves in reading about Tomie. Then have students turn back in their reading logs to the character map that was completed in Lesson 8. Do they have any new information to add? Do they feel they know Tomie any better after having read about more of his experiences?

  Discuss with students what it means to critique a book or a story or a chapter. Explain that to critique is to figure out what is good and what is not as good in a work. Point out that a good critique always uses concrete examples to back up an opinion. That makes the opinion more believable. Ask volunteers to give a brief critique of the book so far.

- **Reading** Remind students that they are nearing the end of the book. Before reading, ask them to think about what they have enjoyed most about the book, and what they wish were different. Students might want

Assigned Reading:
26 Fairmount Avenue:
Chapters 7–9; pp. 42–57

Writing Prompts:
- Change your character map to make it show what you now know about Tomie.
- How are you and Tomie alike? How are you different?
- What was your favorite part of the book? Why?

to pay special attention to the book's ending. Are they satisfied with how the author ended his work?

- **Writing** Students can respond to as many prompts as they want, but encourage them to focus on their character maps and on their favorite parts of the book.

- **Book Club/Fishbowl** Allow extra time for book clubs so that students can discuss the book's ending and reach some kind of closure. Encourage them to share their critiques and to feel comfortable sharing their opinions. Not everyone will have the same view of a character or situation, and that is what makes book discussions interesting.

- **Closing Community Share** Spend time talking about the end of the book. Invite students to share their reading log responses. You might want to review some of the lesson topics that were taught as the students read, such as author's craft, compare and contrast, and questioning.

ASSESSMENT TIP

Evaluation Sheet 9, Book Club Observation Sheet, can help you determine if students are working on, meeting, or exceeding expectations for book club discussions. Closing community share is a good time to bring up and discuss ways to make book club discussions better.

Lesson 14

Literacy Block

Objectives:

- **Guided Reading**

  – Students read instructional-level texts.

  – Comprehension Strategies:
  The Baby Sister—Intertextual connections
  The Popcorn Book—Looking for information
  The Tarantula . . .—Author's craft and visualizing a story

  – Vocabulary: Foster word consciousness by learning about words through definitional and contextual information

- **Guided Reading**

  The Baby Sister

  —**Before Reading** Talk about baby siblings before reading the book. Connect this book to *26 Fairmount Avenue.* Ask students how this book reminds them of *26 Fairmount Avenue.* Explain to students that making connections among the books they are reading can help them become better readers. Tell them that they will be working to make these connections, called intertextual connections.

  —**During Reading** Choral read the book together. Pay special attention to each reader. Listen for fluency, self-correction, and application of reading comprehension strategies. Feel free to stop at several places in the book to ask students if they can make connections between *The Baby Sister* and *26 Fairmount Avenue.*

 GUIDED READING NOTE

After students have been taught a core set of comprehension strategies, the objectives of each group can be tailored to each group's needs. In Lessons 14 and 15, each guided reading group is focused on a different comprehension strategy that is specific to the text they are reading and to the students' comprehension needs.

- **Literacy Centers**
  Students participate in strategy, skill, and theme-extension activities.

Vocabulary:

The Baby Sister:
hospital
chicken pox
schoolyard
bundle
armchair

The Popcorn Book:
refrigerator
kernels
archeologists
colonists
legend

The Tarantula . . . :
deluge
ratcheting
comeuppance
symbiotic

—**After Reading** Students should reread the book twice alone, focusing on comprehending the book and on the intertextual connections they are making.

The Popcorn Book

—**Before Reading** Discuss two ways texts are grouped: informational (nonfiction) and stories (fiction). Discuss the strategies students use to read stories. Then explain that when they read informational texts, they use a different set of strategies. Tell students their goal for reading *The Popcorn Book* is to learn new information.

—**During Reading** Have students read the first half of the book alone twice. Give each student three to five sticky notes. Direct them to place a sticky note on the page where they find information that they have learned from this portion of the book.

—**After Reading** Discuss the information that students found in their books. The group will discover that some students knew more or different facts about popcorn. This is an important point—we all bring different knowledge to a book, but we can all learn something new as we read.

The Tarantula in My Purse

—**Before Reading** Remind students about author's craft. Discuss how students can know that a book is written by a particular author. For example, how could they identify a story or book by Jean Craighead George? As students discuss the question, assess their ability to give answers consistent with George's writings and style.

—**During Reading** Have students read Chapter 8. Tell them to focus on ways that the author makes them really experience the story. Give students two sticky notes each and have them put the notes in the text where they think George did a good job of showing the author's craft.

—**After Reading** Have students come back to the group to share their sticky notes. Discuss how authors show themselves (note the Stories of Self connection) through their stories and talk about how students can also show themselves when they write.

- **Literacy Centers**

   —Choose from the Literacy Center Options for this week on page 165.

   —**Guided Reading Extensions:**

   > *The Baby Sister* During the rereading time, students should make a list of three new connections they found between this book and *26 Fairmount Avenue* or other Tomie dePaola books.

   > *The Popcorn Book* Ask students to choose three things that they learned from this book. Have students draw a picture and write a sentence about their information to share with the class.

   > *The Tarantula in My Purse* Encourage students to identify two or three author crafts they would like to add to their own writing. Have students identify and practice these writing crafts in a paragraph or short story.

   —**Vocabulary (all groups)** Give students lists of vocabulary words chosen for these books. Explain to the class (in either the guided reading group or whole class setting) that there are many ways to determine the meanings of new words. One way is to use context clues, or use information from the story, illustrations, and word clues to decide on word mean-

VOCABULARY NOTE

This activity has students learning vocabulary from their guided reading books, but in the context of a whole class lesson. Students learn how to use contextual and definitional clues to determine the meaning of words. Once introduced, this lesson can be completed in a literacy center or as a whole class activity of about 30 minutes.

ing. Another way is to use definitional clues. This means looking at prefixes, suffixes, and root words to help determine meaning. It can also mean looking the word up in a dictionary if other clues are not enough to understand the word.

Distribute Think Sheet 7. (You may want to provide each student with several copies of the think sheet if the word lists are extensive.) Discuss it with students and provide modeling and scaffolding for students to see how contextual and definitional clues can help them figure out the meaning of an unknown word, while the dictionary can help when they are still unable to decipher a word's meaning.

Have students identify where each word on their lists appears in each book. They will copy the word and the sentence onto the think sheet. Next, students reread the paragraph where each word appears and write what they think the word means on the think sheet using contextual and definitional clues. Students then look up each word in a dictionary and copy the definition onto the think sheet.

Lesson 15

Literacy Block

• **Guided Reading**

The Baby Sister

—**Before Reading** Discuss the book and the intertextual connections that students were able to make between it and *26 Fairmount Avenue* or other dePaola books. Ask students to make additional connections to their own lives and to other texts. Encourage them to look for additional connections as they reread the book.

—**During Reading** Have students reread the book independently twice.

—**After Reading** Discuss any new connections students made between the book and other texts.

The Popcorn Book

—**Before Reading** Discuss some of the drawings that students made the day before. Remind students of ways they need to read informational texts. These include noticing pictures and captions, the table of contents, headings, bold words, the index, and other text structures found in informational books. Ask students if they have any questions about the book that they would like the group to answer. Tell students that as they read the second half of the book they should be looking for new information.

—**During Reading** Give students three new sticky notes each to record new information as they read the second half of the story twice.

—**After Reading** Have students gather to discuss their new information. Emphasize that each person brings different background knowledge to a book, but that everyone can learn something from an informational book.

The Tarantula in My Purse

—**Before Reading** Talk to students about visualizing a story while reading. Discuss how through visualizing a reader can hear, see, smell, and feel objects and emotions expressed in a story. Discuss that it is part of an author's craft to help a reader visualize the story.

—**During Reading** Have students read Chapters 9–10. Remind students that they should use visualizing to feel as if they are right there in the book—like watching a movie picture in their minds.

—**After Reading** Ask the group how the visualizing is going. What are they experiencing as they read? Identify what the author is doing as part of her craft to help her readers feel as if they are in the story. What could the author do better? What can they (the students) do as writers to help their readers feel as if they are a part of a story?

• **Literacy Centers**

—Choose from the Literacy Center Options for this week on page 165.

—**Guided Reading Extensions:**

> *The Baby Sister* Have students each choose three favorite connections and represent them on a piece of paper. Tell students to choose a format such as a paragraph, a concept map, or pictures and sentences.

> *The Popcorn Book* Have students each place their sticky notes on a sheet of paper and write a reflection about the book. In this reflection, they should include some of the information they learned, some of the ways reading informational text is different from reading stories, and some strategies they use while reading informational texts.

> *The Tarantula in My Purse* Ask students to each draw a vivid picture to represent a part of this story. They should write sentences or a paragraph on the picture explaining how the author helped them to feel as if they were in the book. Option: Students can pick one specific event that has happened to them and practice writing about that event with enough detail and craft so that readers feel as if they are right there.

—**Vocabulary (all groups)** Students can continue to work with vocabulary using Think Sheet 7, introduced in Lesson 14.

Lesson 16

Response to Literature:
Feelings

Objectives:
- Connect to the Stories of Self theme.
- Introduce students to *The Canada Geese Quilt.*
- Encourage students to think about the feelings of characters.

Vocabulary:
grouse
Cassiopeia
shards
ruefully
protective
design

Assigned Reading:
The Canada Geese Quilt:
Chapters 1–2

Writing Prompts:
- How do you think Ariel feels about the baby, and about the quilt?
- How would you feel if you were Ariel?
- Describe the relationship between Ariel and her grandmother.

- **Opening Community Share** Introduce *The Canada Geese Quilt* to students. Have students examine the front and back covers of the book and make predictions about the book. Remind students as they read to think about how *The Canada Geese Quilt* reflects a story of self and to try to make intertextual connections to other books.

  Then talk to students about understanding feelings in a book. Explain that part of enjoying and understanding a book is being able to connect with its characters. Explain that authors show how their characters are feeling through thoughts, words, and actions.

- **Reading** As students read, encourage them to put themselves in the shoes of Ariel, the main character. Ask them to notice how the author helps them to understand how Ariel is feeling in the first two chapters.

- **Writing** Urge students to respond to all the writing prompts. However, if some students have been in a situation similar to Ariel's and want to write about that, allow them to do so.

- **Book Club/Fishbowl** Before students join their book club groups, remind them to think about what has gone well in their discussions throughout the unit and what their groups could do better. You may want to review some basic rules for book club discussions, such as being a good listener and not interrupting, letting everyone in the group speak, and not reading directly from their logs. Remind students that this is the last book of the unit, so it is their last chance to use what they've learned to have the best book discussions yet.

 **ASSESSMENT TIP**

Review information you have gathered in your ongoing assessments with your "I Can" statements in mind. Determine if any of the Book Club curricular target areas should be addressed before the end of the unit, with the whole class or with individual students.

- **Closing Community Share** Talk about the book's opening pages. What do students predict will happen to the characters? What do they think of Ariel? What clues does the author give about how characters are feeling? You might want to ask students to think about whether or not this book seems a lot different to them; unlike the last two Book Club books, it is not autobiography but fiction.

Lesson 17

Response to Literature:
Character Relationships

Objectives:
- Revisit the Stories of Self theme.
- Help students use descriptive text and actions to understand how characters feel toward each other.

Vocabulary:
pelleted
curried
tendrils
therapy
determined
energetic
hesitantly
mythology
migrating
appliqued

Assigned Reading:
The Canada Geese Quilt:
Chapters 3–4

Writing Prompts:
- Describe how Ariel's relationship with her grandmother changes.
- How do you think Ariel is feeling?
- Free choice

- **Opening Community Share** Discuss the connection between today's lesson and the Stories of Self theme. Remind students that an important part of this book focuses on Ariel's relationship with her grandmother, her parents, and the new baby. Ask students what they understand about these relationships already and how these relationships reflect self.

Take the time to review scenes from earlier chapters in the novel that show the relationship between Ariel and her grandmother. For example, when Ariel's grandmother encourages her drawing skills, or when Ariel watches in fascination as her grandmother creates another quilt, or when her grandmother tries to ease her fears about the new baby.

- **Reading** As students read, encourage them to pay special attention to the relationship between Ariel and her grandmother. Ask them to think about how the relationship has changed and how Ariel seems to feel about this change.

- **Writing** Students should respond to both prompts as they examine the characters of Ariel and her grandmother. At this point, some students may prefer to have a free choice in writing to allow them to respond to the reading in their own way.

- **Book Club/Fishbowl** Encourage students to share their reading log responses in their book clubs. Students should talk about why Ariel feels so uncomfortable around her grandmother and how she overcomes her discomfort to reach out to her.

- **Closing Community Share** Continue the discussions that began in the book club groups. Do students understand the changes in the relationship between Ariel and her grandmother? Do they think Ariel could have acted differently? Invite students to share their responses with the whole group.

● TEACHING OPTION

Ask students to write about or discuss a person who is very important to them. Have them think about what effect this person has on them, and how it would feel if they could no longer talk to the person in the same way or enjoy some of the same activities with that person. You might have students bring in a photograph or drawing of their special person and write a few lines to go with the picture.

Lesson 18

Comprehension:
Summary, Interpretation

Objectives:
- Connect to the Stories of Self theme.
- Help students explore author's craft.
- Guide students to understand the distinct characteristics of one author's work.

Vocabulary:
None

Assigned Reading:
The Canada Geese Quilt: Chapters 5–6

Writing Prompts:
- What do you think the author wants you to learn from this story?
- Complete the summary sheet (Think Sheet 8).
- Free choice

NOTE: Evaluation Sheets 10–12 allow you to work with students to assess their overall performance throughout this unit and to set goals for future Book Club Plus units.

- **Opening Community Share** Discuss what students are noticing about how the book connects to the Stories of Self theme. Do the students see any connections to their lives and how they feel? Ask volunteers to predict how the book might end. Do students know Ariel well enough to guess how the birth of the baby will affect her? Do they know if her relationship with her grandmother will continue to improve and grow stronger?

Revisit the other books in the unit to help students determine how all the books relate to each other and to the unit theme. Encourage them to look back over their reading logs and recall significant details from the other Book Club books. You might write the following quotations on the chalkboard and read them aloud:

> From *Roxaboxen:* "Not one of them ever forgot. Years later, Marian's children listened to stories of that place and fell asleep dreaming dreams of Roxaboxen. Gray-haired Charles picked up a black pebble on the beach and stood holding it, remembering Roxaboxen."

> From *26 Fairmount Avenue* (when Tomie talks about his drawings of his family on the walls of the new house): "I decided I would give each person in the family a special corner in what was going to be our living room. . . .The plasterers finally came and covered over all my beautiful drawings. I was mad about that, but my grandfather, Tom, told me that was perfect because they'd always be there under the plaster and the wallpaper. That made me feel better."

- **Reading** Have students think about the author's message as they begin reading the end of the book. Tell them that they will later be asked what the author most likely wants readers to learn from this story.

- **Writing** Discuss themes and author's message with the class. Remind students that the theme of the unit is Stories of Self. Each book that the class has read is connected to this theme. Explain to students that another way to look at theme is to ask what the author wants the reader to learn from reading the story. As an example, ask students to think about the book *Judy Moody.* What is the book REALLY about? Students may begin talking about a girl who goes to school. Stop them, and ask them to think about what the book is really about. Continue this discussion until students bring up the idea that the book is about accepting oneself or fitting in or friendship. In this way, challenge students to think more broadly and deeply to explore the concept of theme. Distribute Think Sheet 8, Summary Sheet. It will encourage students to relate all three Book Club books to the unit theme. Encourage students to respond to the first writing prompt and then work on the summary sheet.

- **Book Club/Fishbowl** Students should discuss the author's message, the author's craft, and what they learned from the ending of the book. Students can also work together to finish their summary sheets.

- **Closing Community Share** Talk about how this book fits in with the other books in the unit and with the unit themes. Encourage students to share their summary sheets. Ask students what the land of Roxaboxen, the events surrounding the building of 26

ASSESSMENT OPTION

Have students respond in writing, either individually or in pairs, to the quotations and then use this activity as a means of assessment. Evaluate how well students can put into their own words the meaning of the text and how well they relate the text to the unit theme. Compare this information to your "I Can" statements to decide if students are working on, meeting, or exceeding the standard(s).

Fairmount Avenue, and Ariel's experiences with the geese and her grandmother's quilts have in common. You might add the following quotation from the end of *The Canada Geese Quilt* to the chalkboard next to the other quotations:

> "'They're [the geese] gone again for this year,' she thought. But they'll be back in the spring. . . .Year after year they knew, even the ones that were flying the route for the first time. A knowledge passed on.
>
> "Like Grandma. Grandma taught her things without making it seem like teaching. . . ."

Ask students to think about each quotation. Point out that in all three cases, the narrators are talking about things that have a great deal of importance in their lives. Discuss why the town of Roxaboxen, the drawings of Tomie's family, and Ariel's geese are important. How do these things fit into the story of each life?

Lesson 19

Literacy Block

Objectives:

- **Guided Reading**
  - Students read instructional-level texts.
  - Comprehension Strategies:
    When I Was Young . . . — Retelling versus summarizing
    Family Pictures— Using illustrations and text to tell the story and author's craft
    The Tarantula . . . — Finding important details
  - Vocabulary: Fostering word consciousness, by promoting word play, and making synonym and antonym matching games
- **Literacy Centers**
  Students participate in strategy, skill, and theme-extension activities.

Vocabulary:

When I Was Young . . . :
okra
pasture
mound
cocoa
congregation
baptisms
dusk
hoe
draped

Family Pictures:
border
artisans
entertainers
booths
university
parboil
tortillas
handkerchief

• Guided Reading

When I Was Young in the Mountains

—**Before Reading** Discuss the difference between a retelling and a summary. A retelling is when a student tries to tell the story as written, including every detail. A summary is made up of the most important points in chronological order. Help students focus on summary and the value of choosing the most important points of the story.

—**During Reading** Read the book together as a group, talking about the content and any comprehension strategies students use while reading. Work with students as they try to evaluate details as either important or not important in a summary.

—**After Reading** Have students write a concise summary of the story.

Family Pictures

—**Before Reading** Give students their books already turned to a page of text without the picture showing (cover the picture with construction paper if you like). Read the text aloud as students follow along and ask them to picture this story in their minds. Discuss the pictures that students formed in their minds. Reveal the picture and ask students to look at the picture while you read the text aloud. Discuss how authors and illustrators work together to give the reader a better understanding of the text.

—**During Reading** In pairs, have students read the first half of the book twice. Encourage them to stop and talk about each page as they move through the book.

—**After Reading** Ask students to identify characteristics of Garza's author's craft that would help them to identify a book as hers. Encourage them to use ideas from both the text and the illustrations.

The Tarantula in My Purse

—**Before Reading** Tell students that they are going to concentrate on important details. Often, above-grade-level readers have the misconception that all of the details in a story are important. Let them know that

TEACHING OPTION

Family Pictures is a wonderful story to use with the whole class to learn about author's craft. Garza's vivid watercolors lend several opportunities for extension activities such as students writing and illustrating their own family stories.

The Tarantula . . . :
instinct
enchanted
migratory
polarized
infused
cacophony
taffeta

some are more important than others. As they read, they will be identifying the most important details as well as identifying some less important details.

—**During Reading** Have students read Chapters 11–12. As they read, they should place sticky notes in their books to mark (or write on a piece of paper) three important details and three less-important details.

—**After Reading** Pull the group together and discuss their detail choices. Help clarify through this discussion why some details are more important than others.

- **Literacy Centers**

—Choose from the Literacy Center Options for this week on page 168.

—**Guided Reading Extensions:**

> *When I Was Young in the Mountains* Students should reread the story twice and write a concise summary of the story.

> *Family Pictures* Ask students to start writing a short version of their own family story. They should plan to finish and illustrate it during Lesson 20. You may want to extend the project over several days and have all students in the class participate and have it become a culminating activity.

> *The Tarantula in My Purse* Have students work with details by writing all the important and less important details they identified from the story on pieces of paper. Students can then take turns examining each other's details and categorizing them as important or less important.

—**Vocabulary (all groups)** The vocabulary lists in all of these books are extensive. Students may also find other new words in the books they are reading. Give each group of students index cards or pieces of construction paper cut to card size on which to write each vocabulary word. Then students should look up synonyms or antonyms in a dictionary or thesaurus. Finally, have students make matching memory games with synonyms and/or antonyms. (The center time in this lesson may be taken up with making the game, while students will actually play the game during Lesson 20.)

Lesson **20**

Literacy Block

• **Guided Reading**

When I Was Young in the Mountains

—**Before Reading** Review the summaries that students wrote in Lesson 19. Then write a group summary on chart paper that includes what you all agree are the most important points of the story. Remind students that a summary should answer the *who? what? where? when? why?* and *how?* of a story.

 **TEACHING TIP**

Garza's *Family Pictures* offers an opportunity for students to see English and Spanish written side by side. If you have Spanish-speaking students, this comparison is a wonderful language study. If you don't have students who speak Spanish, invite a visitor who is fluent to help the language come alive.

—**During Reading** Have students practice reading their story twice to improve fluency. Allow them to read aloud so that they can listen to their own reading.

—**After Reading** Have students work in the guided reading and vocabulary centers.

Family Pictures

—**Before Reading** Ask students to share their favorite story details. Discuss Garza's craft as an author and illustrator, defining some points of agreement about her craft. Remind students that it is important to both read the text and examine the pictures to get the whole experience that Garza intended.

—**During and After Reading** Have students work with their partners to read the second half of the story twice. Encourage them to stop and talk about each story as they read it and examine the illustrations.

The Tarantula in My Purse

—**Before Reading** Ask students to choose their most and least favorite chapter. Ask them to identify reasons for these choices. Encourage students to include ideas about how authors use text and sometimes illustrations to convey their meaning. You might ask whether students prefer to have more illustrations and why.

—**During Reading** Have students find their favorite chapter in the book and identify three of the most important details in the chapter and explain why they are important.

—**After Reading** Pull the group back together and collect their papers. Ask them if they have any questions about the book that they can answer as a group.

- **Literacy Centers**

—Choose from the Literacy Center Options for this week on page 168.

—**Guided Reading Extensions and Vocabulary:** Have all groups play their matching memory game created in Lesson 19 with vocabulary words using either synonyms or antonyms. Students reading *Family Pictures* should complete writing and illustrating their own family stories (see notes in Lesson 19).

CENTER OPTIONS

One Book Club *Plus* teacher, Karen Eisele, had students create artistic representations of their family pictures on brown paper bags with water color paints. Kathy Highfield scanned students' drawings into the computer and made a slide show out of her students' family stories that included the text and a voice button so student could tell their family stories in their own voices.

NOTE: The Week 6 activities outlined on pages 168–169 offer opportunities for students to synthesize what they've learned throughout the unit and to further explore unit themes.

Chapter Ten

Framework for a Read-Aloud Unit

Why Teach a Read-Aloud Unit?

The benefits of a read-aloud unit range from developing students' language, literacy, and literature appreciation to broadening their cultural perspectives and building a classroom community. First, hearing a story captures students' attention and fosters learning. Students hear unfamiliar words used in context and add them to their vocabulary. They observe a model of reading fluency. They begin to recognize skillful manipulation of language, which helps them improve their own writing. Their comprehension is reinforced by the teacher's oral implementation of strategies and their own connections between illustrations and text. Second, the nature of a read-aloud program exposes students to more sophisticated, multi-layered literature than they might be able to read independently. This, in turn, enriches their classroom discussion and makes the ideas they take from their reading more meaningful and lasting. Their analysis of what they've heard helps them develop critical faculties. In addition, hearing good literature inspires students to seek out works by the same author or reread books. Finally, the common reading experience provides a unifying background for diverse students and may afford teachers an opportunity to relate lessons from the texts to life in the classroom community.

How Is a Read-Aloud Unit Structured?

Hoffman, Roser, and Battle (1993) identified several factors that contribute to a successful read-aloud experience. These include the choice of quality literature, built-in opportunities for discussion of the literature, designated times for read aloud in the curriculum, optimal grouping of students for the discussion forum, a varied menu of response and extension activities, and the chance to reread selected pieces. This unit incorporates all of these factors as well as a comprehension strategy component to create a well-balanced framework for instruction.

This type of unit adapts well to a variety of scheduling needs. There are numerous ways in which to incorporate a read-aloud framework into your primary-grade classroom. You can organize the main contexts of Book Club—opening community share, reading, writing, book clubs, and closing community share—in a way that works best for you and your students. For instance, you might decide to allocate a large portion of time on one day to an entire Book Club lesson—cycling through the main Book Club components. Or, you might have more success keeping students engaged if you divide a Book Club lesson over more than one day. As with any type of Book Club unit, the amount of time you allocate to the different contexts on any given day or week will vary according to the time of year, the complexity of the book you are reading, and the needs and ability levels of your students. This flexibility is attractive to teachers who need to find creative ways to enhance their work in the classroom with a Book Club read-aloud unit.

The read-aloud sample we provide contains lessons that cover a variety of reading and comprehension skills. Students are asked to respond to their reading in various ways; they practice the techniques of good readers, such as questioning, visualizing, and making connections; they explore theme through writing, discussion, and unit projects; and they practice talking about books through fishbowls and book clubs. The read-aloud context alone is valuable in what it imparts to students. As the teacher in the sample unit, MariAnne George, reads aloud, she often models her thinking to demonstrate how she is using reading strategies, background knowledge and experiences, and note-taking to make meaning. She sometimes jots down a note on large chart paper or sometimes writes on a sticky note to remember a special part of the story or a question she wants to ask later. Thus, the read aloud in Book Club is an important place for students to observe what a skilled, enthusiastic reader does while reading. It is not a setting simply to sit back and listen passively.

Guided reading and other types of literacy instruction were, of course, also part of MariAnne's curriculum. These other areas of instruction took place outside the Book Club format at another time in the day. It is certainly possible to build guiding reading and other types of reading instruction into Book Club. In Chapters 9 and 11, we show how this is done using a context called Literacy Block.

Lessons in this unit contain additional ideas for making connections to other curricular areas (sometimes extending concepts taught within the unit and sometimes bringing in something new). The unit in this chapter links to the general theme of Our Storied Lives, described in Chapter 5, Talk in the

Classroom. Students explore Our Storied Lives in terms of the ethics of behavior and the consequences of our own actions. The books are connected through the theme, What is Truth? Focusing on the value of truth helps young children start to understand the ideals, principles, and practices of our democratic society.

Through this thematic unit, we illustrate how Book Club can be used within a read-aloud program to integrate reading, writing, and talk about books appropriate to primary-grade students' age levels. Of course, this unit can be modified and adapted to fit your specific grade level.

Why Explore the Theme of Truth?

By the time students enter the primary grades, most have absorbed a basic understanding of ethics—including the guiding precept that telling the truth is good, but telling a lie is bad. As students encounter more complex situations, however, this straightforward standard may not always help them to make decisions. Dishonesty takes many forms, some of them difficult to recognize. Sometimes the reason to lie seems to justify the action. And telling the truth, while it would seem to be beyond reproach, may create other problems. This unit is designed to help students explore the many facets of truth and deception, to enhance their awareness of the consequences of their actions, and to develop a greater sense of themselves as individuals who have the freedom to make wise choices. In a larger context, the self-exploration that students undertake in this unit will prepare them for the roles that await them as citizens of a community, a democratic nation, and a global village.

Unit Themes

Through literature, discussion, writing, and other activities, students will explore the importance of truth, the reasons why people act dishonestly, the consequences of lying, and the need to be compassionate. We suggest displaying the following theme-related questions to focus students' discussions throughout the unit.

How is the truth important in my life?

When is honesty the best policy?

How do I feel when someone lies to me? How do I feel when I lie to someone else?

How does my dishonesty affect other people and my relationships with them?

Literacy Skill Instruction

The chart below correlates Book Club curriculum areas to individual lessons in this unit. For details about each curriculum area, refer to the chart on pages 16–17. Lessons are also correlated to the twelve English language arts standards established by the National Council of Teachers of English and the International Reading Association. Numbers in parentheses refer to specific NCTE/IRA standards (see page 136 for a list of these standards).

Curriculum Correlation Chart

Curriculum Area	Lessons in the Theme of Truth
Comprehension	**Lesson 1:** Definitions (1, 3, 11) **Lesson 2:** Fishbowls (2, 3, 11) **Lesson 4:** Making Connections (3) **Lesson 5:** Questioning (3) **Lesson 6:** Sequence Chart (3, 9, 11) **Lesson 7:** Exploration of Theme (2, 3, 5, 9) **Lesson 8:** Book Clubs (2, 3, 6, 11) **Lesson 10:** Visualizing (3) **Lesson 12:** Journal Entry (3, 5)
Writing	**Lessons 1-13:** Daily Log Writing (3, 5, 6, 12) **Lesson 7:** Exploration of Theme (2, 3, 5, 9) **Lesson 12:** Journal Entry (3, 5) **Lesson 14:** Final Project (3, 4, 5)
Language Conventions	**Lesson 1:** Definitions (1, 3, 11) **Lesson 2:** Fishbowls (2, 3, 11) **Lesson 3:** Consequences of Lying (3, 12) **Lesson 8:** Book Clubs (2, 6, 11) **Lesson 14:** Final Project (3, 4, 5)
Literary Aspects	**Lesson 2:** Fishbowls (2, 3, 11) **Lesson 3:** Consequences of Lying (3, 12) **Lesson 4:** Making Connections (3) **Lesson 7:** Exploration of Theme (2, 3, 5, 9) **Lesson 8:** Book Clubs (2, 3, 6, 11) **Lesson 9:** Parts of a Story (2, 3) **Lesson 11:** Character Mapping (1, 3, 8, 9) **Lesson 13:** Theme Thoughts (2, 3, 6, 12) **Lesson 14:** Final Project (3, 4, 5)

Integrating Instruction

This read-aloud unit on truth provides many opportunities for cross-curricular connections particularly with social studies. For your convenience, we've identified links with social studies content based on the ten thematic strands defined by the National Council for the Social Studies (NCSS). A complete listing of the NCSS strands is available on page 137. The chart that follows highlights the four strands that relate to this unit.

Correlation to Social Studies Thematic Strands

NCSS Thematic Strands in Social Studies	Lessons
1. **Culture** Social studies programs should include experiences that provide for the study of culture and cultural diversity.	Lesson 7, Lesson 8, Lesson 9
4. **Individual Development and Identity** Social studies programs should include experiences that provide for the study of individual development and identity.	Lessons 1–14
5. **Individuals, Groups, and Institutions** Social studies programs should include experiences that provide for the study of interactions among individuals, groups, and institutions.	Lessons 1–13
10. **Civic Ideals and Practices** Social studies programs should include experiences that provide for the study of the ideals, principles, and practices of citizenship in a democratic republic.	Lesson 7, Lesson 11

Unit Overview

This chart outlines the complete three-week Truth unit. Book synopses are given on pages 207–209.

Three-Week Unit Overview

This unit has been correlated with the NCTE/IRA Standards for the English Language Arts (see page 136). Numbers in parentheses refer to specific standards.

Week 1: Beginning the Unit

- Teacher introduces the theme of the unit and reviews the Book Club concept.

- The class defines central terms related to the unit theme. (3)

- Students explore the theme through listening to several texts and analyzing the characters and plots. (1, 2, 6)

- Students write different types of reading log responses. (4)

- Students participate in fish-bowl each day and examine the qualities of good discussions. (11)

- Students employ various comprehension strategies such as predicting, making connections, identifying cause-and-effect relationships, questioning, using prior knowledge, and comparing and contrasting to help them understand the texts. (3)

Week 2: Book Club Lessons Continue

- Teacher introduces the class to the folk-tale genre. (6)

- Teacher continues to read aloud portions of a story during each lesson. (1, 2, 9)

- The class reviews the elements of fiction in order to analyze various texts with particular emphasis on the themes of each work. (6)

- Students complete a sequence chart and practice the comprehension strategies of predicting, making connections, questioning, and visualizing. (3)

- Students move from the fish-bowls into book clubs and continue to work on strengthening their discussion skills. (11)

- Students explore issues related to truth and deception.

Week 3: Closing the Unit

- Teacher continues to present varied literature selections to the class. (1, 2)

- The class works together on a character map and a Venn diagram. (3)

- Students write journal entries from the perspective of a main character. (3, 5)

- Students continue to make connections. (3)

- The class completes the cause-and-effect chart, the definitions chart from the first lesson, the connections chart, and theme think sheets. (3)

- Students construct a truth-mobile.

- Students respond to unit theme questions and discuss their insights. (3, 11)

- Students do a final project and present their work. (4, 5, 12)

Synopses of the Featured Books

Book Club Literature

- *A Big Fat Enormous Lie* by Marjorie Weinman Sharmat

   The narrator tells a small lie that assumes monstrous proportions in his mind. Only telling the truth rids him of his lie monster.

- *The Boy Who Cried Wolf* by Tony Ross

   Willy's false alarms allow him to get his own way until one day, when the wolf is real. His appeals for help are ignored with tragic consequences.

Chen Ping and His Magic Axe by Demi

   This Chinese folk tale tells the story of Chen Ping, who loses his axe in a stream. When he is offered the chance to identify a silver or a gold axe as his, he refuses and instead claims his old iron axe. His honesty is rewarded.

- *A Day's Work* by Eve Bunting

   Anxious to find work for himself and his grandfather, Francisco lies about their abilities to garden. Francisco doesn't take home a day's wages but rather some important lessons about integrity and responsibility.

- *The Empty Pot* by Demi

   When all the children in the empire are given a seed from which to grow a flower, Ping appears to be the only one unable to produce anything. He admits his failure. The emperor reveals that because the seeds were cooked and useless, Ping is, in fact, the only honest child in the kingdom.

Harriet and the Garden by Nancy Carlson

   Harriet runs away from the damage she has done to Mrs. Hoozit's garden but decides that she must face the consequences of her actions.

- *The Honest-to-Goodness Truth* by Patricia C. McKissack

   After Libby gets into trouble for lying to her mother, she decides to always tell the truth. But telling the truth can create problems, too.

Liar, Liar, Pants on Fire! by Miriam Cohen

   Alex, the new boy, tries to impress his classmates by telling lies. When he is found out, the other students turn against him, except for Jim, whose acceptance of Alex sets an example for the class.

That's Mine, Horace by Holly Keller

   Horace gives in to the temptation to keep a toy truck, which involves him in a web of deceit. Walter, who owns the truck, shows Horace a way to resolve his conflict.

To Tell the Truth **by Patti Farmer**

Benjamin loses friends when he insists on telling them the truth about their paintings, their athletic ability, and their clothes. Then Benjamin tells the truth about himself and becomes one of them again.

What's So Terrible About Swallowing an Apple Seed? **by Harriet Lerner and Susan Goldhor**

Katie tells her younger sister Rosie that the apple seed she swallowed will grow into a tree inside of her. Rosie believes her. Katie doesn't know how to tell Rosie the truth until one day Rosie discovers it on her own.

Why Mosquitoes Buzz in People's Ears **by Verna Aardema**

This African folk tale shows how a thoughtless comment led to a trail of disasters and the perpetual whining of the mosquito.

Special Classroom Library

Below are some suggestions for theme-related resources with which you might stock your classroom during this unit. Titles with asterisks have been incorporated into optional activities within the lessons.

Alex Did It! **by Udo Weigelt**

Three little rabbits blame all their wrongdoing on a mythical hare named Alex. When a real Alex moves into the woods, they must repair the damage they have done to his reputation and confess their misdeeds.

Annabelle's Un-Birthday **by Steven Kroll**

In this chapter book, Annabelle faces the anxiety of starting a new school. She decides to pretend it is her birthday and invite everyone to a party. She must confess her deception to the class the next day.

Arthur's Computer Disaster **by Marc Brown**

Although Arthur's mother asked him not to use her computer, he does and thinks he's broken it. He tries to get it fixed but can't and must confess to his mother what he did.

The Berenstain Bears and the Truth **by Jan and Stan Berenstain**

Brother and Sister Bear play ball in the house with disastrous results. Their mother is more upset, however, by their deceit, and Brother and Sister Bear resolve never to lie again.

The Children's Book of Virtues **edited by William Bennett**

Several selections in this collection of poems, fables, folk tales, legends, and short stories convey the importance of acting on the truth.

Honest Abe **by Edith Kunhardt**

The life of Abraham Lincoln is traced from his humble beginnings to his death. An incident showing his honest nature is briefly narrated.

* ***Honesty*** **by Kathryn Kyle**

This book provides a basic definition of honesty and offers some relevant situations in which young people would have to decide whether or not to be honest. Included is an explanation of President Lincoln's nickname and a bibliography that suggests further reading and Web sites.

* ***Juan Verdades: The Man Who Couldn't Tell a Lie*** **retold by Joe Hayes**

In this folk tale, Juan's ability to resist temptation and tell the truth is tested. He does so cleverly, saving his reputation and that of his employer.

The Judge **by Harve Zemach**

The story of a judge's inability to recognize the truth is told in verse.

* ***My Big Lie*** **by Bill Cosby**

Little Bill finds out how telling a lie can damage a relationship and cause him to lose the trust of those he respects.

Plato's Journey **by Linda Talley**

Four lies send Plato the goat on an arduous journey to run in a race that doesn't exist. When he returns home, he confronts the animals who lied to him and resolves never to be dishonest himself.

Other Media

* ***Adventures from the Children's Book of Virtues: Honesty: Featuring the Indian Cinderella and Other Great Stories.*** (Videocassette, 30 minutes).

In this animated video, a contemporary boy Zach lies to his father. He sees the error of his ways through the tales his friends tell him, which are based on those found in *The Children's Book of Virtues.*

Lesson 1

Comprehension:
Definitions

Objectives:
- Define terms related to the unit theme.
- Briefly describe the components of Book Club.
- Give students the opportunity to practice the strategy of predicting.
- Discuss the importance of reading logs.

Reading:
The Boy Who Cried Wolf

Writing Prompt:
What do you think happens at the end of the story? Write or draw your own ending.

NOTE: All writing prompts for the Book Club lesson plans in this unit appear on Think Sheet 9. Pass out copies of this sheet so that students can refer to it as they complete each reading assignment.

- **Opening Community Share** Tell students that for the next few weeks, they will be reading (listening to) books about truth. Write the terms *truth, honesty, lies,* and *dishonesty* on a chart. Have students define the concepts from their prior knowledge. Record their ideas on chart paper. Guide students to recognize the relationship between truth and honesty, lies and dishonesty. When people say the truth or act on it, they are honest. When they tell lies or do something that they know is counter to the truth, they are dishonest. Tell students that although each book they will read has different characters and events, each will present some important ideas about truth.

If your class has not been involved in Book Club before, you may want to take this opportunity to explain the components of the program. Tell students that they will be listening to one or two books in each lesson. They will respond to what they've heard by writing or drawing in their logs and then will discuss their responses in small groups. Ask students why they think discussing the books is an important part of these lessons.

Introduce the strategy of predicting by presenting students with a hypothetical situation. For example, you might tell them that every single night, your next door neighbor lets her dog out at eight o'clock and screams for him to come back ten minutes later. What would students guess might happen tonight? Why? After students have guessed, tell them that they just predicted. Predicting is making a logical guess about what might happen later. Ask students for examples of times when they have made predictions. Then explain that they need to listen carefully to the story you are about to read aloud because you will be asking them to make a prediction about the ending.

- **Reading** Read aloud *The Boy Who Cried Wolf.* Stop reading just after Willy meets the wolf and "cries wolf" to the townspeople.

 TEACHING TIP

You may find it helpful to introduce the theme by presenting some possible situations in which students would need to decide whether or not to act honestly. *Honesty* by Kathryn Kyle offers plausible scenarios as well as solutions. Have students explain what they would do in each case. Use their responses as a springboard for defining the terms.

 ADAPTING THE LESSONS

Beginning readers
- Model thinking aloud for each selection.
- Pause frequently while reading to clarify plot developments.
- Provide taped versions of more difficult books for students to listen to a second time on their own.

Explain that students will write or draw their responses to the literature in their reading logs. These reading logs will help them to keep a record of their ideas about the books and will remind them of what they want to discuss. Write the date and the book title on the board for students to copy. (For very young writers, putting the date and title on every reading log entry may be too time consuming. Eliminate it in favor of having students respond to the reading.) Give students today's writing prompt. Circulate as they respond in case they have questions. Emphasize that their ideas are the most important part of their reading log entries.

Have students pair up and share their predictions. Then have pairs exchange ideas with another pair.

- **Closing Community Share** Read the rest of the story. Ask students how their predictions compare to what really happens. What clues within the story point to that particular ending? Ask students what they learned from sharing their ideas with a partner and then a group. Were they surprised by anyone's idea? Did they see the story differently because of something someone else said?

 INTERTEXTUAL CONNECTIONS

My Big Lie by Bill Cosby dovetails nicely with this selection. You may want to read this book aloud to the class. Discuss how *My Big Lie* differs from *The Boy Who Cried Wolf.* Why is that difference important in the Cosby story?

Lesson 2

Language Conventions: Fishbowls

Objectives:
- Review unit theme questions.
- Guide students toward an understanding of the literary element theme.
- Model text-to-self connections.
- Introduce students to the fishbowl model of book club discussion.

Reading:
A Big Fat Enormous Lie

Writing Prompt:
Write about a time when you felt like the narrator of the story.

- **Opening Community Share** Tell students that each of the books in this unit has a theme or a message that the author wants to share with readers. Theme is revealed through the experiences of the characters. Ask students what they learned from what happens to Willy in *The Boy Who Cried Wolf.* Guide students to see that the book shows that lying is dangerous. It also illustrates that when people lie, they lose the trust of others. Hand out Think Sheet 10, Theme Blocks. You may choose to draw a class chart resembling this think sheet. Decide on a theme statement for *The Boy Who Cried Wolf.* Have students record it on their sheets. Explain that there is often more than one theme that can be taken from a story.

VOCABULARY

No vocabulary words have been identified in this unit. You may wish to have students keep a list of words unfamiliar to them from the reading and then define them as a class during each lesson. Or, you might present words from the reading beforehand and illustrate their meaning in your introduction to the book.

Explain that today they will be listening to another book in which the character tells a lie. His experience is a little different from Willy's. Tell students the title of today's selection, and draw their attention to the series of adjectives that describe the lie. What might they expect the book to be about?

Introduce the idea of text-to-self connections by telling students that sometimes readers can see similarities between themselves and what the characters in books do or say or feel. Sometimes the experiences of the characters make readers think of similar situations they have been in. Making connections helps readers better understand the books and become more interested in what happens.

- **Reading** Read aloud *A Big Fat Enormous Lie.* Throughout your reading, model how to make text-to-self connections. Mark passages ahead of time at which to stop and think aloud about how that event or action or feeling reminds you of something in your life. For example, one teacher brought out a connection to the first page of the story. Once she ate a piece of her mother's birthday cake and lied about doing it.

TEACHER RESOURCES

The book *Reading with Meaning: Teaching Comprehension in the Primary Grades* by Debbie Miller offers further ideas for how to enhance students' understanding and appreciation of texts.

- **Writing** Have students respond to the prompt.

- **Book Club/Fishbowl** After students have responded to the prompt, begin fishbowl. We have found it helpful to begin with fishbowls even if your students have been in book club groups before. This provides a good opportunity to talk about effective discussion strategies, good questioning practices, themes, and other areas for discussion. The teacher can provide scaffolding, if necessary, for students before and during fishbowls and can guide the discussion of the whole class after each fishbowl.

- **Closing Community Share** Talk about the fishbowl discussion. What did the group do well? What would be some other strategies to use in a group discussion? What should the other members be doing when one person speaks? Explain that everyone will be participating in future fishbowls, so it is important to know how to make a discussion successful. Then talk about the theme of today's book. Have students articulate their thoughts so you can assess their understanding of the element. They should add a class theme statement to their Theme Block think sheets.

EXTENSION ACTIVITY

Have students illustrate the principle behind the story by constructing their own lie monster. Students' drawings or models should show how the lie grows bigger and bigger until it is overwhelming. For example, students could illustrate this with rubber band balls. The beginning of the lie is a small ball. As time goes on, it becomes huge. Have students take turns presenting their versions of the lie monster.

Lesson 3

Response to Literature:
Consequences of Lying

Objectives:
- Relate consequences of lying with the theme.
- Discuss and chart the consequences of lying.
- Analyze the qualities of a good discussion.
- Familiarize students with different reading log response types.

Reading:
Harriet and the Garden

Writing Prompt:
Respond to either *Favorite Part or Character* or *In the Character's Shoes*. (See Think Sheet 5, Things to Do in Your Reading Log.)

- **Opening Community Share** Start a list of the qualities of a good discussion group. The list should include ideas such as listening to each other's points, using specific examples from the story, adding to each other's ideas, being polite. Tell students to think of these qualities as they meet in their groups today. This might be the time to work with students to generate a list of discussion "I Can" statements that they can keep in mind throughout the unit. Turn to Evaluation Sheets 1 and 13 for examples.

Ask students what the books they have read so far have shown about the effects of lying. Stimulate students' thoughts by giving some examples. Willy loses the trust of the people around him and his life. The narrator in *A Big Fat Enormous Lie* is practically crushed by guilt. Record students' thoughts on a class cause-and-effect chart. Tell students to listen carefully for the consequences of dishonesty in this story.

- **Reading** Read *Harriet and the Garden* to the students.

- **Writing** Hand out Think Sheet 5. Go over Special Story Part and In the Character's Shoes. Discuss with students how responding in different ways in their reading logs is a good way to understand a book better and to improve their book club discussions. Review the qualities of a strong reading log entry, emphasizing the need to use specific details. It might be helpful to show students a sample entry, such as the one below. Then ask students to respond to one of the prompts.

Wednesday April 12   Harriet and the Garden

My special part of the story was when Harriet helped Mrs. Hoozit clean up the garden. She was brave to tell Mrs. Hoozit what she did. They had fun. Harriet felt better. She ate popcorn balls.

- **Book Club/Fishbowl** Conduct book clubs in the fishbowl model today. Give as many students a chance to participate as time permits.

- **Closing Community Share** Display the class cause-and-effect chart. (Yours might resemble the example shown below.) Ask students for their insights from the books read so far about how lying or acting dishonestly affects a person and relationships with others. Today's book clearly shows that as a result of Harriet's dishonesty, she becomes unhappy. After filling in some ideas on the class chart, bring the discussion around to the theme. What message is the author sending the readers through Harriet's experiences?

Conclude the lesson by returning to the list of qualities of good discussions. Have students add what they learned from today's fishbowls. Bring in the importance of questions in discussion groups. Talk about what makes a good question and ways to ask one. For example, a "thin" question is one that can be answered with one word or that stops conversation. A "thick" question makes people think and encourages them to express new ideas.

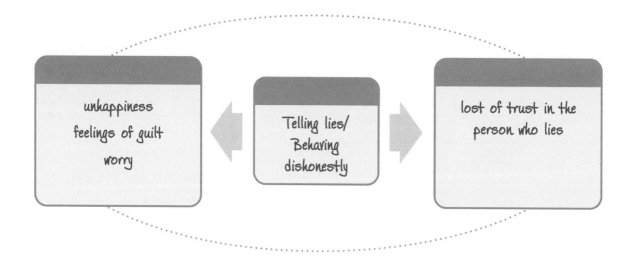

Lesson 4

Comprehension:
Making Connections

Objectives:
- Revisit the theme questions.
- Analyze characters' motives for lying.
- Develop students' ability to make connections between texts.
- Emphasize role of prior knowledge in comprehension of text.

Reading:
Liar, Liar, Pants on Fire!

Writing Prompt:
Respond to *Feelings* on Think Sheet 5, Things to Do in Your Reading Log.

- **Opening Community Share** Ask students what is meant by the words *prior knowledge*. Give a real-life example to help them define the phrase from context. For example, the ice-cream truck has visited their neighborhood at noon each day for the past eight days. At 11:55 A.M. on the ninth day, they hear the sound of chimes. What do they know? Why? Tell students that the knowledge they've accumulated from their own experiences is prior knowledge. So even before the truck comes into sight, they know what is making the sound. Apply this concept to reading. Show the cover of *Liar, Liar, Pants on Fire!* and some of the illustrations. Based on their prior knowledge, what are some of the ideas the students have about the story even before they listen to it?

  Remind students of the text-to-self connections they made in Lesson 2. Explain that they can also make connections between two stories. Making connections between the events or characters in two different texts gives them more insight into the author's message. Have them listen for details about the main character Alex and think about whether he is similar to or different from Harriet.

 **TEACHING TIP**

Gather resources related to the theme in a corner of the room. These might include the supplemental selections described in the Special Classroom Library section on pages 208–209 as well as books on tape and additional videos relevant to the unit. You might wish to build activities that use these resources into the lessons or encourage students to choose from among them when they have unstructured time.

- **Reading** Read *Liar, Liar, Pants on Fire!* to the class.

- **Writing** Have students respond to the writing prompt and move into fishbowl.

- **Book Club/Fishbowl** Alternate participants and observers in fishbowl. Remind students to check the list of discussion "I Can" statements. Discuss connections between the text and themselves and between this story and others. Talk about how the fishbowls worked.

- **Closing Community Share** Analyze similarities and differences between *Liar, Liar, Pants on Fire!* and *Harriet and the Garden.* Ask students if the characters have the same or different reasons for acting dishonestly. Guide them to see that Harriet doesn't want to get into trouble, while Alex lies to make friends. How is Alex's problem solved? Show that while Alex changes his ways, his problem is mostly solved by Jim's kindness. Harriet, on the other hand, must be courageous enough to admit her mistake and suffer the consequences. Then revisit the theme questions and identify further ways that behaving dishonestly affects relationships. Ask students if they have ever lied to get out of trouble, or, as Alex did, to try to make people like them. As a class fill in the theme block for this story. Then identify further ways that behaving dishonestly affects relationships.

Lesson 5

Comprehension: Questioning

Objectives:
- Guide students in making self and text connections with the theme questions.
- Model the comprehension strategy of questioning.
- Update cause-and-effect chart.

Reading:
That's Mine, Horace

Writing Prompt:
What lies does Horace tell in the story? Why?

- **Opening Community Share** Talk about the technique of questioning. Tell students that they already use this strategy when they ask themselves what they think is going to happen. Readers might also ask themselves questions about why the character is behaving a certain way or what a particular comment means. Asking questions helps readers get the most out of the book and keeps them focused on important ideas.

- **Reading** Read *That's Mine, Horace* to the class. Model how to ask questions by thinking aloud throughout the book. Placing sticky notes on pages ahead of time ensures that this modeling exercise goes smoothly. Help students to think beyond the text with such questions as "I wonder what Horace is going to do with that truck he found?" "Why did Horace put that funny sign on his bedroom door?" "I wonder if Horace will ever want to go back to school?"

- **Writing** Have students respond to the prompt. If you are adapting these lessons for beginning readers and writers, remind students that they can draw and label their responses to the "writing" prompts. You may also want to work on a class list of words and phrases to use in responses. Students can then copy this material from the board or chart paper.

- **Book Club/Fishbowl** Emphasize the importance of building on each other's responses in today's fishbowl activity.

- **Closing Community Share** Return to the qualities of a good discussion chart and the "I Can" statements. Students should add new ideas to the chart. Then ask students if there are any effects they wish to add to the cause-and-effect chart. Students should recognize that the initial dishonesty of taking the truck leads Horace to tell further lies. At what point could Horace act honestly? Why doesn't he? Talk about the lessons students might learn from Horace's actions. Conclude by encouraging students to see connections between Walter and Jim from *Liar, Liar, Pants on Fire!* What might students learn from their behaviors? Help students make self and text connections with the theme questions.

Lesson 6

Comprehension:
Sequence Chart

Objectives:
- Make connections (self, text, world) with the theme questions.
- Develop students' ability to make text-to-world connections.
- Work with students to complete a sequence chart.

Reading:
Why Mosquitoes Buzz in People's Ears

Writing Prompt:
Do you agree that the mosquito is to blame for all that happened? Why or why not?

- **Opening Community Share** Tell students that some stories have many events. Explain to students that keeping track of the sequence or order of the events (define *events* if necessary) will help them understand the stories more easily.

  Discuss with students the kinds of connections they have made already. Students should mention text-to-self and text-to-text. Explain that sometimes connections can also be made between what happens in a book and the real world. Either the reader must look to the real world for an answer to a question or the events in the book remind readers of something in real life. It might be helpful to display a connections chart (Text-to-Self, Text-to-Text, Text-to-World) to record links that students find.

- **Reading** Read the story aloud, identifying some text-to-world connections. Think out loud so students can understand your thought process. Place your ideas on the class connections chart in the appropriate column. Discuss the connections you make with the class.

- **Writing** Have students respond to the prompt in their reading logs.

- **Book Club/Fishbowl** The writing prompt raises some important issues related to truth and responsibility. Listen carefully to students' responses in the fishbowl activity. Assess students' ability to present their ideas clearly and to draw upon the text to support their ideas.

- **Closing Community Share** As a class, complete a sequence chart on the board or on chart paper. Ask students what they notice about the events in the second half of the story. Students should point out that the order of events is reversed. Then take some time to build on what students said in the fishbowl activity. First, see if the class comes to a consensus on the mosquito's guilt. Discuss what the author is saying about the consequences of even small lies or thoughtless exaggerations. Add insights from today's lesson to the cause-and-effect chart and work together on a theme statement for the story. Guide students in making connections (self, text, world) with the theme questions.

  Conclude the lesson by examining what students feel is going well in fishbowl discussion and what they are finding difficult. Relate comments to the discussion chart and the "I Can" statements. Write some suggestions on the board that students can implement next time.

Lesson 7

Response to Literature:
Exploration of Theme

Objectives:
- Revisit the theme analyzing the effects of telling lies on others and on relationships.
- Examine aspects of author's craft.
- Review the strategy of questioning.
- Add to theme blocks.

Reading:
A Day's Work

Writing Prompt:
What lessons does Francisco's grandfather teach him?

- **Opening Community Share** Tell students that in the book they are going to read today, the author uses some terms from the Spanish language to add realism. She wants the events and the characters to seem true to life in the setting she has chosen for the story. Write some of the terms on the board: *abuelo, hace frío, bueno, grácias, muy bonito.* Ask students if they recognize any of them. Give students the definitions and tell them to listen carefully for how the words are used in the story. If you have Spanish-speaking students in your classroom, you might ask them to help you and the other students with speaking and understanding the Spanish words. This will help them to see their home language as a strength they bring to the classroom. You might even have them create a lesson for their peers about the terms used in the story.

- **Reading** Remind students of the importance of questioning before, during, and after they read a book. Ask students to write down two or three of the questions that occur to them as you read *A Day's Work*. Stop periodically during the reading to have students share them.

- **Writing** Clarify questions that students have after the story is completed. Then have them respond to the writing prompt.

- **Book Club/Fishbowl** Ask students to look over the suggestions for improving their discussions before moving into fishbowl. Have each group decide on one area to try to improve.

- **Closing Community Share** Talk about students' feelings about their discussion groups. Were they able to improve one area? What other ideas do they have for making their discussion more effective? Add students' ideas to the list of suggestions on the board.

  Have students consider what they learned from this book about the effect of people's actions on themselves and on their relationships with

ADAPTING THE LESSON

Beginning readers

Spread the read aloud over two days. At the end of the first day, have students work together to draw summaries of the story.

Advanced readers

Have student groups prepare readers' theater presentations of scenes from the book and interpret their significance.

CITIZENSHIP CONNECTION

Explain that Francisco's grandfather is not a citizen yet. You might want to hold a class discussion during which each student is invited to contribute a word that captures what it means to be a good citizen. Connect to the unit theme by asking what role truthfulness and honesty play in being a good citizen. Ask why it's important that both people in government and average citizens not lie. Encourage students to give concrete examples to support their ideas. Then make a class word web or another type of chart that displays the words and ideas generated during this discussion.

others. What is Francisco's grandfather's reaction when he realizes that Francisco lied about his gardening knowledge? How does Francisco feel on the drive back to the parking lot? Have students suggest additions to the cause-and-effect chart. Then explore further the meaning of the story by analyzing the reason that Francisco lies. Is a good reason an excuse for lying? As a class, use a web to record reasons that characters have lied or behaved dishonestly. Discuss whether lying is ever okay. Then work as a class to update students' theme blocks. Conclude by asking students what they have learned so far about the importance of truth and honesty in their own lives.

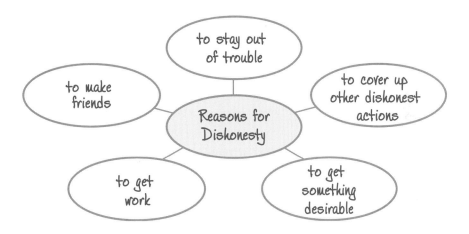

Lesson 8

Language Conventions: Book Clubs

Objectives:
- Guide the students' understanding of how the theme of truth and honesty runs throughout history and across cultures.
- Define the term *genre* and explain folk tales.
- Have students make predictions about the conclusion of the story.
- Move students into book clubs.

Reading:
Chen Ping and His Magic Axe

- **Opening Community Share** Write the word *genre* on the board. Explain that types of writing are known as genres. The type of writing they will hear today is a folk tale. Tell them that they have already read two folk tales in this unit, *The Boy Who Cried Wolf* and *Why Mosquitoes Buzz in People's Ears*. A folk tale is an old story that originally was passed from generation to generation by word of mouth. Explain that folk tales may use animals as main characters or have magical elements woven into the story. Folk tales were meant to entertain listeners, but they often have a theme or message as well. Remind students to listen for that message as you read aloud *Chen Ping and his Magic Axe*.

Remind students that today they will be meeting in book club groups. Identify the similarities and differences between book clubs and fishbowls.

Writing Prompt:
Choose one of the response types from Think Sheet 5, Things to Do in Your Reading Log.

Emphasize to students that the strategies for conducting a successful discussion are especially important in book club groups because the students are in control. Although you will be listening to their conversations, it is their responsibility to keep the discussion focused and moving forward. It is also important for them to use their reading logs to help them contribute good ideas.

Tell students that you will be asking them to make predictions about the story they are about to hear. Remind them that they need to use the clues in the story as well as their own knowledge to make a guess about the outcome.

- **Reading** Read *Chen Ping and His Magic Axe* aloud, stopping when Wing Fat throws his axe into the river.

  Have students draw pictures of what they think might happen in the rest of the story. Have them share their pictures and explain the clues in the story that help them to predict that ending.

  Finish reading the story. Discuss how students' predictions matched up to the actual ending.

- **Writing** Have students respond to one of the log response types and move into the book club groups that you have identified.

- **Book Club/Fishbowl** Briefly remind students of the discussion "I Can" statements and book club etiquette. Walk around and check their progress. Keep this first book club under five minutes so that the talk doesn't lose focus.

- **Closing Community Share** Conclude the lesson by discussing what message the folk tale communicates about truth. Why do students think so many authors explore honesty and dishonesty? Help guide students' understanding of how honesty is an age-old theme and runs across all cultures. Then have students react to their first book clubs. What did they like about them? What would they like to improve?

◆ ADAPTING THE LESSON

You may decide to have your students continue to work in fishbowls. Very young students may not be ready to work independently. However, if you want to introduce them to independent book clubs, you may want to ask a parent volunteer to supervise book clubs on a rotating basis.

◆ TEACHING OPTION

Have students design book jackets for this folk tale or for one of the other books in the unit. Encourage students to convey the message of the story through their illustration.

Lesson 9

Literary Elements:
Parts of a Story

Objectives:
- Make connections from the theme blocks to the unit theme questions.
- Analyze the elements of fiction.
- Compare and contrast texts.

Reading:
The Empty Pot

Writing Prompt:
Which folk tale do you like better, *The Empty Pot* or *Chen Ping and His Magic Axe*? Why?

- **Opening Community Share** Begin today's lesson by introducing the elements of fiction. You may wish to use a chart such as the one shown. Be sure students understand the basic definitions of each element and how each is important in a story by giving examples from books previously read. For example, in *A Day's Work* the author's style includes the use of Spanish words and phrases. The setting of *Why Mosquitoes Buzz in People's Ears* is the jungle. The narrator in *A Big Fat Enormous Lie* is the main character who uses first person or "I" to tell the story.

  Explain that the story they will hear today is also a folk tale. They should listen for ways in which the story is similar to and different from the one they read yesterday—*Chen Ping and His Magic Axe*.

- **Reading** Read *The Empty Pot*.

- **Writing** Have students respond to the writing prompt. Then have them move into their book clubs.

- **Book Club/Fishbowl** Before students begin their discussions, remind them to ask good questions that will help them to think beyond the text. Briefly review the technique of questioning that was introduced in Lesson 5.

ADAPTING THE LESSON

Advanced readers

This selection provides a good opportunity for students to practice their reading fluency. Assign each student a page of the story to prepare to read aloud. Have students do the read aloud instead of you.

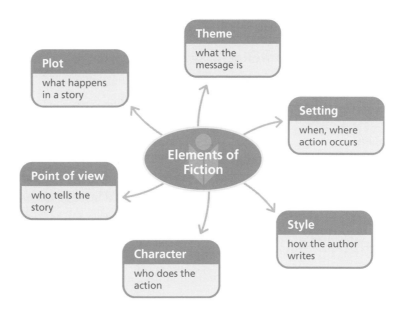

Theme
what the message is

Plot
what happens in a story

Setting
when, where action occurs

Elements of Fiction

Point of view
who tells the story

Style
how the author writes

Character
who does the action

- **Closing Community Share** Explore the similarities and differences between *The Empty Pot* and *Chen Ping and His Magic Axe*, referring to the elements chart. Do students think the themes are the same? If the themes are not the same, what new idea about truth can students take from *The Empty Pot*? Have students add to their theme blocks.

INTERTEXTUAL CONNECTIONS

Read aloud or have students read *Juan Verdades*. Have students compare and contrast Ping and Juan, using a Venn diagram. Discuss what students find. Guide students to analyze the kinds of temptation that both face and the qualities they show in overcoming this temptation.

Lesson 10

Comprehension:
Visualizing

Objectives:
- Introduce the strategy of visualizing.
- Add to cause-and-effect chart.

Reading:
What's So Terrible About Swallowing an Apple Seed?

Writing Prompt:
Has anyone ever told you a "story" that you believed? What happened?

- **Opening Community Share** Explain to students that many times readers are able to enjoy and remember the story more if they visualize or see pictures in their minds of the characters and the events. If an author uses descriptive words and phrases, it helps readers to build this image. To demonstrate, read a highly visual poem. (For example, "It's Raining Pigs and Noodles" from the volume of the same name by Jack Prelutsky gives listeners concrete images.) Ask volunteers to describe what they see in their minds. Discuss how visualizing makes literature more memorable.

- **Reading** Read the beginning of the story aloud. Stop after Katie describes how the tree will look growing out of Rosie's head. Have students use the details to visualize and draw what Rosie will look like after swallowing the apple seed. Then continue reading the story.

- **Writing** Before students respond to the prompt, briefly analyze the elements of the story they have just read.

- **Book Club/Fishbowl** Have students meet in their book club groups. Monitor students' discussion skills and offer assistance where it is needed.

- **Closing Community Share** After students have met in book clubs, ask them to show their visualization pictures. Talk about the similarities and the differences among them. Then ask students to consider what would have happened if Rosie had never found out the truth about the apple seed. What if she had passed on that story to others who also believed it? Discuss the consequences of spreading lies. Have students ever told someone something that they knew was untrue? At the end of class, update the cause-and-effect chart with ideas from the discussion. Help the students make connections from the theme questions.

Literary Elements:
Character Mapping

Objectives:
- Explore reasons why people tell the truth and relate these reasons to the theme questions for the unit.
- Identify reasons why reading a number of texts helps us understand the unit theme more clearly.
- Add to theme blocks.
- Map the character of Libby.

Reading:
The Honest-to-Goodness Truth

Writing Prompts:
- Have you ever had your feelings hurt by someone telling you the truth?
- Have you ever hurt someone's feelings by telling the truth?

- **Opening Community Share** Begin opening community share by drawing a character map on the board. Place the name of Libby in the center. Tell students that the more realistic a character is, the more sides to his or her personality there will be. As students listen to today's story, have them think what Libby's thoughts, words, and actions show about the kind of person she is.

- **Reading** Read *The Honest-to-Goodness Truth* aloud. You may want to pause at important passages to draw inferences about Libby's character from what she is saying and doing.

- **Writing** Have students respond to the writing prompts. Encourage students to be thorough in their responses.

- **Book Club/Fishbowl** Move students into book club groups.

- **Closing Community Share** Discuss how until this point the books in the unit have mostly explored the consequences of telling lies or acting dishonestly. This book explores the effect of telling the truth and the reasons that people tell the truth. Ask students for their reactions to what happens in the book. Is Libby doing something wrong when she keeps being honest? What makes her realize the effect that her words have on others? What kinds of truth has Libby been telling the people around her? Work with students to arrive at some realizations about the responsibility of the truth-teller to use the truth with compassion and wisdom. Suggest that Mama's words might help students to identify the theme of this story. "Sometimes the truth is told at the wrong time, or in the wrong way, or for the wrong reasons." As a class, create a theme statement and take the opportunity to fill in theme blocks for previous stories as well.

Ask students what they learn about Libby's character from her behavior and speech in the story. Together, work on the character map, guiding students to discover more about Libby by making inferences. For example, Libby is upset when she realizes how she has hurt her friends through telling the truth. This reaction shows that Libby is a kind person. She

SOCIAL STUDIES CONNECTION

Tell students that President Lincoln's nickname was Honest Abe. Have students work in pairs to find out why he earned this nickname. (Some of the supplemental sources will be helpful to students who may be less experienced with researching techniques.) Students should report their findings to the class. Then discuss why honesty is an important quality.

hurries to make amends, illustrating that she is willing to take responsibility for her mistakes.

Conclude the lesson by asking students if they have any questions on what was discussed today. Revisit the theme questions. Ask why it's important that we read many different stories that relate to our unit theme. Have children discuss this question. Encourage them to think about the different perspectives of the characters and the variety of problems and solutions they've encountered in their reading. Make a list of their ideas to display.

Lesson 12

Writing: Journal Entry

Objectives:
- Add ideas/connections to the theme questions.
- Give students an opportunity to write a journal entry.
- Explore connections between the book and other books.
- Use a Venn diagram to compare and contrast texts.
- Foster students' reflections on theme.

Reading:
To Tell the Truth

Writing Prompt:
Write a journal entry from Benjamin's perspective. Explain what happened in school when you took the fudge and what you learned.

- **Opening Community Share** Explain that the story students will hear today has some similarities to *The Honest-to-Goodness Truth.* Also tell students that after the read aloud, they will be writing in the form of journal entries in their reading logs. Journals are books in which writers record their thoughts and feelings as well as the important events that occur in their lives—artifacts of their storied lives. A person might write an entry every day. Keeping a journal helps someone to realize what is important in life and what can be learned from daily experiences.

  Ask students to listen for connections they can make between the book and themselves, the book and other texts, and the book and the real world.

- **Reading** Read *To Tell the Truth.*

- **Writing** Have students write their journal entries from the point of view of Benjamin. Encourage students to describe what occurs in school when they take the fudge and then to explain lessons that they learn from their experience.

- **Book Club/Fishbowl** Have students share their journal entries in their book clubs.

- **Closing Community Share** Draw a Venn diagram on the board, and discuss the similarities and differences between today's book and *The Honest-to-Goodness Truth.* This comparison will lead into the other kinds of connections that students have noticed. Update the class connections chart if you have chosen to do one. Then ask students what further ideas about truth they can add to what they discussed in Lesson 11. Is it always good to tell the truth? What do people sometimes confuse telling the truth with? Why is Benjamin's honesty at the end of the story important? Before concluding, have students volunteer the theme of this story.

Lesson 13

Response to Literature:
Theme Thoughts

Objectives:
- Bring closure to the theme of truth through discussion and analysis of theme questions.
- Have students construct a truthmobile.
- Finish and review charts from the lessons.

Writing Prompt:
Write your ideas about one of the unit theme questions.

- **Opening Community Share** Revisit the definitions chart from the first lesson. Ask students what they have to add from the reading and discussion they have done in this unit. Write students' further ideas about the meanings of *truth, honesty, lies,* and *dishonesty* on the chart.

Then look over the cause-and-effect chart. What conclusions might they draw about the effects of lying on the person himself? Discuss with students how something good in the person is lost each time a lie is told or a dishonest action is performed. Guide students to see how difficult it is to regain that good even after admitting the lie or apologizing for a dishonest action. It is easier in the long run to be honest the first time. Then look at the effects of lying on relationships. Why is honesty essential to a relationship? Have students volunteer times that they have lost trust in someone or lost someone's trust because of dishonesty.

TEACHING OPTION

There is no read-aloud segment planned for this lesson. If your schedule allows, you might wish to show a video such as *Honesty: Featuring the Indian Cinderella and Other Great Stories.* Seeing the stories animated might be enjoyable for students and reinforce some of the important ideas in the unit.

- **Writing** Have students choose one of the unit theme questions and respond to it.

- **Book Club/Fishbowl** If possible, extend book clubs today to allow students to share their responses to the theme questions and to construct a truthmobile. Provide each book club with stout construction paper or posterboard, scissors, glue or tape, yarn, and markers. Have students put together a mobile that illustrates all the themes they have discovered throughout the unit.

- **Closing Community Share** Discuss the unit theme questions. Ask students if they have further ideas about truth that they would like to add. Hang students' mobiles around the room.

Lesson 14

Response to Literature:
Final Project

Objective:
Give students an opportunity to show their assimilation of the unit's important ideas.

NOTE: Evaluation Sheet 13, "I Can" Self-Evaluation, is a useful self-assessment tool for younger students. In simple language, it guides students to think about how they performed in the different areas of the Book Club unit. You might want to distribute this form at the end of the unit, work with each student to complete it, and then discuss their responses.

SOCIAL STUDIES CONNECTION

If you are integrating work in this unit with social studies, you might hold another discussion about truth being a core democratic value. Talk about the importance of truth and honesty in the functioning of a democracy. If, in Lesson 7, you created a word web or another type of chart on being a good citizen, include your chart in the discussion.

NOTE: The projects in this lesson may be done individually or in pairs. With beginning writers, you may want to have students write their ideas with the help of a classroom volunteer. You may wish to set aside more than one class for completion of the projects and students' presentations.

- In opening community share, explain that students will be finishing the unit by doing a project. You may wish to have the unit's books in an easily accessible place and display the mobiles and class charts throughout the time that students are working on their projects.

- Depending upon what will best suit your class, you may wish to assign the entire class one specific project or let students choose from the projects described below.

    —**Comic Strip** Have students create a comic strip that illustrates the theme that they consider to be most important. Students should use text and art. Encourage them to draw colorful, oversized frames and to use humor if appropriate.

    —**Truth Award** Have students choose the character from the books in this unit that they feel is the most deserving of a truth award. Students should compose a speech explaining how the character shows the importance of being honest and how he or she demonstrates courage in facing the consequences of his or her mistakes. Students should also design the award to be presented.

    —**Dialogue** Have students write a dialogue between two characters from different books in which the characters share their experiences and their realizations about the importance of truth. Encourage students to develop their dialogues with very specific details from each book and try to establish a realistic tone and manner of speaking.

    —**Skit** Have students write an original script for a short skit in which they teach a lesson about acting truthfully. Have students rehearse their parts and incorporate simple props.

- In closing community share, allow students time to present their projects. Have students think about how their projects reflect what they studied about truth. Then, hold a final discussion in which you revisit unit theme questions and return to "I Can" statements developed at the beginning of the unit.

Framework for Using Book Club *Plus* with Your Basal

Why Teach a Book Club *Plus* Unit with Your Basal?

Nina Hasty, the teacher who developed this unit, taught in a district that mandated the use of a particular basal reading program. Many of the first- and second-grade students in her split-grade-level classroom were struggling to learn to read and not surprisingly, were already becoming disengaged with literacy learning. As a member of the Teachers Learning Collaborative, Nina had been working with other teachers to re-engage young readers and she knew that Book Club *Plus* provided a powerful model for literacy instruction. Like many teachers, Nina was obligated to build her instruction around her basal reading program. Of course, Nina was determined to meet the obligation of providing instruction in reading skills and strategies at students' reading levels using the basal reading program. But she was also determined to integrate literature at her students' age level through the Book Club program. This unit, Stories of Self and Family, provides a framework for integrating Book Club and basal reading instruction through Book Club *Plus*. Through their literacy work in this unit, students read books in a variety of genres, listened to their peers and communicated with them about ideas, and learned literacy skills and strategies and how to apply these strategies independently. In this way, Nina accomplished her goals of increasing her students' achievement and their engagement with reading while meeting the district and state standards and benchmarks.

Structure and Schedule

As you know from previous chapters, Book Club *Plus* combines the use of Book Club with Literacy Block. In a classroom using a basal reading program, the basal selections and their apparatus can be used in the guided reading and literacy center portions of Literacy Block. In this unit, we present Literary Block lessons to show the process of integrating basal materials. In teaching a similar unit, you will want to use your own basal to make decisions about skills and strategies to teach during Literacy Block. As you make your decisions about the basal materials you will use, keep in mind the theme of self and family. We point out the kinds of materials and lessons you might want to look for in your reading program and suggest teaching options to help you tailor the lessons for use with Book Club *Plus.* In this unit, we also introduce strategies for using Book Club *Plus* to support low-achieving students.

During this six-week unit, the class uses the following learning contexts to access literature and to practice skills: book clubs (including fishbowl), reading logs, writer's workshop, literacy centers (including working with words, language arts, and reading), speedwriting, guided reading, shared reading, read aloud, and independent reading. Over the course of the unit, all of these contexts are given their place in the literacy curriculum. This approach makes the unit very flexible and allows you to manage the activities in a realistic way.

Each week students participate in Book Club lessons and Literacy Block. In the first Book Club lesson of the week, the class listens to a read aloud and does a writing (speedwriting) activity. In the second lesson of the week, students go into their book club groups to discuss the Book Club book that all students have read (and reread) at some time during the week. After the discussion, book club groups participate in fishbowls to share what they have discussed. The other three days of the week, students participate in Literacy

	Monday	Tuesday	Wednesday	Thursday	Friday
Week 1	Getting Started Activities				
Weeks 2–6	**Book Club:** • Opening Community Share • Reading • Writing • Book Clubs/ Fishbowls • Closing Community Share	**Literacy Block:** • Guided Reading • Writer's Workshop • Literacy Centers	**Literacy Block:** • Guided Reading • Writer's Workshop • Literacy Centers	**Literacy Block:** • Guided Reading • Writer's Workshop • Literacy Centers	**Book Club:** • Opening Community Share • Reading • Writing • Book Clubs/ Fishbowls • Closing Community Share

* Independent reading is done daily at another time in the day and/or in the reading center. Shared reading is done two or three times a week at a convenient time. Read aloud is combined with Book Club.

Block. Before each Literacy Block lesson begins, the teacher conducts a whole-class lesson on the skill(s) that will be the focus of the guided reading groups. This ensures that all students have access to all the necessary reading skills. Then each group meets for twenty minutes of guided reading or a literacy center, and then students rotate. This combination of contexts supports and challenges all levels of readers. During the final week of the unit, students pull together ideas explored throughout the unit about autobiography, culture, self, and family. The assessment of the students is best done throughout the unit to keep track of the progress of each student. You can use the suggestions for assessment found at the end of this chapter, "I Can" statements (see Chapter 6 and Evaluation Sheets 1 and 13), or your own means of assessment. You might also use center work for additional assessment opportunities each week.

The schedule on page 228 and the Unit Overview chart on page 232 show how the literacy contexts have been allocated. Other scheduling options are presented on page 127.

Why Explore Stories of Self and Family?

This Stories of Self and Family unit focuses students on understanding themselves and their roles within the world. Students at grades one and two are moving from an understanding of self to a broader understanding of family and the world outside the family. Students are introduced to this theme through literature that explores the role of culture in understanding oneself, family, and others. This theme is also strengthened by activities that support reading comprehension and promote the critical thinking that is necessary for students to be successful participants in our society.

Unit Themes

In this unit, students are exposed to many different expressions of the theme of self and family. The books are used in different contexts to support students' exploration of what self and family means. Through the books and book discussions you will examine with students their ideas about autobiography, culture, family, the different people who have helped them become who they are, the ways in which they are the same as and different from their classmates, their roles within their families and community, and what they learn from studying their lives and the lives of others. We suggest that you display big theme questions such as the following for the duration of the unit:

How is my life like a story?

What is family? What makes my family special?

What is culture? How would I describe my culture?

Literacy Skill Instruction

This chart correlates the Book Club *Plus* curriculum areas to individual lessons in the Stories of Self and Family unit. For additional information about each curriculum area, refer to the information in Chapter 2, pages 16–17. Lessons are also correlated to the language arts standards established by the National Council of Teachers of English and the International Reading Association. Numbers in parentheses refer to specific NCTE/IRA standards (see page 136).

Curriculum Correlation Chart

Curriculum Area	Lessons in Stories of Self and Family
Comprehension	**Week 1:** Getting Started (3, 4, 5, 6, 11) **Lesson 1:** Introduction to Book Club (1, 2, 3, 4, 11, 12) **Lessons 2, 19:** Literacy Block: Story Structure (1, 3, 5) **Lesson 3:** Literacy Block: Retelling (3, 5, 12) **Lessons 4, 17:** Noting Details (3, 5) **Lessons 6, 18:** Predicting (3, 6) **Lessons 7, 8:** Literacy Block: Drawing Conclusions (3, 6, 11) **Lessons 9, 10:** Cause and Effect (2, 5)
Writing	**Weeks 2–6:** Writer's Workshop (4, 5, 6, 12) **Lesson 1–23:** Daily Writing (3, 5, 6, 12) **Lesson 4:** Noting Details (3, 5)
Language Conventions	**Week 1:** Getting Started (3, 4, 5, 6, 11) **Lesson 1:** Introduction to Book Club (1, 2, 3, 4, 11, 12) **Lessons 2, 3, 4, 7, 8, 9, 12, 13, 14, 17, 18, 19, 21–23:** Literacy Block: Working with Words (6) **Lessons 2, 3, 4, 7, 8, 9, 12, 13, 14, 17, 18, 19, 21–23:** Writer's Workshop (4, 5, 6, 12) **Lesson 5:** Qualities of a Good Book Club Discussion (3, 4, 11, 12)
Literary Aspects	**Lesson 2:** Literacy Block: Story Structure (1, 3, 5) **Lessons 7, 8:** Literacy Block: Drawing Conclusions (3, 6, 11) **Lessons 11–13:** Compare and Contrast (3, 5, 6) **Lesson 14:** Categorization and Classification (3) **Lesson 15:** Me & the Book (3) **Lesson 16:** Intertextual Connections (3, 6, 11) **Lesson 20:** Autobiography (1, 2, 11) **Lessons 21, 22:** Sequence (3, 4)

Integrating Instruction

The Stories of Self and Family unit provides many opportunities for cross-curricular connections, particularly with social studies. For your convenience, we've identified links with social studies content based on the ten thematic strands defined by the National Council for the Social Studies (NCSS). A complete listing of the NCSS strands is available on page 137. The chart that follows highlights the six strands that relate to this unit.

Correlation to Social Studies Thematic Strands

NCSS Thematic Strands	Lessons and Activities
1. Culture Social studies programs should include experiences that provide for the study of culture and cultural diversity.	**Weeks 1–6**
2. Time, Continuity, and Change Social studies programs should include experiences that provide for the study of the ways human beings view themselves in and over time.	**Lessons 1, 5, 12, 13, 23; Weeks 2–6, Unit Work; Weeks 2–6, Writer's Workshop**
3. People, Places, and Environments Social studies programs should include experiences that provide for the study of people, places, and environments.	**Lessons 1, 3, 5, 10, 13, 15, 16**
4. Individual Development and Identity Social studies programs should include experiences that provide for the study of individual development and identity.	**Lessons 1, 3, 5, 10, 13, 15, 20; Weeks 2–6, Unit Work; Weeks 2–6, Writer's Workshop**
5. Individuals, Groups, and Institutions Social studies programs should include experiences that provide for the study of interactions among individuals, groups, and institutions.	**Lesson 6**

Unit Overview

This chart outlines the complete six-week unit featured in this chapter. Book synopses, weekly planning charts and general procedures for the weeks of the unit are given on pages 233–255.

Six-Week Unit Overview

This unit has been correlated with the NCTE/IRA Standards for the English Language Arts (see page 136). Numbers in parentheses refer to specific standards.

Week 1: Getting Started

- Book Club: Teacher introduces elements of Book Club. Teacher groups students. (11)

- Literacy Block: Class discusses types of centers and practices transitions. Teacher groups students. (11)

- Writer's Workshop: Teacher prepares writer's workshop and discusses it with students. (11)

- Unit Work: Class discusses themes of self and family. Teacher introduces students to the Quilt Writing Project. (4, 11, 12)

- Assessment: See Week 1 planning guide.

Week 2: Book Club and Literacy Block Begin

- Book Club and Literacy Block: See individual lessons for details. (3, 4, 5, 6, 11, 12)

- Writer's Workshop/Unit Work: Class begins Quilt Writing project. (11)

- Assessment: See Week 2 planning guide.

Week 3: Book Club and Literacy Block

- Book Club and Literacy Block: See individual lessons for details. (3, 4, 5, 6, 11, 12)

- Writer's Workshop: Students write inferences and draw conclusions about pictures. (3, 5, 12)

- Unit Work: Small groups brainstorm family stories for the project. (11, 12)

- Assessment: See Week 3 planning guide.

Week 4: Book Club and Literacy Block

- Book Club and Literacy Block: See individual lessons for details. (3, 4, 5, 6, 11, 12)

- Writer's Workshop: Students draft family stories and conference with peers. (4, 5, 11, 12)

- Unit Work: Students make quilt squares. (11)

- Assessment: See Week 4 planning guide.

Week 5: Book Club and Literacy Block

- Book Club and Literacy Block: See individual lessons for details. (3, 4, 5, 6, 11, 12)

- Writer's Workshop: Students revise family stories and edit into a final copy. (4, 5, 11, 12)

- Unit Work: The class quilt is assembled. (11)

- Assessment: See Week 5 planning guide.

Week 6: Book Club and Literacy Block/Closure

- Book Club and Literacy Block: See individual lessons for details. (3, 4, 5, 6, 11, 12)

- Writer's Workshop: Class publishes quilt stories. (4, 11, 12)

- Unit Work: Students present their quilt squares and their stories. (4, 11, 12)

- Assessment: Teacher completes Quilt Writing Project assessment. Students complete self-assessment. (3, 6)

- Assessment: See Week 6 planning guide.

Synopses of the Featured Books

Book Club and Read-Aloud Literature

During this unit, students read and reread the Book Club books at various times during each week. However, each book is initially used as a read aloud. When you read aloud, you create a common literary context for the whole class and you increase opportunities for intertextual connections while providing a model of fluent reading. Following this procedure gives students additional practice and literacy experiences essential to furthering their reading fluency and comprehension.

Aunt Flossie's Hats (and Crab Cakes Later) by Elizabeth Fitzgerald Howard

Each of Aunt Flossie's hats reminds her of a special memory that she shares with Sarah and Susan when they visit her. They especially enjoy the story connected to her best hat because they were there when her hat flew across the water and had to be rescued by a dog. At the end of each trip down memory lane, the girls, their parents, and Aunt Flossie go out for crab cakes, another cherished family tradition.

Bigmama's by Donald Crews

After a long train ride, the narrator and his family arrive at his grandparents' house for the summer. They are greeted with hugs and kisses. Then it's time to explore all the favorite places, to make sure everything has stayed the same since last year. Best of all, there is the anticipation of a whole summer ahead.

Chicken Sunday by Patricia Polacco

The narrator and her friends are determined to buy the beautiful hat in Mr. Kodinski's window for Miss Eula Mae. They even go to his store to ask him if they can earn money for it by doing odd jobs for him. Unfortunately, they arrive at the wrong time, and he thinks they're responsible for pelting his store with eggs. Acting on Miss Eula Mae's advice, they show Mr. Kodinski they are good people and not only earn money for the hat but make a new friend as well.

My Rotten Redheaded Older Brother by Patricia Polacco

Patricia's older brother can do everything better than she can, including eat more raw rhubarb. When her babushka shows her how to wish on a star, Patricia knows that she'll finally win out over her brother. She does. She stays on the carousel longer than he does. But when she finally gets off, she is so dizzy that she falls onto some glass bottles. Her brother has to carry her home and run to get the doctor. Somehow after that, it's okay that he'll always be her older brother.

The Patchwork Quilt by Valerie Flournoy

When Grandma starts the quilt, Tanya is impatient. She can't believe it might take a year to finish. Gradually she begins to understand how stories are woven into the quilt from the scraps of material Grandma includes. Soon Mama is working on the quilt too. Then Grandma falls ill. Determined to finish the quilt, Tanya works constantly until Grandma is well enough to put the last stitches in.

The Quilt Story by Tony Johnston

The quilt stitched with love for Abigail by her mother provides her with security and happiness, even when her family moves. It is put away in the attic and brought out again years later by another child, whose mother repairs it and replaces the stuffing. This little girl's family moves too, but she is comforted by the familiar quilt in a strange place, just as Abigail was.

Tell Me Again About the Night I Was Born by Jamie Lee Curtis

The narrator asks her parents to retell the story about the night she was born. She prompts her parents, reminding them of every detail, from getting the telephone call that she had arrived to flying to pick her up at the hospital to her first nights at home.

Guided Reading Literature

When this unit was used in the classroom, books and selections from a district-mandated basal program were used in guided reading. As you make your decisions about your basal materials, you will want to highlight connections between the basal selections and the themes of this unit. Since you will also be using materials from your basal program, we have not provided specific lessons for guided reading books—although we do suggest strategies that you might want to focus on in your lessons. In addition, you may want to supplement your own selections with the books listed below or the guided reading books and lessons presented in Chapter 9, starting on page 139.

Below Grade Level

A Mother for Choco by Keiko Kasza

Choco is an orphan bird who looks in vain for a mother until he meets Mrs. Bear. Although she doesn't look like she could be his mother, she certainly acts like a mother should. When she takes him home to meet the rest of her children, who are all different too, Choco realizes that he has found his new family.

At Grade Level

Something from Nothing by Phoebe Gilman

When Joseph is a baby, his grandfather makes him a blanket that Joseph cherishes. As Joseph grows older, his grandfather transforms the blanket into a coat, a vest, a tie, a handkerchief, and a button. Then Joseph loses the button. But he keeps the memories and writes the story that will preserve his treasured blanket and grandfather forever.

One of Three by Angela Johnson

The narrator loves spending time with her two older sisters and being one of three. Sometimes, though, she is left behind because she's too young. Then she's one of three with Mama and Daddy, and that's okay too.

Above Grade Level

A Chair for My Mother by Vera B. Williams

After a fire destroys all their possessions, the narrator, her mother, and her grandmother move into a new apartment furnished by friends and family. But there is no comfortable chair for the narrator's grandmother to sit in while she cuts up potatoes or for her mother to relax in after she gets home from her job as a waitress. Finally, they save enough money to buy the perfect chair for the new apartment.

Now One Foot, Now the Other by Tomie dePaola

Bobby is named after his best friend in the world, his grandfather Bob. Bob taught Bobby to walk, told him stories, and did everything with him. Then Bob has a stroke. Now it is Bobby's turn to teach Bob how to walk and to tell him stories.

At and Above Grade Level

Clean Your Room Harvey Moon! by Pat Cummings

When his mother tells Harvey Moon to clean his room on Saturday morning, he is quite sure he can finish in time to watch cartoons. He rushes around, diligently sorting and picking up things. Then his mother comes to inspect what he's done. Unfortunately, she doesn't agree that stuffing everything under the carpet qualifies as cleaning his room so he has even more work ahead of him.

Shared Reading Literature

In shared reading, children sit in small groups and read one book together. The teacher reads the book aloud as the students follow along. This is an interactive reading experience during which the group pauses often to discuss, share, and address questions. Because the teacher reads aloud, this is an opportunity for students to access literature that may be above their instructional reading level, but includes concepts that are appropriate to their age and to the themes covered through this unit. The following titles work well with the unit theme:

The World of William Joyce Scrapbook **by William Joyce**

This colorful autobiography, which Joyce calls a scrapbook, tells the story of Joyce's life through snapshots, stories, and excerpts from his books. He allows readers into his world to see his home, family life, work life, childhood, and elaborate holiday celebrations.

Firetalking (Meet the Author) **by Patricia Polacco**

In this autobiography, the author traces the significant events of her life, attributing her love of storytelling to both sets of grandparents, who sat by the fire in the evening and spun tales for their grandchildren—some true and some that could have happened.

Goin' Someplace Special **by Patricia C. McKissack**

For the first time, 'Tricia Ann is going to the library on her own. She almost turns back after the numerous insults from white people that she endures on the way, but then she remembers her grandmother's example and completes her journey.

Special Classroom Library

The following books about self, family, and quilting are appropriate for your special classroom library during this unit. Allow students to explore the library during reading center and at their leisure to choose texts that match their interests.

Amelia Bedelia's Family Album **by Peggy Parish**

With her trademark literal descriptions, Amelia Bedelia tells the Rogers, her employers, about her family members.

Are You My Mother? **by P.D. Eastman**

Looking for his mother, a baby bird meets a kitten, a hen, a cow, a dog, and finally a big mechanized shovel that sets him back in his nest, just as his real mother returns with dinner.

Babushka's Doll by Patricia Polacco

One day, impatient and demanding Natasha is allowed to play with Babushka's doll, which comes alive and gives Natasha a taste of her own medicine. From that time on, Natasha is much nicer to her grandmother.

The Boy and the Quilt by Shirley Kurtz

This book, which includes instructions for making quilts, tells the story of a boy who finds out firsthand how enjoyable quilt-making can be. With the help of his mother and his sister, he creates a quilt of his own.

The Crazy Quilt by Kristin Avery

The main character, a young bear, finds an interesting quilt made from the clothing of her grandparents and other relatives. She decides to make a crazy quilt of her own out of her family's favorite clothes.

Daddies by Adele Aron Greenspun

The photographs and text pay tribute to the role of fathers in children's lives and describe what fathers need in return.

Families Are Different by Nina Pellegrini

Nico, who was adopted by her parents from Korea when she was a baby, grows to realize that love, not a physical resemblance to each other, brings a family together.

Family Pictures: Cuadros de Familia by Carmen Lomas Garza

In English and in Spanish, using both words and colorful illustrations, the author presents scenes from her childhood. These scenes show her making tamales with her family and picking oranges from her grandparents' trees.

Fly High! The Story of Bessie Coleman by Louise Borden and Mary Kay Kroeger

This biography tells of Bessie Coleman, whose persistence and hard work led her to become the first African American to earn a pilot's license.

Henry and Mudge and the Careful Cousin by Cynthia Rylant

Henry and his big dog Mudge don't know what they're going to do with Henry's perfect cousin, Annie. Finally Henry introduces Annie to the game of Frisbee, which is so much fun that she forgets about staying neat and clean.

The Keeping Quilt by Patricia Polacco

In Patricia's family, a special quilt is used to welcome babies, to provide the canopy for weddings, and to decorate tables for parties. The quilt belongs to Patricia now. She must keep it and all of the memories that accompany it safe for her daughter.

Lucy's Picture **by Nicola Moon**

Lucy uses her imagination and many materials of different textures to make a special picture for her blind grandfather, who says it's the best he's ever seen.

Mama Bear **by Chyng Feng Sun**

When Mei-Mei does not save up enough money to buy the large teddy bear she sees in a shop window, her mother offers her the comfort and warmth she hoped to find in the bear.

New Baby **by Emily Arnold McCully**

Unaccompanied by text, the pictures tell the story of the youngest mouse in the family whose place is usurped by the new baby. Her mother realizes how she is feeling and gives her a special role in caring for the baby.

On Mother's Lap **by Ann Herbert Scott**

Michael says there isn't room for the baby to rock with him and Mother. He finds out, however, that there is always room for one more on his mother's lap.

The Relatives Came **by Cynthia Rylant**

The author describes a memorable summer during which a group of relatives come together for a visit filled with talk and love.

Sisters **by David McPhail**

The special bond that sisters share is celebrated in this story of two sisters. They are alike in many ways, different in others, and love each other dearly.

Tell Me a Story, Mama **by Angela Johnson**

The narrator retells some of her favorite stories from her mother's past, and in doing so, understands the strength of the love that nurtured her mother and is part of her own life.

Thank You, Mr. Falker **by Patricia Polacco**

In this autobiographical story, Patricia can draw beautifully but struggles with reading. Her classmates tease her and she falls behind in her work. Then Mr. Falker, her fifth-grade teacher, recognizes her talents and opens for her the door to the world of words.

Whose Mouse Are You? **by Robert Kraus**

A little mouse takes steps to reunite himself with his family—a mother, father, sister, and new baby brother.

Yo También/Me Too **by Susan Winter**

The narrator of the story, a very young girl, imitates everything her older brother does, from reading books to watching scary movies.

Other Media

Chicken Sunday. (Videocassette, Audiocassette, and CD, 14 minutes)
Patricia Polacco narrates her story, which is one of the Book Club selections in this sample framework. The videocassette also features illustrations from the book.

The Keeping Quilt. (Videocassette, Audiocassette, and CD, 13 minutes)
Patricia Polacco narrates her story, which is a title in the Special Classroom Library in this sample framework. The videocassette also features illustrations from the book.

Thank You, Mr. Falker. (Videocassette, Audiocassette, and CD, 26 minutes)
Patricia Polacco narrates her story, which is a title in the Special Classroom Library in this sample framework. The videocassette features illustrations from the book.

Teacher Resources

***Author Talk* compiled and edited by Leonard S. Marcus**
Fifteen authors share insights about their childhood, the source of their inspiration for writing, and their approach to their craft. Each interview is followed by a short bibliography of the author's work.

***In Love with Quilts* by Leisure Arts, Inc. and Oxmoor House, Inc.**
This book provides a guide to making quilts and includes illustrations and diagrams.

***The Dark-Thirty: Southern Tales of the Supernatural*
by Patricia C. McKissack**
The story "The Chicken Coop Monster" at the end of this collection is appropriate for the self portion of this theme. It talks about how Melissa faces the chicken coop monster and learns that fear itself is the true enemy. With her grandparents' help, she conquers the chicken coop monster. Since this story is within a collection, you may want to consider using it as a read aloud during the unit.

Week 1: Getting Started

Week 1 Planning Guide

Book Club Activities

• Introduce the components of a typical Book Club lesson.   One 30-minute session

Literacy Block

• Tell students what they will be doing in Literacy Block.   5–10 minute sessions 3 times (on Literacy Block days)

Literacy Centers

• Organize the classroom.
• Introduce the students to centers: language arts, phonics, reading.   One 20 minute-session; Ongoing 5-minute reviews of rules when necessary

Unit Work/Writer's Workshop

• Introduce unit themes.
• Begin talking about the Quilt Writing Project.   One 30-minute session; 5-minute unit theme review 2–3 times

Assessment

• Assess students' instructional reading levels.
• Group students according to reading level.   Ongoing

This first week of the unit is used to introduce students to the unit theme and to assess and group students while also teaching them about Book Club, Literacy Block (centers), fishbowl, and speedwriting. The activities can be used in any order you find comfortable. If you are using this unit later in the year, you may be able forgo the assessment and move to the Book Club and Literacy Block lessons starting on page 256. At the end of the first week, you and your students should be ready to dive into Book Club and Literacy Block sessions.

Organization

• If necessary, rearrange students' desks for your centers. (We have suggested centers in this unit but you may choose to create others.) Each reading groups stays together as they rotate through the centers.

PURPOSE FOR EACH CENTER

LANGUAGE ARTS CENTER:
Reinforces the reading strategies taught in guided reading and during whole group instruction.

PHONICS CENTER:
Helps students gain more knowledge about sounds, letters, and words.

READING CENTER:
Gives students access to the Book Club books (and Special Classroom Library books) in many forms; buddy reading, independent reading, through audiotapes, and/or a teacher, teacher's aide, or parent volunteer reading aloud.

- Some teachers like to color-code and label center folders for each group. For example, all reading work could be on red paper and the papers labeled Group "A" Work. Your students may also benefit from a weekly chart of the center activities they are expected to complete. A separate chart can be made for each of the groups. Students cross off the activities they have completed.

Grouping Students

- Throughout the week, assess each student's instructional reading level. You may already have this information. In that case, move directly to grouping the students and introducing Book Club and Literacy Block. If you do not know your students' instructional reading level, you can use the assessments talked about in this book or assessments recommended by your district. A selection of reading inventories are discussed on page 112 and a multi-day writing assessment is described in Chapter 9, pages 155–156.

  A number of word lists have been created as quick and relatively easy ways of initially determining students' instructional reading-group assignments. Some word lists come with informal reading inventories, such as John's Basic Reading Inventory (Johns, 2001). The Dolch Basic Word List has been popular for decades. Since the list has sections ranging from preprimer to third grade, it can give an indication of a student's reading vocabulary. You may also find the information gathered from pretests in your basal helpful.

- Use the data from your assessment to group students in heterogeneous book club groups and homogeneous guided reading groups. There are many different ways to describe homogeneous groupings. For the purposes of this unit, we have used the following terms: Above Grade Level, At Grade Level, Below Grade Level, and Struggling Readers.

Book Club and Literacy Block

- Introduce the idea of Book Club to students. Tell students that they will be reading or listening to books, writing about what they have read or heard, and meeting in groups to discuss their ideas. They will also be meeting as a class to talk about the books. Sometimes groups will participate in a fishbowl. To introduce this concept, show a video of a fishbowl being conducted, or gather some adults or experienced Book Club students from a higher grade level to model fishbowl to your students. You might want to distribute Think Sheet 11, Welcome to the Fishbowl Rules! Explain to students that participating in book clubs and fishbowls will give them an opportunity to think and talk about what they are reading.

- Introduce the concept of speedwriting parties. Nina found that some of her students were intimidated by the idea of writing responses to what they were hearing. She found that speedwriting was something they saw as fun. Students could engage in writing about their thoughts and feelings about a story without getting bogged down by spelling, grammar, and punctuation. The procedure is described in detail in the chart below. Note that throughout the unit, each student in Nina's class had a speedwriting journal as well as a reading log for Book Club. The front cover of each was labeled so that the students would not become confused about the correct writing book to use for each activity. The reading log was used during Book Club writings and the speedwriting journal was used only during designated speedwriting parties.

- Introduce to students what will generally happen during Literacy Block and go over the rules for helping each other when an adult is not present. Practice with the students rotating from center to center. You might want to use a bell, sign, lights, etc., to signal a transition. Work with your students to help them complete transitions quickly. Note: Familiarizing students with the center routine will probably take longer than a week. Try spending a few minutes on each Literacy Block day going over what will be happening in the centers. You may also distribute or display a chart like the one shown on page 243. Students can use the chart to check if they are completing the assigned work.

Speedwriting Procedure

Have students

- listen to or read the story.
- listen to the question or prompt. (Sometimes students freewrite, but often they respond to a teacher prompt. Prompts grow more complex over time. Sample prompts are listed for all lessons that include speedwriting.)
- speedwrite for 3–6 minutes in response to the question or prompt.
- choose an audience to read his or her writing to. (You may want to have students mark their papers with their chosen audience: G for Small Group; T for Teacher; B for Buddy.)

- review the rules. (You may want to distribute Think Sheet 12, Have a Speedwriting Party!, or post the rules on chart paper that you can hang on the board.)
  — Keep your eyes and pencil on your paper.
  — Keep writing until you are told to stop.
  — Cross out your mistakes. Don't erase.
  — Keep going.
  — Have fun.
- share their writing. (read or talk/ listen)

- participate in community share. (Students read and talk about what they wrote to the whole class. Initially this is optional, but gradually all students should be asked to participate. This is a good opportunity for instruction in speaking and listening skills and for the teacher to assess the students (or their speaking and listening skills.)
- turn their speedwriting into a published text. (This is optional. Speedwriting can function as a rough draft if students want to publish.)

Center Work for the week of October 5-7, 1999
Group 1

PHONICS	Write words that have the following Consonant Clusters: pr, fr, sp, br, sk, sl, tr, st Use crayons to write the words on your circles.	Write 4 words that begin with the following diagraphs: th, wh Put each word that you made into a complete sentence.	Say and write each of your spelling words two times. 1. these 2. watch 3. thank 4. dish 5. cash 6. brush	
LANGUAGE ARTS	Grammar Sheet	Naming parts of Sentences	**Complete a Story Map for the story Three Cheers for Tacky**	
LITERACY	Read or Listen to Three Cheers for Tacky on the audio tape.	Read or Listen to Arthur's Pet Business on the audio tape.		
WRITING	Put the Snoopy cartoon together on construction paper anyway that you would like to and make up a story about the cartoon.	Write about "If I had a pet business, what type of pets would I have and what I would do to let people know that I had my own pet business.		

As you do each lesson, please cross if off of your chart. Remember to put your name and date on all papers. Do not rush to complete your work, you
have until Friday afternoon to finish all of your centerwork

▲ Facsimile of sheet describing center activities for a reading group

Theme Introduction and Writer's Workshop

• During this first week, introduce students to the theme of the unit. Start by writing the big theme questions (from page 229) on the board or chart paper and reading them as a class. Ask students to speculate what an autobiography is and what *culture* means. Accept all answers and write them on the chart. Tell students that you will come back to these questions during the unit to add information.

Ask students what a family is, what a family looks like, where some of their family members live, etc. Ask students about family traditions and artifacts that represent their families. Also, ask students about the role each of them plays in the family as an individual. You can use the KWL chart on Think Sheet 13 to record the information students know and want to learn about the concept of family. Students can return to this chart at the end of the unit to record what they learned. Or have students illustrate and label a picture or pictures of a family scene or family members. You may want to have volunteers put their family portraits on a bulletin board to help kick off the Self and Family unit.

► **This student wrote words around a web that conveyed a sense of family as part of the writing process.**

🏷 **QUILT BOOKS**

Some quilt books you might consider placing in your classroom.

- *The Boy and the Quilt* by Shirley Kurtz
- *The Patchwork Quilt* by Valerie Flournoy
- *The Crazy Quilt* by Kristin Avery
- *Firetalking* by Patricia Polacco
- *In Love With Quilts,* Leisure Arts, Inc. and Oxmoor House, Inc.
- *The Quilt Story* by Tony Johnston

• One part of Literacy Block, the writer's workshop, lets students work on their process writing skills. They plan, create rough drafts, revise, and publish their work. During this unit, students have the opportunity to complete a theme-related writing and art project—the Quilt Writing Project. To prepare for writer's workshop, give each student a folder in which to place their work. Also, have quilt books available (see sidebar) for students to examine during the project. Students will use pencils, pens, scissors, crayons, old magazines, glue, and paper during the weeks of this project. While the prompts for writer's workshop fall during the Literacy Block portions of this unit, students can work on their projects whenever it is appropriate.

Explain to students that they will create their own quilt square after reading quilt stories and seeing quilts in books. The students' squares will tell a story about a special place, event, time, etc., that they would want to share with their children and their grandchildren. They will also write about quilts and will describe the significance of their quilt squares. One of the first steps in the project will be for students to create a family word web (as shown above). From the ideas on their word webs, students can write sentences and parts of their stories.

▶ Students created
speedwriting journals
for this unit. They
name their journals
and draw pictures
inspired by the unit
theme.

SPEED WRITING JOURNAL

Name of Journal My family uder a Raibow.

The Crazy Quilt

I would like to have a blue and
green quilt. And I would get
my pices from my old cloths.
And it will bee made out of
sqaure.

wrote to prompt

◀ In this speedwriting
sample, the student
is responding to the
following prompt:
If you could make a
quilt, what would it
look like, where
would you get the
pieces to make the
quilt, and in what
shape would the
pieces be?

You may want to launch this project by showing *The Keeping Quilt* videotape. If you know a teacher or parent who quilts, you might also consider asking that person to speak to the class about quilting and to show the class a few examples. To close the project, you might consider creating a "quilt" from the students' quilt squares and their published writing by taping or stapling them together. Hang the "quilt" on a bulletin board or outside the classroom. Asking students to present their projects to the class gives the class an opportunity to continue discussing the big theme questions as they relate to the project. You might also consider using the presentations as an opportunity to assess students' speaking and listening skills.

Week 2: Book Club and Literacy Block Begin

Week 2 Planning Guide

Book Club

- *The Patchwork Quilt* by Valerie Flournoy (read aloud)
- *Tell Me Again About the Night I Was Born* by Jamie Lee Curtis (buddy reading, audiotape, or independent reading)

Monday and Friday: 30–45 minutes each day

Book Club Activities

- speedwriting party
- community share
- book clubs/fishbowls

Monday: speedwriting 20 minutes, community share 45–60 minutes
Friday: book clubs 20–30 minutes, fishbowls 15–20 minutes, community share 10–15 minutes

Guided Reading and Literacy Centers

- Read from basal text.
  – phonemic awareness
  – letter and word recognition

Tuesday, Wednesday, and Thursday: 20 minutes for guided reading; 20 minutes per center each day

Unit Work/Writer's Workshop

- Launch Quilt Writing Project.
- Revisit theme questions.

Tuesday, Wednesday, and Thursday: 20 minutes each day

Shared Reading

2 or 3 times per week: 10–20 minutes

Week 2 Planning Guide, *continued*

Independent Reading	Daily 10–20 minutes

Assessment Suggestions	
• Review "I Can" statements with students. • Observe students in fishbowl setting.	Ongoing

Book Club and Literacy Block

Students will read, respond to, and discuss Valerie Flournoy's *The Patchwork Quilt* and Jamie Lee Curtis's *Tell Me Again About the Night I Was Born*. Refer to page 256 for Lesson 1 and page 264 for Lesson 5. Students do additional work with the Book Club books in Literacy Block, Lessons 2–4. In Literacy Block, students learn and practice reading and comprehension strategies as they move into, through, and out of the texts.

Guided Reading

Students will meet in small groups to read selections from the district-mandated basal program. Through the reading of these selections, students will focus on learning and/or reviewing such skills as phonemic awareness and letter and word recognition. During the unit, it is very important to help students make connections between their guided reading texts and the themes of this unit. For more detailed descriptions, refer to pages 258, 260, and 262 of Lessons 2–4.

Unit Work/Writer's Workshop

• During this week, have students begin work on the Quilt Writing Project. Students can look at books about quilting and possibly an actual quilt to see how one is constructed. Conducting these introductory activities and giving students time to work and plan together will allow students to generate ideas for their own quilt squares.

• At the end of this week and throughout the unit, you will want to have students revisit the unit theme theme questions and add to a class chart that features responses to these theme questions. Students can revisit these questions in discussions and in writing.

Week 3: Book Club and Literacy Block

Week 3 Planning Guide

Book Club

- *Chicken Sunday* by Patricia Polacco (read aloud/video)
- *Aunt Flossie's Hat (and Crab Cakes Later)* by Elizabeth Fitzgerald Howard (buddy, independent reading, or read aloud)

Monday and Friday: 30–45 minutes each day

Book Club Activities

- speedwriting party
- community share
- book clubs/fishbowls

Monday: speedwriting 20 minutes, community share 45–60 minutes
Friday: book clubs 20–30 minutes, fishbowls 15–20 minutes, community share 10–15 minutes

Guided Reading and Literacy Centers

- Read from basal text.
  - rhyming words
  - prefixes and suffixes
  - drawing conclusions

Tuesday, Wednesday, and Thursday: 20 minutes for guided reading; 20 minutes per center each day

Unit Work/Writer's Workshop

- Brainstorm family stories for project. Write sentences about ideas.

Tuesday, Wednesday, and Thursday: 20 minutes each day

Shared Reading

2 or 3 times per week: 10–20 minutes

Independent Reading

Daily 10–20 minutes

Assessment Suggestions

- Assess students' speaking abilities.
- Observe students' ability to make meaning when reading and listening.

Ongoing

Book Club and Literacy Block

Students will read, respond to, and discuss Patricia Polacco's *Chicken Sunday* and Elizabeth Fitzgerald Howard's *Aunt Flossie's Hats (and Crab Cakes Later)*. Refer to page 266 for Lesson 6 and page 274 for Lesson 10. Students do additional work with the Book Club books in Literacy Block, Lessons 7–9. In literacy centers within Literacy Block, students learn and practice comprehension strategies as they move *into, through,* and *out of* the texts.

Guided Reading

Students will meet in small groups to read selections from the district-mandated basal program. Through the reading of these selections, students will focus on learning and/or reviewing skills such as identifying rhyming words, understanding prefixes and suffixes, and drawing conclusions. As appropriate, make intertextual connections to the Book Club books and highlight ties to the unit themes. For more detailed descriptions, refer to pages 269, 270, and 273 of Lessons 7–9.

Unit Work/Writer's Workshop

Allow students to continue planning and brainstorming ideas for the Quilt Writing Project. Students can continue to list topics and story ideas. Students can then work on writing sentences to support their ideas.

Week 4: Book Club and Literacy Block

Week 4 Planning Guide

Book Club

- *The Quilt Story* by Tony Johnston (buddy reading, independent reading, or read aloud)

Monday and Friday: 30–45 minutes each day

Book Club Activities

- speedwriting party
- community share
- book clubs/fishbowls

Monday: speedwriting 20 minutes, community share 45–60 minutes
Friday: book clubs 20–30 minutes, fishbowls 15–20 minutes, community share 10–15 minutes

Guided Reading and Literacy Centers

- Read from basal text.
  - fluency
  - word recognition
  - comprehension

Tuesday, Wednesday, and Thursday: 20 minutes for guided reading; 20 minutes per center each day

Unit Work/Writer's Workshop

- Make quilt squares.
- Students review unit theme questions and add to their charts about the theme of culture.

Tuesday, Wednesday, and Thursday: 20 minutes each day

Shared Reading

2 or 3 times per week: 10–20 minutes

Independent Reading

Daily 10–20 minutes

Assessment Suggestions

- Monitor students' progress in book clubs and fishbowl.
- Administer self-assessment forms.
- Observe students' understanding of unit theme.

Ongoing

Book Club and Literacy Block

Students will read, respond to, and discuss Tony Johnston's *The Quilt Story.* Refer to page 275 for Lesson 11 and page 282 for Lesson 15. Students do additional work with the Book Club book in Literacy Block, Lessons 12–14. In literacy centers within Literacy Block, students learn and practice comprehension strategies as they move *into, through,* and *out of* the texts.

Guided Reading

Students will meet in small groups to read selections from the district-mandated basal program. Through the reading of these selections, students will focus on learning and/or reviewing skills such as word recognition and comprehension strategies. Make students aware of any connections between their guided reading texts and the unit themes. For more detailed descriptions, refer to pages 277, 279, and 281 of Lessons 12–14.

Unit Work/Writer's Workshop

• Students will continue to work on their story drafts. They can meet with their classmates to help each other revise their pieces. Students can also begin working on their quilt squares.

• Students should revisit the unit themes and add to their charts.

Week 5: Book Club and Literacy Block

Week 5 Planning Guide

Book Club

| *Bigmama's* by Donald Crews (buddy reading, independent reading, read aloud, or video) | Monday and Friday: 30–45 minutes each day |

Book Club Activities

| • speedwriting party
• community share
• book clubs/fishbowls | Monday: speedwriting 20 minutes, community share 45–60 minutes
Friday: book clubs 20–30 minutes, fishbowls 15–20 minutes, community share 10–15 minutes |

Guided Reading and Literacy Centers

| • Read from basal text.
– fluency
– word recognition
– comprehension | Tuesday, Wednesday, and Thursday: 20 minutes for guided reading; 20 minutes per center each day |

Unit Work/Writer's Workshop

| • Revise family stories and edit into final copy.
• Assemble quilt.
• Add to or revise information on the theme question chart. | Tuesday, Wednesday, and Thursday: 20 minutes each day |

Shared Reading

| | 2 or 3 times per week: 10–20 minutes |

Independent Reading

| | Daily 10–20 minutes |

Assessment Suggestions

| • Observe students' progress with a unit project.
• Evaluate students' ability to apply comprehension and vocabulary strategies. | Ongoing |

Book Club and Literacy Block

Students will read, respond to, and discuss Donald Crews's *Bigmama's*. Refer to page 283 for Lesson 16 and page 289 for Lesson 20. Students do additional work with the Book Club book in Literacy Block for this week, Lessons 17–19. In literacy centers within Literacy Block, students learn and practice comprehension strategies as they move *into, through,* and *out of* the texts.

Guided Reading

Students will meet in small groups to read selections from the district-mandated basal program. Through the reading of these selections, students will focus on learning and/or reviewing skills such as fluency, word recognition, and comprehension. You may want to have students discuss briefly how their guided reading texts relate to the big theme questions. For more detailed descriptions, refer to pages 284, 286, and 287 of Lessons 17–19.

Unit Work/Writer's Workshop

Students will do final revisions on their family stories and produce a final copy. Students can then work together to assemble their quilt.

Week 6: Book Club and Literacy Block/Closure

Week 6 Planning Guide

Book Club

- *My Rotten Redheaded Older Brother* by Patricia Polacco (buddy reading, independent reading, read aloud)

Monday and Friday: 30–45 minutes each day

Book Club Activities

- speedwriting party
- community share
- book clubs/fishbowls

Monday: speedwriting 20 minutes, community share 45–60 minutes
Friday: book clubs 20–30 minutes, fishbowls 15–20 minutes, community share 10–15 minutes

Guided Reading and Literacy Centers

- Read from basal text.
  - decoding
  - vocabulary
  - comprehension

Tuesday, Wednesday, and Thursday: 20 minutes for guided reading; 20 minutes per center each day

Unit Work/Writer's Workshop

- Display quilt.
- Plan and complete presentations.
- Revisit unit theme questions for the last time.

Tuesday, Wednesday, and Thursday: 20 minutes each day

Shared Reading

2 or 3 times per week: 10–20 minutes

Independent Reading

Daily 10–20 minutes

Assessment Suggestions

- Review informal assessments conducted throughout the unit.
- Evaluate unit work.

Ongoing

Book Club and Literacy Block

Students will read, respond to, and discuss Patricia Polacco's *My Rotten Redheaded Older Brother.* Refer to page 290 for Lesson 21. Students do additional work with the Book Club book in Literacy Block, Lesson 22. In literacy centers within Literacy Block, students learn and practice comprehension strategies as they move *into, through,* and *out of* the texts.

Guided Reading

Students will meet in small groups to read selections from the district-mandated basal program. Through the reading of these selections, students will focus on learning and/or reviewing skills such as decoding, vocabulary, and comprehension. For more detailed descriptions, refer to page 292 of Lesson 22.

Unit Work/Writer's Workshop

- At this point students will publish and present their work on the Quilt Writing Project. On the project's completion, you can evaluate student work using Evaluation Sheets 14 and 15. Students can conduct peer and self evaluations using Evaluation Sheets 16 and 17.

- Students should revisit and discuss the "big theme questions" and make any final additions to the class chart.

- The teacher will review and evaluate student work and informal assessments that were conducted throughout the unit.

Lesson 1

Language Conventions:
Introduction to Book Club

Objectives:
- Brainstorm ideas about self and family.
- Have students write in response to the book.
- Ask students to share their thoughts about the book.

Vocabulary:
You may want to explain words as you read the book aloud.

Assigned Reading:
The Patchwork Quilt

Writing Prompts:
- Which picture or story was your favorite or least favorite? Why?
- Tell about an artifact that reminds you of family.
- Have you had a family member who was or is sick? How did this make you feel?
- Describe something that you worked on with a family member or a friend.
- Make a connection between Tanya's family and your family.

NOTES:
- Reproducible think sheets and evaluation sheets, referred to throughout this unit, are provided in the back of the book after page 295. These sheets can help students respond to their reading and can help guide assessment.
- All the writing prompts for this unit appear on Think Sheet 14. Pass out copies of this sheet so that students can refer to it as the class completes each reading assignment.

- **Opening Community Share** Begin by talking about the goals for today's lesson. Explain to students that you will be reading aloud and then giving them time to respond to the reading in their speedwriting journals. Tell them that they will then be gathering in their book club groups to talk about the book and discuss their writing. Book club discussions will be followed by closing community share, during which the whole class will gather together to share writing and ideas about the book. Answer any questions they still have about the different elements of Book Club. If necessary, revisit the unit theme before starting to read the book. Have students reflect back on the work they did and the discussions you had in the introductory week of the unit. Another option is to pass around the Book Club books you will be reading during this unit so students can briefly preview the covers and illustrations.

- **Reading** Read aloud *The Patchwork Quilt* by Valerie Flournoy. The book has wonderful illustrations, touches on the idea of a community working together (communities can be families, neighbors, classmates), and reinforces the themes of self and family. Before you read, tell students that they should pay close attention to the story and to the pictures so that they will have the information that they need to participate in the speedwriting party.

- **Writing** Hand out speedwriting journals. Give students the opportunity to decorate their journals for the Stories of Self and Family theme. Start the activity by reading students the writing prompt. Several prompts are listed here. You may want to start with simple prompts for the first few speedwriting activities. You can use prompts that are more challenging when you want to emphasize a particular comprehension strategy or author's craft.

  Review the rules of speedwriting. You may want to hand out Think Sheet 12, Have a Speedwriting Party! and read over the rules with students. Then have students write for 3–6 minutes. Give them some additional time to illustrate their writing and/or to complete any unfinished thoughts or sentences. Stress that they should not erase errors, but cross them out and write the correction above, below, or next to the error.

- **Book Club** Gather students in their book club groups and ask them to read their writing to the group or a person in the group. Have students discuss the writing and talk about the book. Students can spend a few minutes doing this first book club before proceeding to community share.

(If you have time in your schedule, you may want to have students read *Tell Me Again About the Night I Was Born* by Jamie Lee Curtis. The reading of this Book Club book can occur after community share. If your time is limited, students will have the opportunity to access the Book Club books at the reading center on Literacy Block days. Repeated access to these books will help all students participate in Book Club.)

- **Closing Community Share** Have student volunteers read their writing and show their illustrations to their entire community—their classmates. As students read their papers, it is helpful to write down what students read or adlib, since students sometimes forget what they have written. (It is important to allow students who are not proficient in print to adlib—or be a storyteller.) If you write down their story, you will be able to assist them if they ask you to help them with their journal.

After students have shared their writing, talk about the book. Ask them what they learned about families. How would they have felt if they were Tanya? What stories would they like to tell in a quilt?

Give students the opportunity to talk about their Book Club day. What did they enjoy? What could have been better? Brainstorm ways to solve any problems so that the next Book Club day is even better.

ASSESSMENT TIP

During closing community share, you can assess students on their speaking skills and on their comprehension of the writing prompt. You may want to use Evaluation Sheet 5, Checklist for Language Arts Skills that is included at the back of this guide. Use Evaluation Sheets 7–10 for ongoing evaluation of book club groups and reading logs throughout the unit.

Lesson 2

Literacy Block

Whole Class Instruction:
- Story structure
- Long vowels

Objectives:

- **Guided Reading**
Students focus on strategies while reading basal selections.

- **Writer's Workshop**
Students examine quilt books.

- **Open Literacy Block**

In this context, you will use your own district-mandated reading materials. We present skills and strategies that you might want to focus on, but you will also want to refer to the skills and strategies recommended in your basal program.

Before starting Literacy Block with the class, conduct a brief whole-class lesson to familiarize students with the work they will be doing in this part of the unit. This also helps students receive information on skills that will be taught and reinforced within their guided reading groups.

- **Literacy Centers**
  - **Language** Students complete story maps of *The Patchwork Quilt.*
  - **Phonics** Students identify and use long *i* words.
  - **Reading** Students read the Book Club book, *Tell Me Again About the Night I Was Born,* and also read from other theme-related books.

Introduce the idea of story structure. Ask students if they know what it means. Write the definition on the board or place it on a sheet of paper that you can post in your classroom. Reread *The Patchwork Quilt* and ask students to help you complete a graphic organizer of the story structure on the board or chart paper. If possible, keep the graphic organizer posted for students to use as a reference.

Continue your whole-class instruction by reviewing the vowel sound long *i.* Remind students that a long *i* says its "name." Introduce or review the CVCe structure of many words. You might write on the chalkboard words such as *like, fine, mine, nice, kite, side, hide,* and *find.* Tell students that there are words in *The Patchwork Quilt* that have a long *i.* Point out words from the book such as *outside, time, recognized,* and *grandchild.* Write them on the chalkboard and say them aloud to make clear the long *i* sound. Next, write two sentences on the board, read them and ask students which word(s) have the long *i* sound. Circle the words as students respond. Or, write a list of words with long and short *i* on the board and ask individual students to underline or circle the words with the long *i* vowel sound.

The quilt will take <u>time</u> to make.
Tanya wants to go <u>outside</u> to play.
The <u>dime</u> is <u>shiny</u>.

- **Guided Reading**

By this time, you will have chosen the selections to use with each group. Whenever possible, you should use selections that complement the unit theme of Stories of Self and Family and in the course of guided reading, you should help students recognize the connections between their texts and the unit themes. Your objectives with each of your groups will be slightly different, but in all groups, you want to further fluency and enjoyment of reading through the use of comprehension strategies. During this lesson, you may want your struggling readers to focus on phonemic awareness and letter and word recognition. With your other groups, guide students in moving through the text by using context clues to help them determine the definitions of unfamiliar words.

- **Writer's Workshop**

Have students look at the books about quilting that you have gathered. If possible, have students examine a real quilt to look at the construction. This introduction to the project, in addition to the Book Club lesson about *The Patchwork Quilt,* will give students ideas for their own quilt squares.

- **Literacy Centers**

  Students should spend no more than twenty minutes at each center. Before you send homogeneous groups to their first centers, review the objectives of each center. Write them on the board, say them aloud, and/or hand out charts of activities to each group. (See the chart on page 243 for an example.)

  Language Arts With all groups, the focus is on story structure. Have students who are reading below grade level complete a story map of *The Patchwork Quilt.* In this case, you will want to provide a sheet of paper with the questions *Who? Where? Problem? Solution?* on it. As a hint, provide the solution to the main conflict of the story. Students use words, phrases, and sentences to answer the questions. Other groups should complete an entire story map of the text on their own.

  Phonics Have all groups focus on identifying long *i* words. Struggling readers will benefit from circling long *i* words on a list. Other students can practice writing sentences that include words with long *i*. You may also want to use practice sheets that you have in your collection.

  Reading All students will read the Book Club book, *Tell Me Again About the Night I Was Born* by Jamie Lee Curtis. Tell students that they may read independently, with a buddy, or listen to the story on an audiotape (if you have one available). In addition to the Book Club book, direct students to other books about self and family. You can find suggested titles on the special classroom library list, page 236.

- **Close Literacy Block**

  At the end of each Literacy Block lesson, gather students together. Give the class a few minutes to share what they did at centers. Then instruct them to check that all of their work has names and dates on it and that all papers have been put in their work folders. (We say work folders because many teachers use this method to help students organize ongoing and completed work. You may have a different method of organization.) Finally, spend a few moments going over any vocabulary that you highlighted during guided reading. You may also want to review Dolch Sight Words or any vocabulary list that your school requires. This simple closing routine will help students keep their work organized and will serve as a review of the work done at centers.

Lesson 3

Literacy Block

Whole Class Instruction:
- Retelling
- Consonant Digraphs

Objectives:

- **Guided Reading**
  Students focus on strategies while reading basal selections.

- **Writer's Workshop**
  Brainstorm family story ideas. Record them on a word web.

- **Literacy Centers**
  - **Language Arts** Retell a nursery rhyme.
  - **Phonics** Students either work on a *wh* book and illustrate the words, or they list five *wh* words and write riddles with the words.
  - **Reading** Students reread the Book Club book and read from other theme-related books.

- **Open Literacy Block**

Talk about retelling a story with students. Ask students if they know what it means to retell something. Accept all answers before posting the correct answer in the classroom. Ask volunteers to retell all or a portion of the guided reading selection that they read in the previous lesson.

Introduce or review the concept of consonant digraphs. Tell students that a consonant digraph is two consonants that make one sound. Ask students if they know any digraphs and write their answers on the board. Introduce some more digraphs (*sh, th, ch,* and *wh*) Let students know that they will be working with the *wh* digraph. Ask them to name some words with this digraph (*why, what, when*). Remind students that silent letters don't count. For example, the words *knee* or *wrap,* do not start with digraphs. Tricky fact: The *wh* in *whole* is not a digraph. In this case the *w* is a silent letter.

Help students practice the *wh* digraph. Dictate five words for students to write on a sheet of paper or in a word journal. Some examples include *wheat, wheel, when, why, what.* Or, write the words on the board and ask students to read them silently and then write them twice. If appropriate, ask students to use each word in a sentence. (This could be homework.)

- **Guided Reading**

During this lesson, you may want your struggling readers to focus on letter and word recognition. Point out words that are related to the theme of self and family. You might want to ask students to notice words with the *wh* digraph. Focus on reading the words correctly and defining them. With your other groups, focus on fluency and comprehension. Have students practice retelling portions of the selections they are reading.

- **Writer's Workshop**

Continue working on the Quilt Writing Project. Have members of each group of students help each other brainstorm subjects for family stories for the project. Students should create word webs for ideas they want to include in their stories. Remind students to think about the kind of story that was told in *The Patchwork Quilt.*

- **Literacy Centers**

  Review the center objectives with students. Write the objectives on the board or say them aloud.

  Language Arts The focus of this activity is on retelling. Choose a nursery rhyme for the focus of this center. There are many collections of rhymes available on the Internet, or you can choose one from the library. Copy the rhyme onto a sheet of paper with each line or verse separated by space. Have your emergent readers read the poem with a buddy and then illustrate each verse. Then students should cut apart the rhyme, mix up the pieces, and work on "retelling" the rhyme by putting the pieces in the correct order. Other students should read and illustrate the same rhyme and then write a retelling of the rhyme on the back of the sheet.

  Phonics Have your below-grade-level students make a book of words that contain the *wh* digraph. They should illustrate each word and if possible, use the word in a sentence. Sources of words include words you have posted around the classroom and books they have been reading. Students in your other groups should write riddles for five words containing the *wh* digraph. They should exchange their riddles with a partner and see if they can guess the answers.

  Reading Have all students reread the Book Club book, *Tell Me Again About the Night I Was Born* by Jamie Lee Curtis. Tell students that they may read independently, with a buddy, or listen to the story on an audiotape (if you have one available). Encourage students to read or look at the other theme-related books available in the reading center.

- **Close Literacy Block**

  Follow the same procedure as in Lesson 2.

Lesson 4

Literacy Block

Whole Class Instruction:
- Noting Details
- Consonant and Vowel Sounds
- Vowel pair *oo*

Objectives:

- **Guided Reading**
  Students focus on strategies while reading basal selections.

- **Writer's Workshop**
  Students illustrate ideas for the Quilt Writing Project.

- **Literacy Centers**
  - **Language Arts** Students solve and write detail riddles.

  - **Phonics** Create a matching activity for the vowel pair *oo*.

  - **Reading** Students reread the Book Club book and read from other theme-related books.

- **Open Literacy Block**

Ask students if they know what it means to note details. Accept all their answers and remind them that details in the words and the pictures in a story can help them know what a character is thinking. Details also help the reader understand the story. Write a definition together on the board or on a sheet that can be posted in the classroom.

Have students look inside *Tell Me Again About the Night I Was Born* to note details in both the text and illustrations that indicate that the girl is happy, the parents are proud to be new parents, and the dog is happy to have the girl in the family.

Spend a few minutes reviewing the sounds of consonants and vowels. Dictate a few phrases or sentences that use words with long *i* and the *wh* digraph. Remind students to write all the sounds they hear and to read their work to see if it looks right. Repeat words if students need additional help. Then have students dictate sentences for you to write on the board and have students correct their own papers.

> What time is it?
> The whale was white.
> The bike wheel was flat.

Introduce the vowel pair *oo* and go over the sounds that this vowel pair makes. Brainstorm words with the vowel pair, e.g., *school, noon, boot, room, moose, book, look, poor,* and note the different pronunciations. Remind students to be looking for this vowel pair as they read and write. Tell them that it is a difficult pair because it has many different pronunciations.

- **Guided Reading**

During this lesson, you may want to ask your struggling readers to look for the vowel pair *oo* as they read. Remind students to use details from the text and the pictures to help them read fluently. With your other groups, you may want to have students read portions of a selection and then tell some of the details that they noticed in the text and pictures. Ask how these details help them understand the selection.

- **Writer's Workshop**

  Have students illustrate one or two of the ideas that they brainstormed in Lesson 3. Remind them to keep all of this information in their folders to help them write their stories.

- **Literacy Centers**

  Review the center objectives with students. Write them on the board or say them aloud.

  Language Arts For emergent readers, make about fifteen labels to match details that they can find at or close to the center. You might want to write some of the details in the form of riddles. For example, if students are working at desks, you might write *What is brown, has four legs, and doesn't mind being covered in papers?* After students have completed matching the detail labels to items, each student should try with words and pictures to write another detail riddle. Students can swap clues and try to guess the answers.

  Have your other groups write sentences that describe ten details they can observe in the classroom.

  Phonics Have students practice the vowel pair *oo.* You may want to use worksheets provided by your basal program. An activity for all students is to give them a list of words with the vowel pair and then have each student work with a partner to cut pictures out of magazines, newspapers, or flyers to match the words. Possible words for the list include *goose, tool, pool, goo, tooth, boot, roof, food, cook, book, wood.* If students can't find a matching picture, they make illustrations. Have students cut the word list apart and place the words and their pictures in a bag. Students might also write a clue for each word to put in the bag. All students can practice matching the words to pictures and clues. Remind students to read each word aloud and to think about the correct pronunciation.

  Reading Have all students reread *Tell Me Again About the Night I Was Born* by Jamie Lee Curtis. Encourage students to read or look at the other theme-related books available in the reading center.

- **Close Literacy Block**

  Follow the same procedure as in Lesson 2.

Language Conventions:
Qualities of a Good Book Club Discussion

Objectives:
- Review book club discussion and fishbowl procedures.
- Have students write in response to the book.
- Ask students to share their thoughts about the book.

Vocabulary:
again
night
born
phone
airplane
adopt
hospital
nursery
perfect
lullaby
family

Assigned Reading:
Tell Me Again About the Night I Was Born

NOTE: In this chapter, this selection is used as a Book Club book. To see how the same material can be used for guided reading in Literacy Block, turn to Chapter 9.

Writing Prompts:
- Why does the girl want to hear about the night she was born?
- Write two details from the book that tell you the girl is happy.
- Who is telling this story? How do you know?

- **Opening Community Share** Tell students that they are going to work in their book club groups and do some fishbowls today. Review the Book Club discussion rules with students. A suggested list is provided on page 117, but give your students the opportunity to tailor the list.

Hand out reading logs to each student. Talk about the difference between their speedwriting journals and reading logs, explaining that their speed-writing journals are used when the teacher reads a book aloud, asks a question, and gives them a limited time to write. The reading logs, however, are used when students are within a group and writing about a book that everyone has read and that they will discuss in their groups. Remind them that they will be writing questions and thoughts about Book Club books in their reading logs. Discuss ways that a reader can respond to their reading. Distribute Think Sheet 5, Things to Do In Your Reading Log. Focus on one reading response from the think sheet so students do not become overwhelmed. The others can be explained to students at different times throughout the unit when they are asked to respond in different ways. Give students a few minutes to decorate their reading logs for the theme, or ask them to decorate the logs at another time.

- **Reading** In the last three lessons, students have had the opportunity to read *Tell Me Again About the Night I Was Born* by Jamie Lee Curtis. At this time, you may want to discuss the vocabulary words on the list. If you think students have had enough time to read the book, move on to the writing portion of this lesson. If you feel that students need another reading, you may want to read the book aloud and discuss any areas of confusion.

- **Writing** You may want to consider gathering students in their book club groups and allowing them to write and discuss the book as a group. Post the writing prompts or hand out Think Sheet 14, on which the writing prompts appear. Tell students that they only need to respond to one prompt. During these types of meetings, you will want to walk around the room taking notes to help you in assessment. You will also want to take these notes to share with students

🔖 VOCABULARY

We have included a list of vocabulary words from the book. However, the best approach is to allow vocabulary study to arise naturally from reading, writing, and discussion. In this case, you may want to introduce the vocabulary words to students at the reading center where they are first exposed to the book. Or, you may want to ask students to list words they find interesting or difficult. They can then discuss the words in their book clubs. Think Sheet 7 gives one format for recording words during reading.

as they make their first attempts at self-assessment. Finally, you can help each group remain focused.

- **Fishbowl** If this is the first time doing book clubs/fishbowls, you may want to walk the students through the process. You could join a group and have the other students surround the group to observe. You can lead the discussion off by mentioning a specific writing prompt, asking students if they have any questions or comments, and then giving them time to write in their reading logs. Different fishbowl groups can then meet, and you can facilitate discussions and help students to stay focused on talking and writing. Before beginning fishbowl, be sure to establish and review rules. (See Think Sheet 11 and pages 115–117 of this guide for additional information about fishbowl.) Not all book club groups will be able to discuss their books in fishbowl in a single day. You will need to determine how much time you have available and notify the groups that will be asked to be "fish."

  TEACHING TIP
  The teacher who developed this unit set up a rotation of fishbowl groups. She posted this schedule in the classroom for everyone to use.

  Ask students to come to the fishbowl area. Tell them that they can bring their Book Club books and their reading logs to fishbowl. Give each group doing fishbowl 3–6 minutes to talk about the book. Give a few minutes for student observers to make positive comments and suggestions about the discussion. After all the groups have done their fishbowls, you may want to do fishbowl assessments as shown on Evaluation Sheet 3. From fishbowl, the class can move into closing community share.

- **Closing Community Share** Talk about the book with students. Ask them how this book supports the self and family theme. Discuss the fact that the girl in the story is talking about herself but also talking about her family. Focus on experiences that students might share with the main character, e.g., bedtime, parents listening, or a family story. Some students will be interested in talking about adoption and perhaps the term *birth mother*. Remind students that there are many kinds of adoptions and that this is just one kind. If any of your students are adopted, give them the opportunity to share thoughts about this topic.

  Review what happened in book clubs. Ask students what they enjoyed and what could have been better. Are there any things that need to be changed to make the lessons run more smoothly?

  Spend time revisiting the unit's theme questions. Ask students if their answers to any of these questions have changed or become more detailed after the readings or activities they have completed so far. Remind students of these questions throughout the unit.

Lesson 6

Comprehension:
Predicting

Objectives:
- Discuss family traditions.
- Encourage students to make predictions as you read the book.
- Have students write in response to the book.
- Ask students to share their thoughts about the book.

Vocabulary:
No vocabulary, but you may want to explain words as you read the book aloud.

Assigned Reading:
Chicken Sunday

Writing Prompts:
- What traditions does your family have?
- What traditions would you like your family to have?
- What does family mean to you?

- **Opening Community Share** Talk to students about tradition. Tell them that a tradition is a custom, or something that a certain group of people does or says. A tradition is done repeatedly, usually at a certain time or place. Give students some examples of traditions. For example, your school or class may have some traditions that students will find familiar. Ask: In what kinds of traditions do you participate? Do your families or friends have traditions?

  Review the skill of making predictions with students. Tell them that a prediction is a reasonable guess about what will happen later in a story. Remind them that a good prediction is based on the text. Students should read or listen to a story to get clues so that they can predict what will happen next. Tell students that they should also use their own background knowledge to help them make predictions. Encourage them to listen carefully to the story you are going to read.

- **Reading** Read aloud *Chicken Sunday* by Patricia Polacco. As you read the book, pause to note any traditions mentioned in the book (Sunday dinner, dyed eggs, Easter hats, pouring chicken on Miss Eula's grave). Give students a chance to make predictions about what will happen next. Model making a prediction if students are reluctant to speak. For example, pause after you have read the page where the children are having dinner. You might say: "I wonder how the kids can get the hat for Miss Eula. I predict that they are going to try to buy the hat." Encourage students to make their own predictions. (Other opportunities to predict are when the children give the eggs to Mr. Kodinski and how Miss Eula will react when the children give her the hat.) Write the students' predictions on the board. After reading the book, discuss which predictions turned out to be accurate.

- **Writing** Hand out or have students retrieve their speedwriting journals. Place the writing prompts on the board and then read them with your students. Review the rules of speedwriting if necessary. Have students write for 3–6 minutes. Then give them some time to illustrate their writing and/or to complete any unfinished thoughts or sentences.

- **Book Club** Gather students in their book club groups and ask them to read their writing to the group or a person in the group. Have students discuss their responses and talk about anything they found interesting or confusing about the book. You may want to have students read the Book Club book, *Aunt Flossie's Hats (and Crab Cakes Later)* by

Elizabeth Fitzgerald Howard if time permits. Students will also have the opportunity to access the Book Club books at the reading center on Literacy Block days.

- **Closing Community Share** Encourage students who didn't share their writing with the group after the last speedwriting session to read or speak this time. However, sharing should still be optional. Students can participate by listening and responding to what other students contribute.

Return the discussion to traditions. Ask students what they have learned about traditions. You may want to talk about the author of the book, Patricia Polacco. Tell students that this book tells a story about things that actually happened to her as a child. This kind of book is an autobiography, a book that tells about events in the author's life. Ask students if there are things about this book that remind them of other books they have been reading. Students might make some intertextual connections to

▼ *Chicken Sunday* **speedwriting journal entry**

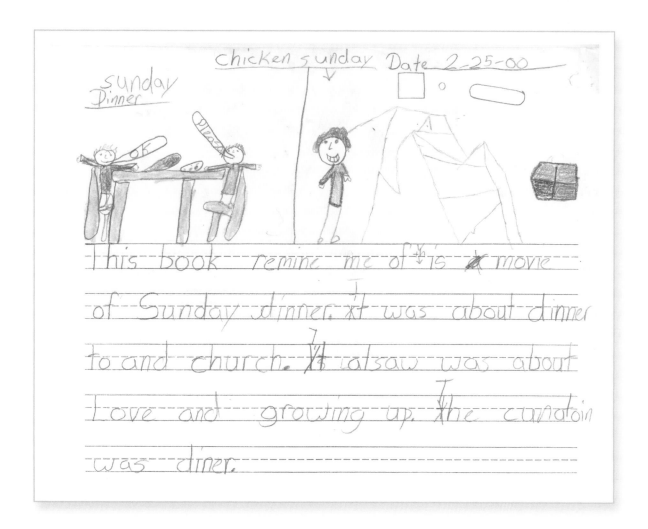

The Patchwork Quilt, Tell Me Again About the Night I Was Born, or other texts they are reading.

Ask students what they think about speed-writing. Is listening to a book and then writing and talking about it changing the way they think about reading?

⬤ **SHARED READING OPTION**

You might want to engage students in shared reading using *Firetalking,* another autobiographical book by Patricia Polacco. Encourage students to make intertextual and thematic connections between this book and *Chicken Sunday.*

Lesson 7

Literacy Block

Whole Class Instruction:
- Drawing conclusions
- Letter/sound correspondence

Objectives:

- **Guided Reading**
  Students focus on strategies while reading basal selections.

- **Writer's Workshop**
  Students write main idea sentences using their brainstorming and webs.

- **Literacy Centers**
  - Language Arts
    Students draw conclusions about pictures.
  - Phonics Students work with letter-sound correspondences.
  - Reading Students read the Book Club book, *Aunt Flossie's Hats (and Crab Cakes Later),* and read from other theme-related books.

- **Open Literacy Block**

Introduce the concept of drawing conclusions. Ask students if they can give a definition. Tell students that not everything they find out from a book is stated directly by the author. Readers need to use clues from the text to draw conclusions, or make decisions, about what the author is saying. Post a definition of drawing conclusions in your classroom.

Model and practice this skill by playing some games. First, play a riddle game. For example, you can ask, "I am round and you can roll or bounce me. What am I?" Ask students how they knew the answer. Point out that they used clues from the question and used what they know about things that bounce to answer the riddle. Another game that you can play with students is to show different facial expressions and ask students to draw conclusions about what your expression says about what you are feeling.

Work with students to practice letter-sound correspondences. You will want to choose letters, digraphs, consonant clusters, and blends that you have been working on. For example, you might choose the letters *l* and *a, b, e, d, c.* Place each letter on an individual index card or write the letters on the board. Give students the sound of a letter and have them identify the letter. Then show the letter to the students and have them give the sound. Finally write CVC (consonant-vowel-consonant) words from the letter cards, e.g., *lab, lad, led, bed, cab.* Call on individual students to read the words by first saying the sound for each letter, then saying the first letter independently as they blend the last two letters together, *l---ab.* Finally, have them blend the initial letter with the rest of the word. You can also have the entire group read these words in chorus.

- **Guided Reading**

  During this lesson, you may want struggling readers to identify rhyming words and prefixes and suffixes as you and they read the story aloud. Help students draw conclusions about the story content. With your other groups, ask students to draw conclusions and point out the clues from the selection. With all groups, help students make connections between what they are reading and Stories of Self and Family.

- **Writer's Workshop**

  Have students read over their individual webs of brainstormed topics and then write and draw main ideas for their quilt stories.

- **Literacy Centers**

  Review the objectives of each center with the class or with individual groups. Write them on the board or say them aloud.

  Language Arts The focus for all students is to draw conclusions. Students reading at a lower level should look through magazines and books to find and cut out pictures or photographs of families. Have them draw conclusions about what the people or family members in the pictures are thinking or feeling. Other students should also be looking for and cutting out pictures, but they should write sentences giving their conclusions.

   TEACHING TIP

  If students in any of your center groups were not able to participate in the previous Book Club lesson, you may want to have the rest of the group update them at the reading center. You will want to have a copy of *Chicken Sunday* at the reading center.

  Phonics Have all groups practice letter-sound correspondences with the letters you chose for the whole-group lesson. Ask below-grade-level readers to form words with magnets, wooden letters, cubes with letters, etc., to match pictures. This kinesthetic activity will help reinforce letter recognition. (Note: If your classroom is equipped with enough computers, you can conduct this activity using phonics software.) Have other students read a short story with *l* (or other letter) words throughout. Have students find the words and write them on a sheet in alphabetical order. Alternatively, you can play a clue word game: I am thinking of a word that has four letters and tells me that you are not on time: LATE.

  Reading All students will read the Book Club book, *Aunt Flossie's Hats (and Crab Cakes Later)* by Elizabeth Fitzgerald Howard.

- **Close Literacy Block**

  Give the class a few minutes to share what they did at centers. Review any vocabulary that you highlighted during guided reading or any vocabulary or spelling list that your school requires.

Lesson 8

Literacy Block

Whole Class Instruction:
- Review drawing conclusions
- Short *u*

Objectives:

- **Guided Reading**
  Students focus on strategies while reading basal selections.

- **Writer's Workshop**
  Continue writing sentences to support brainstormed ideas.

- **Literacy Centers**
  - **Language Arts**
    Students match conclusion sentences to pictures.
  - **Phonics** Students identify words that contain short *u* or write rhyming words.
  - **Reading** Students reread the Book Club book and read from other theme-related books.

- **Open Literacy Block**

  Review drawing conclusions with your students. Read aloud a portion of a picture book and then ask students to draw conclusions about what the characters might do next, or are thinking or feeling. *The Relatives Came* by Cynthia Rylant is a book that lends itself to this activity. Other books are listed in the special classroom library list, page 236.

  Introduce or review the short vowel *u* (or another vowel you are working with in your basal). Tell students that short *u* makes one sound. Give students a word such as *umbrella* to help them hear the sound. As you say and sound out each word/phrase/sentence, let your students know which words are proper nouns and need a capital letter. Reinforce that a sentence begins with a capital letter and ends with a punctuation mark. A few sample words, phrases, and sentences to use in dictation are shown below.

  Words: bug, mug, hug, dull, gull, hull, fun, jump, sun, duck, cluck, jump, bump

  Phrases: snug as a bug, run in the sun, munch on lunch,

  Sentences: The pup dug a hole.; I can hug my mom.; The duck was stuck in the mud.

- **Guided Reading**

  During your guided reading groups, ask students to draw conclusions about the texts they are reading. Model drawing conclusions for all your groups. Ask students who cannot read at grade level to draw conclusions using clues from pictures, and when possible, from the text. Students who are reading more fluently can be expected to state the clues they used.

- **Writer's Workshop**

   Have students continue to work on writing sentences to support their brainstormed story ideas. You may want to have students work in pairs to help each other write sentences that can eventually be used in their stories.

- **Literacy Centers**

   Review the center objectives with students at the beginning of the session. Write the objectives on the board or say them aloud.

   Language Arts Have all groups do an activity where they draw a line from a picture to a sentence that tells what the people in the picture may be thinking or feeling. If you do not have a worksheet that focuses on this skill, you may want to create an activity using pictures and sentences from the previous lesson's language-arts activity. Simply place the pictures on the table with sentences (that you have revised and written on cards) and ask each group to match the pictures and the sentences. Students will be intrigued to notice that some of the sentences they wrote and pictures they cut out have been used as the foundation for this activity.

   Phonics Ask all groups to create rhyming words for the word parts *-ud*, and *-um*. If you have a group of students that cannot write rhyming words, you may want to use or create a paper where students are asked to match a word to a picture. Some possible words for either activity include: *drum, gum, glum, plum, swum; bud, cud, dud, mud, spud, thud.*

   Reading Have all students reread the Book Club book, *Aunt Flossie's Hats (and Crab Cakes Later)* by Elizabeth Fitzgerald Howard. Tell students that they may read independently, or with a buddy, or listen to the story on an audiotape (if you have one available). Encourage students to read or look at the other theme-related books available in the reading center.

- **Close Literacy Block**

   Follow the closing routine that works best for you. Give students a chance to discuss what they have learned during their center work and what connections they see to the unit themes.

Lesson 9   **Literacy Block**

Whole Class Instruction:
- Cause and Effect
- Consonant cluster *cl*

Objectives:

- **Guided Reading**
  Students focus on strategies while reading basal selections.

- **Literacy Centers**
  - **Language Arts**
    Students explore cause and effect.
  - **Phonics** All students practice *cl* words.
  - **Reading** Students reread the Book Club book and read from other theme-related books.

► Students write cause-and-effect statements related to *Chicken Sunday* by Patricia Polacco.

- **Open Literacy Block**

Talk to students about cause-and-effect relationships. Explain that a cause tells why something (event or action) happened and an effect tells what happened as a result of a cause. Emphasize that knowing about cause-and-effect relationships can help students read and understand stories. Reread *Chicken Sunday* by Patricia Polacco (used in Lesson 6) to students. Then work with students to create a cause-and-effect chart either on the board or on chart paper. Prompt students with questions, such as "What caused the children to want to get the hat for Miss Eula? What was the effect of not having enough money?" If your students are ready, you may want to talk about how each cause may have more than one effect, and one effect may have more than one cause. A portion of a sample cause-and-effect chart is shown below.

Review the sounds of consonants and vowels that you have already covered. Then have students write the following words on a sheet of paper: *clap, clip, clump, clam.* Enunciate each letter as you dictate. Then dictate the sentences: *I can clap hard.* and *Dan has two paper clips.* As students write

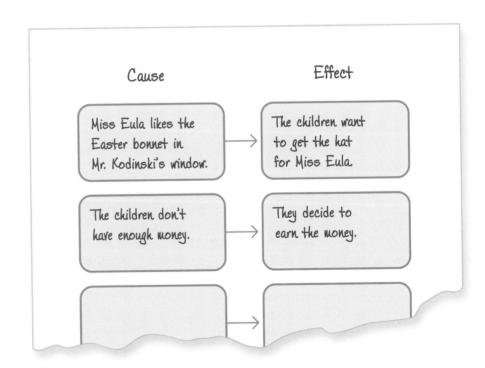

the sentences, remind them that a complete sentence contains a subject and a predicate. Then ask volunteers to dictate the correct spelling of the words and sentences for you to write on the board. All students should correct their papers. You may want to circle the subjects and underline the predicates in the sentences on the board.

- **Guided Reading**

  During this lesson, ask struggling readers to look for the consonant cluster *cl* as they read. Have all students think about and identify cause-and-effect relationships in the selections they are reading. Emphasize that thinking about the cause-and-effect relationships can help students understand the text.

- **Writer's Workshop**

  Have students continue to work on writing sentences to support their brainstormed story ideas. Students can focus on writing detail sentences to support their main ideas.

- **Literacy Centers**

  Review the center objectives with students. Write them on the board or say them aloud.

  Language Arts Give all groups access to *Tell Me Again About the Night I Was Born* by Jamie Lee Curtis. Have students reading below grade level work in pairs to read the book or look at the pictures. Ask these students to match pictures from the book that represent cause-and-effect relationships. For example, phone ringing—people on plane, baby—parents smiling, woman sneezing—mother putting up her hand, baby bottle—baby smiling, diaper—baby crying. Have other students look at the same pictures and write cause-and-effect sentences. You can also use cause-and-effect matching or sentence-completion sheets to practice this skill. However, using *Tell Me Again About the Night I Was Born,* gives you an opportunity to assess students' understanding of the skill and the story.

  Phonics Have students practice the consonant cluster *cl.* You may have materials available for this type of practice. Struggling readers can benefit by practicing matching *cl* words to pictures, while other students can write and illustrate words that contain *cl.* The following list of words are possibilities for this activity: *cloud, clam (or clamshell), clap, class, claw, clay, cliff, clock, cloak, closet, cloth, clown.*

Reading Have all students reread the Book Club book, *Aunt Flossie's Hats (and Crab Cakes Later)* by Elizabeth Fitzgerald Howard. Encourage students to read or look at the other theme-related books available in the reading center.

- **Close Literacy Block**

  You might want to talk about common cause-and-effect relationships that your class encounters during the day, e.g., a bell rings and this causes students to go to lunch.

Lesson 10

Comprehension: Cause and Effect

Objectives:
- Review book club discussion and fishbowl procedures.
- Talk about cause and effect in *Aunt Flossie's Hats (and Crab Cakes Later)*
- Have students write in response to the book.

Vocabulary:
afternoons
boxes
crab cakes
memories
thought
minute
different
exciting
special
favorite

Assigned Reading:
Aunt Flossie's Hats (and Crab Cakes Later)

Writing Prompts:
- Why are Aunt Flossie's hats important to her?
- What things do you keep because they remind you of something?

- **Opening Community Share** Tell students that they are going to work in their book club groups and do some fishbowls today. Your students may benefit from a review of the book club discussion and fishbowl rules. Lesson 5 contains information for talking about discussions and fishbowls.

  Review with students that a cause tells why something (event or action) happens and an effect tells what happened as a result of a cause. Remind students that the author of this book included several stories or memories from Aunt Flossie's past. Ask students what caused Aunt Flossie to remember things that happened in her life. Help students understand that Aunt Flossie kept the hats because they cause her to remember important events in her life.

- **Reading** In the last three lessons, students have had the opportunity to read *Aunt Flossie's Hats (and Crab Cakes Later)* by Elizabeth Fitzgerald Howard. However, you may want to read the book aloud for all students. Go over any portions of the story that students found confusing as they read the book. For example, students may not understand the reference to the Great War (World War I). Tell students that many communities held parades to celebrate the end of the war and to welcome home soldiers.

  Review vocabulary words. Place words that are of particular interest on the board or on a word wall. Talk about the meaning(s) of each word.

- **Writing** Gather students in their book club groups to write reading log responses and discuss the book. Tell students they can write their own responses, use prompts, and/or use Think Sheet 5, Things to Do in Your Reading Log. Remind them to use their reading logs to help them have interesting discussions. You will want to walk around the room taking notes to help you assess students' discussions. Some groups may need help in remaining focused on the book, but you will need to give students time to share what kinds of things they keep to remind them of special events in their lives.

- **Fishbowl** Ask students to come to the fishbowl area. Tell them that they can bring their Book Club books and their reading logs to fishbowl. Give each group doing fishbowl about 3–6 minutes to talk about this particular book. If a book has a great deal of substance, the fishbowls may last longer. Have student observers make positive comments and suggestions about the discussion. After all the groups have done their fishbowls, you may want to do fishbowl assessments as shown on Evaluation Sheet 3.

- **Closing Community Share** Ask students what they thought about the book. Did they feel that the author told the story well? Why or why not? You may also want to help students think about any traditions that are talked about in the book. Are these traditions similar in any way to the traditions that they read about in *Chicken Sunday* during Lesson 6?

● SHARED READING OPTION

This is a good place to include shared reading using *Goin' Someplace Special* by Patricia C. McKissack. Students can discuss what our older relatives give to us. Guide students to understand why Aunt Flossie's stories are so important to her family, and how they affect Susan and Sarah. Then they can focus on Tricia Ann and the influence her grandmother has on her.

Lesson 11

Comprehension:
Compare and Contrast

Objectives:
- Have students compare and contrast elements of the story.
- Have students participate in Book Club activities.

Vocabulary:
quilt
warm
stitch
pretended
wore
tore
once
moved
new
patchwork

- **Opening Community Share** Tell students that comparing means to look at similarities between things, and contrasting means to look at differences. Words that show similarities are *like, common, both,* and *same.* Words that show differences are *unlike, but,* and *however.* Tell students that authors sometimes use comparison and contrast in their stories to help the reader understand the setting.

- **Reading** Read aloud *The Quilt Story* by Tony Johnston. Encourage students to listen for things that are the same and things that are different. As you read the story, stop periodically to ask if your students have any questions. Have students think about how the girls are similar and different. During your reading, define words for your students. You can pick from the words listed in the column at left and add your own. Words that

Assigned Reading:
The Quilt Story

Writing Prompts:
- How are the girls alike?
- Compare and contrast the two families.
- How do you know that there are two different times in this story?

you want your students to have access to during the week can be put on your board or word wall.

- **Writing** Place the writing prompts on the board and then read them with your students. Have students get their speedwriting journals ready. Remind students to pick one writing prompt (or assign one for the class). Have students write for 4–6 minutes. Then give them some time to illustrate their writing and/or to complete any unfinished thoughts or sentences.

- **Book Club** Gather students in their book club groups and ask them to read their writing to one person in the group. Have each pair of students discuss the similarities and differences they noticed about the characters and setting in the story. Note: Students will be reading and examining *The Quilt Story* throughout the week. They will have the opportunity to discuss other aspects of the book during Lesson 15.

- **Closing Community Share** Encourage students to talk about the similarities and differences they noticed between the book's characters and the settings. Did the comparisons and contrasts that the author included help students understand the changes in setting and time? Some students might want to compare and contrast what they heard and saw during the read aloud with aspects of their own lives.

Discuss how *The Quilt Story* expresses the importance of family. Have students talk about how the family in *The Quilt Story* is similar to and different from their own families. Guide students to think about how families care about each other and do things for each other.

● **ASSESSMENT OPTION**

Meet with students individually to discuss their performance thus far in this unit. Preview self-assessment sheets that students might be asked to complete. Take a few minutes to set goals for the next few weeks. Ask students to talk about what they are learning.

Lesson **12**

Literacy Block

Whole Class Instruction:
- Comparing and Contrasting
- Past tense

Objectives:

- **Guided Reading**
  Students focus on strategies while reading basal selections.

- **Writer's Workshop**
  Students draft family stories, conference, and begin making quilt squares.

- **Literacy Centers**
  - **Language Arts** Students compare and contrast objects.

  - **Phonics** Students add *-ed* to a list of verbs.

  - **Reading** Students read Book Club book, *The Quilt Story* by Tony Johnston, and read from other theme-related books.

- **Open Literacy Block**

  Ask the class to compare two students and contrast two students. You may want to begin the activity by comparing and contrasting yourself to a student. (I have a blue sweater. Natalia has a green sweater. We both have brown hair.) Write students' comparison and contrast statements on the board. Read the statements aloud.

- Discuss forming the past tense of a regular verb by adding *-ed*. Write sentences on the board using the present tense. Underline the word in the present tense and ask students to come up to the board and rewrite the sentences using the past tense. After several students have had a turn, suggest a verb and ask the class to dictate sentences using the present tense for you to write on the board. As a class, decide how to write the verb in each sentence in the past tense.

I walk my dog.	She quilts a blanket.
I walked my dog.	She quilted a blanket.

- **Guided Reading**

  Help struggling readers focus on comprehension, phonemic awareness, and word recognition through their instructional-level text. Other groups should focus on fluency, comprehension, and word recognition. With all groups, you will want to encourage students to examine similarities and differences among the characters, settings, or themes of the selections.

- **Writer's Workshop**

  Have all students use the sentences that they have been writing to begin a draft of their stories. Remind students that their writing and their quilt square need to tell a story about a special place, event, or time that they might want to share with their children and grandchildren. Tell students that they can conference with another student if they need help. You will also want to have materials available for students to start making their quilt squares.

 QUILTING TIPS

The quilt squares can be made from a variety of materials. You may want to give each student a sheet of construction paper or cardboard to use as a base. Tell students that their squares should not be bigger than the sheet of paper. Provide markers, scrap paper, glue, magazines, and other materials for students to use. Remind them that the written story and the quilt square should work together to tell a story that they might want to tell to their children and grandchildren.

- **Literacy Centers**

  With students, review the objectives of your centers. Write them on the board or say them aloud.

  Language Arts Gather a number of objects, such as two teddy bears, toys, pictures, or picture books. Have struggling readers work in pairs to verbally compare and contrast the objects. Other students should complete a Venn Diagram to compare and contrast each set of objects.

  Phonics Give all groups a sheet with words in the present tense. Have students change the words from the present tense to the past tense by adding *-ed.* Words that you may want to use include *quilt, sew, play, add, need, dress, fish, walk, wish, land.* You may think of other theme-related words. For additional practice, have students use some of the words in sentences with both the present and past tense form of each word.

  Reading All students will read the Book Club book, *The Quilt Story* by Tony Johnston. In addition to the Book Club book, place other theme-related books in the center. You may want to rotate your book selection at this time. Students may have had the opportunity to look at all the books in the center during the past few weeks.

- **Close Literacy Block**

  Give the class a few minutes to share what they did at centers and to put away their work. Review any vocabulary that you highlighted during guided reading. Talk to students about the progress they made with their quilt stories and how their stories relate to the big theme questions.

Lesson 13

Literacy Block

**Whole Class
Instruction:**
- Review comparing and
  contrasting.
- Adding *-ing* to create
  verb participles

Objectives:

- **Guided Reading**
  Students focus on
  strategies while reading
  basal selections.

- **Writer's Workshop**
  Students continue
  drafting their stories
  and making their quilt
  squares.

- **Literacy Centers**
  - **Language Arts**
    Students compare and
    contrast by writing or
    drawing.
  - **Phonics** Students
    work with verb
    participles.
  - **Reading** Students
    reread Book Club
    book.

- **Open Literacy Block**

Draw a Venn diagram on the board. Have the class compare and contrast one of the following: summer/winter, a quilt/a blanket, bread/pie. Ask all students to fill in the Venn diagram as you write words and phrases on board. Remind students that they can use Venn diagrams to help them understand parts of a story.

Introduce or review forming verb participles. Tell students that these are verbs that can work with other verbs to tell the reader that an action is ongoing. Write the following sentences on the board.

> I am quilting a blanket.
> She is playing hide and seek.
> We are taking a test.

Discuss each example and underline the base verb. Show students that they can make participles by adding *-ing*. Discuss that if a word (take) ends in *e*, they need to drop the *e* before adding *-ing* (taking).

- **Guided Reading**

At this time, you may want to make some notes about how students in various groups are progressing with their instructional-level selections. You can observe students' fluency, word recognition, and comprehension. These notes will help you move students among groups as necessary.

- **Writer's Workshop**

Remind students to read over what they wrote in the previous lesson to check it for errors. Students can work with partners to help them revise their stories.

- **Literacy Centers**

If necessary, review the center objectives with students at the beginning of the session. Write them on the board or say them aloud.

Language Arts Have all students use a Venn diagram or another graphic organizer to compare and contrast one or two of the following pairs: a horse and a car, a candle and a lamp, a new house and an old house. All students can write and/or illustrate and label their ideas.

Phonics Have struggling readers break apart words on a list, e.g. *looking = look + ing.* Possible words include *quilting, looking, talking, going, playing, making, taking, walking.* Assess students' ability to add the *e* to the end of words such as *making* after taking off *-ing.*

Ask your other groups to read a short paragraph, such as the sample below, and correct errors by adding *-ing.* If you don't have time to reproduce a paragraph for students to use, you can ask them to copy the paragraph from the board and then correct it.

> Macy and Ted are look (looking) at a small quilt in a store. She is take (taking) a long time to decide. The quilt costs a lot of money. Ted is speak (speaking) to the people in the store. He thinks the store can sell the quilt for less. Macy and Ted walk to another store. She is smile (smiling) because she found the same quilt for less money.

Reading Have all students reread the Book Club book, *The Quilt Story* by Tony Johnston.

- **Close Literacy Block**

Review any vocabulary that you introduced during guided reading. Discuss with students whether reading other books about quilting (in the reading center) has helped them understand *The Quilt Story.*

Lesson 14

Literacy Block

Whole Class Instruction:
- Categorization and Classification
- Letter/sound correspondence

Objectives:

- **Guided Reading**
  Students focus on strategies while reading basal selections.

- **Writer's Workshop**
  Students continue drafting their stories and making their quilt squares.

- **Open Literacy Block**

Explain to students that groups of items that all have something in common are often given a name or phrase that identifies all of them. Read aloud *Clean Your Room, Harvey Moon* by Pat Cummings (see the Guided Reading Literature on page 234). Then write the heads *Toys and Games* and *Clothes* on the board. Ask students to use ideas from the book and their own ideas to add words to each category. Write their suggestions under the correct heads.

At this time, review letters and sounds that you have introduced. These may include letters and sounds introduced throughout this unit in addition to letters/sounds that you have introduced during other parts of your curriculum. Say each letter, cluster, or digraph and ask students to give

- **Literacy Centers**
  - **Language Arts** Students categorize objects.
  - **Phonics** Students play with letters to make words. Some groups write riddles for each word.
  - **Reading** Students reread Book Club book.

you the sound. Then make a sound and ask students to give you the letter or letter combination that represents the sound.

- **Guided Reading**

Use your chosen instructional-level texts with each group.

- **Writer's Workshop**

Students should continue writing the drafts of their family stories and constructing their quilt squares. Suggest to students that they review what they have written and add details that will help their readers understand the sequence of events. Remind students that they need details to support their main ideas and that they can look at the sentences they wrote earlier in the unit for ideas.

- **Literacy Centers**

Review the center objectives with students. Write them on the board or say them aloud.

Language Arts Have a stack of magazines and/or newspapers on the table. Ask students reading below grade level to cut out and paste pictures in two categories. For example, you could give them a sheet with the categories Family and Moving. Other students can be given the same categories and asked to write words that fit in the categories.

Phonics Have letter cards available for each student in a group. Have struggling readers create words with two to four letters. If you think they will have difficulty completing the task, give them picture cards and ask them to "write" the words to match the pictures. After they complete each word, they should say the word. For example, you can give a picture of a dog and then ask students to use the letter cards *d, o, g,* to write the word. Alternatively, you may have a computer program that helps students practice letter/sound correspondence.

Students in other groups can use the same letter cards to create words. Include consonant blends and clusters in their cards. Students should read the words aloud as they create them. After they have created five to six words, challenge them to write a riddle for at least two of the words they created. They can ask each other the riddles.

 **VOCABULARY**

Tell students that they might be finding words in the Book Club book that are difficult or unfamiliar to them. Remind them that they can record these words in their reading log and talk about these words during book club discussions or in any of the closing activities. If you have started a "word wall," you can add to the wall as students read and find more words.

Reading Have all students reread the Book Club book, *The Quilt Story* by Tony Johnston. Encourage students to read or look at the other theme-related books available in the reading center.

- **Close Literacy Block**

Follow your closing routine. Give students the opportunity to talk about center work they found interesting. Some students may want to talk about classifying words and pictures into categories.

Lesson 15

Response to Literature:
Me & the Book

Objectives:
- Review book club discussion and fishbowl procedures.
- Have students write in response to the book.
- Ask students to share their thoughts about the book.

Vocabulary:
Review vocabulary covered in Lesson 11 in addition to words noted by students.

Assigned Reading:
The Quilt Story

Writing Prompts:
- What happens when each girl moves? How does each girl feel?
- How do you make yourself feel better when you are sad? Is there someone or something that can make you feel better?

- **Opening Community Share** Students have read *The Quilt Story* several times at this point. In Lesson 11, they worked on comparing and contrasting elements of the story. In this lesson, the focus is on having students use a response type called Me & the Book. In this kind of response, students write or draw (in their reading logs) about something in the book that reminds them of a situation or event from their own lives. The writing prompts give them two ideas.

  Review the vocabulary you covered in Lesson 11. Ask students if there are other words they found interesting or confusing. Add these words to your word wall for the unit. Students may want to look at their copy of *The Quilt Story* to help them remember how the words were used.

- **Reading** To vary their reading, students may form pairs and read *The Quilt Story* aloud to each other. Have students concentrate on reading fluently and with expression.

- **Writing** Hand out students' reading logs. Give them a few minutes to respond to the book. You may want to post the writing prompts or hand out Think Sheet 14. Remind students to try a Me & the Book response type.

- **Book Club** Students will focus their discussions on their own experiences of moving or feeling sad. Remind students to listen carefully to each other and to observe how their personal experiences are like events and situations in the book.

- **Fishbowl** Follow the same procedure as in previous lessons. Encourage students to show their Me & the Book thoughts and highlight them during closing community share.

- **Closing Community Share** Focus the discussion on the connections students described in their logs and fishbowl discussions, emphasizing that books will become much more meaningful if they relate them to their own lives. In particular, ask students to share stories from their own lives in which they felt sad or worried and somebody or something comforted them. Have students think about the saying "Home is where the heart is," and relate this to the book and to their own lives.

  Guide students in a review of the big theme question, How would I describe my culture? Return to the charts the class has been working on and ask students to add or revise information about the idea of each student's culture. Ask students if they think everyone has a distinct culture, and why or why not.

Lesson 16

Literary Aspects: Intertextual Connections

Objectives:
- Have students make intertextual connections.
- Encourage students to think about setting in books.

Vocabulary:
station
conductor
horse and wagon
record player
kerosene lamps
dipper
outhouse
roosted

Assigned Reading:
Bigmama's

Writing Prompts:
- Why do you think the family members call their grandmother Bigmama?
- Make a connection between this story and *Chicken Sunday*.
- How is farm life different from city life?

- **Opening Community Share** This unit offers a good opportunity for students to make intertextual connections between books. Review the term *intertextuality*. If necessary, explain that one book or movie might remind us of another book or movie because of similar characters, story lines, settings, or themes. Invite students to make intertextual connections between books and movies they've seen and *The Quilt Story* that they finished in Lesson 15. Make the connection between intertextual connections and the comparing and contrasting that the students did in the last few lessons.

  End opening community share with a discussion of the literary term *setting*. Explain that the setting of a book is the time and place in which it occurs. Encourage students to listen for details that illustrate time and place as you read the story. Ask students to think about how the setting might affect characters in a book.

- **Reading** Read aloud *Bigmama's* by Donald Crews. Explain words and concepts as you read the book aloud. Some of the terms listed on the left may cause confusion. Encourage students to think about the setting of the book. Is there anything about the setting that reminds them of other books they have read?

- **Writing** Choose one of the writing prompts for speedwriting and write it on the board. Read it with your students. Have students get their speedwriting journals ready. At this point in the unit, you may want to give students 3–4 more minutes to write and 10 minutes or longer to finish their illustrations.

- **Book Club** Gather students in their book club groups and ask them to read their writing to one person in the group. Have the students discuss the setting of the story. Students will be reading and examining *Bigmama's* throughout the week.

- **Closing Community Share** Encourage students to talk about the setting of the book and any intertextual connections they can make to other books and/or movies.

Lesson 17

Literacy Block

Whole Class Instruction:
- Noting Details
- *Y* acting as a vowel

Objectives:

- **Guided Reading** Students focus on strategies while reading basal selections.

- **Writer's Workshop** Students revise family stories and begin editing into final copies.

- **Literacy Centers**
  - **Language Arts** Students demonstrate knowledge of details.
  - **Phonics** Students work together to say words and write which long vowel sound they hear.
  - **Reading** Students read Book Club book, *Bigmama's*.

- **Open Literacy Block**

Tell students that pictures, words—everything in a story consists of details. These details can help a person understand the story and what characters are thinking. Ask students to give you examples of details from books they have been reading. You may also want to note details from various basal selections that you have been using in guided reading. Prompt students to think about how authors are describing characters: are the character(s) happy/sad/angry? How does the author make that clear through details?

Break students into small groups and have each group look through a few stories to find words that end in *y*. Write the words on the board and read the list with the students. Then ask what they hear at the end of the words. Explain that in many words that end with a *y*, the *y* makes the long *i* or *e* sound, e.g. *try, puppy.*

- **Guided Reading**

Help struggling readers focus on word recognition and comprehension through their instructional-level texts. Other groups should focus on fluency, word recognition, and comprehension. Ask all students to pay attention to details in the texts they are reading.

- **Writer's Workshop**

  Have students work on revising their stories. Remind them that the goal is to create final copies of the stories to publish with their quilt square. Encourage students to look over their quilt squares and make the finishing touches.

 **TEACHING TIP**

Parent volunteers can help students edit stories for publication. You may also find a parent who is willing to type the students' stories onto a computer. The parent should work with each student.

- **Literacy Centers**

  Talk briefly to your students about the goals for centers today.

  Language Arts Have struggling readers work to complete sentences with details from *Bigmama's*, while other students write details they find in *Bigmama's* on a separate sheet of paper. When writing your sentences, you may want to think about how they can be used to provide evidence that your students are comprehending various words and concepts. Example sentences for the activity are provided below.

  > It took a _____ (long) time to reach Bigmama's.
  > When the _____ (train) reached Cottondale, it was nearly empty.

  Phonics For this activity, mix up your groups. Have struggling readers work with average or higher level readers. Each pair of students will read and say aloud a list of words ending in *y*. The following are some words you may want to use: *bunny, cry, empty, every, friendly, mummy, my, nearby, nearly, only, silly, scary, tiny, try, very.* You will want to tailor the list to the needs and abilities of your students. As the pairs of students read the words, they should write which long vowel sound they hear at the end of each word.

  Reading All students will read the Book Club book, *Bigmama's* by Donald Crews. Have students read independently, with a buddy, or listen to the story on an audiotape. If students are using an audiotape to access the story, make sure they have a copy of the book. Remind all students to be thinking about how the setting affects the people in the book.

- **Close Literacy Block**

  Give the class a few minutes to share what they did at centers and to put away their work. Talk to students about the progress they made with their quilt stories.

  Encourage students to think about *Bigmama's* in terms of their Quilt Writing Project. Are there ways that this book can help them think about their writing? Is *Bigmama's* a story that they might want to tell their children or grandchildren. Why?

Lesson 18

Literacy Block

Whole Class Instruction:
- Have students make predictions.
- Work with vowel pairs, *ow, ou.*

Objectives:

- **Guided Reading** Students focus on strategies while reading basal selections.

- **Writer's Workshop** Students continue revising stories and start assembling quilts.

- **Literacy Centers**
  – **Language Arts** All students make predictions about pictures.
  – **Phonics** Students practice with vowel pairs, *ow, ou.*
  – **Reading** Students reread Book Club book and read from other theme-related books.

- **Open Literacy Block**

Talk to students to help them understand that in predicting, the objective is to make a guess about what you think will happen next. To make a prediction, a person will use what he or she has read, heard, or seen.

Read the class a story to practice predicting. Choose a theme-related book that students will not have encountered at the reading center or in the special classroom library. Show the book to the students and ask them to make predictions using information from the title of the story and the cover art. Write all their predictions on the board. As you read the story, ask students what they think will happen next, and if that thing happens, what will happen after that. Refer back to their original predictions as appropriate.

After the predicting mini-lesson, ask students if they know any words with the vowel pairs *ow,* or *ou.* Write their examples on the board. Say each word and then have the students repeat the words. Ask students what sound the vowel pairs make. Have volunteers use the words in complete sentences. Write the sentences on the board or on chart paper.

- **Guided Reading**

As you are teaching each guided reading lesson, gather information about students. Since the unit is coming to an end, examine "I Can" statements to determine the progress of your students. This type of assessment can also help determine if a child is ready to move to a different reading group.

- **Writer's Workshop**

If you have decided to have students attach or tape together their quilt squares into a class quilt, begin the process now. It may take several days for the entire quilt to be completed. Be sure you consider how you want to integrate the students' writing into the design. A parent volunteer or aide may be required for help. If your display areas are small, you may want to make several smaller quilts.

- **Literacy Centers**

Write center objectives on the board or say them aloud.

Language Arts Have all groups look at pictures to discuss and predict what they think will happen next. Magazines, newspapers, posters, and paintings, are all sources of pictures for this activity.

Phonics Have your struggling readers draw a picture for each of the following words and label it: *cow, snow, out, grow, crow, round.* Ask your other students to write a list of rhyming words for *snow* and *round.*

Reading Have all students reread the Book Club book, *Bigmama's* by Donald Crews. Encourage students to read or look at the other theme-related books available in the reading center.

- **Close Literacy Block**

Review any vocabulary that you introduced during guided reading. Talk to students about how their quilt looks. Ask what is interesting about the quilt squares or the process of putting them together.

Lesson 19

Literacy Block

Whole Class Instruction:
- Examine story structure with students.
- Review letter/sound correspondences.

Objectives:

- **Guided Reading**
  Students focus on strategies while reading basal selections.

- **Writer's Workshop**
  Students continue putting together final versions of their stories and the class quilt.

- **Literacy Centers**
  - Language Arts
    Students practice determining story structure.

- **Open Literacy Block**

Help students understand the parts of a story and identify information they get from each part. For this activity, you can use either the Book Club book or an appropriate basal selection. Reread the story for students. On the board or chart paper, draw the story map. An example story map is provided on the next page. Work with students to fill in the information. Review how each part of the story supports the goals of the author in conveying the story.

Do a quick review lesson of letters and sounds you have introduced. Say each letter, cluster, or digraph and ask students to give you the sound. Then make a sound and ask students to give you the letter or letter combination that represents the sound.

- **Guided Reading**

Use instructional-level texts with each group to complete a story map. Struggling readers may at this time be able to complete the activity with some assistance.

– **Phonics** All students practice letter/sound correspondences with available phonics games.

– **Reading** Students reread Book Club book and read from other theme-related books.

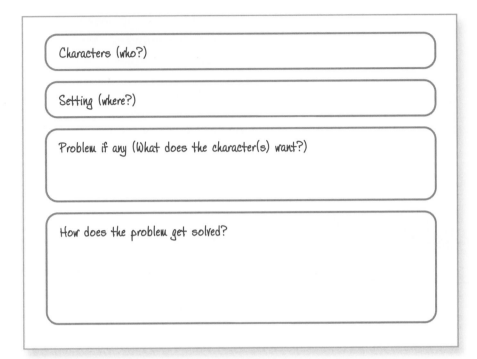

Characters (who?)

Setting (where?)

Problem if any (What does the character(s) want?)

How does the problem get solved?

▶ **Story Map**

• **Writer's Workshop**

Continue completing stories and the quilt. Tell students this project must be completed within the next week. Some students may need extra time to work on the project.

• **Literacy Centers**

Write the center objectives on the board or say them aloud.

Language Arts For this activity, provide copies of a story that you have already read with students. Also provide a blank copy of a story map, such as the one above. Struggling readers can examine the book and either draw or cut out pictures (from magazines, etc.) to place on a story map. Other groups can draw and write to complete the story map. Encourage students to discuss the activity and help each other.

Phonics Provide several phonics games, flashcards, or phonics worksheets for students to practice letter/sound correspondences. These activities should be organized by instructional level for your groups. If you have computers available, you may want to have students use phonics software.

Reading Have all students reread the Book Club book, *Bigmama's.* You may want to vary this activity by having pairs of students read the book to each other. Struggling readers can describe what they see happening in the pictures of the story. Remind them to think about the times they have heard the story read to help them with this activity.

- **Close Literacy Block**

  Follow your closing routine. Give students the opportunity to talk about center work they found interesting.

Lesson 20

Literary Elements: Autobiography

Objectives:
- Review the characteristics of autobiography.
- Identify elements of *Bigmama's* (and other Book Club books) that are autobiographical.
- Ask students to participate in fishbowls.

Vocabulary:
Review vocabulary covered in Lesson 16 in addition to words noted by students.

Assigned Reading:
Bigmama's

Writing Prompts:
Give students the same set of writing prompts as in Lesson 16. Ask them to look back in their reading logs and choose a different prompt and respond to it.

- **Opening Community Share** *Bigmama's* and the other Book Club books provide many opportunities to highlight the characteristics of autobiography. Ask students what the word *autobiography* means—an autobiography is an account written by the author about his or her life. Remind students that they have discussed this term at other times during the unit. Point out the big theme question, discuss the shared reading selection *The World of William Joyce Scrapbook,* or talk about how the students' Quilt Writing projects all contain elements of autobiography. Then ask students to talk about how *Bigmama's* is an autobiographical story. Have students state other autobiographical stories they have heard or read in this unit. This might be a good time to distinguish between a story written in an autobiographical style— a story that is fiction but is written as if it were an autobiography—and a true autobiographical account.

  SHARED READING OPTION

  Use William Joyce's *The World of William Joyce Scrapbook* for shared reading. This is a unique example of how one person chooses to present his autobiography, and students can talk about the aspects of his life that he highlights and why.

- **Reading** Take this opportunity to assess students' fluency. Have pairs of students read the story to each other. Walk around the room making notes about how individual students are progressing in fluency. You may want to focus only on a portion of your class during a session. In that case, spread this activity over several Book Club days.

- **Writing** Hand out students' reading logs. Give students a few minutes to respond to the book. You may want to post the writing prompts or hand out Think Sheet 14. Encourage students to try a new response type, e.g. Author's Craft or Feelings. Remind students to look at Think Sheet 5, Things to Do in Your Reading Log.

- **Book Club** Look for evidence of growth in the areas of listening and speaking as students share their reading log entries in their groups. Encourage students to listen carefully to what people have to say about the book and respond thoughtfully.

- **Fishbowl** Follow the same procedure as in previous lessons. As this unit nears completion, you will want to review the assessments that you have conducted during the unit. Listen to students' conversations for evidence of growth in the use of comprehension strategies, listening, and speaking. You may want to use one of the checklists included in the Evaluation section starting on page 315.

- **Closing Community Share** Discuss culture with the class. Help students make intertextual connections among *Bigmama's, Chicken Sunday,* the shared reading books *The World of William Joyce Scrapbook* and *Goin' Someplace Special,* and the other books that students have read during the unit. How does each book reflect the culture of the author and/or the characters? What similarities and differences do your students notice between what they are reading and their own lives?

  This would be a good opportunity to add or revise information on the big theme question charts that students have worked on during the unit. Is there anything that the class would like to say about the *What makes my family special?* question based on today's discussion?

Lesson 21

Comprehension:
Sequence

Objectives:
- Introduce or review sequencing.
- Have students use sequencing as a strategy for checking their comprehension of a story.

- **Opening Community Share** Introduce or review sequencing with your students. Tell students that the sequence of a story is the order in which the events happen. Remind students that thinking about the sequence of the story can help them understand what is happening. They can also write about the sequence of events in response to a story.

  Refer to an experience that the entire class has shared. It might be a picture book, poem, movie, field trip, or the daily class routine. Ask the class to generate a list of two or three important events from the experience. Help students decide between important events and details and ask the class to arrange the events in the order in which they happened.

Vocabulary:
weasel
awful
terrible
worst
better
set a record
challenged
rotten
redheaded
rhubarb
puckers
wish
carnival
incredible
carousel
stitches
passed out
special
relationship

Assigned Reading:
My Rotten Redheaded Older Brother

Writing Prompts:
- What things does your sister or brother do to bother you?
- What can you do better than your sister or brother? Why can you do that thing better?
- Does your grandmother or another adult give you advice? What does the person say to you?

Discuss why sequencing is important. Guide students to see that it helps them understand a story, helps them write their own stories, and is useful for retelling or discussing a story.

Have the class brainstorm several visual ways to represent a sequence of events. Show students that they can use lists, charts, and story boards to help them record sequence. Ask students to practice sequencing by creating a sequence of story events in their speedwriting journals.

- **Reading** Read aloud *My Rotten Redheaded Older Brother* by Patricia Polacco. Before or during your reading, talk about words for which your students may need definitions and/or help reading. You can pick from the words listed in the left-hand column and add your own. Encourage students to listen for the sequence of events in the story.

- **Writing** Have students pick a writing prompt and then write for 4–7 minutes. If necessary, review the speedwriting rules. Remind students that they will be sharing their writing with their classmates.

- **Book Club** Have students work either as a group or in pairs to share their speedwriting ideas. Students will be reading *My Rotten Redheaded Older Brother* throughout the week. They will have the opportunity to discuss other aspects of the book during Lesson 20.

- **Closing Community Share** Take this opportunity to encourage students to make intertextual connections between *My Rotten Redheaded Older Brother* and other books they have read during this unit. Some students may notice how the illustrations that Patricia Polacco did in *Chicken Sunday* have a similar feel to the illustrations in *My Rotten Redheaded Older Brother*. Others may notice some connections to the home in *Bigmama's*. Encourage students who haven't been active participants in discussions to make comments.

This is the last set of lessons for this unit. You will want to start wrapping up the unit with the class. Students will need to finish their writing projects, and you may want to talk to them about how any presentations of their work will be done. You will also want to give students time to think about the big theme questions and what they have learned about self, family, and culture throughout this unit.

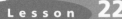

Lesson 22

Literacy Block

Whole Class Instruction:
- Sequencing
- Words that begin with *bl* (or other letters)

Objectives:

- **Guided Reading**
  Students focus on strategies while reading basal selections.

- **Writer's Workshop**
  The class publishes the quilt(s) and family stories.

- **Literacy Centers**
  - **Language Arts** Students sequence information.
  - **Phonics** Students create a *bl* book.
  - **Reading** Students read Book Club book, *My Rotten Redheaded Older Brother,* and read from other theme-related books.

- **Open Literacy Block**

  Review sequencing. As a class, go through *My Rotten Redheaded Older Brother* and the students' speedwriting books. Sequence all of the things that the sister and brother tried to do better than each other. Ask students to dictate this information in complete sentences. Write the sentences on the board or on chart paper.

  Work with students on words that begin with *bl* (or other letters you are emphasizing). Ask students to say the sound and volunteer words that begin with *bl.* Dictate phrases, words, or sentences containing the *bl* combination for students to write. Collect the papers as a form of assessment.

- **Guided Reading**

  Help all students focus on decoding, vocabulary, and comprehension through their instructional-level books.

- **Writer's Workshop**

  Have all students work to prepare their writing for publication. If you are not using a computer, students should copy over their work neatly and follow any other publication guidelines you have in your classroom. The Writing Process Checklist, on Think Sheet 3 may help students decide if their work is ready to be published. Encourage students to act as reviewers for each other.

- **Literacy Centers**

  Review your center objectives with the class.

  Language Arts Have struggling readers paste a set of pictures in sequence. This can be an arbitrary set of pictures showing a sequence such as planting a seed and watching it grow into a plant, or you may want to show a set of pictures for any of the Book Club books or your guided reading selections. Give other students a topic (or several topics to choose from) and ask them to write out the steps in sequence. Possible topics: getting ready for school, the morning routine in your classroom, making a sandwich.

  Phonics Have all students make mini *BL* books with words and illustrations. You may want to make the blank books ahead of time.

Reading All students will read the Book Club book, *My Rotten Redheaded Older Brother* by Patricia Polacco. If you have been rotating books in and out of the reading center, you may want to place a large variety of books in the center for the last part of the unit. Students can revisit books that they have read in the past weeks and think about the intertextual connections and the connections to the big theme questions.

- **Close Literacy Block**

Some of your students may be ready to talk about their quilt squares and their stories. You could start your presentations today. However, you may want to spend a few minutes going over the rules for being a good audience and a good presenter. The presentations are a good opportunity to assess students on their listening and speaking skills. A checklist appears on Evaluation Sheets 4 or 5 or create a checklist of your own.

Lesson 23

Response to Literature:
Wrap-Up Options

Objectives:
- Review skills and strategies.
- Bring closure to the theme through discussion and analysis of theme questions.
- Proceed with conclusion of Quilt Writing Project.

Note: The following is a list of activities you might consider for the last few days of the unit. You will need to determine which activities are most suited to your classroom.

- **Skill Review** As appropriate, review comprehension strategies and phonics skills covered in the lessons of the unit. Look back at students' center work and/or your informal assessments to decide if your students need additional instruction in any areas.

- **Book Club** Conduct a final Book Club lesson. Ask students to read *My Rotten Redheaded Older Brother* and respond to a writing prompt. You can choose a prompt from Lesson 21 or ask students to write about how the book supports the the unit themes. For example— What parts of this story are autobiographical? What does this book show about families? What kind of culture does this family have? If there is time, have several of the book club groups discuss the book in fishbowls.

- **Theme Thoughts** Revisit the big theme questions. Ask students what they have learned from the reading and discussion they have done in this unit. Write students' ideas about self, families, and culture on the board. Discuss how students' ideas about these big theme questions have changed over the course of the unit. Remind students to draw upon their experiences with the Book Club books and any other books they read during this unit to support their ideas.

- **Quilt Writing Project** Continue with student presentations, or conduct a final discussion of the Quilt Writing Project. Talk about what students liked about the project and what they think they learned. You may want to have individual students fill out Evaluation Sheet 16, Quilt Writing Project Self-Assessment. Students can also complete evaluations of other students' projects. Evaluation Sheet 17 can help students focus their thoughts about the qualities of the projects.

- **Assessment** Throughout the unit, you have been assessing students' progress with informal assessments and reviews of their work in Book Club and in your centers. The evaluation section offers a Quilt Writing Project assessment check-list (Evaluation Sheet 14) and also a rubric (Evaluation Sheet 15) that you may want to use as you review the folders students have been keeping for writer's workshop and their final projects. Additionally, you and your students can use the "I Can" statements to evaluate student progress. You might find either Evaluation Sheet 1 or 13 useful for incorporating "I Can" statements into your process.

● ASSESSMENT OPTION

Have students complete evaluation sheets 11 and 12. These sheets will help them to set goals for the next Book Club *Plus* unit.

Think Sheets

The think sheets in this section are blackline masters that you can copy for your class. A few of the sheets are specific to the frameworks outlined in Chapters 9–11, but most of them can be used with any Book Club *Plus* unit.

Name _____ Date _____

Responding to the Readings

Theme Questions

- How is my life like a story?
- What do I learn from studying my own life and the lives of my classmates?
- What is autobiography?
- What is culture?

Roxaboxen

- Roxaboxen is . . .
- What and where is Roxaboxen?
- How do you pretend?

- Why do you think the author wrote about Roxaboxen?
- If you were a character in *Roxaboxen*, who would you be and what would you do?
- Who built Roxaboxen?
- Draw a picture of the house you would build in Roxaboxen.

- Roxaboxen is . . .
- How does this book make you feel?
- How is *Roxaboxen* like an autobiography?
- Write the important events of the story in sequence.

26 Fairmount Avenue

Chapter 1; pp. 1–8

- Have you ever felt like Tomie?

- What is the worst storm you have ever experienced?

- What do you think Tomie's family will find when they go to the new house?

Chapter 2; pp. 9–15

- Compare and contrast Tomie's relationship with his grandparents to your relationship with your grandparents.

- Describe your grandparents and great grandparents.

Chapter 3; pp. 16–23

- Make a character map of Tomie.

- List the characters in the book.

- Have you ever experienced what Tomie did at the theater? How did it make you feel? Compare your experience with his.

Chapter 4; pp. 24–31

- How is the time of Tomie's childhood different from our present time?

- What style of writing and art does Tomie dePaola use in his story?

Chapters 5–6; pp. 32–41

- What do you remember about kindergarten?

- Write some good questions about the book that you can discuss in your book club.

26 Fairmount Avenue, continued

Chapters 7–9; pp. 42–57

- Change your character map to make it show what you now know about Tomie.

- How are you and Tomie alike? How are you different?

- What was your favorite part of the book? Why?

The Canada Geese Quilt

Chapters 1–2

- How do you think Ariel feels about the baby and about the quilt?

- How would you feel if you were Ariel?

- Describe the relationship between Ariel and her grandmother.

Chapters 3–4

- Describe how Ariel's relationship with her grandmother changes.

- How do you think Ariel is feeling?

- Free choice

Chapters 5–6

- What do you think the author wants you to learn from this story?

- Complete the summary sheet (Think Sheet 8).

- Free choice

Name _____ Date _____

Tripod

Critical Response

- Discuss the author's purpose. Why did he or she write the book?

- Critique the book. What parts did you like best/least?

- Give your opinion of the story or the characters.

Personal and Creative Response

- Explain how the story reminds you of people and events in your own life.

- Write a letter to a character in the story,

- Write a poem or draw a picture about something you read.

Author's Craft

- Talk about this author's special style. Is the writing funny, serious, or exciting?

- Identify interesting words and phrases that the author uses.

- Tell how this author's writing reminds you of another book you read.

Name _____ **Date** _____

Writing Process Checklist

Content

_____ I completed the assignment.

_____ I answered the question or writing prompt.

_____ I included details that support my ideas.

_____ I tried to make my writing interesting.

Organization

_____ My writing is clear to a reader.

_____ I organized details in a way that makes sense.

Conventions

_____ I included a title, my name, and the date.

_____ All words are spelled correctly.

_____ All sentences use correct grammar.

_____ I used proper punctuation and capitalization.

Snapshot of Me

Sequence
Sometimes it's important to remember story events in the order they happened. Make a sequence chart, map, or list of these events. Tell why you think the sequence is important.

Intertextuality
Sometimes what you read makes you think about another book you've read or a movie you've seen. Tell what this story reminds you of and explain why.

Me & the Book
Sometimes what you read makes you think about your own life. Write about an event or a character in a book. Tell why it reminds you of your life.

Summary
Sometimes it is important to summarize all or part of the story. Write a summary. Tell why you decided to summarize this particular part.

Things to Do in

Feelings
Sometimes a book makes you feel a certain way. Write about that feeling. Tell why the book makes you feel that way. You can also write about what the characters in the book might be feeling.

Character Map
You can draw a map of a character in the story. Include personality traits, descriptions, actions, and anything you think is interesting about that character.

Prediction
Think about the story and predict what you think will happen next. You can predict an event, the next chapter, or how the story might end.

In the Character's Shoes
You can pretend that you are the character. You can write or draw about what you would do or think in the same situation.

Favorite Part or Character
In each book you can usually find a favorite (and least favorite) part and character. Write about these things. Tell why you like or dislike them.

Author's Craft
Sometimes authors paint pictures with words. They use interesting language, create funny situations, or write great dialogue. Give examples of things the author does that make you enjoy the story.

Story Picture
When you read, pictures can form in your mind. Draw these pictures of characters, settings, and events in your log. Write some words or a sentence under each picture. Tell what it is and why you drew it.

Compare/Contrast
Tell how two things—two characters, two stories, yourself and a character—are alike and different. Write your comparison in sentences or use a chart.

Your Reading Log

Critique
Sometimes when you're reading, you might think, "This is really great!" Other times you might think, "If I were the author, I would do this differently." You can write about things the author does well and things the author could do better.

Questions for Your Group
Sometimes you'll wonder about things in the story. Write questions to ask members of your group so they can help you understand the story better. You can also ask group members how they feel about the story.

Point of View
You might think an author does not tell enough about the thoughts and feelings of a character. You can write from a character's point of view to help explain his or her thoughts and feelings.

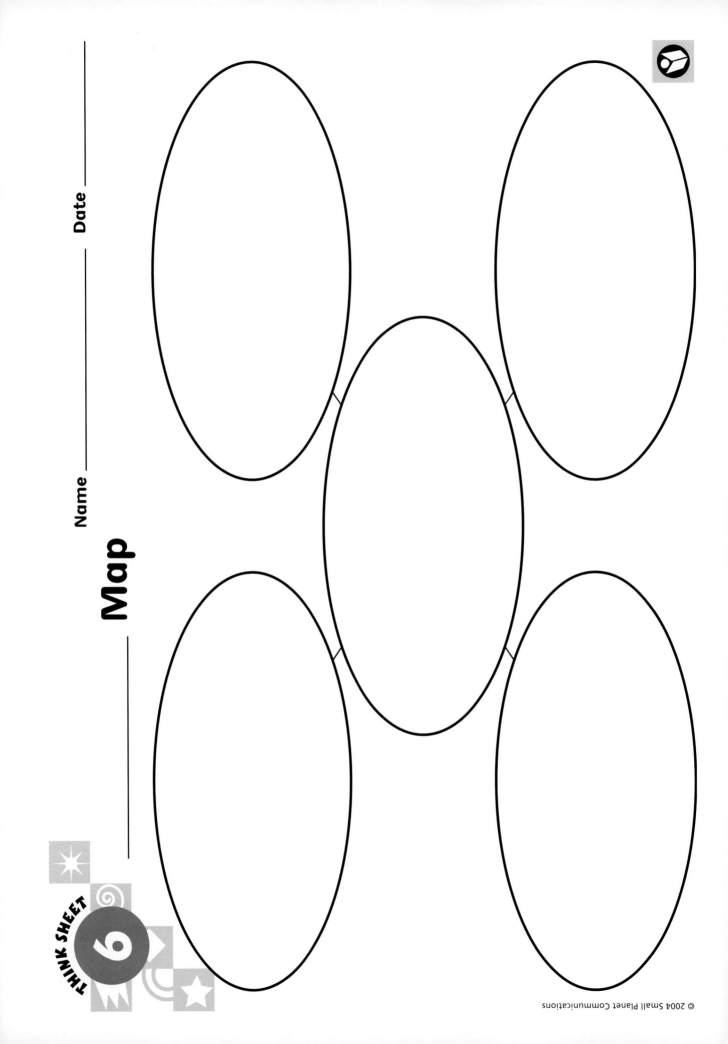

Map

Name

Date

Words of Value

Write the word on the line. Next, write the sentence from the book.
Then write your definition of the word on the lines. Check your
definition in the dictionary. Write the dictionary definition on the lines.

Word: _____   **Sentence in Book:** _____

_____

My Definition: _____

_____

Dictionary Definition: _____

_____

Word: _____   **Sentence in Book:** _____

_____

My Definition: _____

_____

Dictionary Definition: _____

_____

Word: _____   **Sentence in Book:** _____

_____

My Definition: _____

_____

Dictionary Definition: _____

_____

Name _____ Date _____

Summary Sheet

Roxaboxen

Summarize the story.

_____

_____

What is the theme of the story?

_____

26 Fairmount Avenue

Summarize the story.

_____

_____

What is the theme of the story?

_____

The Canada Geese Quilt

Summarize the story.

_____

_____

What is the theme of the story?

_____

Responding to the Readings

Theme Questions

- How is the truth important in my life?
- When is honesty the best policy?

- How do I feel when someone lies to me? How do I feel when I lie to someone else?

- How does my dishonesty affect other people and my relationships with them?

The Boy Who Cried Wolf

What do you think happens at the end of the story? Write or draw your own ending.

A Big Fat Enormous Lie

Write about a time when you felt like the narrator of the story.

Harriet and the Garden

Respond to either *Favorite Part or Character* or *In the Character's Shoes.* (See Think Sheet 5, Things to Do in Your Reading Log.)

Liar, Liar, Pants on Fire!

Respond to *Feelings* on Think Sheet 5, Things to Do in Your Reading Log.

That's Mine, Horace

What lies does Horace tell in the story? Why?

Why Mosquitoes Buzz in People's Ears

Do you agree that the mosquito is to blame for all that happened? Why or why not?

A Day's Work

What lessons does Francisco's grandfather teach him?

Chen Ping and His Magic Axe

Choose one of the response types from Think Sheet 5, Things to Do in Your Reading Log.

The Empty Pot

Which folk tale do you like better, *The Empty Pot* or *Chen Ping and His Magic Axe*? Why?

What's so Terrible about Swallowing an Apple Seed?

Has anyone ever told you a "story" that you believed? What happened?

The Honest-to-Goodness Truth

- Have you ever had your feelings hurt by someone telling you the truth?
- Have you ever hurt someone's feelings by telling the truth?

To Tell the Truth

Write a journal entry from Benjamin's perspective. Explain what happened in school when you took the fudge and what you learned.

Theme Blocks

Title: _____

Theme: _____

Title: _____

Theme: _____

Title: _____

Theme: _____

Title: _____

Theme: _____

Title: _____

Theme: _____

Title: _____

Theme: _____

Title: _____

Theme: _____

Title: _____

Theme: _____

Title: _____

Theme: _____

Title: _____

Theme: _____

Title: _____

Theme: _____

Name _____ Date _____

Welcome to the Fishbowl Rules!

If you are a fish:

- Talk

- Listen

- Connect

If you are watching the fish:

- Think

- Listen

- Connect

- Make positive comments about what the fish did right.

- Tell what you think they could do to have a better discussion.

Have a Speedwriting Party!

Rules

1. Ready, set, go!!

2. Speedwriting is timed.

3. Keep your eyes and pencil on the paper.

4. Keep going! Don't stop to ask for help with ideas or spelling.

5. If you make a mistake, don't erase. Cross it out and keep going.

6. Get your ideas on paper.

7. Stop when the teacher tells you to.

8. Always write in your Speedwriting journal.

9. Share what you have written.

10. Speedwriting is a party, not a test. HAVE FUN!

**Everyone can play!
Everyone is a winner!
Everyone is a writer!**

KWL Chart

Name _____   Date _____

What I KNOW	What I WANT to know	What I LEARNED

Responding to the Readings

Theme Questions

• **How is my life like a story?**

• **What is family? What makes my family special?**

• **What is culture? How would I describe my culture?**

The Patchwork Quilt

• Which picture or story was your favorite or least favorite? Why?

• Tell about an artifact that reminds you of family.

• Have you had a family member who was or is sick? How did this make you feel?

• Describe something that you worked on with a family member or a friend.

• Make a connection between Tanya's family and your family.

Tell Me Again About the Night I Was Born

• Why does the girl want to hear about the night she was born?

• Write two details from the book that tell you the girl is happy.

• Who is telling this story? How do you know?

Chicken Sunday

• What traditions does your family have?

• What traditions would you like your family to have?

• What does family mean to you?

Aunt Flossie's Hats (and Crab Cakes Later)

- Why are Aunt Flossie's hats important to her?

- What things do you keep because they remind you of something?

The Quilt Story

- How are the girls alike?

- Compare and contrast the two families.

- How do you know that there are two different times in this story?

- What happens when each girl moves? How does each girl feel?

- How do you make yourself feel better when you are sad? Is there someone or something that can make you feel better?

Bigmama's

- Why do you think the family members call their grandmother Bigmama?

- Make a connection between this story and *Chicken Sunday*.

- How is farm life different from city life?

My Rotten Redheaded Older Brother

- What things does your sister or brother do to bother you?

- What can you do better than your sister or brother? Why can you do that thing better?

- Does your grandmother or another adult give you advice? What does the person say to you?

Evaluation Sheets

The evaluation sheets in this section provide assessment tools for both you and your students. Some sheets give you a framework for observing and assessing your students' work. Others guide students to set learning goals for their participation in Book Clubs and Literacy Block and then to self-assess their progress. For more information on assessment in the Book Club *Plus* program, see Chapter 6.

Name _____   **Date** _____

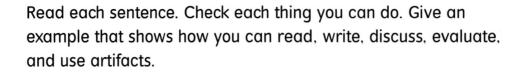

"I Can" Self-Evaluation

Read each sentence. Check each thing you can do. Give an example that shows how you can read, write, discuss, evaluate, and use artifacts.

Reading

I CAN make meaning when I read.

◯ I can retell a story in my own words.

◯ I can make meaning when I read a variety of texts.

◯ I can make connections between my own life and what I am reading.

◯ I can make connections within and between texts.

◯ I can figure out a theme from my reading.

_____

_____

Writing

I CAN write to communicate my ideas.

◯ I can use writing for different purposes and audiences.

◯ I can show "me" in my writing.

_____

_____

Discussion

I CAN contribute to a good book club discussion.

◯ I can stay on topic when I talk.

◯ I can share my feelings and ideas.

◯ I can respect other people's ideas and opinions.

◯ I can build on other people's ideas.

◯ I can bring others into the discussion.

_____

_____

Evaluation

◯ I CAN show and/or tell what I learned and how I learned it.

_____

_____

Culture

I CAN use artifacts to describe—

◯ my own cultural heritage.

◯ other people's cultures.

◯ similarities and differences across cultures.

I CAN define culture and how cultures change.

_____

_____

(Based on "I Can" statements developed by the Teachers Learning Collaborative.)

Artifact Activity

✂ ....

Name: _____ Date:_____

What is the artifact? _____

Can the student explain clearly the meaning behind the artifact?

_____

Additional comments:_____

_____

_____

_____

✂ ....

Name: _____ Date:_____

What is the artifact? _____

Can the student explain clearly the meaning behind the artifact?

_____

Additional comments:_____

_____

_____

_____

Name _____ Date _____

Book _____

Learning from the Fishbowl

Please circle the best answer to each question.

1. What type of conversation did the group have?

Good   Could improve   Not good

2. Did everyone have a chance to talk?

   Yes   No

3. Did the students talk about the book?

   Yes   No

4. Can you suggest ways to make their fishbowl better?
   Write them on the lines.

   _____

   _____

   _____

   _____

Quick Assessment Checklist

EVALUATION SHEET 4

Writing

Responds to a prompt

Writes for many purposes

Uses different response types

Keeps a personal journal

Uses punctuation correctly

Uses capitalization correctly

Maintains subject-verb agreement

Other

Reading

Uses comprehension strategies

Relates personal experiences to reading

Comprehends story sequence

Other

Listening/Speaking

Uses props

Speaks in complete thoughts

Summarizes

Other

Checklist for Language Arts Skills

Name of Student:	Efficient	At Beginning Stages	Non-Efficient	Comments
Speaking				
Positions hands at side or holding paper				
Makes eye contact with audience at least once				
Speaks loud enough for everyone to hear				
Positions paper so people can see speaker's face				
Makes minimum movement while speaking				
Other				
Writing				
Understands the writing process: Planning, Drafting, Revising, Publishing				
Composes a grammatically-correct sentence				
Writes sentences that flow to make sense				
Uses punctuation correctly				
Writes to a prompt				
Is able to go back and edit some mistakes				
Other				
Reading				
Can summarize a story				
Makes predictions to see what the story may be about				
Can point out details				
Can identify the main idea				
Uses context clues to help understand words that are unfamiliar				
Uses reading strategies to help with reading				
Decodes/breaks down parts of words— sounds out letters				
Comprehends what was read/read aloud				
Can compare/contrast items and characters				
Understands cause-and-effect relationships				
Other				

Checklist for
Language Arts Skills,
continued

Name of Student:	Efficient	At Beginning Stages	Non-Efficient	Comments
Phonics				
Can identify blends and sound them out				
Can identify and sound out consonants				
Can identify vowels and sound out short vowels				
Can identify vowels and sound out long vowels				
Other				
Listening				
Maintains eye contact on speaker				
Assumes sitting position to show attentiveness				
Does not move a lot or play around				
Answers question(s) about what the speaker read				
Knows when to clap because he/she is paying attention				
Other				
Book Club Discussions				
Can disagree without arguing				
Takes turns speaking and listening				
Discusses the contents of the book				
Discusses how the content made him/her feel (in general)				
Discusses how the content made him/her feel about self				
Discusses how the content make him/her feel about his/her family				
Discusses why he/she thinks the author wrote the book				
Discusses if the content of the book made him/her aware of any issues or concerns				
Other				

Unit _____ **Date** _____

Fluency Checklist

Student's Name	Uses Expression	Observes Punctuation	Smooth	Appropriate speed/volume	Uses decoding skills	Miscues	Self-corrects

Name _____

Reading Log Self-Assessment

Dates										
Features										
I focus on big ideas, key questions, and main characters.										
I use evidence from the book and my life.										
I use many response types.										
My writing is clear and makes sense.										
I date and label each entry.										

Book Club Checklist

Name _____

Features	Dates										Comments and Concerns
I stayed on topic.											
I made intertextual connections.											
I shared ideas about the topic.											
I asked good questions.											
I listened to the conversation.											
I built on other people's ideas.											
I supported my ideas with evidence.											

Book Club Observation Sheet

Student's Name	Shares Log	Shares Ideas	Listens & Responds	Asks Questions	Off-Task Behaviors

Each ✔ means the student exhibited this behavior.

Overall rating
(Mark next to name.)

✳ exceptional
+ good/okay
— not good
O not participating at all

Off-Task Behaviors Key

1. writing in log
2. playing with pencil or other object
3. digging in desk
4. talking with someone else in group, not about Book Club topic
5. getting out of group to wander

Comments: _____

_____

_____

_____

_____

Name _____   **Date** _____

Book Club Self-Assessment

1. How did your group do in this unit? What did people do well?
    What do they need to work on?

    _____

    _____

    _____

    _____

    _____

2. How did you do as a member of a book club?

    _____

    _____

    _____

    _____

    _____

3. What can you do to have better discussions in the next unit?

    _____

    _____

    _____

    _____

    _____

Setting Goals for My Book Club

Think about the features of a good book club discussion. Choose two of these features as personal goals. Write the features in the chart. Then write how you will meet your goals.

Features of a Good Book Club Discussion	Why I Selected Each Feature	How I Will Meet My Goals
1.		
2.		

Name _____ **Date** _____

Setting Goals for My Reading Log

1. Choose one of the best entries in your reading log. Tell why you like it and what's good about it.

   _____

   _____

   _____

   _____

   _____

2. Now pick a log entry that's not so good. Why don't you like it? How can you make it better?

   _____

   _____

   _____

   _____

   _____

3. Use this information to set goals for your next reading log.

   Goal 1: _____

   _____

   Goal 2: _____

   _____

   _____

Name _____ **Date** _____

"I Can" Self-Evaluation

Read each sentence. Tell how you can do each thing.
Use examples.

I can retell a story in my own words.

_____

_____

_____

I can stay on topic when I talk.

_____

_____

_____

I can stay on topic when I write.

_____

_____

_____

I can describe the theme of a book.

_____

_____

_____

_____

(Based on "I Can" statements developed by the Teachers Learning Collaborative.)

Name _____

Checklist for Quilt Writing Project

Writing Process Criterion:	there	not there
• Plan		
• Draft		
• Revise		
• Publish		
Comments:		

Drawing of Quilt Criterion	based on writing	not based on writing
Describe the drawing:		
Comments:		

Listening Criterion:	yes	no
• Eye contact on speaker		
• Sitting position to show attentiveness		
• Not moving a lot or playing around		
• Answers question(s) about what the speaker read		
• Knows when to clap, because he/she is paying attention		
Excellent (5 items) Good (3–4 items) Fair (1–2 items)		
Comments:		

Speaking Criterion:	yes	no
• Hands positioned at side or holding paper		
• Eye contact with audience at least once		
• Voice tone loud enough for everyone to hear		
• Paper is positioned so people can see speaker's face		
• Minimum movement while speaking		
Excellent (3–4 items) Good (2 items) Fair (1 item)		
Comments:		

Discussion with Peers Criterion:	yes	no
• Student takes turns talking.		
• Students listen to speaker by using eye contact or summarizing what speaker said. (Indicate one or both)		
• Student can disagree without an argument.		
• Student can explain opinions/thoughts/views/beliefs. (Indicate which ones)		

Name _____

Rubric for Scoring Quilt Writing Project

Put a check mark in the column that applies to the student's paper.

Planning:
○ Excellent—word web made with 4 or more ideas
○ Good—word web made with 3 ideas
○ Fair—word web made with 2 ideas
○ Poor—word web made with 1 idea

Comments: _____
_____
_____
_____

Drafting:
○ Excellent—all phrases/sentences came from ideas on the word web
○ Good—most phrases/sentences came from ideas on the word web
○ Fair—1–2 phrases/sentences came from ideas on the word web
○ Poor—no phrases/sentences came from ideas on the word web

Comments: _____
_____
_____
_____

Publishing:
○ Excellent—no mistakes
○ Good—1 mistake
○ Fair—2 mistakes
○ Poor—more than 2 mistakes

Comments: _____
_____
_____
_____

Name _____ **Date** _____

Quilt Writing Project Self-Assessment

1. What does your quilt square show?

2. How does your story tell about your quilt square?

3. Why will you want to tell this story to your children or grandchildren?

4. Which books helped you during your project?

5. Did you follow the writing process by planning, drafting, revising, and publishing?   YES   NO

6. Which part of the writing process was easiest? Which was the most difficult? Why?

7. If you presented your project to the class, do you think you spoke clearly? Why or why not?

Quilt Writing Project Student Assessment

Name: _____ Date: _____

What does the quilt square show? _____

_____

_____

Does the story tell about the quilt square? _____

_____

_____

Is the student's project about family? _____

_____

_____

Did the student speak about the project? Yes/No

If the student presented the project, could you hear the student speak? Yes/No

Comments: _____

_____

_____

_____

_____

_____

Bibliography

Literature for Students

Aardema, Verna. *Why Mosquitoes Buzz in People's Ears.* New York: Dial Books, 1975.

Avery, Kristin. *The Crazy Quilt.* Palisades, California: Goodyear Publishing Co., 1994.

Bennett, William J. *The Children's Book of Virtues.* New York: Simon and Schuster, 1995.

Berenstain, Jan, and Stan Berenstain. *The Berenstain Bears and the Truth.* New York: Random House Books for Young Readers, 1983.

Borden, Louise, and Mary Kay Kroeger. *Fly High! The Story of Bessie Coleman.* New York. Margaret K. McElderry Books, 2001.

Brill, Marlene Targ. *Margaret Knight: Girl Inventor.* Brookfield, CT: Millbrook Press, 2001.

Brown, Marc. *Arthur's Computer Disaster.* Boston: Little, Brown & Co., 1997.

Bunting, Eve. *A Day's Work.* New York: Clarion Books, 1994.

————. *Smokey Night.* San Diego: Harcourt Brace & Co., 1994.

Cannon, Janell. *Stellaluna.* New York: Harcourt Brace & Co., 1993.

————. *Verdi.* New York: Harcourt Brace & Co., 1993.

Carle, Eric. *Flora and Tiger: 19 Very Short Stories from My Life.* New York: Philomel Books, 1997.

Carlson, Nancy. *Harriet and the Garden.* Minneapolis, MN: Carolrhoda Books, 1999.

Cleary, Beverly, et al. *It's Great to Be Eight.* New York: Scholastic, 2000.

————. *It's Terrific to Be Ten.* New York: Scholastic, 2000.

Cohen, Miriam. *Liar, Liar, Pants on Fire!* New York: William Morrow & Co., 1985.

Cosby, Bill. *My Big Lie.* New York: Scholastic, 1999.

Crews, Donald. *Bigmama's.* New York: HarperTrophy, 1998.

Cummings, Pat. *Clean Your Room, Harvey Moon!* New York: Aladdin Books, 1994.

Curtis, Jamie L. *Tell Me Again About the Night I Was Born.* New York: HarperCollins, 1996.

————. *When I Was Little: A Four-Year-Old's Memoir of Her Youth.* New York: HarperCollins, 1993.

Dahl, Roald. *The BFG.* New York: Puffin Books, 2002.

————. *Boy: Tales of Childhood.* New York: Puffin Books, 1986.

————. *Charlie and the Chocolate Factory.* New York: Puffin Books, 1989.

D'Arc, Karen S. *My Grandmother Is a Singing Yaya.* New York: Orchard Books, 2001.

Demi. *Chen Ping and the Magic Axe.* New York: Dodd, Mead & Co., 1987.

————. *The Empty Pot.* New York: Holt, 1990.

dePaola, Tomie. *The Art Lesson.* New York: Putnam, 1997.

————. *The Baby Sister.* New York: Putnam, 1999.

————. *Nana Upstairs & Nana Downstairs.* New York: Puffin, 2000.

————. *Now One Foot, Now the Other.* New York: Putnam, 1981.

————. *The Popcorn Book.* New York: Holiday House, 1978.

————. *Tom.* New York: Putnam, 1997.

————. *26 Fairmount Avenue.* New York: Putnam, 2000.

————. *What a Year!* New York: Putnam, 2002.

Eastman, P. D. *Are You My Mother?* New York: Random House, 1960.

Farmer, Patti. *To Tell the Truth.* Toronto: Stoddart Kids, 1997.

Feng Sun, Chyng. *Mama Bear.* Boston: Houghton Mifflin, 1994.

Flournoy, Valerie. *The Patchwork Quilt.* New York: Dial Books, 1985.

Galdone, Paul. *The Gingerbread Boy.* New York: Clarion Books, 1983.

Gardiner, John R. *Stone Fox.* New York: HarperTrophy, 1988.

George, Jean Craighead. *The Tarantula in My Purse: And 172 Other Wild Pets.* New York: HarperTrophy, 1997.

————. *There's an Owl in the Shower.* New York: HarperTrophy, 1997.

Gilman, Phoebe. *Something from Nothing.* New York: Scholastic, 2000.

Greenspun, Adele Aron. *Daddies.* New York: Philomel Books, 1992.

Hayes, Joe. *Juan Verdades: The Man Who Couldn't Tell a Lie.* Retold by Joe Hayes. New York: Orchard Books, 2001.

Helmer, Marilyn. *Three Tales of Trickery: Little Red Riding Hood/Hansel and Gretel/Rumpelstiltskin.* Tonawanda, New York: Kids Can Press, 2002.

Howard, Elizabeth Fitzgerald. *Aunt Flossie's Hats (and Crab Cakes Later).* New York: Clarion Books, 1995.

Hyman, Trina Schart. Ill. *Little Red Riding Hood.* New York: Holiday House, 1987.

Johnson, Angela. *One of Three.* New York: Orchard Books, 1995.

————. *Tell Me a Story, Mama.* New York: Orchard Books, 1992.

Johnston, Tony. *The Quilt Story.* New York: Puffin Books, 1996.

Joyce, William. *Bently & egg.* New York: HarperTrophy, 1997.

————. *Dinosaur Bob and His Adventures With the Family Lazardo.* New York: HarperTrophy, 1995.

————. *George Shrinks.* New York: HarperTrophy, 2003.

————. *The Leaf Men and the Brave Good Boys.* New York: HarperTrophy, 2001.

————. *Rolie Polie Olie.* New York: HarperCollins Children's Books: Laura Geringer imprint, 1999.

————. *The World of William Joyce Scrapbook.* New York: HarperCollins, 1997.

Kasza, Keiko. *A Mother for Choco.* New York: Puffin Books, 1996.

Keller, Holly. *That's Mine, Horace.* Hong Kong, China: Greenwillow Books, 2000.

Kimmel, Eric. *Anansi and the Magic Stick.* New York: Holiday House, 2002.

————. *Anansi and the Talking Melon.* New York: Holiday House. 1995.

Kinsey-Warnock, Natalie. *The Canada Geese Quilt.* New York: Puffin Books, 2000.

Kraus, Robert. *Whose Mouse Are You?* New York: Macmillan Co., 1986.

Kroll, Steven. *Annabelle's Un-Birthday.* New York: Atheneum, 1991.

Kunhardt, Edith. *Honest Abe.* New York: William Morrow & Co., 1998.

Kurtz, Shirley. *The Boy and the Quilt.* Intercourse, PA: Good Books, 1991.

Kyle, Kathryn. *Honesty: A Level Three Reader.* Chanhassen, Minnesota: The Child's World, 2002.

Lalli, Judy *I Like Being Me: Poems for Children About Feeling Special, Appreciating Others, and Getting Along.* Minneapolis, MN: Free Spirit Publishing, 1997.

Leisure Arts, Inc. and Oxmoor House, Inc., *In Love with Quilts,* 1993.

Lerner, Harriet, and Susan Goldhor. *What's So Terrible About Swallowing an Apple Seed?* New York: HarperCollins, 1996.

Lester, Helen. *Tacky the Penguin.* Boston: Houghton Mifflin, 1990.

Lobel, Arnold. *Frog and Toad Are Friends.* New York: HarperCollins, 1979.

Lomas Garza, Carmen. *Family Pictures: Cuadros de Familia.* San Francisco: Children's Book Press, 1993.

MacLachlan, Patricia. *Sarah, Plain and Tall.* Torrance, CA: Frank Schaffer Publications, 2000.

Mak, Kam. *My Chinatown: One Year in Poems.* New York: HarperCollins, 2001.

Marcus, Leonard S., Compiled and edited. *Author Talk.* New York: Simon & Schuster, 2000.

Martin, Rafe. *The Rough-Face Girl.* New York: Puffin Books. 1998.

Maruki, Toshi. *Hiroshima No Pika.* New York: William Morrow & Co., 1982.

McCully, Emily Arnold. *New Baby.* New York: HarperCollins, 1998.

McDermott, Gerald. *Raven: A Trickster Tale from the Pacific Northwest.* San Diego, CA: Harcourt, 2001.

McDonald, Megan, *Judy Moody.* Cambridge, MA: Candlewick Press, 2002.

McKee, David. *Elmer.* New York: McGraw-Hill, 1968.

McKissack, Patricia C. "Chicken Coop Monster." *In the Dark-Thirty: Southern Tales of the Supernatural:* 111–122. New York: Knopf, 1992.

————. *Flossie and the Fox.* New York: Dutton Books, 1986.

————. *Goin' Someplace Special.* New York: Simon & Schuster, 2001.

————. *The Honest-to-Goodness Truth.* New York: Atheneum, 2000.

McLerran, Alice. *Roxaboxen*. New York: Puffin Books, 1992.

McPhail, David. *Sisters*. New York: Harcourt, Inc., 2003.

Mills, Lauren A. *The Rag Coat*. Boston: Little, Brown & Co., 1991.

Moon, Nicola. *Lucy's Picture*. New York: Puffin Books, 1997.

Myers, Walter Dean. *Angel to Angel: A Mother's Gift of Love*. New York: HarperTrophy, 2000.

———. *Brown Angels: An Album of Pictures and Verse*. New York: HarperTrophy, 1996.

———. *Glorious Angels: A Celebration of Children*. New York: HarperTrophy, 1997.

Parish, Peggy. *Amelia Bedelia's Family Album*. New York: HarperTrophy, 2003.

Paulsen, Gary. *My Life in Dog Years*. New York: Yearling, 1998.

Pellegrini, Nina. *Families Are Different*. New York: Holiday House, 1991.

Polacco, Patricia. *Babushka's Doll*. New York: Aladdin Books, 1995.

———. *Chicken Sunday*. New York: Philomel Books, 1992.

———. *Firetalking (Meet the Author)*. Katonah, NY: Richard C. Owen Publishers, Inc., 1994.

———. *The Keeping Quilt*. New York: Aladdin Books, 2001.

———. *My Rotten Redheaded Older Brother*. New York: Aladdin Books, 1998.

———. *Pink and Say*. New York: Philomel Books, 1994.

———. *Thank You, Mr. Falker*. New York: Putnam, 1998.

Ransom, Candice. *Little Red Riding Hood*. New York: McGraw-Hill Childrens Publishing, 2001.

Ross, Gayle. *How Rabbit Tricked Otter: And Other Cherokee Trickster Stories*. New York: Parabola Books, 2003.

Ross, Tony. *The Boy Who Cried Wolf*. New York: Puffin Books, 1991.

Rylant, Cynthia. *Henry and Mudge and the Careful Cousin*. New York: Aladdin Books, 1997.

———. *The Relatives Came*. New York: Aladdin Books, 1993.

———. *When I Was Young in the Mountains*. New York: Viking, 1985.

Scott, Ann Herbert. *On Mother's Lap*. New York: Clarion Books, 1992.

Sharmat, Marjorie Weinman. *A Big Fat Enormous Lie*. New York: Dutton, 1978.

Steptoe, John. *Mufaro's Beautiful Daughters: An African Tale*. Pine Plains, NY: Live Oak Media, 2003.

Stevens, Janet. *Coyote Steals the Blanket: A Ute Tale*. New York: Holiday House. 1994.

———. *Old Bag of Bones: A Coyote Tale*. New York: Holiday House, 1997.

———. *Tops & Bottoms*. San Diego, CA: Harcourt, 1995.

———. *The Tortoise and the Hare*. New York: Holiday House, 1985.

Stevenson, James. *When I Was Nine*. New York: William Morrow & Co., 1986.

Talley, Linda. *Plato's Journey*. Kansas City, Missouri: Marsh Media, 1998.

Waber, Bernard. *Ira Sleeps Over*. Boston: Houghton Mifflin, 1987.

Weigelt, Udo. *Alex Did It!* New York: North-South Books, 2002.

Williams, Vera B. *A Chair for My Mother*. New York: HarperTrophy, 1984.

Winter, Susan. *Yo También/Me Too*. New York: Lectorum Publications, Inc., 2002.

Wisniewski, David. *Golem*. New York: Clarion Books, 1996.

Woodson, Jacqueline. *The Other Side*. New York: Putnam, 2001.

Zemach, Harve. *The Judge*. New York: Farrar, Straus and Giroux, 1988.

Ziefert, Harriet. *Little Red Riding Hood*. New York: Puffin Books, 2000.

Audiovisual References

Adventures from the Children's Book of Virtues: Honesty: Featuring the Indian Cinderella and Other Great Stories. Los Angeles, CA: Porchlight Entertainment. 1996. Videocassette.

A Visit with Tomie dePaola. 25 minutes. New London, NH: Whitebird, Inc. 1996. Videocassette.

Chicken Sunday. Narrated by Patricia Polacco. 14 minutes. Holmes, NY: Spoken Arts Media. 1992. Videocassette, Audiocassette, and CD.

The Keeping Quilt. Narrated by Patricia Polacco. 13 minutes. Holmes, NY: Spoken Arts Media. 1993. Videocassette, Audiocassette, and CD.

Thank You, Mr. Falker. Narrated by Patricia Polacco. 26 minutes. Holmes, NY: Spoken Arts Media. 1999. Videocassette, Audiocassette, and CD.

References

Applebee, Arthur N. *The Child's Concept of Story.* Chicago: University of Chicago Press, 1978.

Au, Kathryn H. "Constructing the Theme of a Story." *Language Arts* 69, no. 2 (1992): 106–111.

———. "Elementary Programs in the Context of the Standards Movement." In *Administration and Supervision of Reading Programs.* 2nd ed. Edited by Shelley B. Wepner, Dorothy S. Strickland, and Joan T. Feeley. New York: Teachers College Press (2001): 42–58.

———. "Literacy Research and Students of Diverse Backgrounds: What Does It Take to Improve Achievement?" Plenary Presentation at the Annual Meeting of the National Reading Conference, Miami, FL, December, 2002.

———. "Participation Structures in a Reading Lesson with Hawaiian Children: Analysis of a Culturally Appropriate and Instructional Event." *Anthropology and Education* 11 (1980): 170–180.

———. "Using the Experience-Text-Relationship Method with Minority Children." *The Reading Teacher* 32, no. 7 (1979): 677–679.

Au, K. H., and C. Jordan. "Teaching Reading to Hawaiian Children: Finding a Culturally Appropriate Solution." In *Culture and the Bilingual Classroom: Studies in Classroom Ethnography,* edited by H. T. Trueba, K. H. Au, and G. P. Guthrie. Rowley, MA: Newbury House, 1981: 139–152.

Au, Kathryn H., Jacquelin H. Carroll, and Judith R. Scheu. *Balanced Literacy Instruction: A Teacher's Resource Book.* Norwood, MA: Christopher-Gordon Publishers Inc., 1997.

Au, Kathryn H., Taffy E. Raphael, Susan Florio-Ruane, and Rand Spiro. "Seeing Worlds in Grains of Sand: Cases, Complexity, and Cognitive Flexibility in the Teachers Learning Collaborative." Final Report to the Center for Improvement of Early Reading Achievement (CIERA). Ann Arbor: The University of Michigan, 2002.

Bakhtin, Mikhail M. *The Dialogic Imagination.* Austin: University of Texas Press, 1981.

Barnes, Douglas. "Talking and Learning in Classrooms: An Introduction." *Primary Voices K-6* 3, no. 1 (1995): 2–7.

Barton, David. *Literacy: An Introduction to the Ecology of Written Language.* Cambridge, USA: Blackwell, 1994.

Birkerts, Sven. *The Gutenberg Elegies: The Fate of Reading in an Electronic Age.* New York: Fawcett Columbine, 1994.

Bishop, Rudine S. "Multicultural Literature for Children: Making Informed Choices." In *Teaching Multicultural Literature in Grades K–8,* edited by Violet J. Harris. Norwood, MA: Christopher-Gordon Publishers, Inc., 1992: 39–53.

Block, Cathy C., and Michael Pressley. "Best Practices in Comprehension Instruction." In *Best Practices in Literacy Instruction.* 2nd ed. Edited by Lesley M. Morrow, Linda B. Gambrell, and Michael Pressley. New York: Guilford, 2003: 111–126.

Book Club *Plus* Network, The. "What Counts as Teacher Research?: An Essay." *Language Arts* 77, no. 1 (1999): 48–52.

Bromley, Karen. "Building a Sound Writing Program." In *Best Practices in Literacy Instruction.* 2nd ed. Edited by Lesley M. Morrow, Linda B. Gambrell, and M. Pressley. New York: Guilford, 2003: 143–165.

Bruner, Jerome. *The Culture of Education.* Cambridge, MA: Harvard University Press, 1996.

Carroll, John A. "A Model for School Learning" *Teachers College Record* 64 no. 1 (1963): 723–733.

Davey, Beth. "Think Aloud: Modeling the Cognitive Processes of Reading Comprehension." *Journal of Reading* 27 (1983): 44–47.

Dole, Janice A., Gerald G. Duffy, Laura R. Roehler, and P. David Pearson, "Moving from the Old to the New: Research on Reading Comprehension Instruction." *Review of Educational Research* 61, no. 2 (1991): 239–264.

Duke, Nell K., and Victoria Purcell-Gates "Genres at Home and at School: Bridging the Known to the New." *The Reading Teacher* 57, no. 1 (2003): 30–37.

Egan, Kieran. *The Educated Mind: How Cognitive Tools Shape Our Understanding.* Chicago, IL: Chicago University Press, 1997.

Elbow, Peter. *Writing Without Teachers.* 2nd ed. Oxford University Press, 1998.

Erickson, Frederick. "Culture in Society and in Educational Practices." In *Multicultural Education: Issues and Perspectives.* 3rd ed., edited by James Banks and Cherry A. McGee-Banks. Boston: Allyn & Bacon, 1997: 32–60.

Florio-Ruane, Susan, Jennifer Berne, and Taffy E. Raphael. "Teaching Literature and Literacy in the Eye of Reform: A Dilemma in Three Acts." *The New Advocate* 14, no. 3 (2001): 197–210.

Florio-Ruane, Susan, Nina L. Hasty, and Tracey Beasley. "Quilting a Curriculum: A Pilot Literacy Unit on Family Stories." Paper presented at the the Annual Meeting of the Michigan Council of Teachers of English. Grand Rapids, Michigan: 2000.

Florio-Ruane, Susan, and Taffy E. Raphael. "Reading Lives: Creating and Sustaining Learning about Culture and Literacy Education in Teacher Study Groups." In *Talking Shop: Authentic Conversation and Teacher Learning,* edited by Christopher M. Clark. New York: Teachers College Press, 2001: 64-81.

Florio-Ruane, Susan, Taffy E. Raphael, Kathy Highfield, and Jennifer Berne. "Re-engaging Youngsters with Reading Difficulties by Means of Innovative Professional Development." In *Improving Reading Achievement Through Professional Development,* edited by Dorothy S. Strickland and Michael L. Kamil. Norwood, MA: Christopher-Gordon Publishers Inc., 2004: 129–148.

Florio-Ruane, Susan, with Julie deTar. *Teacher Education and the Cultural Imagination: Autobiography, Conversation, and Narrative.* Mahwah, NJ: Lawrence Erlbaum, 2001.

Fountas, Irene, C., and Gay Su Pinnell. *Guided Reading.* Portsmouth, NH: Heinemann, 1996.

Freire, Paulo. *Teachers as Cultural Workers.* Translated by Donaldo Macedo, Dale Koike, and Alexandre Oliveira. Boulder, CO: Westview, 1998.

Galda, Lee. "Mirrors and Windows: Reading as Transformation." In *Literature-Based Instruction: Reshaping the Curriculum,* edited by Taffy E. Raphael and Kathryn H. Au. Norwood, MA: Christopher-Gordon Publications, 1998: 1–11.

Gambrell, Linda B., and Janice F. Almasi (eds.). *Lively Discussions: Fostering Engaged Reading.* Newark, DE: International Reading Association, 1996.

Gavelek, James R., and Taffy E. Raphael. "Changing Talk About Text: New Roles for Teachers and Students." *Language Arts* 73 (1996): 24–34.

George, MariAnne, Taffey E. Raphael, and Susan Florio-Ruane. "Connecting Children, Culture, Curriculum, and Text." In *English Learners: Reaching the Highest Level of English Literacy,* edited by Gilbert G. Garcia. Newark, DE: International Reading Association, 2002.

Grattan, Kristin W. "They Can Do It Too!: Book Club with First and Second Graders." In *The Book Club Connection: Literacy Learning and Classroom Talk,* edited by Susan I. McMahon and Taffy E. Raphael. New York: Teachers College Press. 1997: 267–283.

Graves, Michael F., and Susan Watts-Taffe. "The Place of Word Consciousness in a Research-Based Vocabulary Program." In *What Research Has to Say About Reading Instruction,* 3rd ed., edited by Alan E. Farstrup and S. Jay Samuels. Newark, DE: International Reading Association, 2002: 140–165.

Hansen, Jane. "An Inferential Comprehension Strategy for Use with Primary Grade Children" *The Reading Teacher* 34, no. 7 (1981): 665–669.

Hansen, Jane, and P. David Pearson. "An Instructional Study: Improving the Inferential Comprehension of Good and Poor Fourth-Grade Readers." *Journal of Educational Psychology* 75 (1983): 821–829.

Hoffman, J. V., N. L. Roser, and J. Battle. "Reading Aloud in Classrooms: From the Modal Toward a 'Model'." *The Reading Teacher* 46, no. 6 (1993): 496–503.

Johns, Jerry. *Basic Reading Inventory.* Dubuque, IA: Kendall/Hunt Publishing Company, 2001.

Keene, Ellin O., and Susan Zimmermann. *Mosaic of Thought: Teaching Comprehension in a Reader's Workshop.* Portsmouth, NH: Heinemann 1997.

Kotch, Laura, and Leslie Zachman. *The Author Studies Handbook: Helping Students Build Powerful Connections to Literature.* New York: Scholastic, 1995.

Kurstedt, Rosanne, and Maria Kourtras. *Teaching Writing with Picture Books as Models.* New York: Scholastic, 2000.

Lamme, Linda L., Vivian Cox, Jane Matanzo, and Mike Olson. *Raising Readers: A Guide to Sharing Literature with Young Children.* New York: Walker, 1980.

Langer, Judith A. *Envisioning Literature: Literary Understanding and Literature Instruction.* New York: Teachers College Press, 1995.

Lehr, Susan S. *The Child's Developing Sense of Theme: Responses to Literature.* New York: Teachers College Press, 1991.

Lionni, Leo. "A Color of His Own." *Share: Invitations to Literacy.* Boston: Houghton Mifflin, 1997.

McMahon, Susan I., and Taffy E. Raphael, with Virginia J. Goatley and Laura S. Pardo. *The Book Club Connection: Literacy Learning and Classroom Talk.* New York: Teachers College Press, 1997.

Miller, Debbie. *Reading with Meaning: Teaching Comprehension in the Primary Grades.* Portland, ME: Stenhouse, 2002.

Moll, Luis. D. "Bilingual Classroom Studies and Community Analysis: Some Recent Trends." *Educational Researcher,* 21, no. 2 (1992): 20–24.

Nieto, Sonia. *The Light in Their Eyes: Creating Multicultural Learning Communities.* New York: Teachers College Press, 1999.

Ogle, Donna M. "K-W-L: A Teaching Model That Develops Active Reading of Expository Text." *The Reading Teacher* 39, no. 6 (1986): 564–570.

Paris, Scott G., Marjorie Y. Lipson, and Karen K. Wixson. "Becoming a Strategic Reader." *Contemporary Educational Psychology* 8 (1983): 293–316.

Pearson, P. David, Janice A. Dole, Gerald G. Duffy, and Laura R. Roehler. "Developing Expertise in Reading Comprehension: What Should Be Taught and How Should It Be Taught?" In *What Research Has to Say to the Teacher of Reading.* 2nd ed. Edited by Alan E. Farstrup and S. Jay Samuels. Newark, DE: International Reading Association, 1992.

Raphael, Taffy E. "Teaching Question-Answer Relationships, Revisited." *The Reading Teacher* 39, no. 6 (1986): 516–522.

Raphael, Taffy E., and Kathryn H. Au (eds.). *Literature-Based Instruction: Reshaping the Curriculum.* Newton, MA: Christopher-Gordon Publications, 1998.

Raphael, Taffy E., and Kathryn H. Au. *Super QAR for the Testwise Student.* Bothell, WA: The Wright Group, 2002.

Raphael, Taffy E., Karen Damphousse, Kathy Highfield, and Susan Florio-Ruane. "Understanding Culture in Our Lives and Work: Teachers, Literature Study in the Book Club Program." In *Reconceptualizing Literacy in the New Age of Multiculturalism and Pluralism.* Language, Literacy and Learning series, vol. 1., edited by Patricia R. Schmidt and Peter B. Mosenthal. Greenwich, CT: Information Age Publishing Inc., 2001.

Raphael, Taffy E., Susan Florio-Ruane, and MariAnne George. "Book Club Plus: A Conceptual Framework to Organize Literacy Instruction." *Language Arts* 79, no. 1 (2001): 159–168.

Raphael, Taffy E., Susan Florio-Ruane, Marcella Kehus, MariAnne George, Nina Hasty, and Kathy Highfield. "Thinking for Ourselves: Literacy Learning in a Diverse Teacher Inquiry Network." *The Reading Teacher* 54, no. 6 (2001): 506–607.

Raphael, Taffy E., Marcella Kehus, and Karen Damphousse. *Book Club for Middle School.* Lawrence, MA: Small Planet Communications, 2001.

Raphael, Taffy E., Laura S. Pardo, and Kathy Highfield. *Book Club: A Literature-Based Curriculum,* 2nd ed. Lawrence, MA: Small Planet Communications, Inc., 2002.

Rosen, Harold. *Stories and Meanings.* Sheffield, UK: The National Association for the Teaching of English, 1987.

Short, Kathy G., and Junardi Armstrong. "Moving Toward Inquiry: Integrating Literature into the Science Curriculum." *The New Advocate* 6, no. 3 (1993): 183–199.

Sipe, Lawrence R. "The Construction of Literary Understanding by First and Second Graders in Oral Response to Picture Storybook Read-Alouds." *Reading Research Quarterly* 35, no. 2 (2000): 252–275.

———. "Talking Back and Taking Over: Young Children's Expressive Engagement During Storybook Read-Alouds." *The Reading Teacher* 55, no. 5 (2002): 476–483.

Sipe, Lawrence, and Jeffrey Bauer. "Urban Kindergartners' Literary Understanding of Picture Storybooks." *The New Advocate* 14, no. 4 (2001): 329–342.

Spandel, Vicki. *Creating Writers Through 6-Trait Assessment and Instruction.* New York: Longman, 2001.

Taylor, B. M., P. D. Pearson, K. Clark, and S. Walpole. "Reading Growth in High-Poverty Classrooms: The Influence of Teacher Practices that Encourage Cognitive Engagement in Literacy Learning." *The Elementary School Journal* 104 (2003): 3–28.

Taylor, B. M., P. D. Pearson, D. S. Peterson, and M. Rodriguez. "The CIERA School Change Project: Using Research, Data, and Study Groups to Improve Classroom Reading Instruction and Increase Students' Reading Achievement." Research Report. Ann Arbor, MI: University of Michigan, Center for the Improvement of Early Reading Achievement. (in press)

Valencia, Sheila W. "How Will Literacy Be Assessed in the Next Millennium?" *Reading Research Quarterly* 35, no. 2 (2000): 248–249.

Valencia, Sheila W., and Sue Bradley. "Engaging Students in Self-Reflection and Self-Evaluation." *Literacy Portfolios in Action* by Sheila Valencia et al. Fort Worth, TX. Harcourt Brace College Publishers, 1998: 174–218.

Vygotsky, Lev S. *Mind in Society: The Development of Higher Psychological Processes,* translated by Michael Cole, Vera John-Steiner, Sylvia Scribner, Ellen Souberman. Cambridge, MA: Harvard University Press, 1978.

Young, Kelly M. "Book Club for Early Primary Grades" Illinois Reading Council Journal 29 no. 4. (2001): 20–26.

Index